Culture
and Society in
France
1848-1898

STUDIES IN CULTURAL HISTORY
SERIES EDITOR:
Professor J. R. Hale

Culture
and Society in
France
1848-1898

Dissidents and Philistines

F. W. J. HEMMINGS

Charles Scribner's Sons *New York*

A—8.71 (I)

Printed in Great Britain.
Library of Congress Catalog Card Number 73-110683
SBN 684-12578-1

Contents

List of Illustrations

THE PLATES

THE PLATES cont.

Acknowledgment

The author and publishers would like to thank the following for permission to reproduce photographs.

Claude O'Sughrue (12); Cliché des Musées Nationaux (1, 18, 25, 27); The Burrell Collection, Glasgow Art Gallery and Museum (13); Giraudon (30); Henry P. McIlhenny Collection, Philadelphia, Pa. (29); Librairie Hachette 9 and 15) from *Victor Hugo and His World*; The Mansell Collection (3, 16); Musée Rodin (28); Nationalmuseum, Stockholm (20); National Gallery London (17); Princetown University Press (map of Paris and illustration 18 rom D. H. Pinkney, *Napoleon III and the Rebuilding of Paris*.

Introduction

De la foule à nous, aucun lien.
Tant pis pour la foule,
tant pis pour nous surtout.
                    Gustave Flaubert

It seems fair to say that art would never have come into being if there had not been a strong demand for its products, and that no artist has ever worked solely for the love of his art and for the peculiar satisfaction that comes of its successful prosecution. No fashioner of sonnets or sculptures, no composer, no painter has ever been able to banish more than fleetingly from his mind some image of the public before whom his finished work would be set: some reader sitting in the shade of a tree, a girl deciphering a score before a piano perhaps, or a little knot of people scrutinizing a portrait hung over a fireplace. Victor Cousin's slogan, 'art for art's sake', makes very little sense unless it is construed to mean 'art for the art-lover's sake'; and the art-object itself has never been more than the high-tension cable along which an alternating current flows between artist and public.

The urge to seek or to create a public is, obviously, stronger in some artists than in others; but even the most hermetic of poets has moved among a small circle of initiates, the most *avant-garde* of artists could not have persevered without the knowledge that his work was earning some appreciation, if only among the few who were trying to develop art in the same direction and along the same lines. There have always been those who, out of arrogance or, conversely, modesty, have proclaimed that their work was intended for an enlightened minority. Stendhal dedicated *La Chartreuse de Parme* 'to the Happy Few', and confided to Balzac that he did not expect his novel to bring him much renown until 1880—40 years or more after it was published. Yet he was as conscious as anyone of the extent to which the expectations of their contemporaries may affect the quality and style of a writer's or an artist's work. No Frenchman ever admired Shakespeare more than did Stendhal, who nevertheless acknowledged that the 'rhetoric' in Shakespeare reflects the compulsion he was under to 'make comprehensible such and such a situation in his drama to a coarse public more distinguished for courage than subtlety'.[1] Stendhal does appear, indeed, to have been inclined to attribute more importance to social factors than to any others when it came to explaining the form that artistic activity takes in any given country or at any given era. 'The arts,' he declared in his *Vie de Rossini*, 'are the product of the entire civilization of a nation and of all its customs, even the most baroque and ridiculous.' In a letter to one of his closest confidants he instanced the case of Michelangelo, often criticized for his hardness and gracelessness, but unfairly, since these qualities arose from the oppressive nature of the religious spirit in his age. But how can the art-historian properly appreciate the masterpiece he is studying unless he knows such things? 'This kind of froth called the fine arts is the necessary product of a certain fermentation. If you are to explain the froth you must explain the nature of the fermentation.' And in another simile, for Stendhal unusually elaborate, which occurs in one of the concluding chapters of his *Histoire de la peinture en Italie*, he wrote: 'Just as the twig, that buoyant flotsam of the forest, follows the direction of the torrent that bears it, alike over the cataracts and through the twisting detours of the mountain passes, and later over the plain when the torrent has become a slow and majestic river, now high, now low, but always on the surface of the water, even so do the arts follow civilisation.'

Stendhal was undoubtedly right: in every age the artist has responded to social pressures; the nature of his work cannot but reflect the demands made on him by the public of his time. But, while it may not be too difficult to establish the form this response of artist to clientèle has taken, it remains always in the highest degree hazardous to theorise about the causal connections between social and cultural development. For the two never march in step. In some periods of history the artist appears to be content to give his public what they seem to want; at others he is at pains to give them only what he thinks they ought to have. Occasionally, to use Stendhal's metaphor, he will allow himself to be borne along the current unresisting, but there are eras, such as the one we are concerned with in this book, when to do so appears to him a betrayal of some deeper allegiance. In a sense, however, the greater the reaction to a pressure, the stronger the proof that that pressure exists.

The period of 50 years surveyed here seems to have been characterized, as no previous period was in France, by a marked hostility on the part of all the great artists—the writers and painters most noticeably—towards the society in which they lived and for which they were obliged to work. A deep chasm yawned between the creative genius on the one side, and the vast majority of ordinary citizens on the other, whether they belonged to the working class, too hard driven by economic pressures or too poorly educated to appreciate the works of art and literature that were being produced, or whether they were members of the middle and upper classes, who in disappointment or incomprehension turned for preference to purveyors of inferior art-substitutes. Flaubert's complaint: 'between us and the crowd there exists no link, unhappily for the crowd, unhappily for us above all'[2] might as well have been made by Baudelaire, by Cézanne, by Rodin, or by a dozen others. Artists and writers formed a dissenting and antagonized minority in a society which was, however, by no means under the impression that art and literature were superfluous to its spiritual health.

The artist's alienation from the society of his time was matched by the dislike and distrust with which he was regarded by all the prosperous and influential members of that society. Evidence of this animosity is tragically plentiful. The leading exponents of literature and the arts were harried in every way. Some were driven into exile, in 1851 and again in 1871. Others were prosecuted in the courts because of the supposed perniciousness of their works: they were fined and imprisoned under the Third Republic as under the Second Empire. Those who did not actually fall foul of the law suffered neglect and bitter poverty because of the incomprehension of the public reinforced by the obtuseness of the critics. Never was there a time when more money was poured out to reward third-rate painters, meretricious playwrights, and pretentiously dull architects, and so little spared to sustain the not inconsiderable number of very fine artists and writers who were active at the time.

Not surprisingly, the latter tended to react with disdain if not with denunciatory fury. Even when, like Zola, they professed a liking for their age, this was only because they detected in it the seeds of a better future. A few capitulated, abandoned all dignity, and contented themselves with the role of entertainer. Others retreated into historicism, into pure subjectivity, into aestheticism, or into various experiments designed to call into being an autonomous art-world. But in so far as the artist still tried to concern himself with the contemporary situation, he had to adopt the only course open to him in a selfish and repressive society: to hold a mirror up to it. In one form or another realism, whether it actually went under that name or under the name of naturalism or impressionism, is the true hallmark of great art during this period.

The reasons for these deep dissensions would appear to be partly political and partly social. At the beginning, the collapse of democratic socialism in 1848, so mortifying to the liberal intelligentsia, induced a distaste for political activity which extended, with very few exceptions, to every member of the cultural élite for almost the whole of the remainder of the century. All through history there have been writers—Machiavelli and Francis Bacon, Goethe and Chateaubriand—who have distinguished themselves in public service. In France, after the failure of the February Revolution, such a duplication of roles ceased to be a possibility. It is easier to imagine Mallarmé running a pawnbroker's business than setting out to become a representative of the people and a minister of state, as it seemed quite natural that Lamartine should do.

The social reasons are bound up with the emergence of a meanly materialistic spirit among the class that by and large controlled the fortunes of the country. The practical man of affairs was not exactly a new phenomenon. He began making his presence felt under the July Monarchy and Balzac's later novels give him a considerable place: in *La Comédie humaine* he is named Crevel, Cardot, Nucingen, Du Tillet. Flaubert called him M. Dambreuse, Zola, Aristide Saccard; he was M. Walter in Maupassant's *Bel-Ami* and Bernard Jansoulet in Daudet's *Le Nabab;* the poets usually referred to him as Croesus. Such figures represented the big men, the *brasseurs de millions,* looked up to, envied, and admired by the smaller fry, the shopkeepers and factory-owners who constituted the backbone of the reactionary force that broke Lamartine in 1848, applauded Louis-Napoleon in 1851, supported him until 1870, smashed the Commune in 1871 and fought a rearguard action against the rising threat of socialism for the rest of the century. This was the real governing class, presiding over and profiting from the transformation of France into a modern industrial power. Knowing that it faced serious opposition, both from militant labour and from those critics within its own ranks who represented, perhaps, its 'bad conscience', it tended to be conservative where social mores were concerned and to react strongly against any challenge to the traditional values that afforded it a spurious justification and gave it social cohesion. Hence the pressure brought on artists to conform, the instinctive hostility to anything new in art, for anything that was new automatically came under suspicion of being subversive.

The innovating artist or writer could be dealt with in various ways: censorship could be used to silence him, ridicule to discourage him. The critics who were the spokesmen of the governing class continued to defend the classical tradition in the teeth of insurgent realism, because it was old and safe and could be taken for granted. It meant little to them that this tradition was outworn and could, in the nineteenth century, support only a puny, derivative art. But the most effective weapon in the armoury of the monied middle classes was the economic one. Because they alone disposed of the surplus wealth of the country, they alone controlled the market for cultural products and were in a position to deny the dissident author or painter a living (except in the rare cases when he happened to be a *rentier* himself).

If eventually the ranks of the philistines were broken, this came about principally thanks to the impact of foreign art, in the wake of the national humiliation of the Franco-Prussian War which suggested to the French that their cultural status no less than their military prestige had doubtless been overvalued. In the late 1880s and in the last decade of the century the stuffiness of the atmosphere was to some extent relieved as horizons widened. But it should not be forgotton either that, as the period drew to its close, a new generation was reaching maturity: the French Forsytes were growing old and impotent and the sons did not always subscribe to their fathers' system of values.

These, at least, appear to be the chief reasons why in this half-century the best of French culture was at odds with its immediate beneficiaries. Like all broad theoretical constructs, such an explanation cannot, and is not meant to, fit every aspect of a complex situation: but it may serve as a useful guide through the labyrinth of the cultural history of the period that stretches from the founding of the Second Republic to the explosion of the Dreyfus Case.

[1] *Racine et Shakspeare* (1823): pp. 51–2 in the Divan edition of Stendhal's works.
[2] Letter to Louise Colet, April 24th, 1852: see below, p. 114.

one

The Poet on the Barricade

History, it is said, never repeats itself; now and again, however, it comes surprisingly close to doing so. In the winter of 1848, and again, exactly 50 years later, in the winter of 1898, two middle-aged writers, whose work had made them famous far beyond the frontiers of France, suddenly took it on themselves to intervene decisively in their country's affairs at a moment of crisis when the professional politicians, through incapacity or unwillingness, hung back or shrank away. They stayed in the limelight only a few months; then disgrace or persecution forced them into retirement or exile. Nevertheless, their intervention had lasting repercussions, and even when, in the course of time, these effects dwindled into imperceptibility, the memory of each writer's stand remained, and still remains, as an exemplary symbol of the power that the artist can, on rare occasions, exert in matters of public policy.

Socialism and the Poets

It was on February 24th, 1848 that the 57-year-old Alphonse de Lamartine left the Chamber of Deputies, already invaded by an armed mob, and made his way with difficulty, arm in arm with the timid, fat, perspiring time-server Ledru-Rollin, through the streets filled with an excited throng, towards the Hôtel de Ville. Here, after feverish consultations with the other left-wing notables who were to form the provisional government, yielding, perhaps against his better judgement, to the insistent promptings of his colleague Louis Blanc and the clamorous demands of the revolutionary crowds gathered in the torch-lit square, Lamartine appeared on the balcony and proclaimed the establishment of the (Second) Republic.

And on January 13th, 1898, Émile Zola, also by a remarkable coincidence aged 57, published in the newspaper *L'Aurore* the open letter to the President of the (Third) Republic in which, by asserting roundly that the Jewish officer Alfred Dreyfus had been wrongfully sentenced four years previously by an army court, he precipitated that confrontation between the forces of chauvinism and racialism and those of liberalism and tolerance which, under the portentous name of 'the Affair', was to split the nation from top to bottom and, indirectly—for *J'Accuse* was not strictly a political manifesto—to polarize political thought and activity in France right down to the outbreak of the First World War.

These two events must be regarded as exceptional. For the most part, during the 50 years' interval that separates them, the writer will revert, collectively and individually, to one or other of his customary roles: that of inactive witness, ironic commentator, or ineffective protester; he is prophet, pure craftsman, or introspective bystander. Never again, during those 50 years, will he have the opportunity, nor perhaps the incentive, to seize the helm as did Lamartine in 1848 or to rock the boat as did Zola in 1898. This survey will therefore be largely concerned with a period of history during which cultural and political activities are pursued in dissociation: but it opens at a moment in time when, exceptionally, the two forms of activity merge, a moment when the leading literary figures of the age, all the great surviving luminaries of the Romantic movement, stepped boldly into the political arena. Lamartine for a brief spell controlled the fortunes of the Provisional Government. Hugo engaged in strenuous though ultimately unsuccessful efforts to build his political fortunes on the heaving slopes of the newly erupted republican volcano. George Sand had the ear of the temporary rulers of France and did her best to push the new Republic even further to the left. Even such reactionary minded writers as Balzac and Vigny tried to get themselves elected to the National Assembly; Eugène Suë, 'the friend of the poor', succeeded in so doing. Many members of the younger generation of writers, apprentice poets with a glittering future, joined the exasperated working men on the barricades in February and June.

Revolutions in France never repeat themselves, since every one—from the lawyers' revolution of 1789 to the students' revolution of 1968—is made by a different group of dissidents. The 1848 Revolution, with its theme song:

> *Chapeau bas devant la casquette,*
> *A genoux devant l'ouvrier!*

was an explosion of working-class resentment against the governing middle classes; in this respect it resembles the Paris *commune* of 1871; but it was unique in being the only revolution in which the artist attempted to play an active and influential part, by swaying crowds with his oratory, moulding

1 Meissonier, *La Barricade* (fragment). Executed 1848, exhibited 1850 as 'A Memory of Civil War', this oil painting of a contemporary scene reveals an unusual aspect of Meissonier's talent

2 'The People in the Throne-Room', contemporary lithograph depicting an incident in the invasion of the Tuileries Palace by the revolutionary mob

3 George Sand: portrait dating probably from the late 1840s

opinion by his manifestoes, or, in the last resort, by discharging his weapons against his adversaries in arms. The poet-militant was a new phenomenon in France, distantly modelled, perhaps, on Byron, whose death in defence of the principle of political freedom 24 years earlier remained a glowing inspiration. But the notion that the poet had some kind of social mission, a duty of sorts to lead the disinherited, as Orpheus had led Eurydice, from the murky under-world of poverty, superstition, and exploitation into the uplands of a social utopia running with milk and honey—this extravagantly un-Byronic idea had been current since the 1830 Revolution. Henri de Saint-Simon himself had for a long time been reluctant to accord a place of any importance in his ideal society to the artist; but his followers remedied the omission, establishing a new hierarchy in which the writer, the sculptor, the painter were seated on thrones elevated above the rest of humanity. In his pamphlet *Du passé et de l'avenir des beaux-arts*, published only a few months before the outbreak of that earlier revolution which had established Louis-Philippe on the throne, Émile Barrault, one of the most eloquent of Saint-Simon's disciples, pro-claimed that 'the artist alone, by the power of that sympathy that allows him to embrace the divine and the social order, is worthy to lead humanity'. First it would be necessary that art should be purified and regenerated, that anti-quated or frivolous forms, the novel, tragedy, comedy, should be consigned to the limbo of forgotten things. But thereafter truth and beauty will be linked:

> poetry which has, down to our day, reflected exclusively either the material or the moral universe, will be the sublime expression of these two domains reunited; and at the sound of these new chords, pagan mythology will fade away as a false and unworthy mode of representation. Finally, music, painting, and sculpture will lend their assistance to the efforts of eloquence and poetry in temples that architecture will have renewed under the influence of a more complete inspiration. Such are the delights reserved for our descendants when a new religion, summoning all men to the feet of the same altars, shall have appeared on earth. . . . *Henceforth the arts will be our form of worship, and the artists our priests.*[1]

In one way or another most of those who, in the first half of the nineteenth century, drafted blue-prints for the millennium were careful to reserve to the artist a place of honour in their projected new society. Charles Fourier, for example, though he expected no revelations from the poets—how could there be any, when the principal and indeed sole revelation had already been vouchsafed to humanity by Fourier himself?—looked to them none the less to propagate the word. He pointed out how wretched their material condition

B

was under the current dispensation, their independence a mirage, their field of action rigorously circumscribed. In his phalansterian society there would be boundless opportunities for the writer, the musician, the painter to pursue their perennial objectives, fame and money, or rather, 'money and fame, to be more precise,' writes Fourier, 'for one must start with the more ardently desired of the two prizes.'

Whatever the incentives they saw fit to offer, it is clear that these worthy visionaries, the 'utopian socialists' as Marx later dubbed them, were prepared to go to considerable lengths to win the artist over to their side and secure his co-operation in the founding of the ideal society. His response was less whole-hearted than might have been hoped. George Sand was the writer who came nearest to fulfilling the expectations of the saint-simonians who, deeply impressed by her early novels, showered gifts on her and even offered to elevate her to the position of 'lady pope'—an honour which she politely declined. It was true that in Le Compagnon du tour de France (1840) she had committed the fault of harking back to an imaginary—and idealized—past, instead of seeking in contemporary conditions the seeds of the future; on the other hand Le Péché de M. Antoine (written on the very eve of the Revolution) could easily be read as a work of propaganda on behalf of the Fourierists: it featured the description of a model village indistinguishable from a co-operative phalanstery. But Mme Sand was something of an exception; for the most part the principal writers of the Romantic generation, those who came to the fore in the late 1820s and early 1830s, regarded the saint-simonians with some distrust when they did not actually satirize them, as did, for instance, Stendhal in his pamphlet D'un nouveau complot contre les industriels.

At the same time, the general encouragement to pay some attention to the direction in which society was moving undoubtedly had its effect. Plato's recipe for the good society, that philosophers should become kings, had been flatteringly modified: the poets were now to become prime ministers. This part of the programme, at least, was taken seriously, by Victor Hugo as well as by his elder, Lamartine. For some years before the 1848 Revolution both these poets had been prominent members of the nation's assemblies. Lamartine had stood for election as early as 1831. That year he published a pamphlet, De la politique rationnelle, in which he summarized the political ideals that were to guide him throughout his life, and—more significantly still—an Ode sur les révolutions. Having narrowly missed election on his first attempt, he presented himself successfully for another constituency and took his seat in the Chamber in 1833. It was in 1838 that, in the course of a parliamentary debate, he threw out the famous phrase: 'La France est une nation qui s'ennuie'

—a condemnation of Louis-Philippe's unexciting but undeniably sensible foreign policy which historians have been quoting ever since: in a single pregnant sentence Lamartine expressed, as perhaps only a Romantic poet could have done, the latent dissatisfaction of the people with their rulers that permitted the emergence of a revolutionary situation ten years later.

As for Hugo, rather than submit himself to the undignified hurly-burly of a parliamentary election, he was content to wait until, in 1845, a royal ordinance conferred on him a life peerage and a seat in the Upper Chamber. '*M. Victor Hugo est nommé pair de France: le roi s'amuse*', commented one wit, making neat play with the title of one of Hugo's romantic verse dramas, the one from which Verdi derived the plot of *Rigoletto*. It was an open secret that Hugo owed his elevation to the good offices of Princess Helen of Mecklenberg-Schwerin, Duchess of Orleans, a great admirer of his poetry who had been his friend and ally ever since they first met in 1837, shortly after her marriage to the heir to the throne of France. Princess Helen was a woman of taste and culture; unfortunately she was known to be ambitious and strong-willed as well, and her patronage of Hugo did him little good in the eyes of the general public. As early as 1841 the satirical paper *La Mode*, anticipating what might happen if she became Queen of France, published a spoof list of the members of her first ministry. Victor Hugo was to be premier besides holding the portfolio for War; Lamartine would be in charge of naval matters; Musset and Théophile Gautier were allotted the ministries of finance and foreign affairs. Evidently for *La Mode* it was not altogether inconceivable that the hour might be at hand when the poet would discard the laurel wreath for the statesman's top-hat.

The February Revolution

The parallel drawn at the beginning of this chapter between Lamartine's action in 1848 and Zola's in 1898 has obviously a limited value. Two writers, at an interval of exactly 50 years, make a dramatic incursion into affairs of state. But whereas Lamartine's assumption of power was the logical and, up to a point, predictable culmination of a decade and a half of orthodox political activity, Zola's motivation was strictly non-political. Though he had always been an interested observer of political life and had even, for the space of a year at the end of the Franco-Prussian War, followed the calling of parliamentary journalist, he had never expected, never even desired, to have any part in the conduct of his country's affairs. That Dreyfus had been wrongfully convicted of espionage, and that those responsible for this miscarriage of justice wilfully refused to admit their error, never struck him at the time as having anything to do with party politics; and if, as part of the process of righting a wrong suffered by an innocent individual, passions were aroused which in the long run might have far-reaching political implications, this was incidental and in a sense outside Zola's calculations. In the storm that he had inadvertently conjured up, the sorcerer's apprentice stood aside as far as events allowed him, leaving it to others to canalize, control, and direct to their advantage the forces he had unleashed.

The difference is not in any important degree attributable to a difference in temperament or personal situation between Lamartine and Zola. Both men earnestly desired a radical improvement in the lot of the less fortunate members of society; both entertained the same lofty concept of the writer's duty to humankind. In a sense it could be said that Zola was a 'man of '48' born out of his time: his novel *Travail*, written after his intervention in the Dreyfus Affair, was largely inspired by the doctrines and ideals of Charles Fourier, though by 1901 these had a decidedly dated air. The real distinction to be drawn between Lamartine and Zola is that when Lamartine's hour struck, the nation was fully prepared to accept the idea that an eloquent writer might become a political leader; not only had the saint-simonians declared this to be a natural and desirable development, but there had been at least one outstanding precedent. Chateaubriand, whose influence on the Romantic generation in France had been decisive, provided a striking illustration of a literary career mutating into a political one; and Chateaubriand was still alive when the 1848 Revolution broke out. Zola, on the other hand, who arrived in Paris ten years after the collapse of the Revolution, spent his whole life under the shadow of its failure. The divorce between the world of culture and the world of politics had already been made absolute, and in the tradition in which he grew up there were only two roles open to the artist who had a political conscience: that of a helpless onlooker, a Cassandra whose warnings were never heeded, or that of the pretentious fly of the fable, sitting on the hindquarters of society's coach-horses, making absurd claims to steer and drive when he was simply being carried along.

Alphonse de Lamartine, with his aristocratic name and lineage and the aristocratic appeal of his mellifluous alexandrines, might seem to have been the least qualified of men to head a popular revolt. Marx himself, referring to the phenomenon of Lamartine's leadership, acknowledged that 'this was actually no real interest, no definite class; this was the February Revolution itself, the common uprising with its illusions, its poetry, its imagined content, and its phrases'.[2] Like everyone else, Lamartine was taken completely by surprise by the turn of events. Nobody expected a revolution at just that time; experience had shown that revolutions never, in any case, broke out in mid-winter. The parliamentary opposition hoped for a change of ministry and some reform of the electoral law; it was, in fact, the action of the government in prohibiting a reformist banquet that precipitated the catastrophe. Difficult though it is for posterity to appreciate their logic, progressives in France in the late 1840s seem to have reached the conclusion that the best way to come to the aid of the starving poor was to sit down to a heavy meal. In this particular instance it was planned that the diners and their supporters should assemble at the Madeleine and march in procession via the Place de la Concorde to the Champs Élysées where the banquet was to be held. These arrangements failed to please the Minister of the Interior, and there was an angry exchange in the Chamber between him and Odilon Barrot, leader of the opposition, following which Barrot summoned a meeting of opposition deputies in his house. Most of them voted in favour of abandoning the demonstration; informed of this decision, Lamartine, who had not been present when it was taken, declared that, if the Place de la Concorde was empty the following day and every other deputy stayed away, he would march on his own, 'taking my shadow behind me'.

In fact, he was far from finding himself alone. At least one other poet was in the Place de la Concorde the following afternoon (Tuesday, February 22), together with a large crowd of excited students[3] and angry workers, among whom moved mounted police to prevent the formation of compact gatherings. Baudelaire, along with Courbet and two other friends, watched the scene from behind the parapet of a little garden bordering the square. Suddenly a group of rioters debouched hurriedly from one of the side-streets, pursued by a detachment of municipal guardsmen with fixed bayonets. One of the fugitives, who was unarmed, dodged round a tree, slipped up, fell, and was immediately pinned to the ground, a bayonet thrust through his chest. Horrified, Baudelaire and Courbet set off for the offices of *La Presse* to report the atrocity.

Two days later, on the Thursday, it was the editor of *La Presse*, Émile de Girardin, who confronted Louis-Philippe with a printed sheet setting out the terms under which the monarch was to signify his abdication in favour of his grandson, the ten-year-old Comte de Paris. The newspaper editor, in connivance with Hugo, had hoped to persuade the old king to nominate Princess Helen regent rather than one of the Comte de Paris' uncles; but Louis-Philippe demurred; he was not over-fond of his daughter-in-law. It was left to Hugo, with the tacit support of Odilon Barrot, to try and ensure the acceptance of his royal patroness as regent, even though the Chamber had not pronounced on the question and had in fact, after the accidental death of the Duke of Orleans in 1842, specifically enacted that his widow could not be invested with the regency should the young heir enter on his reign as a minor. Hugo went first to the Hôtel de Ville, where his proclamation was coldly received, then to the Place de la Bastille where he encountered violent opposition from the working-class crowd. His pleading was drowned with cries of 'No regency! Down with the Bourbons!', and when, to illustrate his point that a constitutional monarchy was the best guarantee of political liberties, Hugo cited the example of Queen Victoria, he was howled down by the anglophobe artisans. The lower orders, at least, had made up their minds that only a republic would suit them; the tide of popular emotion washed away Hugo's hopes and ambitions at this juncture, but Lamartine, more flexible or more attuned to the times, rode it. Late in the evening, as we have already recorded, he yielded to the clamour and proclaimed the Republic from the balcony of the Hôtel de Ville.

Earlier in the day another man of letters, also a national celebrity, Honoré de Balzac, had been following a column of insurgents heading for the Tuileries Palace. Balzac was not among those who hailed the Revolution with relief or gratitude; though he had little liking for the régime of Louis-Philippe, he anticipated nothing but disorder and economic collapse if a republic were to be substituted. His private affairs, as usual, were in no very healthy state, and civil commotion could do nothing but damage to the sales of *La Comédie humaine*. He had started on a play, but what hope was there of full houses when even the cab-drivers were too terrified to risk themselves in the streets at night? At the Tuileries, on the 24th, he was disgusted—or so he said—to see the rabble smashing mirrors and chandeliers, ripping gold fringes from the red velvet curtains, and pillaging the royal library to make bonfires of the books. But he was not averse to seizing the opportunity of adding to his private collection of curios by pocketing the odd knick-knack, and was especially delighted at being able to rescue from the flames a few torn-out sheets from the exercise books of the two young princes of the blood.

Another witness of the sack of the Tuileries was young Gustave Flaubert, who had come up from Rouen the day before with his inseparable friend Louis Bouilhet. They were parted in the crowd; Bouilhet the poet found himself press-ganged into building a barricade, until a large paving-stone fell and crushed his foot. But the two met up again and were able to see what Balzac saw: Flaubert recorded the scene 20 years later, in *L'Éducation senti-mentale*, probably the only major work of literature for which the Revolution can take direct credit. There is a graphic scene in the novel where Frédéric Moreau, together with his friend the bohemian writer Hussonet, watch the throne being borne aloft by bearded proletarians and heaved, with difficulty, out of the window.

Thereupon a joyful frenzy exploded as if, in place of the throne, a future of unbounded happiness had opened out; and the people, not so much to avenge themselves as to assert their sovereignty, smashed and tore the mirrors and the curtains, the chandeliers, the candlesticks, tables, chairs, stools, all the furniture, down to albums of drawings and tapestry baskets. Seeing the victory was theirs, wasn't it right to have fun? The rabble, in a spirit of irony, dressed up in lace and cashmere shawls. Gold fringes encircled the sleeves of workmen's overalls, hats with ostrich feathers decked the heads of blacksmiths, tarts wound ribbons of the Legion of Honour round their waists as sashes. . . .

Then the fury darkened. An obscene curiosity drove the intruders to search every cupboard and every cranny, open every drawer. Ex-convicts thrust their arms into the beds of princesses and rolled about on top to compensate for not having them there to rape. Others, with more sinister looks, padded around silently, looking for something to steal; but the press was too great. Through the openings of the doorways, down the enfilading apartments, nothing could be seen against the gilding but the dark throng of the common people under a cloud of dust. Everyone's chest was heaving; the heat grew more and more oppressive; the two friends, fearing suffocation, left.

In the antechamber, standing on a heap of clothes, a prostitute was posing as the statue of liberty, motionless and with glazed eyes, terrifying.

Lamartine as Leader

The Revolution of 1848 never had a chance of establishing working-class rule; but for a few days or a few weeks it was possible to entertain the illusion that a new social order had dawned, and there must have been many men, many young men particularly, who experienced the same emotions as Flaubert attributes to Frédéric: 'The magnetism of enthusiastic crowds had communicated itself to him. He sniffed delightedly the stormy air, full of the reek of gunpowder; and yet he shivered under the surge of an immense love, a supreme, all-embracing tenderness, as if the heart of all humanity were beating in his breast.' For others, of course, there was every reason for alarm: business slumped, money became scarce, industrials plummeted. Government stock was quoted well below par, while on the foreign exchange the pound sterling shot up in terms of the franc. There were hundreds of bankruptcies, but it was also a good time for profiteers. At a brilliant *soirée* given at the beginning of March by the Girardins, Balzac found himself surrounded by speculators; anyone with any ready cash was investing in property, the one sure value in those troubled times. He himself was unlucky enough to have put his money in railway shares which were quoted at a quarter of their former value. The collapse in confidence remained a grim memory for thousands of small capitalists and even shopkeepers for years after, and contributed retrospectively to the horror aroused by this unprecedented insurgence of the have-nots against the establishment.

Throughout these critical weeks Lamartine remained a reassuring figure, using his powers of oratory to pacify and tranquillize the over-excited citizens of Paris. The first time he had occasion to display his lion-tamer's talent was on the day after the proclamation of the Republic, when a mass of demonstrators besieged the Hôtel de Ville, demanding that the new régime should adopt the red flag as its banner. Standing on a chair, Lamartine improvised an indignant oration: 'I shall repudiate unto death this flag of blood, and you should repudiate it even more vigorously than I. For the red flag you are waving has never been borne further than the Champ de Mars, where it was trailed in the blood of the people in 1791 and 1793, while the tricolour has travelled all over the earth, proclaiming the name, the glory, and the freedom of the motherland!' His audience's memories were long enough to catch Lamartine's allusion. On July 17th, 1791, a popular demonstration, designed to bring about the abdication of Louis xvi, had been held on the Champ de Mars. It was suppressed by the authorities who declared martial law, hoisted the red flag and sent in troops of the National Guard to disperse the demonstrators: some 50 of these were killed in the ensuing massacre. Lamartine's phrase was on everyone's lips for the next few weeks though, as Flaubert observed, while everyone was prepared to stand under the shadow of the tricolour, each man secretly pledged allegiance to one of the three colours exclusively: the socialist to the red, the legitimist to the white, the orleanist to the blue.

Lamartine's policy, at home and abroad, was to gain a breathing space for the Republic by the exercise of caution and moderation. The office he held in the Provisional Government was that of Minister for Foreign Affairs; in this capacity the only initiative he took was to circularize all French diplomatic representatives abroad, instructing them to assure the chancelleries of Europe that the *status quo* would be observed and that France had no aggressive intentions. At home, it seems reasonable to assume that Lamartine was primarily responsible for some of the more humane measures introduced by the government in those early days, including the abolition of the death penalty for political crimes and the legalization of the departure abroad of the former royal family (Louis-Philippe found refuge, as his successor Louis-Napoleon was to do a little more than 20 years later, in Victoria's England).

No doubt such mildness was intended to reassure those who feared that the Second Republic might vie with the First in exacting vengeful reprisals against its enemies; as has been observed already, no revolution ever takes the same course as its predecessors, if only because the moderates know what excesses they should take precautions to avoid. But Lamartine had a difficult task to convert the hard-core revolutionaries. Challenged by a crowd of demonstrators on the question of the abolition of the death penalty, he exclaimed incautiously: 'What! if Louis-Philippe were here, is there anyone who would want to harm the poor old man?' These words infuriated the more intransigent of the republicans, who raised their weapons; a bayonet grazed Lamartine's cheek. Undaunted, he continued: 'Yes, start with me, if you are looking for a victim. Butchers! do you think you represent France?' Lamartine's courage and eloquence never seem to have failed him. After this episode he was, as he deserved to be, acclaimed and conducted home in triumph by his admirers.

The question, who did represent France, if France was not truly represented by those who had seized power in Paris in February, was one which had still to be settled. Lamartine seems to have regarded himself as conducting a holding operation until such time as general elections held throughout France should settle the course of future developments and the speed at which social reforms should proceed. But in the stormy and uncertain atmosphere of the time, with the government liable at any moment to be held to ransom by the most dangerous, volatile and dissatisfied elements of the capital's population, clearly the sooner elections were held and the general will of the nation ascertained, the better. In this Lamartine was at loggerheads with his colleague, the socialist Louis Blanc, who would have preferred elections to be deferred until the country as a whole had learned to accept republican institutions. On March 17th, partly at Louis Blanc's instigation, a large body of workers assembled in the Place de la Concorde and once again marched on the Hôtel de Ville, the seat of government. Here they unfurled the red flag, intoned the Marseillaise, and demanded, through their spokesman Blanqui, the adjournment *sine die* of the elections or, in default, their postponement for a minimum of two months. As usual it fell to Lamartine to address them, which he did with firmness and fire, upholding the government's decision to seek the verdict of the polls at an early date, and once again the poet's speech, and even more his spirit, prevailed over the passions of the crowd. But historians incline to trace the downward curve of Lamartine's popularity to this final confrontation with the disaffected workers whom, from this point on, he exerted himself to charm rather than to convince. A good liberal democrat, as we should call him today,

Lamartine feared a dictatorship of the proletariat no less than the dictatorship of some military adventurer or royal despot. These 'anarchic and
malignant crowds,' as Duveau expresses it, appeared to him as 'the unconscious instrument of counter-revolution.'[4]

It was another writer—curiously, one who, by reason of her sex, was
automatically debarred even from casting a vote—who, a month later,
thanks to an oversight or else by deliberate trickery, almost succeeded in
forcing the government to declare its intention of annulling the elections if
these should result in the return of a conservative majority to the National
Assembly. George Sand had been entrusted with the drafting of a series of
official bulletins intended to explain and justify governmental policy; the
bulletins were distributed all over France and posted in every *commune*. None
of them bore a signature, but it was understood that each was checked and
authorized for publication by one or other of the ministers. The 16th
Bulletin, dated April 15th, slipped through this net; in it, George Sand
argued boldly that a *putsch* might be justified if the outcome of the elections
was unfavourable to republican (i.e. working-class) interests:

> The elections, if they do not bring about the triumph of social truth, if
> they are the expression of the interests of a single caste, extorted from the
> trusting loyalty of the people, these elections, which ought to be the
> salvation of the Republic, will without a doubt be its perdition. There will
> then be only one solution for the people who raised the barricades : they will
> have to manifest their will a second time and adjourn the decisions of a
> misleading national representation.

It is true that George Sand added, with uncharacteristic piety: 'Will
France require Paris to resort to this remedy, extreme and deplorable as it
would be? God forbid !'

The 16th Bulletin caused the utmost consternation and indignation not
only among middle-class voters but also among leading members of the
government, who were prompt to disown it. It marks, as her principal
biographer has said, 'the end of the literary participation of George Sand in
the affairs of the Provisional Government.'[5] We have still to see how this
participation started.

Writers on the Hustings

Of all the literary figures who had a hand in the establishment of the Second
Republic, it was George Sand who devoted herself most whole-heartedly to
the triumph of the programme of social reform it implied. She was ensconced

in her country house at Nohant when the barricades went up; like everyone else, she was disconcerted by this unexpected development, and judged the outbreak of street violence to be no more than the public repercussions of some parliamentary wrangle between Thiers and Guizot. She wrote anxiously to her son Maurice, urging him to come home: 'I recommend that you should avoid going wandering in that area, for it is easy to get oneself a bayonet wound with no advantage for the cause. If it was necessary for you to sacrifice yourself for your country, as you know I would not stop you. But to get yourself knocked on the head for Odilon Barrot and company, that would be too absurd.'[6] However, Maurice remained where he was, so on February 27th George Sand abandoned work on her autobiography and came to Paris.

There, a revelation awaited her. Everything she had dreamed of for years and hoped for seemed to be coming true. The letters she wrote in the early days of the Revolution are overflowing with optimism and enthusiasm; the euphoria that every generous spirit seems to have felt at the time permeates every line, an emotion akin to that which excited Wordsworth, by his own account, in the first stages of an earlier revolution. George Sand's 'bliss was it in that day to be alive' comes over in phraseology less melodious but in accents just as lyrical:

Long live the Republic! What a dream, what enthusiasm and at the same time what discipline, what order in Paris!

I am just back, having hurried thither in time to see the last barricades open before my feet. I saw the nation in all its majesty, sublime, candid, magnanimous, the people of France united in the heart of France, in the heart of the world; the most admirable of the peoples on earth! I spent many a night without sleeping, many a day without resting. We are out of our mind, intoxicated, enraptured to have fallen asleep in the mire and to wake up in heaven. . . .

The Republic is won, it is established; we would all rather perish than let it slip from our grasp. The government is composed of men who are for the most part excellent, each of them, taken singly, somewhat inadequate to a task that would demand the genius of Napoleon or the heart of Jesus. But the collective effort of all these men who have heart or mind or will-power suffices. . . . [7]

This letter was written from Nohant on March 9th, George Sand having returned to the country a couple of days before, partly in order to settle her financial affairs, partly so as to preside over the installation of Maurice as the new republican mayor of the local *commune*, but also to discover for herself how people in her beloved Berry were reacting to the situation. She was gravely disappointed on this last count; the natural conservatism of the farmers and villagers was, if anything, reinforced by their apprehension lest the 'red peril' from Paris should invade the countryside.

To overcome this lethargy and allay these fears, George Sand suggested to the authorities that working-class agents should be despatched into the provinces to educate their fellow citizens in the ways of republicanism. (We shall see, a little later, how the young poet Leconte de Lisle was sent into the fastnesses of Britanny, in accordance with this policy, there to engage in vain attempts to spread the gospel according to Fourier.) Already George Sand was worried about the outcome of the elections which, sooner or later, would have to be held in order to create a properly mandated legislature. In the first issue of the newspaper, *La Cause du peuple*, which she founded on her return to Paris, she professed herself prepared to accept the verdict of the ballot-box, whatever it might be: but circumstances, as we have seen, caused her to modify this confident line of approach. Like many other newspapers founded under the Second Republic, *La Cause du peuple* had a short life: only three numbers were printed, at weekly intervals through the month of April. George Sand herself provided virtually all the copy for each issue, and it is in the columns of this ephemeral sheet that we may best discover what she hoped for of the Republic and what kind of 'brave new world' she expected it to usher in. Her major theme was that the immense gulf between rich and poor was certain, in time, to be closed: private wealth would disappear or rather, merge with social wealth; equality between classes would supersede the tyranny of one class over another, co-operative effort would replace competitive strife. All this was to be achieved by peaceful methods and by the sheer force of circumstances: 'gradually society will move from poverty to affluence and from affluence to plenty, avoiding all violent collisions with those obstacles that duty enjoins us to turn.'[8] These candid words seem to express the very essence of the gentle optimism and pathetic inexperience that marked this first venture in social revolution.

Meanwhile the electoral campaign was gaining impetus, both in Paris and in the provinces. Universal male franchise having been conceded, and eligibility extended to all men over the age of 25, what Flaubert later called a '*vertige de la députation*' gripped the most improbable candidates. They included a number of men of letters: Alfred de Vigny and his more prolific but less well remembered contemporary Victor de Laprade; François Ponsard, who since the failure of *Les Burgraves* in 1843 had replaced Hugo as the premier dramatist of France; and Alphonse Karr, novelist, satirical journalist and wit, who in the later stages of the Second Republic, after the revolution had spent its force, was responsible for the famous remark: '*Plus ça change, plus c'est la même chose.*' None of these had any success at the polls; but their evident readiness to exchange the quiet of their studies for the hurly-burly of the Palais Bourbon—assuming their disinterestedness was unaffected by the lure of a deputy's emoluments—is remarkable testimony to the public-spiritedness of authors in 1848. It is certain that never before or since did poets show themselves so conscious of the fact that politics are too important a matter to be left to the politicians.

Even Balzac, whose novels are strewn with disobliging reflections on the institutions of parliamentary democracy, declared his readiness to represent his fellow citizens in the Republic's legislative assembly. How is one to account for this apparent *volte-face*? Events since February had deepened his pessimism. He was disturbed to find the boulevards overrun with roughnecks, and noted that on Palm Sunday no more than 50 carriages could be seen in the Champs-Elysées in place of the thousands that had paraded there the previous spring. The Republic seemed to be confirming his worst premonitions: 'We have *liberty* to starve to death', he wrote, '*equality* in poverty, and street-corner *fraternity*.'[9]

Having decided to stand as candidate, he discovered he could not spare the time to tour the numerous clubs that had sprung up overnight in Paris, one function of which—as readers of *L'Éducation sentimentale* will remember—was to provide an audience for prospective representatives. Instead, he addressed a letter to the president of one of them (the Club of Universal Fraternity) which was duly inserted in *Le Journal des Débats* and *Le Constitutionnel*.[10] The writer began, in peremptory fashion, by stating his view that 'it is superfluous for men whose life and works have been public property for 20 years to make professions of faith'. Electors were, by implication, advised to re-read *La Comédie humaine*. The profession of faith he nevertheless goes on to make is succinct and could be paraphrased as follows: if we must have a republic, let it at least be a durable régime; France must not be made a guinea-pig for fresh political experiments every 15 or 18 years. Not surprisingly, when the elections were held on April 23rd, Balzac collected no more than a score of votes. The outstanding success of his new play, *La Marâtre*, in May went some way to console him for this rebuff; unfortunately, fear of being caught in street disturbances caused too many Parisians to stay at home, and the manager, Hostein, decided after only six performances to take the play off and close the theatre temporarily. Balzac, disgruntled, accepted an invitation to visit some old friends in the country. The catastrophic insurrection of June 24th–26th occurred when he was still at Saché, 'providentially', he remarked, 'for my bulk would have offered too easy a target for the rebels'. In July he was back on the boulevards, predicting a new restoration (of the Comte de Chambord, the grandson of Charles x, whom the legitimist party still hoped to see crowned one day as Henry v), and laying plans, in that eventuality, to secure appointment as ambassador of France either at the Court of St James or at St Petersburg. His only difficulty was to decide which of the two posts would suit him better. Auguste Vacquerie, the young dramatist who happened to be the recipient of these confidences, listened in silence as Balzac went on to deplore the fact that Victor Hugo had compromised himself by rallying to the Republic. 'What a situation he might have hoped for when Henry v returns! He could have aspired to any position. . . . Ah! why did he have to solicit the votes of the electors? why did he allow himself to be returned to parliament?' Vacquerie, a close friend and ardent admirer of Hugo, objected timidly that Balzac too had been a candidate. 'Oh, but it's different for me', retorted the novelist with a smirk: 'I didn't get elected.'

The Collapse of Socialism

In fact, Hugo had been in two minds whether to seek election to the new Assembly. He had been pressed to do so in April, but had confined himself to publishing a 'Letter to the Electors' in which, without soliciting their votes, he signified that he would accept the mandate if it were offered him; it was not. Then, in June, he contested a by-election with the backing of a committee of conservatives and was returned with a comfortable majority. Thus, after the mortification he endured in February, when his *confrère* Lamartine had gauged so much better than he the political climate of the moment, he was able to stage an honourable return to public life just when Lamartine was being forced out of it.

It is true that the April elections had been something of a triumph for the elder poet. Under the constitution, candidates were allowed to contest more than one constituency, and Lamartine was carried to the head of the list in eight different departments and in Paris, where he polled over a quarter of a million votes; in all, one and a half million Frenchmen registered a wish to have him represent them. But it was a victory in which Lamartine, in so far as he may still have counted himself a friend of the working man, could not take unalloyed pride. George Sand's forebodings had been justified by the event: the elections had strengthened the moderates, while the socialists had been severely mauled. The left-wing intellectuals had scraped derisory polls: Pierre Leroux had collected less than 50,000 votes, Victor Considérant, leader of the Fourierist *école sociétaire* and editor of an influential socialist paper, fewer than 30,000, while Cabet, the gentle communist, author of the utopian *Voyage en Icarie*, had fared even worse. When Lamartine took his seat in the new Assembly, it was noticed that those who shouted '*Vive Lamartine!*' drowned out those whose slogan was still '*Vive la République!*' The representatives of the people in any case lost no time in putting Lamartine in his place. When they came to choose the five deputies who were to constitute the executive commission (the so-called 'pentarchy'), they gave more votes to Arago, the astronomer, who had been Minister of the Armed Forces under the Provisional Government, to Garnier-Pagès, the former Minister of Finance, and to Marie, the creator of the National Workshops, than to Lamartine. The members of the Constituent Assembly 'valued Lamartine as the man who had done away with the red flag and taught the workers a sharp lesson on March 17th and April 16th. They accepted him as the siren whose songs should lull Caliban to sleep . . . '[11]

Caliban was awake and active again on May 15th, but on this occasion Lamartine's siren songs were less effective than the bayonets of the National Guard. The pretext for this new demonstration was the Polish question; but the fate of a remote, dismembered nation was no more than a rallying-cry; what the socialist leaders secretly hoped for was, by a *coup* similar to that of February 24th, to overthrow the reactionary régime imposed on them by the ballot-box and so give fresh impetus to the social reforms that the Provisional Government had been able only to pencil in. Headed by Blanqui and by the mysterious, red-bearded demagogue Aloysius Huber, a man rumoured to be in the pay of the police and acting as an *agent provocateur*, the demonstrators massed in the Place de la Bastille, proceeded along the boulevards to the Place de la Concorde, then crossed the Seine and streamed into the Palais Bourbon. Hugo was to describe the scene graphically in his reminiscences:

> Picture an invasion of the Senate by the vegetable market; gangs of ragged men trooping or rather streaming down past the pillars of the lower galleries and even of the higher ones, entering the chamber, thousands of banners waving everywhere, frightened women with hands upraised, rioters standing on the desks of the press-reporters, the corridors seething, everywhere heads, shoulders, mouths yelling, arms outstretched, fists clenched, no one speaking, everyone shouting.[12]

Suddenly Huber leapt on to the rostrum and pronounced the Assembly dissolved 'in the name of the people misled by its representatives', and the demonstrators rushed out of the Chamber to tread the time-honoured path to the Hôtel de Ville, there to set up a new revolutionary government.

According to a well-learned drill, names were written on pieces of paper, thrown down to the crowd and approved by acclamation. But the National Guard had matters under control within an hour or so. An officer burst into the room where Barbès was drafting decrees and asked him what he was doing. 'I am a member of the new provisional government', came the answer; 'I order you to withdraw.' 'Is that so? Well, in the name of the old one, I am putting you under arrest.' The other insurgent leaders were rapidly rounded up; only Blanqui who, sensing trouble, had left the Hôtel de Ville unobserved a few moments before the arrival of the troops, succeeded in evading the police for a fortnight.

No very important part had been allowed Lamartine in this tragi-comedy. He had tried to argue with the demonstrators on the threshold of the Palais Bourbon, and he had spoken words of encouragement to the National Guard. But it was clear that political passions in France were more polarized than ever, and the situation was uncomfortable for a man who owed his prestige to what success he had had in the past in holding together a nation threatening to fly apart at the centre. In any case the country was inexorably moving towards the acceptance of strong-arm methods, whether of the right or of the left. Correctly, Lamartine saw it as a portent that in the by-elections of June 4th–5th Louis Bonaparte was elected in three departments. 'France is lost', he exclaimed. 'After the model comes the copy; after the Ogre, the mini-ogre (après l'Ogre, l'ogrillon).' On June 12th he tried, and failed, to persuade the Assembly to issue orders to the civil authorities for the Prince's arrest (a law of 1816, confirmed in 1832 and never revoked, made it illegal for any member of the Bonaparte family to set foot on French territory). He resigned from the 'pentarchy' in protest, then, weakly, withdrew his resignation.

He did resign finally, together with his four colleagues, on June 24th. As Sainte-Beuve commented in his diary: 'It can be said, of the fall of the Executive Committee, and of Lamartine in particular, that they literally lost their foothold in blood—in pools of blood.'[13] The blood was shed in the fierce June insurrection provoked by the dissolution of the National Workshops, an institution set up under the Provisional Government which, whatever its defects, did at least represent a first, tentative application of the principle that the state had a duty to provide employment for every able-bodied citizen. But its financing had run into serious difficulties, and in addition it was found that the National Workshops acted as an irresistible magnet for all the unemployed workers in the neighbouring country districts: their presence in the capital was feared by respectable burghers as yet another factor making for insecurity and instability. After weeks of hesitation the government

4 'Victor Hugo and Emile de Girardin attempting to elevate Prince Louis-Napoléon', a celebrated political caricature by Daumier published in *Le Charivari*, 11 December 1848. See p. 27

5 'Interior of a Paris Club', (see p. 33). Note the segregated republican ladies in the balcony

6 Charles Baudelaire, photographed by Nadar

finally summoned up its courage and, on June 21st, promulgated a decree calling to the colours the younger workers and dispersing the rest round the provinces. On the following day, with menacing shouts of 'Bread or lead! (*Du pain ou du plomb!*)', a delegation of workers waited on Marie, the minister principally responsible. He was unable to satisfy them. On Friday, June 23rd the crowds were singing an old revolutionary song to which they had fitted new words:

> *Ah! ça ira, ça ira, ça ira!*
> *Lamartine à la lanterne, Lamartine on le pendra!*

Lamartine was bearing the whole blame for a policy in which he had merely acquiesced. At midday the first barricade went up, near the Porte Saint Denis; the first casualties were two prostitutes, 'beautiful, dishevelled, terrible' as Hugo described them, who, one after the other, mounted the barricade, lifted their skirts up to their waists, and dared the National Guards to fire into the belly of a woman. The National Guards had not the slightest compunction in doing so. In the three-day battle that subsequently raged, Lamartine displayed his usual courage, riding on horseback wherever bullets were flying, side by side with Cavaignac, the general commanding the operations, and doing his utmost to persuade the insurgents to lay down their arms. But resistance ceased only after thousands had been killed on both sides; summary executions disposed of the surviving leaders; as for the rank and file, they were rounded up and deported in batches to Algeria, men and women alike.

After the blood-bath, Lamartine was only occasionally to be seen in Paris. Elections for the presidency were due in December, and he let his name go forward without any serious expectation of being chosen for supreme office. His defeat at the polls, however, was humiliating: only 17,910 votes, against Cavaignac's one and a half million. But even the popularity that Cavaignac owed to his firmness in dealing with the situation in June could not stand against the tidal wave that swept to power the one man who had played no part at all in the revolution, but had simply allowed the others to pull the chestnuts out of the fire for him: Louis Bonaparte.

Victor Hugo and Louis Napoleon

The most experienced politicians were mistaken in their estimates of this man, this incomprehensible visionary so much out of touch with the French scene that even his accent was foreign, who stammered, seemed not to know what he wanted and generally gave the impression of being the least Napoleonic of men; was it even certain that Bonapartist blood really flowed in his

C

veins? Ledru-Rollin dismissed him as an imbecile, Thiers as a cretin who could be led by the nose. Victor Hugo, who staked his political future on this enigmatic figure, was more grievously deceived, and reacted with greater bitterness, than either of these.

Hugo took his seat in the Constituent Assembly heavily committed to the middle-class conservatives who had voted him in. He spoke, on June 20th, in favour of De Falloux' proposals for liquidating the National Workshops, and in the course of this speech warned his listeners against the 'two monsters' which were 'roaring in the darkness, waiting to spring: civil war and the servile war, the lion and the tiger'. Within days the lion and the tiger were at each other's throats. Hugo's sympathies throughout the June insurrection were totally engaged on the side of the forces of repression. As has been said by one of the least prejudiced students of his political career: 'it cannot be denied that in this open manifestation of the class struggle, the author of Les Misères allied himself with the bourgeoisie against the workers.'[14] It would have been astonishing if he had done otherwise. Even though the humanitarian note struck in certain of his writings (Claude Gueux, Le Dernier Jour d'un Condamné) might seem to link him with a writer like George Sand, he did not share, and never had shared, her zeal for a better social order, her impatience with the continued existence of the grosser forms of economic injustice. Hugo had never been a socialist and was not, at this stage, even a radical: at best a mild progressive, with enlightened ideas about universal primary education; but he was opposed to any infringement of the rights of property owners. He was, after all, one himself—he was one of the rare authors of the period whose pen had enabled him to pile up a small private fortune: there is no conservative so double-dyed as your self-made man. The motto of the newspaper L'Événement, which he launched on August 1st, 1848, was: 'Haine vigoureuse de l'anarchie, tendre et profond amour du peuple'. But Hugo's love of the people, tyrannically paternalistic, resembled his love for his mistress Juliette Drouet, whom he would not even suffer to leave her apartment without his knowledge and express permission.

In the latter part of 1848, Hugo's principal political enemy—in his own eyes—was General Cavaignac; not, however, because of the ruthlessness with which this stalwart servant of the Republic had put down the workers' revolt, but more probably because of a sharp exchange he and Cavaignac had had in the Chamber and from which Hugo had emerged bedraggled: the poet was a poor debater, a hesitant orator, and had none of Lamartine's gifts of brilliant improvisation. He foresaw that the only candidate for the presidency who could possibly elbow Cavaignac aside was Louis Napoleon. He had a private conference with the Prince some time in October, which appears to have satisfied him, for *L'Événement*'s pro-Napoleonic campaign opened on October 28th; it is significant that Girardin's paper *La Presse* turned itself similarly into a propaganda organ for the Bonapartist cause about the same time.[15] In the Chamber, Hugo voted consistently for every measure that might facilitate his patron's election to the presidency, and opposed every amendment to the constitution that might have jeopardized it. He even wanted to negative an amendment introduced by Buchez designed to compel the new president to swear allegiance to the constitution and the Republic in the presence of the National Assembly; ironically, it was precisely Louis Bonaparte's violation of this oath, which at the time Hugo argued should not even be required of him, that later constituted a principal article in the long requisitory that the disappointed and exiled poet was to fulminate against the new Emperor of the French.

Did Hugo hope, eventually, for a portfolio in the Prince-President's first ministry? On the face of it, this seems unlikely: his ambitions were at once more nebulous and less prosaic; he would have preferred the role of untitled *éminence grise*, acting as a secret counsellor rather than as a privy councillor. An invitation to dinner at the Élysée seemed to promise much but, in spite of the new President's graciousness in engaging him in private conversation, nothing came of it beyond the offer of an embassy: Madrid or Naples. Was Louis Bonaparte trying to rid himself decently of this faintly embarrassing supporter? In the Chamber, Hugo continued to figure as a staunch adherent of the executive power, one of the 'king's men'; but the uneasy honeymoon ended in October 1849 when a speech he made on the question of the expedition to Rome came near to compromising the President with the Catholic right.

Thereafter, the poet could steer only one course if he was to rescue his political fortunes from shipwreck. The image he now sought to project was that of the anti-Catholic, anti-monarchist opposition leader; sooner or later, he guessed, Louis Bonaparte would be compelled to enlist his aid against the conservative majority in the Assembly, if only to prevent a restoration of one or the other branch of the exiled royal family. Leading articles in *L'Événement*, whether written or merely inspired by Victor Hugo—the editorial staff included his two sons, Charles and François-Victor—tended to use such typically tendentious historical arguments as that, since Charles x lost his throne when he fell out with Chateaubriand, and Louis-Philippe after Lamartine joined the opposition, it behoved Louis Napoleon Bonaparte, if he wished to continue in power, to pay greater heed to the advice of Victor Hugo.

Isolated and distrusted, Hugo pursued his lonely path serenely; isolation and distrust were, after all, the conditions under which the Romantic hero traditionally grew to greatest stature. The three speeches he made in the Chamber between January and May 1850 must rank among his noblest. The first was directed against the *loi Falloux* which he called, with every justification, 'a law of oppression masquerading as emancipation'. On the pretext of freeing education from state control, in effect it granted the Church, as the only body with the resources to do so, licence to set up, administer and staff its own schools in competition with those of the state; it ended the public monopoly of secondary education which had been so admirable a feature of the system inaugurated by Napoleon I. In another of his speeches Hugo assailed, in vain, the proposal to limit the franchise to citizens who could prove three years' residence in the same locality—a blatant piece of class legislation, since the three million voters, representing 30 per cent of the electorate, who were to be disenfranchised belonged for the most part to the body of migrant or seasonal workers or to the poorer sections of the community who, because they were not on the tax-collector's roll, could not prove continuous residence.

His remaining intervention was designed to mobilize opinion against the proposal to introduce the penalty of deportation for political offences. It was in this speech that Hugo formulated, not for the first time, his understanding of the cleavage between politics and art embodied in the myth of the impractical visionary and the hard-headed man of affairs, a myth which for the rest of the century bedevilled every attempt to apply civilized standards to political life. Hugo was commenting ironically on the embarrassment he detected among politicians whenever the word *conscience* was introduced into a debate. 'They tell us we understand nothing of business, that we lack a political sense, that we are not to be taken seriously and—how can I say it?—well, the truth is, they call us something very rude, they use the most vulgar insult they can think of: they call us *poets*!'[16]

By the mere force of circumstance, Hugo was being driven willy-nilly into the ranks of the socialists, a decimated and temporarily leaderless group. *L'Événement* began mooting the possibility of Hugo's candidature at the next presidential elections, due to be held in 1852. The newspaper was being harried by the authorities and subjected to heavy fines, while its staff—including both Hugo's sons—were in and out of prison. Then, on July 14th, 1851, a debate was initiated in the Chamber on a bill to prolong the president's period of office beyond the statutory four years. Louis Bonaparte, playing a game of double bluff, had probably discounted its failure: a three-quarters majority was necessary for a revision of the constitution, but his calculation seems to have been that the deputies, seeing he was seeking to alter it by due process of law, would not suspect that he was secretly planning to overthrow it by violent means. Hugo intervened in the debate on July 17th, in the face of derisive interruptions—for everybody knew that he had hopes of the presidency himself. He alone, among all those who spoke against the proposal, had the courage—or the bad taste—to make it an occasion for a personal attack on the Prince-President and a ruthless denunciation of his schemes. 'What! because there was once a man who won a victory at Marengo and who reigned, you think you should reign, you whose only victory has been at Satory? . . . What! after Augustus, Augustulus? What! because we have had Napoleon the Great, we must needs have Napoleon the Little?'[17] This last phrase, *Napoléon le Petit*, appeared so felicitous, at least to its coiner, that he used it later as the title of the first propaganda broadside he launched from abroad against the Second Empire.

On December 2nd, the anniversary of the coronation of his uncle, Louis Napoleon struck. A handful of opposition deputies, including Thiers and Cavaignac but not Hugo, were arrested in the small hours: notices were plastered on the walls announcing the suspension of the constitution. Hugo escaped from his house, met a few of his political allies in secret and helped them draw up a proclamation branding Louis Napoleon as a traitor and declaring him an outlaw. It was pathetically ineffective. He spent the next two days wandering about the streets, trying in vain to arouse a largely apathetic population. By December 4th opposition had been crushed by a show of force and Hugo went into hiding until, on the 11th, bearing a false passport, he took the train to Brussels. He owed his safety less, perhaps, to the disguise he wore than to the policy Louis Napoleon had adopted of placing no obstacles in the way of those of his opponents who wished to leave the country; their flight did at least save him the embarrassment of having to lock them up.

The End of the Second Republic

As it happened, Hugo was the only prominent French author, if one excepts the doctrinaire socialists, who was obliged to go into exile as a consequence of the *coup d'état*. Balzac was already in his grave. Lamartine, now an ailing sexagenarian, heard the news from a sick-bed. After his crushing defeat at the presidential elections he had spent the first few months of 1849 putting his affairs in order and writing his *Histoire de la révolution de 1848*, a lengthy piece of apologetics which appeared on July 13th and was eagerly read. Later that month he was elected to the Legislative Assembly, where the occasional speeches he made were listened to respectfully and politely ignored: he had not a shred of political power left. 'A noble soul,' as his nobly born bio-grapher sums him up, 'who had no understanding of the sordidness and prosaic mechanics of political intrigue and bargaining. Hence, the politicians dismissed him disdainfully as a poet. A poet he was, God be praised, and it is to be regretted that he did not remain one.' It is evident that the Marquis de Luppé, in writing this epitaph,[18] has accepted implicitly the line of demarca-tion drawn by a later society—a society whose assumptions are still, to a certain extent, conditioned by memories of the fiasco of 1848—between what is and what is not the poet's business. Lamartine's earlier reputation as the supreme exponent of introspective romanticism undoubtedly fostered in him some generous illusions; he was not the best judge of men and was poorly versed in the Napoleonic art of choosing trustworthy henchmen and inspiring their loyalty. In addition, his greatest gift, that of persuasive oratory, was subject to the law of diminishing returns: he spoke too well for people to take him altogether at his word. He did, of course, achieve some note-worthy successes; probably only Lamartine, one of whose verse-collections was entitled *Harmonies poétiques et religieuses*, could have accomplished the almost impossible task of bringing into accord, at least for a few vital weeks, all the conflicting interests that were eddying in the revolutionary maelstrom. In the end it became clear that the objectives he was striving to harmonize were essentially contradictory. He favoured the rule of law and the establish-ment of an ordered society, yet he wanted something like justice for the exploited classes, and this could have been achieved only at the cost of rend-ing the fabric of the existing social order. Conservatives regarded him with suspicion because of his supposed secret dealings with the 'reds', while, viewed through working-class eyes, he appeared shifty, untrustworthy, a gentleman and therefore one of 'them'.

As for George Sand, having, as we have seen, fallen into disgrace in government circles through her incautious advocacy of a socialist coup to banish the spectre of a reactionary legislature, she was compelled, between mid-April and mid-May 1848, to take a back seat. Her own newspaper having ceased to appear, she became a contributor to Thoré's *La Vraie République*, for which Barbès and Leroux also wrote. In her articles she continued to press her favourite ideas, arguing that there was no risk of immediate communism, and that communism was in any case nothing new or particularly frightening, being simply the application to social affairs of the teaching of the Gospels. Her communism was, needless to say, pre-Marxist.

The failure of the working-class demonstration of May 15th finally destroyed George Sand's hopes. It is probable that she had some hand in the plans for the take-over: Barbès later wrote to her: 'Your name very nearly

figured among those who were to form my government of May 15th.'
Rightly or wrongly, she believed herself to be in serious danger, burnt all
papers that might compromise her (including, regrettably, most of the diary
she had been keeping that year) and fled to Nohant from which safe refuge
she did not emerge for another eighteen months. Not that she found much
to console her or restore her peace of mind in the quiet of the country. The
most absurd rumours were circulating among her neighbours about her
terrorist activities during the Revolution. 'In the provinces,' she wrote to
Thoré, 'you have only to be a republican to be branded a communist; and if
by chance you are a socialist republican, ah! then you are believed to drink
human blood, to be a slayer of little children, a wife-beater, a bankrupt, a
drunkard, a thief, and you risk being knocked on the head in the woods by
a ploughboy indoctrinated by his master or the parish priest.'[19]

She went on sending the occasional article for publication in *La Vraie
République*, including a courageous defence of Barbès, then under lock and
key at Vincennes. Then she returned to literature proper and wrote the most
charming of her rustic idylls, *La Petite Fadette*. The preface she composed for
this work in September 1848 seems to voice the whole deeply felt agony of
the Romantic generation to which George Sand belonged, who had welcomed the Revolution with such high hopes, only to see them all dragged
in the mire. This preface reaffirms the Romantic belief in the supreme value
of art, considered as a force that transcends the artist and exists independently
of him; but the idea is also expressed that there are periods in history when,
in despair at the apparent invincibility of political injustice, the devotees of
art must fall silent and put their trust in the future both as artists and as social
idealists:

> Art is like nature, always beautiful; like God, always good; but there are
> times when it has to exist as a mere abstraction until some later date, when
> it will manifest itself again to worthier adepts. Its breath will then re-
> awaken lyres that have long been silent; but can it ever make vibrate those
> that the tempest has broken? Today, art is in travail of decomposition in
> readiness for some future burgeoning. It is like all human things in time of
> revolution, like the plants that die in the winter to live again in the spring.
> But time kills many a seed. What does it matter to nature that there should
> be some flowers, some fruits the fewer? What does it matter to mankind that
> some voices should be silenced, some hearts stilled by sorrow or by death?
> No, art cannot console me for the knowledge that truth and justice are
> today crucified on earth. Art will live on without us. Superb and immortal
> like poetry, like nature, it will continue to smile on our ruins.

Leconte de Lisle and Louis Ménard

Each of the poets and novelists discussed so far in this chapter belongs to that generation of writers who reached maturity and won celebrity in 1830 or before and who, by 1848, had largely spent their literary capital; only Hugo had still to write his most important poetry and his single major contribution to the art of the novel. In order to complete the picture of the impact of the Revolution on men of letters, it is necessary to say something about a younger group of writers for whom the events of 1848 and 1851 were even more traumatic, occurring as they did at the very outset of their literary careers. Once again we shall select a sample of representative poets who, by the variety of their reactions and behaviour, may be considered to illustrate the different ways in which political events affected members of their generation.

Three years before the Revolution broke out, Charles-Marie-René Leconte de Lisle, the son of a sugar-planter, was kicking his heels in idleness on an island in the Indian Ocean when he received through the post the offer of a position on the staff of the Parisian newspaper *La Démocratie pacifique*. The proposal was transmitted to him by a former fellow student at the University of Rennes, where he had pursued his legal studies in a desultory and ineffectual manner between 1838 and 1843. At Rennes Leconte de Lisle had spent less time on the *Code* than on the articles he turned out for an ephemeral literary review, *La Variété*; his contributions betray the deep admiration he felt for the literary work of George Sand and also for Lamennais' social catholicism. 'From Lamennais' brand of messianism to socialism was but a short step', as one of his biographers remarks.[20]

La Démocratie pacifique was a daily paper which had been founded in 1843, along with a monthly magazine called *La Phalange*, by a group of Fourier's disciples led by Victor Considérant. Leconte de Lisle was in no sense a convinced fourierist, but he was a sympathizer, and among the pieces of verse that he published in *La Phalange* in 1845 a few, 'Les Épis', 'La Robe du Centaure' notably, could at a pinch be interpreted allegorically as propaganda for the cause. More clearly, they provided strong evidence of Leconte de Lisle's technical mastery of his medium, a fact quickly noticed by two young Parisian poets, Thalès Bernard and Louis Ménard. Thalès Bernard discovered Leconte de Lisle's address, and he and Ménard paid the new poet a call. Later they introduced him to Théodore de Banville who at this date had already published his first two verse collections, *Les Cariatides* and *Les Stalactites*. These young men, who were all of an age—being in their late twenties— were equally addicted to poetry and, though in this their competence varied, to Greek literature. But all kinds of intellectual inquiry attracted them. Thalès Bernard was an enthusiastic student of the newly founded science of comparative mythology, while Ménard was passionately interested in chemistry and even made some notable chemical discoveries until a laboratory explosion caused him to abandon his researches. Each of them, though again with varying degrees of confidence and fervour, looked forward to the revolution which, they anticipated, would sweep away the existing social order. 'The hour will come when everything will necessarily collapse', Leconte de Lisle wrote to a correspondent in Reunion Island. 'With what joy I shall descend from the heights of serene contemplation in order to play my part in the battle and see for myself the colour of the blood of brutes and cowards. The time is drawing close, and the nearer it comes the more I feel that I am a child of the Convention and that the work of death has not been completed.'[21]

The writer was not quite the fire-eater that these ferocious effusions might suggest, but there can be no question of the unbounded enthusiasm with which, after the initial surprise, he and Ménard greeted the outbreak of the Revolution. Having been sickened in his youth by the barbarous treatment meted out to the negro labourers on the plantations of his native island, Leconte de Lisle was deeply interested in the plans being prepared by the Provisional Government for the emancipation of all slaves in French settlements overseas. A commission was appointed on March 4, 1848, to investigate the problem. The planters' representatives were quick to protest, whereupon Leconte de Lisle, with admirable disinterestedness (since his own family's fortunes depended on the maintenance of the system of slave labour) organized a counter-protest among the young men from the colonies resident in Paris. On April 27th the decree of emancipation was promulgated; it was one of the very few measures taken by the Provisional Government which was never subsequently repealed or tampered with. But Leconte de Lisle's father, not surprisingly, retaliated by cutting off the small allowance he had been paying his son.

Both Leconte de Lisle and Ménard were active in support of the republican clubs which Ménard called, in the account of the Revolution which he later published in Louis Blanc's paper Le Peuple, 'the temples of the new religion'. In the impressions he records of these gatherings there is no trace of the farcical pretentiousness that characterized them in Flaubert's view. According to Ménard, 'it was magnificent to see these men who, only shortly before, had been seeking in wine or in the debased spectacles of the playhouses some relaxation from their toil, for gathering every evening to listen to the good tidings, the gospel of justice, and drink the word of life that fell from the lips of the initiates.'[22] The club to which Leconte de Lisle belonged entrusted him that spring with a flattering but taxing mission: along with a number of other young republicans, he was ordered into the provinces, his business being to explain the policies of the Provisional Government and win adherents to the revolutionary ideology in the still benighted backwaters of France. His destination was Dinan in Britanny, where he had stayed some years before in the family of a cousin of his father's, a solicitor. Leconte de Lisle was present at the planting of a tree of liberty, founded a '*Club républicain démocrate*', delivered some speeches—but achieved very little; according to one account, he so infuriated his audience at a public meeting that he was compelled to leap out of a window to escape being lynched.

Sensitive introvert that he was, Leconte de Lisle emerged sobered and disillusioned by these experiences. He understood well enough the political temper of rural France to divine the massive swing to the right that the April elections for the Constituent Assembly would produce. 'It [the Assembly] will be composed of bourgeois and royalists. It will vote good old-fashioned reactionary laws, will allow the social and political order that prevailed under Louis-Philippe to subsist indefinitely and—who knows?—will shortly impose on us a new monarchy.' But France deserved nothing better. 'What a dirty, disgusting race humanity is! Is there any limit to the stupidity of the common people? They are doomed to live in harness for all eternity, incapable of doing without saddle and bit. For this reason, if we continue to do battle, it will not be for their sake, but in defence of our sacred ideal. Let it perish of hunger and cold, this nation so easily fooled, which will shortly be engaged in massacring its true friends!' These bitter words occur in a letter to Ménard written at the end of April.[23] A little later, hearing of the arrest of his friend Paul de Flotte in the round-up of socialists after the abortive *coup de main* of May 15th, Leconte de Lisle gave way to utter despair.

The question whether, and if so to what extent, he was involved in the street fighting in June cannot be satisfactorily settled; the testimony is conflicting. Henri de Régnier later recounted that the poet had told him he had helped to man a barricade and, when it was overrun, had escaped and made his way to the river to wash his face which was black with gunpowder. The story that Ménard and he presented the insurgents with the formula for gun-cotton, a recently invented explosive, is almost certainly apocryphal. But Leconte de Lisle himself later testified that he was arrested and spent 48 hours in prison.

Whatever they were, these final experiences completed his disillusionment in politics; if he continued to believe in socialism as an ideal, he had lost all faith in the leaders, 'too stupid, too ignorant'. He made up his mind to dabble no more in politics and to devote himself instead to his art for the remainder of his life, scraping a living as best he could as a teacher of the classical languages. Here we have the characteristic disengagement of the poet from socio-political activity, his withdrawal into an unreal world of the historical imagination, which will be so marked a feature of the Parnassian movement during the Second Empire.

> How can the artist fail to recognize [he wrote to Ménard] that all these men devoted to the crudities of action, to the utterance of vapid clichés, tirelessly trotting out the petty, pitiable theories of our times, are not moulded in the same clay as he? ... How can he fail to be repelled by the grossness of their emotions, the platitude and vulgarity of their ideas? Does even the language they speak resemble his? ... The great works of art weigh more heavily in the scales than five hundred million text-books on socialism and democracy. I like to think—and God forgive me for making so monstrous a comparison—that Homer's works will count for rather more than Blanqui's in the sum total of the moral achievement of humanity.[24]

Whether Ménard—who read this outburst in a letter his friend addressed him on September 7th—attempted or not to argue Leconte de Lisle into a less embittered frame of mind, is something we shall never know; but it does appear that he was less ready than his friend to abandon his earlier illusions. The *Prologue d'une révolution*, which as we have noted appeared first in instalments in *Le Peuple*, was published in book form in 1849; its author was immediately prosecuted and given a 15 months' prison sentence which he evaded by the simple expedient of buying a one-way train-ticket to Brussels. The enforced leisure of exile encouraged Ménard to start cultivating his art once more. One of the poems he wrote at this period, 'Adrastée', a paean in honour of the working-class victims of the June insurrection, deeply impressed Karl Marx, whom Ménard met in London. He wrote a sadder, quieter protest against the referendum which white-washed Louis-Napoleon's seizure of power; this poem, 'Cremutius Cordus', can be read as his resigned farewell to earlier revolutionary dreams:

> *L'idéal qu'avait rêvé ma jeunesse,*
> *L'étoile où montaient mes espoirs perdus,*
> *Ce n'était pas l'art, l'amour, la richesse,*
> *C'était la justice; et je n'y crois plus.*

Having undertaken not to engage further in political activity, Ménard was allowed to return to France in 1852, and for the duration of the Second

Empire confined himself to scholarly research and the writing of works of pure erudition. Henri Peyre maintains that his republican fervour had simply been transferred from the present to the distant past, and that the interest he took in the working of Athenian democracy was a substitute for the forbidden pleasure of studying the more practical issues of nineteenth-century socialism. Be that as it may, it is undeniable that, in Ménard's case no less than in Leconte de Lisle's, disillusionment at the course taken by the Second Republic was entire and profoundly corroding.

Baudelaire and the Revolution

It is an astonishing fact that no poet had a closer acquaintance with the barricades, wherever they were set up in Paris between February 1848 and December 1851, than the cool, caustic, self-controlled aesthete Baudelaire. We have already seen how Courbet and he, quivering with excitement, watched the throng of demonstrators in the Place de la Concorde on the first day of the Revolution. The following morning (February 23rd) he joined forces with a group of friends, among them Champfleury and a certain Charles Toubin, whose later reminiscences constitute the sole reasonably reliable source of information available to us about Baudelaire's activities during those crucial days.[25] Starting from the Café de la Rotonde, near the École de Médecine in the Latin Quarter—the famous *Brasserie* which was to become known as the headquarters of the realist school—they crossed to the right bank and tried to make their way towards the Place du Châtelet where they could hear the sound of firing. The barricades they kept encountering forced them to follow a circuitous route, but eventually they reached the Boulevard du Temple, where they learned that the King had dismissed Guizot. Thinking all the commotion would now die down, they dispersed, but met again that evening for dinner. Baudelaire gave the impression of being, writes Toubin, 'enchanted with what he had seen during those two days. The opening scene in the drama had deeply interested him; but the end disappointed him and in his view the curtain had fallen too soon. I can never remember seeing him so light-hearted, so active for a man normally of sedentary habits. His eyes were sparkling.' The curtain, of course, was far from having fallen, and on the morrow (February 24th) Toubin came across him standing behind a half-built barricade, armed with a shining new double-barrelled gun and wearing a splendid yellow leather cartridge belt round his waist: Baudelaire had joined with the insurgents in raiding a gunsmith's shop.

Such reckless espousal of the cause of social reform was a reaction that none of those who knew him at the time would have predicted. Ernest Prarond, who was as close to Baudelaire as anyone, having been associated with him ever since they were at school together, testifies: 'In those days when we used to stroll around, endeavouring only to clothe forms and colours in words, Baudelaire did not simply disdain politics, he professed a positive contempt for it; neither he, nor any of us felt anything but pity for the inferior art practised by leaders of men. Consequently, the excitement my friend exhibited astonished us all.'[26] It has continued to astonish Baudelaire's biographers and commentators especially since, in all his published writings before 1848, he expresses opinions so extravagantly reactionary both in manner and content that some doubt persists as to whether they were intended to be taken altogether at face value. There is the notorious dedication of his *Salon de 1846* 'to the Bourgeois' which begins: 'You are the majority—in number and intelligence; therefore you are strength—and strength is justice.' Elsewhere in the same pamphlet Baudelaire declared that whenever he saw a policeman beating up a republican in the street he was filled with profound satisfaction and felt like urging the policeman to even greater brutality.[27] How does one square such retrograde sentiments with Baudelaire's behaviour only two years later and the very practical support he then gave to the republican movement?

According to one ingenious and attractive explanation, it was from sheer fractiousness that Baudelaire displayed this aggressive anti-republicanism in the years immediately preceding the Revolution. To be an overt reactionary was, at that period, little short of scandalous, and to scandalize his contemporaries was always Baudelaire's favourite pastime. While all right-thinking citizens were ridiculing Louis-Philippe, denouncing the soulless reign of the bankers and captains of industry, and declaring their attachment to the cause of reform, the 'imp of the perverse' in Baudelaire drove him to proclaim exactly contrary opinions. There is no doubt some truth in this, but at the same time it is important not to exaggerate Baudelaire's lack of consistency. In February 1848 he joined a people in arms. Before then, as Prarond implies, it was not the people's aspirations that he condemned, but the people's leaders, and for them his aversion remained unaffected and undiminished by the events of the year of revolution.

The indispensable key to his attitude is to be found in a text never published during Baudelaire's lifetime and still too often overlooked by those concerned to expound his political thought.[28] The opening lines of *Assommons les pauvres!* can be translated approximately as follows:

I had shut myself up in my room for a fortnight, surrounded by the kind of books that were popular at that time (this was some sixteen or seventeen years ago): treatises on the art of making the nations healthy, wealthy and wise in ten easy lessons. I had in this manner digested—ingurgitated, I should say—all the elucubrations of these contractors for the public weal, including those whose remedy is that the poor should all accept slavery and those who preach to them that they are monarchs unjustly deprived of their kingdom. It is scarcely to be wondered that I had reached a condition bordering on vertigo or addle-headedness.

The implied sneer at the works of the doctrinaire socialists who provided the shaky theoretical foundations of the 1848 Revolution cannot be missed; if Baudelaire's account of their teachings is deliberately distorted, it is still recognizable and, besides, the clue provided by the dating ('some sixteen or seventeen years ago') is in itself sufficient: *Assommons les pauvres!* was written probably about 1864-5.

The rest of the prose-poem tells how, finding a decrepit pauper stationed outside a tavern, Baudelaire, instead of giving him alms, threw himself on the fellow without warning and began cudgelling him mercilessly. To his delight and relief the beggar retaliated with spirit, blacked both the poet's eyes and knocked out several of his teeth. Getting to his feet, Baudelaire pulled out his purse and shared the contents with his assailant, overjoyed at having established, if in so outrageous a fashion, that the poor are capable of securing justice for themselves without any help from vapid visionaries whose remedies, if applied, would prove more devitalizing than the social evils that beset them.

It is, in fact, arguable that no real discrepancy exists between the political views Baudelaire expressed before and after the Revolution and the activities he engaged in during it. He was as dismayed as was Marx by the moral and intellectual flabbiness of the early socialist writers, but he was better able than any other poet of his age to identify himself with the aspirations of the down-trodden. He stood with them on the barricades—not only in February, but also in the far more dangerous street fighting in June. Le Vavasseur, who had been a friend of Baudelaire's since his student days, records how, in the concluding stages of that ultimate insurrection of the proletariat against the property-owners, he met the poet in the company of Pierre Dupont, 'nervous, excited, in a state of feverish agitation ... I had never seen Baudelaire in such a mood. He was perorating, declaiming, boasting, fidgeting to rush off to martyrdom. "They have just arrested De Flotte", he said. "Was it because they could smell gunpowder on his hands? Smell mine!" And then socialist tirades, the apotheosis of the bankruptcy of society, etc.'[29]

Baudelaire *lived* the Revolution, and had only contempt for those who mouthed phrases about it. He adopted the habit of attending the meetings of republican clubs in the weeks preceding the April elections in order to interrupt the candidates' flights of oratory and, with a show of sarcastic interest, ask them their views on difficult questions of domestic and foreign policy. For a fortnight that summer he acted as secretary of an opposition paper, *La Tribune nationale*, with a strongly anti-socialist line; he signed nothing, but it is not difficult to recognize his style in this or that article attacking 'idiots guided by fixed ideas, pretentious utopians who cannot sustain the shock of a contradiction'.[30] Baudelaire himself was admirably fitted to cope with contradictions, he who claimed that he could appreciate why a man might 'desert one cause in order to find out what it felt like to serve a different one'. Everywhere is discernible the same dandified disdain for the inky-fingered theorist; and invariably it is combined with an authentic admiration for the man who, when all else fails, betakes himself to the barricade, relying on his own courage. 'Faith in progress is a doctrine for the lazy', he wrote in that astonishing collection of maxims, *Mon Cœur mis à nu*, composed, of course, many years after the events we are concerned with. 'There can only be progress (genuine, that is to say moral, progress) in the individual and through the individual himself.'

Mon Cœur mis à nu provides the only evidence we have that Baudelaire was also involved in the fighting in December 1851. There is a brief entry that runs as follows: 'My fury at the *coup d'état*. How many shots were fired at me! Another Bonaparte, the shame of it!' The ease with which the Republic was overthrown strengthened Baudelaire's contempt for the passive mass of the people (an attitude which needs to be carefully distinguished from the solidarity he felt with the struggling proletariat, the revolutionary in arms). 'All in all, at the bar of history and of the French people, it must be accounted one of Napoleon III's great glories that he demonstrated how anyone who chooses can, by making sure of the telegraphic service and the state printing press, govern a great nation. They are fools who think that such things can be accomplished without the consent of the people.'[31]

The abrupt extinction of the Second Republic does seem temporarily to have cured Baudelaire of his interest in politics: as he expressed it to his old friend and enemy Ancelle, *'le 2 décembre m'a physiquement dépolitiqué'*. But towards the end of his life, when republicanism was once more able to raise its head as institutions became liberalized, this interest revived and Baudelaire asked himself retrospectively what had been the nature of his intoxication in 1848. Various answers could be given, he decided. 'The thirst for vengeance. The *natural* pleasure one takes in acts of demolition. Literary intoxication; reminiscences of one's reading.' He then refers to the great working-class manifestation of May 15th which came close to establishing a socialist régime. 'Still the desire for destruction', he adds: 'a lawful desire, if all that is natural is lawful.' As for the street battles in June, what did they prove? 'The madness of the common people and the madness of the middle classes. The natural love of crime.' In interpreting these admittedly ambiguous and truncated reflections, one is struck by the threefold repetition of the word *natural*, underlined on its first occurrence. In Baudelaire's system of thought, nature was opposed not merely to art, but to civilization also and to the working of the Divine Spirit on earth; a faithful disciple of Joseph de Maistre, Baudelaire embodies an extreme reaction against Rousseauism. That 'all that is natural is lawful' was not a proposition he subscribed to: on the contrary, it was the kind of heresy he was constantly inveighing against. His celebrated philosophy of dandyism springs from an idealization of the artificial; dandyism is nothing more than a controlled and disciplined suppression of natural reflexes. 'Can the Dandy be imagined addressing the people', Baudelaire asked, 'save to insult it?' The dandy yields to no natural emotion, however generous.

Revolt is natural, therefore blasphemous, sinful, satanic. It is not for nothing that the few pieces of socialistic poetry that Baudelaire included in the *Fleurs du Mal* are grouped under the title 'La Révolte', and that the most effective of them is a poem called 'Les Litanies de Satan'. But that is not the whole picture. The unique dipolarity of Baudelaire's thought means that what is damnable, considered from one viewpoint, becomes hallowed, seen from another, and that these viewpoints can be adopted by the poet almost indiscriminately. The two 'postulations', towards God and towards Satan, are 'simultaneous'. From Satan's vantage-point, the saints on the right hand of the Throne are in hell; Lucifer's fall could as accurately be denoted an ascent. Baudelaire wondered about his intoxication, his *ivresse*, in 1848; but he did not regret it, let alone condemn it, even in 1866. One recalls that the *Petits poèmes en prose* include one short piece with the significant title 'Enivrez-vous': 'One should always be intoxicated. . . . With wine, with poetry, or with virtue, it matters little.'

Thus Baudelaire represents among his contemporaries a special and perhaps unique case: the failure of the Revolution did not so much disillusion as disintoxicate him. Along with thousands of others he had been able to give rein, in February and in June 1848, to his 'lawful', natural, satanic lust for revolt and destruction. The *coup d'état* meant the enthronement of 'unlawful', unnatural, but divine authority, and Baudelaire does not hesitate to speak of the 'providentiality' of Napoleon III.

By the zest with which he flung himself into public disorder, as well as by the masochistic fervour with which he acquiesced in the re-establishment of order under the autocracy, Baudelaire epitomizes the whole trend of the cultural reaction which, after 1851, went hand in hand with political reaction. Republicanism became a crime, and the artist accepted it as such. 'Myself', Baudelaire wrote arrogantly, 'when I consent to be republican, I do evil knowingly.' He was not far from regarding republicanism as an aspect of original sin. 'We have all of us got the republican spirit in our veins, as we have the pox in our bones; we are democratized and syphilized.' Just as syphilis was the punishment for the sin of sexual promiscuity, so republicanism, an infection equally incurable, was to be regarded as punishment for the crime of social promiscuity, of prostituting oneself to the masses.

Notes

[1] Quoted (in the original) by H. J. Hunt, *Le Socialisme et le romantisme en France* (Oxford, 1935), pp. 34–5. (My italics.)

[2] Quoted by Georges Rudé in the introduction to the English translation of Georges Duveau's *1848: the making of a revolution* (London, 1967).

[3] The students met on the evening of February 21st in the office of their newspaper *L'Avant-Garde* and resolved to defy the ban; accordingly they marched on the Place de la Concorde from the direction of the Sorbonne.

[4] Duveau, *op. cit.*, p. 85.

[5] Wladimir Karénine, *George Sand, sa vie et son œuvre*, vol. IV (Paris, 1926), p. 74.

[6] George Sand, *Correspondance*, vol. III (Paris, Calmann-Lévy, 1883), p. 3.

[7] *Ibid.*, pp. 9–10.

[8] *La Cause du peuple*, April 16th, 1848. Quoted by Karénine, *op. cit.*, p. 67.

[9] 'Nous avons la *liberté* de mourir de faim, l'*égalité* dans la misère, la *fraternité* du coin.' Letter to Mme Hanska, quoted in André Maurois, *Prométhée ou la vie de Balzac* (Paris, 1965), p. 564. Balzac appears to have been adopting the words of a popular song, the text of which may be found in M.-L. Pailleron, *George Sand et les hommes de 48* (Paris, 1953), pp. 105–6. It ran as follows: 'Liberté de mourir de faim, Égalité dans la misère. Fraternité Selon Caïn, Voilà ce que Ledru-Rollin Nous offre dans sa circulaire.' The reference is to Ledru-Rollin's circulars addressed to the *commissaires provinciaux*, the Republican equivalents of the *préfets*. In the second of these, he told them: 'Vos pouvoirs sont illimités. Agents d'une autorité révolutionnaire, vous êtes révolutionnaires aussi.'

[10] The text is reproduced in Balzac, *Correspondance*, vol. V (Paris, Garnier, 1969), pp. 294–6.

[11] Duveau, *op. cit.*, p. 109.

[12] *Choses vues*, vol. I (Paris, Ollendorff, 1913), p. 349.

[13] *Les Cahiers de Sainte-Beuve* (Paris, 1876), p. 104.

[14] E. M. Grant, *Victor Hugo during the Second Republic* (Harvard U.P., 1935), p. 11.

D

[15] Daumier executed one of his best political cartoons of the year (it was published in *Le Charivari*, Dec. 11, 1848) on the subject. Hugo and Girardin are holding up a plank on which Prince Louis Bonaparte is balancing—a reference to the Frankish custom of elevating a new king on a shield. But Hugo has only half raised his side, as though doubtful about the propriety of what he is doing, and the future Napoleon III, booted, spurred, and wearing a tricorn, is looking down at his unreliable supporter with an expression of mingled alarm and displeasure.

[16] *Actes et paroles*, vol. 1 (Paris, Albin Michel, 1937), p. 197.

[17] *Ibid.*, p. 257. Certain allusions require to be clarified. Louis Napoleon had reviewed units of the French army at Satory a few weeks previously and had been acclaimed with shouts of *Vive l'Empereur!* Augustulus was the name of the last Roman Emperor in the west, deposed by Odoacer in 476 A.D. after reigning for only a year.

[18] *Les Travaux et les jours d'Alphonse de Lamartine* (Paris, 1942), p. 390.

[19] Quoted by Karénine, *op. cit.*, p. 114.

[20] Edmond Estève, *Leconte de Lisle, l'homme et l'œuvre* (Paris, n.d.), p. 41.

[21] Quoted by Estève, *op. cit.*, p. 66.

[22] Quoted by Henri Peyre, *Louis Ménard* (Yale U.P., 1932), p. 65.

[23] Estève, *op. cit.*, p. 68.

[24] *Ibid.*, p. 70.

[25] They were published, under the heading 'Souvenirs d'un septuagénaire', in the *Revue de France*, 1925–6. An analysis will be found in Jules Mouquet and W. T. Bandy, *Baudelaire en 1848* (Paris, 1946), pp. 9–11.

[26] See E. & J. Crépet, *Baudelaire* (Paris, n.d.), p. 76, n.l.

[27] See Baudelaire, *Curiosités esthétiques*, ed. H. Lemaître (Paris, 1962), pp. 97–100, 191–2.

[28] Not, however, by Laurence Lerner. See the opening pages of his essay on Baudelaire in *French Literature and its Background: the Early Nineteenth Century*, ed. J. Cruickshank (Oxford U.P., 1969).

[29] Quoted by Crépet, *op. cit.*, p. 82. On Pierre Dupont, see below, p. 78.

[30] *La Tribune nationale*, May 31, 1848.

[31] *Mon cœur mis à nu*, viii, xliv.

[32] *Ibid.*, viii.

two

The Blue-Pencil Régime

Theatre Censorship

Government censorship has had a long and inglorious history in France. Its better advertised severities have been directed against the staging of supposedly subversive plays, like Molière's *Tartuffe* and Beaumarchais' *Mariage de Figaro*, though it is noteworthy that neither of these two *causes célèbres* resulted in anything more than a temporary intermission in performances. The system of preventive censorship, or of the issue of licences for the staging of all new plays, dates back to the end of Louis xiv's reign, and in the course of the two succeeding centuries such rules as had been formulated were applied, sometimes with extreme harshness, sometimes with relative leniency, in accordance with the whims and fears of successive administrations. In few areas did government policy impinge more directly on the literary scene. There were brief periods (as between 1791 and 1794) when, officially at least, complete liberty obtained; while at other times (notably under the First Empire) censorship of the most rigorous kind was enforced. By comparison, the repression practised under the Second Empire was mild and less effective than is sometimes claimed. Its vacillating and arbitrary functioning arose from a basic uncertainty as to what constituted subversion in a literary and artistic context, the difficulty being always to distinguish between what was plainly outrageous and what was no more than amusingly audacious. The theatres were expected to provide entertainment while respecting current shibboleths; the two aims were not always absolutely compatible. Second-Empire society, which was stuffy and gay in turns and often simultaneously, could never quite make up its mind whether it preferred to be titillated or bored.

In any case it would be wrong to attribute the re-establishment of theatrical censorship (abolished in the early days of the Second Republic) to the government of Napoleon III. State control of the theatres was re-introduced before the Prince-President seized power. After the first few months of exhilarating freedom in 1848, the Republican government had second thoughts; a commission was appointed to examine and report on the general state of the entertainment industry. When the question of the re-imposition of censorship came up for consideration, members of the commission were of two minds: Alexandre Dumas and Victor Hugo were for leaving it to theatre managers to decide for themselves whether a given play was fit for public performance, while others, including the eminent but now elderly dramatist Eugène Scribe and Jules Janin, the most widely read theatre critic of the day, expressed themselves in favour of a return to the old system of preventive censorship. The reactionaries won the day, and on August 1st, 1850 a law was passed prohibiting all dramatic productions that had not previously been examined and authorized by an official board of censors. It was understood that this board would be a branch of the civil service. At the beginning it was attached to the Ministry of the Interior; but, since the administration of the censorship, involving as it might conferences with dashing young authors and alluring actresses, promised a gratifying break from the normally tedious routine of bureaucratic memo-writing, some furious in-fighting seems to have taken place among the various ministries as each advanced reasons for having these duties allocated to them. The Ministry of the Interior was eventually forced to yield up the censorship office to the Ministry of State; after that it passed under the care of the Imperial Household; then the Ministry of Fine Arts made good its claim, until finally it was adjudicated to the Ministry of Education. Curiously—and fortunately—it never came under the wing of the Prefecture of Police.

The commissioners started work on August 4th. Their instructions were, firstly, to 'clean up' the theatres (in the more dignified language of official-dom, to 'put an end to the licentiousness prevalent on the stage'); and, secondly, to ensure that no anti-religious or socially subversive play should be seen. The immediate result was that, in place of the attractive list of shows from which Parisians could choose in the summer of 1850, a much drabber series of plays were billed for the autumn season. As usual, the extinction of permissiveness inaugurated the reign of dullness.

One instance of the censorship's activities under the Second Republic will suffice as an example. The first night of a revival of Musset's play Le Chandelier had taken place on June 29th, 1850 at the Théâtre Français, now rechristened the Théâtre de la République. Arsène Houssaye, who had recently been appointed manager, was anxious to renovate the out-dated repertoire of this, the most ancient of French playhouses; he was, besides, a close friend of Musset's. *Le Chandelier*, a fast-moving, light-hearted comedy of intrigue with a happy if slightly scabrous ending, had been written many years previously and published in the *Revue des Deux Mondes* without any real expectation that it would ever be performed. In 1848 it had a first, short and unsuccessful run at the Théâtre historique, before an audience of apprentices and shop-assistants accustomed to a regular diet of straightforward melodrama; the subtleties of Musset's dialogue were quite beyond them. But in 1850, *Le Chandelier* went down extremely well with the more sophisticated *habitués* of the Théâtre Français; for all the sniffs and snorts of outraged prudes, it played to full houses throughout the summer. This comedy of Musset's has parts for four principals: a rich, elderly, middle-class cuckold; his young, pleasure-loving wife; Clavaroche, her current lover, an officer from the nearby garrison; and, finally, 'le chandelier'. The word was a slang term applied to the unsuspecting young man whom a faithless wife will pass off as her gallant in order to divert the suspicions of a jealous husband. It is on Clavaroche's suggestion that Jacqueline chooses the innocent adolescent Fortunio as her 'chandelier'. But Fortunio is far from insensible to Jacqueline's charms; his juvenile ardour eventually touches her, and the play ends with Fortunio displacing Clavaroche—for the time being.

It was this ending that the censors, when they viewed the play, judged to be inadmissible: stage adulteresses must be made to repent, and not be allowed to persist in their wickedness with a fresh and charming partner. Baroche, the minister, suggested privately to Houssaye that *Le Chandelier* had better come off; then, when Houssaye turned a deaf ear, despatched him a curt, written order. Houssaye, who stood in no great awe of cabinet ministers, wrote back inviting Baroche to come and see the play for himself. In the course of the last act he brought the author along to the minister's box, introduced the two men, and Musset's courtly charm completed the work of conversion already partly achieved by the play. But it was only a reprieve; complaints continued to reach the censor's office. Musset hoped to avert an outright ban by changing the ending of *Le Chandelier*: Fortunio was to enlist in the army, emigrate to America, or by some other desperate course leave Jacqueline free to lead a life of blameless domesticity with the greybeard, her husband; thus the sanctity of the marriage bond would be upheld. All this was to no avail; nothing would satisfy Baroche now but that performances should be stopped. *Le Chandelier* was not seen again by Parisian audiences until 1872.

This first brush with the censorship thoroughly frightened Musset, who had been counting on his plays, long thought to be dramatically unviable, to provide him in his declining years with that steady income which had eluded him ever since, after his father's death in the cholera epidemic of

1831–2, he had had to rely on what earnings his pen could provide. Rather than forego his share of box-office receipts, he trimmed, altered and emasculated his other plays to bring them into line with the new standards of decorum. Before *André del Sarto* was put on at the Odéon, he changed the original ending and killed off Cordiani instead of allowing him to elope with Del Sarto's wife; he also went through the text with great care, weeding out every word that might imply that the guilty lovers had actually consummated their adultery. A year later it was Arsène Houssaye once more who produced for Musset his *Caprices de Marianne*, and again a number of cuts were made, less for the purpose of sparing the feelings of the theatre-going public than with the idea of placating the members of the all-powerful board of censors.

The procedure adopted by these gentlemen when a new play was submitted to them was to begin by reading the manuscript with scrupulous attention, taking care not only that the plot itself and the various situations should be inoffensive, but that no phrase in the text should be allowed to stand which could possibly bear a doubtful construction. The censors were adept at seeing sly allusions and *double-entendre* where none had been intended. After this, the custom was to summon to their office both author and manager for consultation, as it was politely termed; this gave the other side the opportunity to accept with a good grace the deletions and modifications which the guardians of public morality thought desirable. If the necessary accommodation was reached—that is, if the author did not judge that his work had been so cruelly mauled that he preferred to withdraw it—then the play would go into rehearsal. An inspector attended the dress-rehearsal, so as to ensure that the changes imposed by the censorship had been duly incorporated into the acting version; he also had the ticklish task of ensuring that costume and dances did not conflict with the demands of delicacy. Only when all these hurdles had been cleared was the play licensed for public performance.

Clearly much depended on the personality of whatever minister happened to be in charge. For a period during the early years of the Empire the man who had responsibility for dramatic censorship was Auguste Romieu, who owed his portfolio to the fact that under the Second Republic he had written a pamphlet called *Le Spectre rouge* in which he predicted that the nation would sink into ruin and anarchy unless it gave absolute power to Louis-Napoleon. His appointment as Minister of Fine Arts was greeted at first with relief and satisfaction by most dramatists, who were confident that a fellow like 'Coco Romieu' would be bound to show himself reasonably accommodating. He had been a notoriously gay dog in his youth and had even written a vaudeville, *Le Sous-Préfet s'amuse*, which was performed in

1849 and which was certainly no very austere work of art. But alas, like George Colman the Younger in England, the licentiousness of whose own plays had deceived many into supposing that he would be lax in the exercise of his duties as chief censor, Auguste Romieu proved to be quite inflexible when it came to judging the morality of other men's work. It was he who threatened to have Arsène Houssaye dismissed from his post as director of the Théâtre-Français if he persisted in keeping Hugo's *Marion Delorme* on the repertory after the poet had revealed himself as an enemy of the régime. However, the sternest censor to hold office under the Empire was no doubt Walewski, who not only pounced on the slightest deviation from the norms of decency but went so far as to issue a stern warning to all playwrights not to attempt even to submit a play which might infringe them. The most conspicuous of his acts of authority was to ban *Les Diables noirs*, one of the productions of that stodgy but very popular disciple of Scribe's, Victorien Sardou.

In the absence of any hard-and-fast principles, personalities counted for a great deal in the functioning of the censorship. There were cases of plays being banned and then, the right strings having been pulled, of the ban being lifted; thus, Augier's *Les Lionnes pauvres* was finally authorized in 1858, in despite of the censorship, thanks to the personal intervention of Prince Napoleon. Many a playwright needed only to wait for a change in the directorship of the board of censors; here, the best documented case is undoubtedly that of Alexandre Dumas and the difficulties he encountered in getting *La Dame aux Camélias* past the censors.

This play, depicting a courtesan with a heart of gold who conveniently dies in the last scene so as to enable the man who loved her and wronged her to return to a life of respectability, could be judged harshly, according to present-day standards, for its failure to grapple with the problem of the ambiguous morality displayed by a society which excused the men who availed themselves of the services of a woman like Marguerite Gautier, and yet simultaneously condemned the woman herself for providing these services. Possibly, too, Dumas could be censured for casting a pleasing veil of romantic melancholy over the brutal sordidness of the *cocotte*'s daily, or rather nightly activities, in much the same way as Murger, in his *Scènes de la vie de bohème*, chose to glamorize the depressing realities of the way of life of the Latin Quarter *grisettes* of the same period. But it was for none of these reasons that the play was judged to be morally pernicious; rather, it was for his sheer audacity in giving the leading part to a fallen woman that Dumas found himself faced, initially, with a flat refusal on the part of the censorship to license the play. This veto, however, did not cause the management of the

Théâtre du Vaudeville to suspend rehearsals, for it was known that the author had a good friend in the Duc de Morny, one of the men closest to the Prince-President. On Morny's advice, Dumas submitted the text to a trio of competent critics and playwrights (Jules Janin, Léon Gozlan and Émile Augier) who drafted a favourable report on it. Morny took the report to Louis-Napoleon, who initialled it and sent it on to Léon Faucher, the minister responsible at the time for dramatic censorship. Faucher refused, however, to give way to this gentle pressure and the original interdiction was maintained.

Accompanied by his father, of *Three Musketeers* fame, Dumas then paid the minister a call, but was denied an audience. Instead, the two men were interviewed by the permanent secretary, who told them not to expect any change in policy so long as Faucher was in power. Dumas armed himself with patience, but had not long to wait; in the cabinet reshuffle that followed the *coup d'état* it was Morny himself, ironically, who replaced Faucher. Within a few days of assuming office he summoned the members of the board and read them a stiff lecture, not just on their misplaced zeal in prohibiting performances of *La Dame aux Camélias*, but on their equally reprehensible short-sightedness in having, a few months earlier, sanctioned the production of Balzac's *Mercadet*. This play, a satire on speculators, had been given its first two performances at the Théâtre du Gymnase on August 23–24, 1851. It had been a wild success; when the curtain fell on the second night, the actor taking the leading part was given a standing ovation. But on the third day the theatre bills were covered with stickers announcing that the play had been withdrawn. It emerged that various influential members of the banking and stockbroking community had protested to Faucher that they were being maligned, traduced, caricatured, libelled and lampooned, and that the national economy would certainly suffer in consequence. Faucher had the theatre closed for a day while he took Balzac's text home to read; evidently his conclusions were that the protests should be overruled, since he made no difficulty about re-authorizing the production. The mere threat of a ban proved an added stimulus to popular interest, and for the rest of its run (72 performances) *Mercadet* played to full and enthusiastic houses.

Morny recalled the circumstances, blamed his predecessor's thoughtless handling of the case, and proceeded to give the commissioners the benefit of his own opinion in the firmest possible way: this was that financiers, who render the state no small service, have a right to be shielded from the darts of impertinent satirists; whereas no offence is given to any influential section of the community by revealing that young men about town habitually frequent the houses of loose women. This was an unusual, but still, a tenable point of view; more importantly, it was the point of view held by the minister, and no time was lost in licensing *La Dame aux Camélias*. As for *Mercadet*, it was not seen again in Paris for 17 years.

Shortly before the Second Empire passed into history, Dumas wrote a preface to a re-edition of *La Dame aux Camélias* in which he reviewed the operation of the censorship over the period during which he had worked as a professional dramatist. The conclusion he reached was that the censorship was no bad thing. If a play was unlucky enough to be banned at the outset, and lucky enough later to be authorized (and all banned plays are sooner or later authorized) the publicity it will have received will amply compensate the author for anything he may have suffered by the delay. The censorship may or may not be harmful to the dramatic art, but it certainly cannot harm, Dumas asserts optimistically, the individual dramatist: 'it makes brisker business for us than we could make with our unaided efforts.' A preventive censorship is the ideal kind: 'Once a play has been passed—and in the long run it cannot but be passed—how secure we feel! how soundly we sleep! The censorship has authorized the play, therefore the play is innocuous; and if the government objects, all we need say is: "That's nothing to do with us. Address your complaints to your own board of censors, it's their job to stop trouble." '

If there were no preventive censorship there would be something much worse: direct police action against the offending theatre or else, in the knowledge that this was a possibility, the private censoring of an author's work that every manager would engage in for fear of prosecution in the courts. Nowhere, claimed Dumas, was there a civilized country which had been able to dispense with censorship, and France under Napoleon III was less obscurantist than England under Queen Victoria: in that supposed haven of political liberty, no playhouse would have dared to stage *La Dame aux Camélias*.

Dumas was no doubt right. In mid-Victorian England—though the blame must be laid less on the 1843 Act than on the morally repressive effects of the methodist revival—a far more asphyxiating climate prevailed than in France under the Second Empire. Taboos being stronger this side of the Channel, it was that much harder for the dramatist to break new ground and deal frankly with socially relevant subjects, with the result that, anti-libertarian though it was, Louis-Napoleon's régime did witness a freer flowering of the dramatic art than any that was seen in Great Britain up to the end of the century. Augier, Sardou, Dumas *fils* himself, Pailleron and Labiche make up a group of writers more often pedestrian (save for the last-named) than brilliant, technically masters of their craft, and not without glimmerings of a social conscience. Their plays have not, even today, sunk into complete oblivion, and were undeniably superior to the best that was being shown concurrently on the London stage, where audiences were being regaled by nothing more sophisticated than Dion Boucicault's dramas of Irish life and Tom Taylor's naïve attempts at social comedy.

It would not be altogether true to say that the drama flourished under the Second Empire in spite of the censorship; rather, it did so because the censorship functioned in so uncertain, capricious, and half-hearted a fashion. The governing class was not, on the whole, composed of men moved by strong religious or moral principles; these new rulers of France had schemed and fought for power, and now that they had secured it they intended to enjoy its fruits. For them, the function of the theatre was to provide an evening's entertainment *'entre les plaisirs de la table et ceux du lit'*, as the saying goes; and if the entertainment was novel, saucy, even spicy, they liked it all the better, and were disposed to be indulgent towards the author even if he occasionally overstepped the bounds of decorum. And so, as time went by, and especially under the more relaxed conditions obtaining in the latter part of Napoleon III's reign, the board of censors grew less and less inclined to interpret their instructions too strictly.

Their rulings were, in any case, sometimes flouted, more often slyly circumvented. Up until 1861, at least, there remained one big loop-hole in the law: no penalties had been provided against deliberate disregard of the censor's instructions regarding cuts and alterations in the text. At the dress-rehearsal and for the first few performances, the passages that had been blue-pencilled would be obediently omitted; but, as performance succeeded performance, the cuts would be imperceptibly restored by the players, or the author would even add new matter that the censor had never seen. This practice led to the creation, in December 1861, of a new office, that of *Commissaire-inspecteur des théâtres et spectacles de Paris*. This functionary's duties were to attend occasional performances, armed with a prompt-copy of the play that was running. However, even this safeguard sometimes proved inadequate. At one theatre (the Porte-Saint-Martin) the possibility of unwelcome visitations had been foreseen and due provision made for the eventuality: as soon as the inspector appeared the actors, obeying a pre-arranged signal, reverted to the authorized text. One sees why Dumas was able to describe the censorship as a 'sleepy duenna whose keys are easily stolen by the Muse whenever she wishes to roam the countryside.'

On the other hand, the censorship operated with extreme efficiency when it came to ensuring that no theatre should serve as an arena for political debate and that no work should be performed which might serve the interests of the régime's critics. A play about the events of 1848, written by a republican deputy, Glais-Bizoin, was refused a licence outright. The commission, in its report, made no secret of the reasons for the absolute veto they had imposed. 'These scenes in which the odious vituperations of socialism against law and order are voiced in all their violence and brutality, and which recall the blackest days of revolution, appear to us quite inadmissible.' Similarly, a proposal to stage an adaptation of Musset's *Lorenzaccio* was turned down on the grounds that even though the setting was sixteenth-century Florence, a play that presented tyrannicide as being in certain circumstances excusable could not possibly be licensed for performance before the subjects of Napoleon III. When the play offended simply by the occasional incautious outburst, the censors could be satisfied with a few deletions. Émile Augier had given it to one of the characters in *La Pierre de touche* to express the view that 'society was ill ordered' and, elsewhere, to advance the theory that 'the rich man was, in the design of Providence, no more than the poor man's treasurer'. Augier had to consent to the suppression of these inflammatory remarks.

Religion was quite as much a taboo subject as politics, of course, and any play that tended to throw discredit on the Church, like Sardou's *La Dévote*, came under just as much suspicion as one that reflected adversely on any aspect of the imperial régime. The melodrama drawn from Victor Hugo's historical novel *Notre-Dame de Paris*, which had proved a magnet for popular audiences when it was first performed in 1850, was never shown under the Second Empire. The embargo had nothing to do with the political odium Hugo had incurred, but was due simply to the presence in the play of the unchaste priest, Claude Frollo.

Dramatists learned further that it was not merely inadmissible to hold up to ridicule a minister of the Crown or a minister of the Church, but inadvisable to suggest that even quite lowly employees of the state were capable of improper conduct. Two one-act sketches written for the Palais-Royal in 1852 had to be revised, the first because it showed a postman neglectful of his official duties, the second because there figured in it a customs officer who accepted bribes. In short, if a play was no more than unseemly, it had a fair chance of slipping through the censorship's net, even if mangled in the process; but it was immediately pounced on if it embodied the slightest hint of political or social criticism.

Censorship of the Press

With all this, it remains true that officialdom treated with far greater leniency those who wrote for the stage than it did writers whose works issued from the printing press, whether novelists, essayists, or poets. The greater potentialities for mischief of the printed word, indelible and immutable where the spoken word was fugitive and impermanent, were fully recognized, and it was in the control it exercised over books and periodicals that the censorship showed itself most inquisitorial, most tyrannical, and from the cultural point of view most stultifying. And yet, as we view them in the light of our rich experience of twentieth-century police states, the efforts of the régime to impede the expression and diffusion of ideas that it considered subversive seem almost ludicrously fumbling and ineffective. If the Second Empire provided a discouraging climate for literature and the arts, this was more because of the philistinism of the general public than in consequence of the repressive measures that were put into force after the *coup d'état*.

These measures were aimed in the first place at muzzling the press. Whether or not journalism should be properly regarded as a branch of literature, it is a fact that throughout the second half of the nineteenth century no very firm line of demarcation can be drawn between those who wrote books and those who wrote for the papers. At a period when the copyright law had no application beyond the national frontiers, when publishers in Belgium and Germany could with impunity issue pirated editions of best-selling novels and smuggle them back into France, when an author normally drew no fee in respect of translations of his works, when in his own country his publisher was more likely to offer him a small lump sum for the right to 'exploit' his book over a given number of years than to propose regular royalty payments, the newspaper or magazine prepared to purchase, at so much a line, the right to serialize his novel before it was published in volume form afforded the writer one of the few sources of revenue on which he could confidently rely. Apart from this, it often happened that the young man with ambitions to make his name, in due course, as a novelist, an historian, a literary critic or a poet, would serve an apprenticeship to his craft by acting as a freelance journalist and feature-writer. The professional reporter (although the word itself passed from English into French as early as 1829) was still a comparative rarity.

This being so, it is easy to see how the rigid control of the press instituted by the government of Napoleon III threatened, indirectly but none the less seriously, the livelihood of the writer and hence the very existence of a healthy, independent literature. Quite simply, the new laws drove out of circulation a great number of newspapers both in Paris and in the provinces. (Admittedly, those that remained outnumbered those that can be found in present-day France, but in 1852 the newspaper was virtually the sole vehicle for the dissemination of information and the presentation of comment on issues of moment.) The extinction of so many daily or weekly periodicals reduced many a man of letters to destitution or drove him to embrace some other career. As Du Camp put it with dry irony: 'under the Convention, during the Re public, journalists were sent to the guillotine; under the Second Empire things improved: it was only the journals that were guillotined.' But Du Camp's tone is less light-hearted when he comes to sum up the process by which a political censorship became, or tended to become, a literary censorship: 'The decree of 17 February [1852] was not simply directed against political journalism, but incidentally struck at and ruined those writers who depended on newspapers for their livelihood, either as dramatic critics, art critics, novelists or scientific popularizers.'[1]

The decree mentioned by Du Camp was that which inaugurated the régime under which the press was to live for the greater part of the Second Empire. Its 36 articles included every restrictive clause that earlier régimes had thought of, together with several others designed to extinguish whatever residual liberty had been formerly permitted to political journalists. Actually, within living memory, it had only been during a brief period in 1848 that newspapers had been truly free, to the extent of not even being required to pay caution-money. The system of *cautionnement* had been introduced by Guizot in 1819: anyone who wished to start a newspaper was required to deposit a sum of money with the Treasury, nominally as security against any fines that the courts might impose, but actually in order to ensure that the press should reflect the views of the conservative, moneyed classes, and of no others. The size of the deposit had fluctuated through the years and was always in inverse ratio to the liberality of the régime and also to the degree of security it felt it enjoyed: any crisis that exacerbated the nervousness of the central government could result in an increase in the caution-money exacted.[2] Under the terms of the 1852 press law, the deposits rose to 50,000 francs for newspapers published in Paris; a slightly smaller sum was required of any would-be newspaper proprietor publishing in the provinces.

However, there was nothing new in the principle of this impost. Similarly, in stipulating that any periodical dealing with 'politics or social economy' required government approval before it was allowed to appear, the authorities were merely reviving a precautionary device which had had a long history. The intention was not, however, to abolish at a stroke all anti-government newspapers and so suppress every kind of public criticism of national policy; the Second Empire was not a totalitarian state and had no plans to create a government monopoly of the communications media. Established newspapers representing the views of monarchists (like the Orleanist *Journal des Débats* and the Bourbon legitimist *Gazette de France*) continued to appear; so did the moderate republican paper *Le Siècle* and also Girardin's *La Presse*, which could be said to follow a cautiously independent line. The most left-wing paper of all, among those that could be read in Paris in the 1850s, was *Le Charivari*, in which Daumier's famous cartoons were appearing. It is an interesting fact that the reason why Daumier devoted his talents to immortalizing the foibles of representative members of the middle and lower classes was that direct political caricature was no longer permitted. The only form of preventive censorship introduced by the February decree was, as it happened, in respect of illustrations: these had to be submitted to the prefect of police before the blocks were made.[3]

For all this, it must be admitted that relatively few opposition papers were circulating in the early years of the Second Empire. These few, however, prospered; their circulation figures increased at an alarmingly rapid rate. In the early sixties, worried at the spectacle of so much power being concentrated in the hands of a few unfriendly editors, the government decided to abandon their earlier policy of discouraging the foundation of new opposition papers. Profiting from this apparently relaxed atmosphere, the Orleanists launched *Le Temps* and the republicans *L'Avenir national*. But, contrary to all expectations, the appearance of these competing journals did not bring about any measurable decline in the number of subscribers to the *Débats* and the *Siècle*: there was, it seemed, a large unsatisfied demand for anti-government journalism, not of course because the population at large had grown disillusioned with the imperial régime at this date, but simply because the *esprit frondeur* of the French was reasserting itself. In some provincial districts the situation was even more disturbing from the administration's point of view than it was in the capital. Though there might be only one opposition paper printed in a *département*, it had so large a following that the *préfet* was often reluctant to threaten it with suspension, however dangerous he might consider its line, for fear of the resentment his action might arouse among the local people. Even in its most authoritarian phase, the régime remained uneasily aware that its continuance in power depended on the consent of the majority, and that in the long run public opinion had to be conciliated.[4]

The need to secure preliminary authorization did not apply to periodicals abstaining from comment on current affairs and public policy, and in consequence there were numerous attempts at this time to found magazines dealing purely with cultural issues. The difficulty was always to treat such matters in a political void; the authorities were only too apt to smell treason in the most innocent of passing remarks. Picture galleries were administered by the state: was it safe to make even a mildly disparaging reference to the choice of canvases on view and their arrangement on the walls? Members of the Comédie Française were, up to a point, state employees: was it prudent to comment on the quality of their acting? In a serious article dealing with some aspect of the history of imperial Rome it was all too easy for the police to imagine that some parallel was intended with conditions in contemporary France. The offending journalist might incur no worse a penalty than a trifling fine; but the paper was suspended. Rather than risk such a calamity, the editor preferred to act as his own censor, and carefully blue-pencilled his staff's copy with one eye on the office of the prefect of police.

'Obstacles and pitfalls on all sides beset the newspaper and those who wrote for it', comments one journalist in his memoirs. 'Self-censored in the first instance, re-read and corrected with meticulous care by his editor, superintended in the last resort by the printer who was responsible before the law for everything that came off his press, stifled and hamstrung, attracting the thunderbolt and yet tied to the lightning-conductor, seated on the powder-barrel and condemned to strike the tinder-box, the journalist of 1860 was truly a victim tortured by the imperial régime.'[5]

If, more often through carelessness than deliberate design or desire to be provocative, the journalist committed one of the numerous offences listed in the law on the press, he went before a *cour correctionnelle*, where he was tried by a magistrate whose own career depended on his subservience to the administration, and who was therefore strongly disinclined to listen to his plea of innocence. There was no possibility of the case being tried before a jury in a *cour d'assises*. But it was only when a journalist flagrantly flouted the law that he was prosecuted at all; it was no part of government policy to arouse sympathy for persecuted writers by trying to force verdicts against them when the circumstances were doubtful. The authorities had other means of bringing recalcitrants to heel. The law provided for the issue of warnings to newspapers (by the Minister of the Interior in Paris, or by the prefect of the department in the provinces) if any objectionable matter were published, even though such publication did not actually constitute a contravention of the law. A warning, if disregarded, could be followed by suspension of the paper and, after a certain number of such provisional suspensions, by its outright suppression.

The contents of books, no less than of magazines and periodicals, came under careful scrutiny. The accession lists of public libraries were vetted, and all politically subversive or religiously offensive literature mercilessly proscribed. Especial care was taken to monitor the sale of books by the pedlars (*colporteurs*) who for generations had been bringing the products of the provincial and Parisian presses to the remoter villages and farmsteads of France. After July 28, 1852 every copy of every book so sold had to bear the rubber stamp of the local *préfet*'s office. The stock of reading matter in the bookstalls of railway stations was similarly scrutinized in case it should contain unsavoury material; Champfleury—to name but one victim—was disturbed to find that his novel *La Succession Le Camus* was being denied to travellers because it included an episode in which a gang of urchins throw jam over the statue of a church dignitary.

Censorship of the printed word was, in short, as stringent as the methods of control available at the time allowed it to be. It was, however, discreetly exercised and its operations were not publicly advertised. The word went out that writers hostile to the régime were to be coaxed rather than coerced; but if they insisted on biting the hand that fed them, they had their teeth drawn. The intellectual élite were submitted to polite pressure if—as not infrequently happened—they held salaried appointments in the university world, and there was no hesitation in breaking their careers if they resisted. Both Jules Michelet, who had occupied the chair of history at the Collège de France since 1838, and Étienne Vacherot, who had replaced Victor Cousin as professor of philosophy at the Sorbonne in 1839, were dismissed their posts when they refused to subscribe to an oath of allegiance to the Empire. For publishing a satirical poem directed against Sainte-Beuve's proposals for the financial encouragement of writers sympathetic to the régime, Victor de Laprade, professor of French literature in the University of Lyons, similarly forfeited his chair. When Renan delivered his inaugural lecture as professor of Hebrew at the Collège de France, the minister who had been responsible for his appointment, Gustave Rouland, realized with dismay that his nominee had an original mind and held unconventional views which he was not afraid of expressing. Renan was forbidden to deliver any further lectures and an alternative job was found for him in the Bibliothèque Nationale, where opportunities to make mischief would be more circumscribed; he turned it down. Then he compounded his original offence: he published his *Vie de Jésus*, a work of scholarship which was also a great popular success, to the indescribable scandal of the leaders of the Church. This time his chair was suppressed, exactly two and a half years after it had been created. The orthodoxy required of university teachers, whether in their *ex cathedra* pronouncements or in their published writings, was religious as well as political.

The men whom we have named were prominent and established figures. It is almost impossible to estimate the full effect of the stifling intellectual atmosphere of the Second Empire on the younger generation of writers who were still making their way, though the history of the early career of Hippolyte Taine, full of rebuffs and disappointments, gives some measure of this.

Because it was so difficult and dangerous to write about serious topics, all the verve and intelligence of the newcomers tended to be expended on frivolities. The Second Empire witnessed a debasement of the tone of the press, a trivialization of the reading-matter offered, which was only partly due to the increasing invasion of the communication media by commercial values.[6] Faced with an embargo on serious discussion of questions of import, editors had to offer subscribers something else for their money; and accordingly, their cub-reporters were instructed to glean whatever amusing scandal they could by listening in to café conversations, pumping indiscreet ladies' maids, and hanging round actresses' dressing-rooms. The gossip-column came into being, under the benevolent eye of the leading personalities of the régime. When an outraged minister protested about the intrusion of the press into private life, the Duc de Morny merely laughed. 'Provided they don't talk politics, let them say what they like!' In fact, it was rare for those whose private affairs became public property to object; many of them were not altogether displeased with this gratuitous publicity. The real victims were the journalists who were obliged to spend their days scurrying around in search of spicy stories to use as copy. 'It is impossible to reckon', wrote Zola shortly after the collapse of the régime, 'how many intelligences have been devoured by the trivial journalism made fashionable by the Second Empire.'[7] Maxime du Camp was even more specific in his diagnosis of the evil. 'This or that young man who, in the space of ten years, has written a thousand articles based on drawing-room tittle-tattle, and has worn himself out at this trade, might have written three or four good novels, or one or two volumes of poetry which would have enriched the literary heritage.'[8] The rise and fall of Lucien de Rubempré, which Balzac chronicled in his *Illusions perdues*, was repeated *ad infinitum* and *ad nauseam* under the Second Empire.

Writers in the Dock

It is one of the more baffling of the paradoxes of the time that this type of banal muck-raking in the popular press was combined with rigorous demands for a high moral tone in serious literature. Underlying this double standard was the unspoken assumption that sly allusions to infringements of the moral code could be tolerated: their outright exposure and discussion could not. Prudery and starchiness were by no means incompatible with covert salaciousness; but frankness, even if combined with an exemplary austerity of moral purpose, was labelled 'realism,' and this word, the full implications of which will be examined in a subsequent chapter, was one that carried the most sinister and damaging implications.

E

Moreover, the censorship drew no very clear distinction between 'realism', which tended in its view to corrupt morals, and political criticism which risked weakening the sinews of government. To disregard conventional reticence in sexual matters was to qualify for a certificate of bad citizenship. 'Where you see an immoral man, a debauchee, you see also a demagogue and an anarchist. Revolt against moral prescriptions and divine laws engenders revolt against society and human laws, and reciprocally.'[9] Unorthodoxy of any kind, moral, literary or political, was alike suspect; the innovating artist was as great a danger to society as the faithless wife or the socialist working man. The only safe writers were those who wrote nothing that could jolt the average, non-political middle-class supporter of the régime out of his unthinking euphoria. The prosperous *père de famille* who could be counted on at election time to vote for the official candidate was one whose tastes were satisfied by the art of Horace Vernet and Meissonier, by the novels of Paul de Kock or Octave Feuillet, and by Offenbach's catchy tunes. At all costs it was imperative that he should be left undisturbed, secure in his conviction that his values were unassailable, that his spiritual lethargy lay under no threat, and that his material interests were best served by the continuation in power of those to whom he dutifully if grudgingly paid his taxes.

It may be that the ludicrously ill-advised court-cases brought in the same year (1857) against Flaubert for publishing *Madame Bovary* and Baudelaire for publishing *Les Fleurs du Mal*, had some underlying political motivation; but it is certain that the main reason why it was decided to proceed in this way against the greatest novelist and the greatest poet of the age was that their works were disturbing and therefore demanded to be suppressed. A law had been in force since 1819 prohibiting the publication of books that constituted an 'outrage to public and religious morality and to good morals.' Under the Second Empire the only change made was one of procedure: it was decreed that, in future, cases brought under the 1819 act were to be regarded in the same light as offences against the press laws. The accused were no longer to have the benefit of a jury trial, but were to be dealt with summarily by a magistrate presiding over a *tribunal correctionnel* whose more usual duties were to pass prison-sentences on pickpockets, ponces and pederasts.

Action was taken against Flaubert before his novel had appeared in book form and when it was still being serialized in the *Revue de Paris*; the question therefore arises whether the authorities were not just as anxious to seize the opportunity of having the magazine, with its notoriously liberal tendencies, suppressed, as they were to have the book, with its supposedly immoral thesis, proscribed. Du Camp, one of the two editors of the *Revue de Paris*, was convinced that the indictment of *Madame Bovary* was a mere pretext.

'The *Revue de Paris*', he tells us in his memoirs, 'was under close surveillance; although we had deposited caution-money, we never published political articles; but our contributors included professors who had resigned after the *coup d'état* and former ministers of the Second Republic. . . . We had already been given several warnings; a conviction in the courts could lead to our being suppressed.' Flaubert too, before the trial, thought it likely that the attack was politically motivated, 'because they want at all costs to extermi-nate the *Revue de Paris*, which the government finds irritating; it has had two warnings already, and it is very clever to suppress it for an attack on religion.'[10]

No one today would describe *Madame Bovary*, as Flaubert here describes it, as 'an attack on religion', and it is scarcely conceivable that he had ever intended it to be read as such; after all, he had expressly pilloried Voltairean anti-clericalism in the person of Homais. But orthodox Roman Catholics cannot have been gratified by the portrayal of the village priest, Bournisien, with his grubby cassock and his feeble puns, nor by the account Flaubert gave of Emma's convent-school education, nor yet by his brilliantly devasta-ting analysis of the way eroticism and religiosity blend in her nature; finally, his handling of the death-scene could not have failed to give offence to the devout. It may well be that in bringing this case the government was at least as anxious to placate religious opinion as to destroy the *Revue de Paris*. If there had been a serious conspiracy to do away with the magazine, one imagines the prosecution would have been conducted a little less half-heartedly and that a more determined effort would have been made to secure a conviction. As it was, the authorities probably got the verdict they wanted. Flaubert was censured but not censored; he was denied the benefits of martyrdom, and Michel Lévy was left free to issue the book later in the year. Similarly, the *Revue de Paris* was not victimized. It continued to appear —for a while—and was suppressed only the following January, in accordance with certain emergency security measures taken after the attempt made by Orsini on the life of the Emperor.

Whatever may have been the immediately determining factors, the funda-mental reason for the decision to prosecute was no doubt much more deep-seated. If it is true that any modern government must rely, to a greater or lesser extent, on concealment of awkward facts, then any artist who sets out to reveal a portion of the social truth is bound to be regarded as a nuisance. Even though Flaubert made no overt criticism of the régime in his novel (and it should not be forgotten that both *Madame Bovary* and the other great work of realism that Flaubert published under the Second Empire, *L' Éducation sentimentale*, were set in the era that preceded the *coup d'état*), the mere example of frank reporting and fearless analysis was dangerous because it could be infectious. The line of argument adopted by the public prosecutor, Ernest Pinard, is in this respect extremely significant, ridiculous though his rhetoric may have been. As was to be expected, he made extensive use of quotation, and among the passages he read out was Flaubert's description of Emma undressing in front of her lover, 'ripping apart the thin cord of her stays which hissed round her hips like an adder gliding . . . ', etc. Pinard acknowledged this passage to be 'an admirable description from the point of view of the talent employed, but an execrable one from the point of view of morality. Yes, Monsieur Flaubert is expert at embellishing his pictures with all the resources of art, but without the restraints of art. He uses no gauze, no veils, he gives us nature in all its nudity, in all its crudity.' Pinard used textually the same phrase (*avec toutes les ressources de l'art, mais sans les ménagements de l'art*) later in his speech, when he declared that his objections extended beyond the particular novel that the court was examining, and embraced 'the kind of literature that Monsieur Flaubert cultivates and which he exploits with none of the restraints of art but with all the resources of art: that is, the descriptive kind, realistic painting'. The peroration included a forthright denunciation of realist literature as such, 'not because it depicts the passions—hatred, vengeance, love—the world turns on these, and art is obliged to depict them; but because of the unbridled, unrestrained fashion in which they are depicted. Art that knows no rule is not art; it is like a woman who goes about without any clothes.' Flaubert heard this last assertion with sardonic glee; later, when the trial was just a bad memory, he and his friends would repeat the phrase with guffaws: 'art that knows no rule has no more right to be called art than a woman without clothes has the right to be called a woman.'

When, later the same year, Baudelaire was brought to trial for allegedly publishing a blasphemous obscenity—to wit, *Les Fleurs du Mal*—rumours were current that this was being done on the express instructions of the Minister of the Interior himself, Billault, who considered himself slighted by the court's inability to secure a verdict against *Madame Bovary*. Baudelaire was warned to expect trouble—Leconte de Lisle had told him it was proposed to confiscate the entire edition—and busied himself, just as Flaubert had done, with attempts to enlist support among influential colleagues. Mérimée, who was best placed to help, having the ear of the Empress herself, unfortunately thought the volume 'very mediocre'. The timorous Sainte-Beuve claimed he would suffer disgrace if he were to praise *Les Fleurs du Mal* in *Le Moniteur*; nevertheless, to Baudelaire's vast surprise a review did appear in this paper, over the signature of Édouard Thierry, which gave him intense satisfaction; it was, indeed, a most glowing tribute, in which he was spoken of as the equal of Dante. Other reviews were written—by Barbey d'Aurevilly for *Le Pays*, by Asselineau for *La Revue française*—but were not allowed to appear: the editors, when they referred the question to the Ministry of the Interior, were told it would be inadvisable to make any reference to *Les Fleurs du Mal* in the press. Evidently bureaucratic processes were as blindly capricious under the Second Empire as under any other régime: that the one favourable review of the book should have appeared in the government-sponsored *Moniteur*, while other papers were being warned against printing a word in its support, was a striking illustration of the formidable inefficiency of the censorship's repressive machinery.

Pinard, who conducted the case for the prosecution, used the same arguments in attacking *Les Fleurs du Mal* as he had resorted to in respect of *Madame Bovary*: he claimed, simply, that this was a work of realism, and therefore obscene. 'His principle, his theory', he declared of Baudelaire, 'is to paint everything, to lay everything bare. He delves into the innermost recesses of human nature; he uses, to render it, strong and striking tones; he particularly exaggerates the hideous aspects; he magnifies inordinately so as to create the impression, the sensation.' Here, Baudelaire was being accused not merely of realism, but of impressionism too, long before impressionism was invented.

The judges, in motivating their verdict, implicitly accepted Pinard's argument; they ordered the excision of certain poems because, as they expressed it, those poems 'inevitably result in the excitement of the senses by the crude, immodest realism they employ'. The word was used in a very special sense. Nowadays any critic, if asked which part of *Les Fleurs du Mal* exhibits the most obvious realistic elements, would no doubt refer the inquirer to the section entitled 'Tableaux parisiens'. But no strictures were passed at the trial on poems like *Les Aveugles*, *Le Jeu*, *Les Petites Vieilles*, and the two *Crépuscules*. If one looks for a common denominator in the compositions that were condemned, one realizes—without the slightest surprise, it must be said—that every one of them is heavily erotic. All the same, they comprised no more than a small minority of the numerous erotic poems that are to be found in the *Fleurs du Mal*, with its so-called 'cycle de la Vénus noire', 'cycle de la Vénus blanche', etc. The poems that Pinard denounced and the somewhat smaller group that the court decided were pornographic were those in which Baudelaire had referred directly or by means of similes to portions of the female body that are normally kept covered. It was because of the

> *deux beaux seines, radieux*
> *Comme des yeux*

or the 'bouts charmants de cette gorge aiguë', it was on account of the description of the girls of Lesbos who

> de leur corps amoureuses
> Caressent les fruits mûrs de leur nubilité,

of the 'molle enchanteresse' with her

'Boucliers provoquants, armés de pointes roses'; it was, in short, because (according to the opening words of Les Bijoux) 'la très-chère était nue', that Baudelaire was found guilty of outraging public morality. The identification of nudity with crudity still held. Tartuffe cannot have flourished his handkerchief more energetically in front of Dorine's décolletage than did the magistrature of the Second Empire before Jeanne Duval's.

An identical prudishness had inspired the proceedings put in train against the brothers Goncourt. Their trial took place four years earlier than the two just discussed, but attracted far less attention since the accused, in 1853, were still unknown in the world of letters; further, their alleged offence against 'public morality' had been made not in a book, but in an article published in Le Paris. This was a newspaper with an impressive editorial staff. Murger, Banville, Aurélien Scholl and Alphonse Karr all wrote for it. Gavarni was under contract to produce a lithograph for every issue. The editor was a cousin of the Goncourts, a certain Pierre-Charles de Villedeuil, whose independent attitude towards the new régime may conceivably have been at the bottom of the court action taken against the two brothers: he was accused of failing to solicit invitations to the Tuileries and of refusing to wait in ministers' antechambers if they happened to be too busy to receive him on the spot.

The article that was singled out as offending the proprieties bore the unmomentous title: 'Voyage du no. 43 de la rue Saint-Georges au no. 1 de la rue Laffitte', and consisted in a whimsical account of the various art dealers' shops that could be encountered on this Parisian itinerary. One of the canvases on display that the authors happened to mention was a Diaz painting of a pair of underclad lovers in voluptuous embrace; rather than attempt to describe it in their own words, the Goncourts contented themselves with borrowing a few lines by the Petrarchan poet Jacques Tahureau where Venus is spoken of as

> Croisant ses beaux membres nus
> Sur son Adonis qu'elle baise.

It was for quoting these lines that the Goncourts were put on trial. They were indignant, but also frightened: an uncle of theirs with connections had made inquiries and had passed on to them the information that the procureur-

général, De Royer, was forecasting a prison-sentence which, he said, might be remitted if they petitioned the Emperor to exercise his prerogative of mercy.

A charge based on no more serious an imputation than that the accused had quoted a short passage from the works of a minor sixteenth-century poet might have seemed difficult to sustain; all the more so since the Goncourts were able to show that the verses had already been reproduced once, without causing any uproar, in the epoch-making study of French renaissance poetry written by Sainte-Beuve, a work that had been publicly commended by the Académie Française.[11] But the prosecutor was all fire and fury none the less, and denounced the brothers as being 'apostles of physical love'. Defending counsel took the pusillanimous but prudent course of introducing evidence of the two Goncourts' blameless private life, instancing as proof of their fundamental decency that they were looked after at home by an old woman who had been in the family service for 20 years.

Having heard the legal arguments on both sides the presiding magistrate, for no obvious reason, adjourned the case. In the week that elapsed before it was re-opened, De Royer lost his position as *procureur-général* to Gustave Rouland, who for political and personal reasons was well disposed towards the Goncourts. But although, thanks to these ministerial musical chairs, the case ended with their acquittal, they were not allowed, any more than Flaubert, to emerge without a stain on their characters. They were found not guilty of the intention of outraging public morality, but blameworthy in so far as they had succeeded in doing so.

Of the four writers involved in the three court cases so far mentioned, one only—Baudelaire—incurred a specific penalty, and even then the fine imposed on him, 300 francs, was not staggeringly heavy.[12] But, acquitted or not, these writers undoubtedly remembered, and resented all their lives, the indignity to which they had been subjected. The secrecy surrounding obscenity trials, which could not be reported, let alone commented on, in the press, increased their discomfort. It was, as the Goncourts noted in their diary, *une justice sans écho*; if found guilty, only the nature of their offence would be mentioned, and in such terms as to make it hard for the uninitiated to realize that they were in any way to be distinguished from 'a sodomite or an Ignorantine friar given to stroking little boys.'[13] The persecution complex that Edmond de Goncourt developed in later life, especially after the death of his brother, had many sources of which the fright he was given in 1853 was undoubtedly one. Flaubert's misanthropy, and Baudelaire's pessimism, were deepened by their experiences. In Baudelaire's case, his indignation was increased by the knowledge that his mother, by her second marriage the wife of an ambassador, was suffering exquisite embarrassment in the circles in which she moved from the circumstance that her son had been publicly branded a pornographer.

Beyond this, it has to be admitted that not all the court actions brought against men of letters under the Second Empire ended with a grudging acquittal or a small fine. Prison sentences were occasionally imposed. Some of these might have been merited, if one concedes the principle that authors of licentious works unredeemed by literary merit deserve to be jailed. *Les Filles de plâtre*, the seven-volume novel for which Xavier de Montépin was brought to trial in February 1856, arguably fell into this category: the author can hardly have had any other purpose in composing it than to take his profit from the wide sales that fiction of its sort, however ill-written, invariably commands. The title was a transparent reference to that of Théodore Barrière's high successful drama, *Les Filles de marbre*, the argument of which was that the courtesan is rarely the good-hearted, self-sacrificing, misjudged and ill-used heroine that Dumas had made her out to be in *La Dame aux Camélias*. If Montépin's tediously naughty ramblings conserve any interest for literary historians, this lies only in the probably fortuitous resemblance of one of its scenes to the opening chapter of Zola's *Nana*.[14] The judges who heard the case were not impressed by Montépin's plea that his intention had been purely didactic: to expose and condemn the shameless practices of the 'filles de plâtre'; he was fined 500 francs and given a three-month prison sentence. Having served it, and earned thereby a useful notoriety, he emerged to pursue his dubious activities undeterred and unrepentant.

The case of Catulle Mendès, also charged under the law of May 19, 1819, was rather different from that of Montépin. Almost as precocious and almost as big a blackguard as, a generation later, Rimbaud was to prove,[15] Catulle Mendès embodied to perfection the name he bore, declared George Moore, 'with his pale hair, and his fragile face illuminated with the idealism of a depraved woman ... An exquisite artist, he is the muse herself, or rather, he is one of the minions of the muse ... He never wrote an ugly line in his life, but he never wrote a line that some one of his brilliant contemporaries might not have written.' Mendès was only 20 when he founded *La Revue fantaisiste* with a star cast of contributors which included, besides veterans like Gautier, Baudelaire, and Arsène Houssaye, a group of newcomers many of whom were destined to become ornaments of the Parnassian, naturalist and symbolist movements: Albert Glatigny, Villiers de l'Isle Adam, Alphonse Daudet and Stéphane Mallarmé.

It was in the *Revue fantaisiste* that Mendès published his light-hearted, slightly *risqué* verse narrative entitled 'Le Roman d'une nuit'. In the traditional setting of a carnival night students roar their bawdy ditties, fiery-cheeked lovers embrace, tipsy harlequins reel through the streets, and incontinent monks dally with serving-wenches in taverns. The public prosecutor, when he read out in court selected passages from this fantasy, was astonished to hear himself applauded by members of the public: it was not his diction that had prompted this tribute, but Mendès's metrical skill and coruscating imagery. The trial, which took place in July 1861, was regarded by the literary world as an opportunity to demonstrate against the persecution of writers by the régime. Both Flaubert and Baudelaire, the two most eminent men to have endured this persecution, were present, as were a crowd of Mendès' younger supporters, long-haired Parnassian poets flaunting waistcoats of outrageous hues.

Although in law a minor, Mendès was sentenced to a month's imprisonment which he served at Sainte-Pélagie, traditionally the detention centre for dissident intellectuals and political prisoners: other inmates included the obdurate old revolutionary Auguste Blanqui, opposition journalists like Albert Sirven of *Le Gaulois* and Jules Vallès, and even the occasional university professor like Etienne Vacherot who was awarded a three-months' sentence when his treatise *La Démocratie* was condemned by the courts in 1862. The prison may have been a grim old place, but it seems to have held few terrors for the writers who were sent there and who were lodged separately from the ragtag and bobtail of ordinary delinquents, in a building known as the Pavillon des Princes. Here they were free to furnish their rooms as they chose and to vary the meagre prison fare by having cooked meals sent in from neighbouring restaurants. One well-heeled writer even had his two manservants to wait on him, and enjoyed daily visits from his wife and daughter. It appears, in short, that everything was done to make life not just tolerable, but as agreeable as possible for those convicted of offences against the press laws and 'public morality.' Journalists were even permitted and given facilities to pursue their professional activities while in prison, and examples are on record, particularly under the so-called 'liberal' Empire, of newspaper writers prosecuted and sentenced for offences against the press laws which they had contrived to commit while 'doing time' for identical offences committed earlier.[16]

There were those who were not displeased to escape from the frenetic atmosphere of the *salle de rédaction* to the peace and quiet of a well-appointed prison cell: the Virgilian tag, *deus nobis haec otia fecit*, seemed to Vallès to apply very aptly to spells in Sainte-Pélagie. Certainly nobody is on record as having ever tried to escape, though a cartoonist from *La Lune* once, for a lark, knotted his sheets together and lowered a mattress from his cell window; the sentinel, glimpsing it in the dark, let off a round, to the huge amusement of the other prisoners. Quite apart from the incidental amenities they found there, a prison sentence tended to be regarded by left-wing journalists as a signal mark of distinction. In 1866, when Prévost-Paradol was elected to the French Academy, his concierge, bringing up the pile of congratulatory letters that had come through the post, asked him shyly if he was being sent to prison.

In short, a curious ambiguity seems to have marked the administration's attitude towards the recalcitrant writer. It was felt necessary that he should be kept in check but, since it so often happened that he was a member of the very class on which the régime leaned most heavily for support, he could not be treated with the severity that his kind encounters in the monolithic, classless societies that have arisen since 1917. This analysis receives support from the fact that persecution of authors in the courts did not by any means cease with the overthrow of the Second Empire: some of the most scandalous, if not the most notorious examples date from the first two decades of the Third Republic, which suggests that the use of the law-courts to clamp down on certain forms of writing was primarily a device by the well-to-do middle classes to maintain their ascendancy, and had really very little to do with the buttressing of caesarism. In 1874 Barbey d'Aurevilly was threatened with prosecution for publishing *Les Diaboliques*, a collection of lurid short stories bearing the stamp of an outdated romanticism, which by no stretch of the imagination could be called indecent. The attorney-general decided eventually against bringing the suit, but the confiscation and destruction of all unsold copies of the book were ordered as a precautionary measure. Thus, both author and publisher suffered financial loss though it was never proved that they had broken the law. On the other hand, the case against Jean Richepin's *Chansons des Gueux* did come before the court in 1876. Eight of the poems in the collection were condemned as obscene, and Richepin had to go to prison for a month; but he did derive some benefit from the scandal, since his book, which might well have passed unnoticed otherwise, was reprinted several times in rapid succession even though the new editions were, perforce, expurgated.

In 1881 the law governing the censorship of printed books underwent a small modification: cases were in future to be heard before a jury. In practice, this made less difference than had been expected. In 1884 a young writer, Louis Desprez, the author of a notable critical study—one of the very first to be published—of the naturalist movement in literature,[17] brought out a novel of rural life written in collaboration with a younger friend, Henri Fèvre. At this date, if one excepts Balzac's unfinished work *Les Paysans* and a few short stories by Maupassant, no one in France had attempted to depict the lives of villagers and farm-workers with any degree of honesty. This is what Desprez and Fèvre tried, with some success, to do in *Autour d'un clocher*. The novel was a little disjointed and lacked any unifying theme beyond that provided by the furtive amours of the local priest and the local schoolmistress; but it did represent a well-meant attempt to open up a new field in French fiction.

The old law, 'outrage to public morality', was once more invoked. Fèvre was too young to stand trial, but Desprez appeared before a jury consisting of two or three shopkeepers, one or two small rentiers and property-owners, a mason, a carpenter, and other good men and true, humble citizens anxious only to do what their 'betters' expected of them. Vainly, Desprez protested that the only jury fit to pronounce on his case would be one composed of 'masters of contemporary literature'. Zola had advised him to throw himself on the mercy of the court. Desprez had been a cripple since childhood, and, standing there between the burly police guards, looked a frail, pathetic figure. Unfortunately, he insisted on taking up a defiant and arrogant attitude, and nothing his advocate said could soften the impression he made. He served his month's sentence at Sainte-Pélagie, not, however, in the 'Pavillon des Princes' but among the ordinary prisoners. When Zola and Alphonse Daudet went to see him on visitors' day, he would not shake hands for fear of the vermin he might pass on to them. After his release, desperately ill, he crept back to the cottage he owned in the country and stayed there, bed-ridden, until acute bronchitis carried him off less than a year later.

The lamentable affair could not be hushed up. Zola, in particular, refused to keep silent, and published a violent protest in *Le Figaro* on December 9th, 1885.[18] He accused the authorities point-blank of committing a juridical murder. 'The stupid law that was passed in order to halt the dirty trade of a handful of guttersnipes has claimed as its victim a poor boy who promised to develop into a writer of distinction. Always the same dread of freedom, that dread which one fine day will fasten a dictator's yoke on our necks.'

Hugo, poet-militant

There remained one violently critical and protesting voice which the censorship of the Second Empire was powerless to silence. Under the protection of the flag of Great Britain, Victor Hugo was able with impunity to direct against the new ruler of France such a stream of denunciation and invective as no modern European head of state had ever had to endure. The diatribe was devastating and, if it did nothing to loosen the grip in which the population was held, it cannot have failed to bring encouragement and fresh hope

to those Frenchmen living at home who still counted on the eventual triumph
of democracy, secularism and social justice. The strenuous efforts made by
Napoleon III's administration to prevent the dissemination of Hugo's
writings within the country constitute the clearest proof of how damaging
they were reckoned to be.

We last saw Hugo, disguised as a workman, boarding the train for
Brussels. His stay in the capital of the recently established kingdom of
Belgium lasted seven months. He arrived in a strangely optimistic frame of
mind, belligerent and more exhilarated than depressed by the experiences he
had undergone since December 2nd. On the 19th he wrote to Auguste
Vacquerie: 'I have just come away from the fight during which I was able to
demonstrate in some small measure what kind of a man a poet is. These
bourgeois will realize at last that the mind is as valiant as the belly is timorous
. . . ' He lost no time in laying plans for the propaganda war he proposed to
carry out against Louis-Napoleon, and spoke to Jules Hetzel about a scheme
for 'constructing a citadel of writers and publishers from which we shall
bombard Bonaparte.' He had grandiose ideas of entering into partnership
with other great European political exiles like Kossuth and Mazzini and
publishing from London an international newspaper to further the interests
of enslaved nations all over the world. He met and talked with fellow
refugees from Paris, like Noël Parfait, Arago and De Flotte; he received a
number of literary men, including Jules Janin, Alexandre Dumas and Émile de
Girardin, who came on short visits. These conversations gave him the idea
of presenting a record of his own experiences, supplemented by the narra-
tives of others who had witnessed the immediate aftermath of the *coup d'état*,
in the form of a book to be called *Faits et gestes du 2 décembre*. Later he
invented a more arresting and more significant title: *Histoire d'un crime*.
Professor Barrère, linking this title to the other, *Les Châtiments*, which Hugo
used for his later volume of satirical verse, has some pertinent observations
to make on the strange tension that kept Hugo's whole mind, over the period
1851-3, stretched between the two poles represented by the concepts of
crime and punishment.[19] As invariably happened with him, the word was
substituted for the reality. It might have been objected—and, in fact, Jules
Janin was to make this very point, in no spirit of carping criticism—that
there was something a little incongruous, a little impertinent even, in the
circumstance that the 'crime' was being 'chastised' by the poet who, as much
as anyone, had made its perpetration possible; for it was Hugo, by his sedu-
lous cultivation of the 'Napoleonic legend' in the 1830s, who paved the way
for the nephew's success in reaping the political harvest of the uncle's posthumous celebrity.[20]

The *Histoire d'un crime* was not published at this time. Hugo stowed it away in the famous travelling trunk which contained all his half-finished manuscripts (and which very nearly slid to the bottom of the English Channel when he was embarking, later, in a rough sea to cross from Jersey to Guernsey), and waited till 1877 before taking it out again, revising and publishing it. 1877 was the year when the danger of a monarchical restoration was at its height; once more, republican institutions were in manifest peril; the moment was therefore well chosen for the release of Hugo's history of an earlier, successful *coup*.[21]

He did, however, complete *Napoléon le Petit* while in Brussels: it was written in one burst, between June 14th and July 12th. Its publication had to be carefully timed. The Belgians were known to be busy rushing through a bill which would make it an offense to publish attacks on the head of a friendly state. There was also a risk that, once the book had appeared, the French authorities might retaliate by confiscating Hugo's property and assets in France. His wife was accordingly told to dispose of all effects that she could not readily remove, and to take ship from Le Havre to Southampton, joining him ultimately in Jersey. On August 1st the poet himself sailed from Antwerp to London, where he spent 'three dismal days' before setting off for the little island in the Channel where he proposed to spend the remainder of his exile. 'Nature', writes Thibaudet, 'had prepared for Victor Hugo a comfortable St Helena, within sight of the French coast. For the next 20 years, he was to fulfil the decorative functions of émigré and witness what had fallen to Chateaubriand under the July Monarchy.'[20] The ill-omened resemblance between the name of Napoleon 1's final place of exile and that of the chief town of Jersey, if it did not occur to Hugo himself, certainly struck his companions. Auguste Vacquerie, who had escorted Mme Hugo and her daughter Adèle on their double journey across the Channel, observed in a letter to Paul Meurice (still in a Paris prison): 'This charming, well-wooded, well-watered isle, this other Eden, reveals itself to us under the aspect of a pile of barren, scorched rocks. We look in vain for a tree in leaf. St Helier looks suspiciously like St Helena.'[23]

If Hugo's large family—his wife and daughter, his two grown-up sons Charles and François-Victor, not to speak of the faithful Juliette Drouet who had followed him to Brussels and now settled down at his side in Jersey— were less than enchanted by their surroundings, the poet himself was far too engrossed in his literary and political activities to be conscious of the indignity of being forced to 'eat the bitter bread of banishment.' *Napoléon le Petit* had been published. 'They tell me', he wrote to a friend, 'that my little book is infiltrating into France and dripping, drop by drop, on to Bonaparte. It may well end by making a hole. . . . Since my arrival here they have done me the honour of trebling the establishment of customs officers, policemen and police spies at St Malo. The fool is raising a bristling barrier of bayonets to try and keep the book out of the country.' Hugo was not exaggerating. On August 2nd, 1852 a circular from the Ministry of the Interior warned customs officers on all frontiers and coastlines of impending attempts to smuggle copies of *Napoléon le Petit* into France by inserting them into hollowed-out lumps of coal, hiding them in carts with false bottoms, or sending single sheets through the post. Considerable ingenuity was, in fact, used to foil the vigilance of customs officers on the Normandy coast. Copies were placed inside hermetically sealed boxes which were then dropped at prearranged spots along the rocky coast by Jersey fishermen at high tide, ready to be picked up at low tide by local people collecting seaweed. The seaweed was loaded on to carts and transported inland for processing; it was manifestly impossible to search every consignment of the messy stuff. Once out of sight of the excisemen, it was a simple matter, on some quiet country road, to open the boxes and transfer the printed volumes to a hawker's pack.[24] The *colporteurs* made big profits on their illegal and clandestine sales, but deserved to: they incurred grave risks, if caught, not just of being heavily fined and sentenced to long terms of imprisonment, but—even worse—of losing their licence and hence their livelihood.

Napoléon le Petit, distributed in this way inside France in spite of all efforts to suppress it, found in addition thousands of readers in neighbouring French-speaking countries and, in its English and Spanish translations, penetrated to all parts of Europe and America. But Hugo was not content to leave matters there. In October 1852 he started work on a series of verse satires and within eight months had written enough to make up a substantial volume— the famous *Châtiments*. Originally he may have wanted simply to finish settling his personal score with Napoleon III: the first titles he toyed with (*Le Chant du Vengeur, Rimes vengeresses*) hint at this. 'The wretch having been toasted on one side only, I am turning him over on the gridiron', he wrote to Alphonse Esquiros. But the vein of private vendetta soon ran out, and vaster themes were broached. Hugo composed the poems in a state of fierce concentration, possessed, obsessed by his subject, spurred on by his anger, indignation and resentment, and also by the over-optimistic calculation that the régime would shortly collapse. The book was ready some time before it could be published. An expurgated version was on sale in Brussels at the end of 1853; the unexpurgated edition bore the fictitious imprimatur: 'Geneva and New York: Imprimerie Universelle, St Helier.'

Poetry directly inspired by contemporary political events rarely wears well. If *Les Châtiments* is still exciting to read, this survival it must owe to its specifically poetic qualities, to its verve, its variety, its inventiveness; the passion that sustains it is authentic, and the fervour never seems to flag. Much of it is, of course, 'occasional verse', requiring for its full appreciation a close acquaintance with the day-to-day development of the political scene in France through the year 1852. Certain names (often ingeniously used as rhyme-words) recur obsessively, like those of Morny, Louis-Napoleon's bastard half-brother and right-hand man, Sibour, the archbishop who consecrated the *coup d'état* with a Te Deum celebrated at Notre-Dame, Saint-Arnaud, a general who had won a reputation for bravery in Algeria and had a soldier's contempt for the niceties of parliamentary rule, Troplong, a lawyer who became president of the Senate under the Empire, and Maupas, a zealous administrator whom Napoleon made chief of police at Paris; it was Maupas who, when a subordinate hesitated about making arrests without sufficient evidence of treason, answered: 'My agents will introduce the evidence themselves into the homes of the accused.' The Emperor himself is referred to by a variety of insulting nicknames, of which Mandrin and Cartouche (who were famous robbers and highwaymen executed in the eighteenth century) are the least outrageous.

Around this central target, composed of the usurper and his immediate circle of supporters, the shafts of invective scatter to hit all manner of acquiescent bystanders, all those groups in the country that connived at the destruction of the Republic or actively collaborated with the destroyers: the army officers who organized the street massacres, the judges who so lightly passed sentence of execution, deportation or imprisonment on Napoleon's political enemies, the financiers and large-scale employers of labour who welcomed the new régime because it promised them an era of steady business expansion, the clergy, finally, who gave their blessing to the Empire because the Empire stood for a restoration of religious values.

The best of the poems in the collection are those least dependent on the inspiration provided by day-to-day events. Hugo made effective play with the theme of the contrast between the giant Uncle and the pigmy Nephew, especially in the long, sombre poem *L'Expiation*. The image of the sea, which he had of course constantly before his eyes when composing *Les Châtiments*, bears a continually shifting weight of symbolic significance. *Nox* is couched in the form of an acrimonious dialogue between the poet, who wishes to think only of the social and political evils stalking his country, and the sea which, with its serene and timeless impassivity, tempts him to forget his mission. Elsewhere the sea provides a convenient and effective personification of the common people, whom Hugo trusts eventually to overwhelm and wash away the vicious tyranny of Bonaparte. *Le Bord de la mer*, perhaps the most sombre piece in the collection, turns on the question whether political assassination is justifiable, and reaches an affirmative conclusion; conscience speaks to the poet, in the very last line, to tell him:

> *Tu peux tuer cet homme avec tranquillité.*

Even though the statement is immediately contradicted by the succeeding poem (*Non*), this uncompromising advocacy of tyrannicide shocked even those of Hugo's contemporaries who shared his hostility to the imperial régime.[25] More characteristic is the reiterated assertion that the punishment of the guilty man will lie in the verdict that history will pass on his acts, and in the contempt in which posterity will hold him. The poem *Sacer Esto* takes its title from the curse pronounced on certain classes of criminals who, under the old law of Rome, were condemned to become untouchables: they were sacred in the sense that it was sacrilegious to have anything to do with them. Hugo's visionary gift was never better vindicated in the event. Almost exactly 20 years later his enemy was to expire, shunned and forsaken by all, shamed by defeat and racked by disease, in the quiet little Kentish town of Chislehurst.

Meanwhile the poet, pacing the shingle of the Jersey beaches, remained free to raise his own clamorous protest, confident that it could not fail to hasten the day of reckoning. Hugo saw the application of the Biblical story of the fall of Jericho: he himself was Joshua, the trumpets he was blowing (*'clairons de la pensée'*) would in time shatter the walls and lay waste the city. Elsewhere, in a clever pastiche of a La Fontaine fable, Louis-Napoleon is presented as the monkey dressed up as a tiger, who terrorizes the neighbourhood until the huntsman (Hugo himself) arrives to strip him of his disguise. In the most dignified of this group of poems, *Ultima Verba*, Hugo pledged himself never to set foot again on his native land until the Empire had fallen and the Republic had been re-established; even if all his fellow refugees allow themselves to be tempted by offers of amnesty, even if he is the only exile left in exile:

> If there remain but ten, I shall be one of ten;
> If only one be left, that one will be myself!

Hugo held firm to this resolution, even though the régime endured far longer than he had anticipated; he was nearly 70 when circumstances finally made it possible for him to return. The years of exile, especially the first two or three, were uncomfortable and sometimes stormy. A number of political refugees from France had settled in Jersey, attracted by the fact that it was

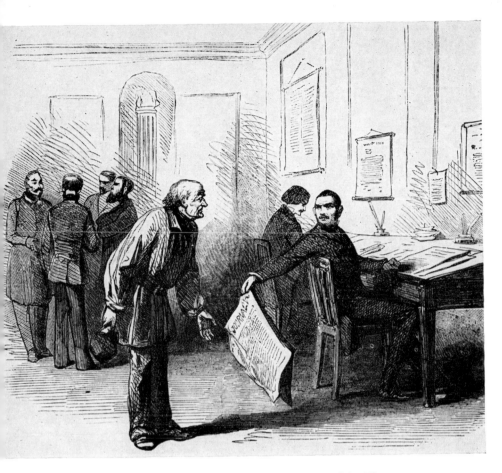

7 'Office of the Newspaper Police'. This drawing, which appeared in *The Illustrated London News* a month after the *coup d'etat*, shows a printer's devil accepting a censored proof-copy of his newspaper

8 Edmond and Jules de Goncourt. One of Nadar's photo-portraits, showing the brothers at about the time they were sent for trial (see pp. 62–3)

French-speaking territory though part of the United Kingdom. Most of them had been living there long before Hugo arrived, having fled from Paris after the collapse of the socialist republic in June, 1848. Most of them again, unlike Hugo, had scanty resources, and a number were working-class people; however much he sympathized with them, he found it impossible to prevail on his own family to let him receive them in Marine Terrace, the rented house where he was living, and the long conversations he had with Pierre Leroux took place out of doors.

The islanders themselves, and even some of the leading Tory politicians at Westminster, were inclined to cast suspicious glances at this crew of ragged revolutionaries. Their cause evoked scant sympathy in Whitehall. England had lost very little time in recognizing Napoleon III as *de jure* ruler of France, and the state visit that Victoria paid in 1855 was intended to cement friendly relations between the two countries. It drove the French republicans to despair: one of them, Félix Pyat, a refugee living in London, delivered a bitter personal attack on the Queen for lending herself to this ignoble charade in which, so he declared, she had sacrificed her regal dignity, her aristocratic pride, her patriotism and even her womanly modesty, for the love of the brigand Napoleon. Pyat's violent manifesto was reproduced by the Jersey refugees in their newspaper *L'Homme*, whereupon the fury of the loyal islanders knew no bounds; there was talk of lynching the foreigners, but fortunately the governor had sufficient authority to pacify local sentiment by expelling three of the ringleaders, two Frenchmen and an Italian. Hugo was approached by a delegation of his fellow countrymen and agreed to draw up and sign a protest against this high-handed action, so little in keeping with traditional British tolerance; the only result was that he was given three days to pack and leave the island. On October 31st he embarked for Guernsey.

Here he led a quieter life and gradually became accepted by the inhabitants. The charitable activities that Mme Hugo engaged on impressed local opinion favourably, and the social standing of the poet was enhanced by the obvious esteem in which he was held by the Bailiff of Guernsey, Sir Stafford Carey, and his highly cultivated daughter. Hugo made regular trips to the continent of Europe, and was greeted wherever he went with admiration and adulation. The works he published after *Les Châtiments* added greatly to his reputation, even inside France, for Napoleon III's administration did not choose to proscribe his non-political writings. When *Les Contemplations* were ready for the press Paul Meurice, at Hugo's request, paid a visit to the head of the Sûreté, a certain Pierre-Hector Collet-Meygret, who happened to be a former member of the staff of *L'Événement* and conserved all his old admiration for Hugo as a poet. Paul Meurice's mission was none the less delicate, as

F

Hugo had stated that he would never consent to submit *Les Contemplations* for preliminary inspection by the censorship. Collet-Meygret was satisfied, however, with Meurice's solemn assurance that the new volume included nothing that could be construed as an attack on the régime, and *Les Contemplations* was in due course published openly. It was a great popular success, the first edition selling out within a few days, in spite of the efforts of official criticism to ridicule it. Sainte-Beuve, prudent as ever, refrained from reviewing the book.

The size of Hugo's following in France can be judged from the fact that he was able to ask his publisher, Lacroix, for the record sum of 300,000 francs for the rights of his long-awaited novel, *Les Misérables*, in 1862; even so, Lacroix is said to have netted half a million within four years of its publication. Once again, the politically inspired hostility of the critics could not interfere with the sales of the book;[26] Sainte-Beuve, still cautious about what he put into print, was heard to declare that Hugo 'had won the greatest success of the age, stolen from under the nose of a government which is, after all, extremely powerful'. Then, in 1864, occurred the episode of the Shakespeare banquet. A committee had been set up to organize the tricentenary celebration of Shakespeare's birth. They decided to hold a banquet, with Hugo as guest of honour; since it was obvious that he would not be present, the plan was to leave one chair empty, like Banquo's, at the head of the table. The government, however, got wind of the project and banned the banquet.

A marked softening in the official attitude towards Victor Hugo became noticeable in the last five years of the Empire. His *Chansons des rues et des bois* (1865) accorded so well with the frivolous, gracefully licentious atmosphere of the period that it could almost be regarded as a conciliatory gesture on the part of the *grand absent*. The bland eroticism that characterized this new collection of verse might have been expressly designed to captivate the public that delighted in Carpeaux' suggestive sculpture and Baudry's sugary nudes. At all events it constituted further proof of Hugo's extraordinary versatility. No one could deny that the aging poet, obdurate and fanatical though he remained, constituted one of the principal glories of French culture, and when the Paris Exhibition of 1867 was being arranged, it was realized that to exclude Hugo would be more dangerous than to accord him his rightful place. The decision was taken to stage a revival of *Hernani*. Since the *coup d'état* no theatre manager had ventured to put on any of his plays, apart from Houssaye whose audacious production of *Marion Delorme* in the very first weeks of the Empire has already been recalled, and Hugo, hearing of the proposal, was filled with misgivings, fearing that the authorities might have it in mind to plant police agents in the audience to create an uproar. But the only protests on the first night came from members of the public who knew the play by heart and noticed where, for the sake of observing the conventions, some of the more outrageous lines had been modified. Mme Hugo attended the performance, along with Théophile Gautier, Théodore de Banville, Émile de Girardin, Auguste Vacquerie and many another of the exile's old friends. The excitement was tremendous, the applause deafening. 'Nothing', wrote Janin in the *Journal des Débats* the following day, 'could be compared with the celebration of this unexpected return.' True, it was not yet a return in person; but the occasion did mark the triumph of the pen over the sword, of genius over the gendarme. The censorship had at last been driven into retreat, disarmed by the overwhelming force of popular acclaim.

Notes

[1] Maxime Du Camp, *Souvenirs littéraires* (Paris, 1892) II, 34, 42.

[2] Thus, a by-product of Fieschi's attempt on the life of Louis-Philippe in 1835 was that caution-money was put up from 24,000 fr. to 100,000 fr.

[3] Rather daringly, Gustave Doré inserted a note in the *Journal pour rire* shortly after the *coup d'état*: '*MM. les dessinateurs ont l'honneur de vous faire part de la perte douloureuse qu'ils viennent de faire en la personne de dame Caricature, récemment décédée.*'

[4] In addition there is some evidence that sections, at least, of the opposition press were secretly acquired and 'managed' by the Ministry of the Interior: a newspaper editor who decided, for one reason or another, to go over to the government might be instructed to maintain ostensibly his former hostile line: the authorities were quick to realize that indoctrination of the public was less effective when the medium was known to be controlled by the government than when they unsuspectingly read an editorial in a newspaper they believed to be free of such control. See D. I. Kulstein's extremely well documented study, 'Government Propaganda and the Press during the Second Empire', *Gazette*, vol. x (1964), pp. 125–43.

[5] Hector Pessard, *Mes petits papiers* (Paris, 1887), pp. 8–9.

[6] It was in 1836 that Émile de Girardin revolutionized the financing of newspapers (and piled up a fortune for himself in the process) by selling *La Presse* at less than cost price, and bridging the gap by the sale of advertisement space.

[7] *La Cloche*, 11 July 1872.

[8] Du Camp, *op. cit.* p. 52.

[9] These statements, which occur in a circular issued to Justices of the Peace by the Prefect of Toulon only a few days after the *coup d'état*, are quoted in Howard C. Payne, *The Police State of Louis Napoleon Bonaparte* (Seattle, 1966), p. 146.

[10] Du Camp, *op. cit.*, pp. 144–5; Flaubert, *Correspondance* (Paris, Conard, 1910, III, 91.

[11] *Tableau historique et critique de la poésie française et du théâtre français au XVIᵉ siécle*, 1828.

[12] Moreover it was reduced, on appeal, to 50 francs.

[13] E. & J. de Goncourt, *Journal, mémoires de la vie littéraire* (Monaco, 1956), I, 90.

[14] See Auriant, 'Xavier de Montépin, romancier réaliste, moraliste et poète baude-lairien', *Mercure de France*, vol. 279 (1937), pp. 620–31.

[15] Théophile Gautier, whose daughter Judith he married, nicknamed Catulle Mendès 'Crapule M'embête'. He is said to have disgraced himself by getting drunk at Victor Hugo's funeral.

[16] See Philip Spencer, 'Censorship by imprisonment in France, 1830–1870', *The Romanic Review*, vol. 47 (1956), pp. 27–38.

[17] *L'Évolution naturaliste*, Paris, 1884.

[18] Reprint in *Les Lettres et les Arts* (Paris, 1908), pp. 265–8.

[19] *Hugo, l'homme et l'œuvre*, (Paris, 1952,) p. 120.

[20] The ode 'Lui' in *Les Orientales* (1828) was the poem in which Hugo first demon-strated clearly his admiration for Napoleon I:

> 'Les chants volent pressés sur mes levres de flamme,
> Napolèon! soleil dont je suis le Memnon.'

On the whole question, see M. Descotes, *La Légende de Napoléon et les écrivains français du XIXᵉ siécle*, Paris, 1967.

[21] He caused to be printed on the title-page of *Histoire d'un crime* the following note: '*Ce livre est plus qu'actuel; il est urgent.*'

[22] *Histoire de la littérature française de 1789 à nos jours* (Paris, 1936), p. 296.

[23] Quoted by Paul Hazard, 'Avec Victor Hugo en exil', *Revue des Deux Mondes*, vol. 60 (1930) p. 391.

[24] See Léon Deries, 'Policiers et douaniers contre Victor Hugo', *La Grande Revue*, vol. 85 (1914), pp. 635–44.

[25] '*Il y a dans les Châtiments un vers odieux, un vers coupable qui fait l'effet de la tache de sang de Lady Macbeth . . .*', wrote Louis Etienne, in an otherwise enthusiastic study of the work which appeared in *La Revue des Deux Mondes*, June 15, 1869.

[26] A remarkably well documented survey of critical reactions will be found in Max Bach, 'Critique et politique: la réception des *Misérables* en 1862', *PMLA*, vol. 77 (1962), pp. 595–608.

three

The Realists

Realism and its Opponents

In 'Le Saut du tremplin', the best-known poem in his collection *Odes funambulesques* (published in the same year as the *Fleurs du Mal*, 1857), Théodore de Banville confronts us with a muscular, semi-divine clown who, in one enormous leap, bursts through the canvas ceiling of the circus-tent and 'goes spinning off among the stars'. This mythical acrobat clearly represents the poet, Banville himself;[1] and a central feature of the poem is the prayer he addresses to his springboard, adjuring it to hurl him higher in the air than ever before, where he can no longer see the rows of spectators, the grocers and the notaries in their 'cruel black dinner-jackets.'

> *Plus loin! plus haut! je vois encor*
> *Des boursiers à lunettes d'or,*
> *Des critiques, des demoiselles*
> *Et des réalistes en feu.*

We can recognize, in this catalogue of Banville's *bêtes noires*, all the anti-poetic scarecrows of the time: stockbrokers with gold-rimmed spectacles, critics (that tiresome, obtuse race of parasites), and the gaunt, prissy, school-mistressy *demoiselles*. But what are the 'realists' doing in this company, and why are they described as being 'on fire'? For its proper understanding, this line needs to be glossed by referring to another poem in the *Odes funambulesques*, entitled simply 'Réalisme', in which Banville shows the realists as fiery-faced for no other reason than that they are beer-sodden:

> *Ils se sont tous grisés de bière chez Andler,*
> *Et les voici qui vont graves, les yeux en l'air,*
> *Rouges pourpres, dirait Mathieu, quant au visage.*

Andler was the name of the German-Swiss proprietor of a left-bank restaurant called La Rotonde, or, by the initiated, simply 'La Brasserie'. Champfleury, who knew it well, gives a graphic description of it in his *Souvenirs et portraits de jeunesse*: he talks of the great hams festooned by strings of sausages which depended from the ceiling, of cheeses on the side-tables as big as millwheels and barrels of sauerkraut on the floor. In this odoriferous and appetizing atmosphere, Gustave Courbet could be observed sitting before a copious midday meal almost any day of the week in the early 1850s; his studio was conveniently situated in the same street, rue Hauteville. Around him would gather a motley company of fellow artists, Corot, Bonvin, and Daumier; of art-critics like Jules-Antoine Castagnary, Armand Silvestre, and now and again Baudelaire; together with a sprinkling of other literary men, Champfleury himself, his disciple Duranty, Jules Vallès. A heterogeneous group to have a common label put on them, but Banville was not interested, just here, in the niceties of categorization.

And Mathieu? Gustave Mathieu was born in George Sand's part of the country, and it was she who originally showed him kindness and encouraged his literary bent. Possibly, too, she was responsible for fanning the republican ardour which inspired the poetry that gave him a brief celebrity in 1848. Mathieu's name was indissolubly linked with that of Pierre Dupont. The two poets fought side by side in the streets in December 1851 and boldly continued, after the establishment of the Empire, to pump out socialist propaganda in the form of popular songs which were listened to by workmen, bohemians and plain-clothes policemen at the Estaminet lyrique, a forerunner of the Montmartre cabarets of the Third Republic. Dupont was a rather more gifted poet than Mathieu. Baudelaire thought well enough of him to compose a preface for his *Chants et chansons* in 1851, while Champfleury, writing in *L'Artiste* in 1852, publicly inducted him into the company of the realists.

Thus, Banville's allusions can be traced to their contemporary and anecdotal sources, but his manifest aversion to these fiery-faced, beery democrats remains unexplained. No doubt it was largely nourished by the realists' deliberately provocative sorties against the poets. The only poetry Champfleury enjoyed was, so he declared, 'La Marseillaise', or else the after-dinner ditty, 'Béranger's spicy or sentimental witticisms'. Duranty saluted *Les Contemplations* with a long and insolent review in his journal *Le Réalisme*, on which Henry Murger passed an equitable though devastating verdict when he said that Duranty was behaving like a dog lifting its leg against the portals of Notre-Dame. If Murger was offended, Banville must have been infuriated, for Hugo was one of his gods: his admiration for the older poet bordered on fanaticism, and the slightest criticism savoured of blasphemy.

In addition Banville knew that his gibes against realism, while they might leave the realists indifferent, would win him the approving grin of the *boulevardier*; and Banville was very much the *boulevardier*'s poet, elegant, flippant, his verses stuffed with in-group allusions: Thibaudet called him 'the Offenbach of poetry'. To be witty at the expense of this lumpish crew of beery, pot-bellied, blear-eyed 'realists' was a diversion indulged in by every dashing young dandy at the time, for there are none so old-fashioned as the trend-setters in any age.

The very real anger and disgust aroused by the realists during the decade in which they first came to public notice was more seriously motivated, however, than Banville's trivial sarcasms might suggest. Their doctrine, and much more blantantly the first-fruits of this doctrine which were the canvases of Courbet, called sharply into question the age-old belief that the whole mission of art was to give visible form to beauty, however the concept of beauty might be interpreted, and that an understanding of beauty, whether intuitively attained or laboriously acquired through education, was what determined the acquisition of taste. This faith, the roots of which reach back to the High Renaissance and beyond that, no doubt, to Plotinus and the neo-Platonists, had of course undergone certain important modifications in the course of time, but the central dogma had never before been assailed. The leading theoreticians of the eighteenth century had rejected the concept of an aesthetic absolute in favour of a system of relative variables; as Voltaire put it, a toad would imagine Venus in the form of a female toad, but this did not mean that the toad was lacking in aesthetic sense. Later, Mme de Staël suggested that race, climate, latitude, customs, religion, and national history, all these might influence what people regarded as constituting the beautiful in art. But neither the Abbé Du Bos, who was the first writer in France to challenge the notion of absolute beauty, nor Voltaire nor Mme de Staël doubted for one moment that the aim of art was to create or distil the beauty that was present in nature only in a dormant or inchoate state.

Nor was this belief seriously impaired by the Romantic revolution that Mme de Staël helped to promote. Whatever arguments Hugo may have used in the preface to *Cromwell* and elsewhere, to justify adding the grotesque and the sinister to the catalogue of aesthetically valuable elements, neither the Romantics themselves nor post-Romantics like Gautier seriously believed that crude, unadorned, unprocessed reality could be incorporated just as it was into the work of art. The typical reaction to such a suggestion— still falteringly and obliquely advanced, at the time—is to be found in Vigny's essay, 'Réflexions sur la vérité dans l'art', which was printed as a preface to the fourth edition (1829) of his historical novel *Cinq-Mars*. 'What value have the arts', wrote Vigny, 'if they are no more than the reduplication and repetition of existence? Ah! good God, we see enough of it all around us, that gloomy, disenchanting reality.' In the 1840's, notwithstanding the example given by the landscape painters of the Barbizon school, the idea that beauty might emerge from straightforward representation of the model still faced immense resistance. Art was defined by Baudelaire, in his *Salon de 1846*, as 'une mnémotechnie du beau': he meant that it was a device for recording what is conserved as beautiful in the memory.[2] 'Now an exact resemblance ruins one's remembrance', he continued. 'There are wretched painters for whom the smallest wart is a great good fortune. Not only are they careful not to forget it, but they needs must make it four times as big as it is.' This is the kind of objection that *salonniers* were to raise time and again in their criticisms of Courbet's painting: but Baudelaire was writing several years before Courbet put his first realist canvases on show.

Apart from the aesthetic counter-arguments, there were other reasons for the widespread hostility to realism which are traceable to its iconoclastic ideology. Academic art, to which realism was opposed and which it hoped to supersede, was linked through the long-standing system of public patronage, official rewards and honours, and state-supported teaching centres, to the established order. That the status of the fashionable and popular products of the École des Beaux-Arts was endangered by the emergence of new methods and new preoccupations which seemed to have little in common with the great traditions of the past, would not in itself have mattered so much if the central government had not developed a vested interest in the maintenance of the artistic *status quo*. Partly because the Second Empire laid such store by outward display and attached such importance to the acknowledged supremacy of French art throughout the world, a movement which seemed to threaten this supremacy from within by challenging its dearest assumptions was easily construed as a danger to national pride and prestige. At least one attempt was made, as we shall see, to persuade Courbet to modify his intransigence in return for official support and approval. On another occasion a minister of the Crown (Fould) took it on himself to use the full weight of the authority that his position gave him in order to denounce the realists and all their works.

There was another sense in which realism could be regarded as the opposition art *par excellence* under the Second Empire. Deliberately and, it would seem, provocatively, it sought its inspiration and its subjects among the less privileged classes of society which academic art had tended to ignore— though, all through the seventeenth and eighteenth centuries there had been painters (Le Nain, Chardin, Greuze) and novelists (Sorel, Marivaux, Restif de La Bretonne) who had found their models in the fields and farmyards, in the back rooms of small shops or the servants' hall, and discovered in these lowly settings the scenes they wished to paint and record. In literature, this tradition had persisted thanks to Balzac, Eugène Suë, George Sand and other novelists of lesser calibre. In art it had fallen into abeyance and into corruption until, as we shall see, first Millet, then Courbet revived it.

In one respect, however, realism did command support from all except the most reactionary. Its advocacy of modernism, at least where subject-matter was concerned, was fully in line with the progressive spirit of the age. There was a negative and a positive aspect to this. Modernism, with its slogan: 'Who will deliver us from the Greeks and the Romans?' implied in the first instance a crusade against debased, conventional, or bogus classicism. If the Greeks and the Romans were so hard to evict (as late as 1875, Cabanel's *salon* painting was a long-tressed Venus shown slowly ascending a winding flight of steps towards a cloud-girt classical temple, the mythical apple in her hand, the traditional doves fluttering about her feet), this was not through any genuine nostalgia for the simplicities of antiquity. The real reason for its retention was that the mythological setting permitted the study of the nude, which the conventions of the period forbade in any other context. It was for infringing these conventions that Manet's *Déjeuner sur l'herbe* aroused such a storm of protest and execration in 1863. But Courbet had already shown the way, by refusing to paint a nude except in situations where a woman would naturally be naked, having just removed her clothes to bathe or (as in *L'Atelier*) to pose. His criticism of Aimé Millet's allegorical statue of Youth, on the grounds that the girl was shown nude, was peevish, certainly, and obtuse, but also revealing. In real life you never see young women standing about without any clothes. 'She ought to have been given a dress; where's her dress?'

The positive side of modernism was epitomized in Baudelaire's celebrated prediction: 'That man will be the *painter*, the true painter, who first succeeds in revealing the epic aspect of modern life, and who helps us to realize, by the use of line and colour, how great, how poetical we are in our cravats and our polished boots.' Baudelaire looked for such a prodigy in vain: the artist who approached nearest to his ideal was Constantin Guys, a minor draughts-man and water-colourist whom he extolled a little extravagantly in a mono-graph significantly entitled 'Le Peintre de la vie moderne'.[3] Some of Guys' most interesting work, done in the Crimea, appeared in the *Illustrated London News*; which suggests that realism, in its guise of modernism, is best sought for first not among those who painted on canvas and framed their pictures for public exhibition, but among the humbler, industrious confraternity of those who recorded the passing scene or commented on current events in a form suitable for reproduction in the pages of illustrated newspapers and magazines. The name of Honoré Daumier presents itself immediately. One of the very few sayings attributed to this modest, taciturn artist is the un-emphatic remark: '*Il faut être de son temps, que je vous dis*'—'I tell you, you must stick to your own time.'

Honoré Daumier, lithographer

The development of art in the nineteenth century and the various trans-formations it underwent owed much to contemporary advances in techno-logy. In this respect, the artist may be said to have been far more a child of his age than the writer. First of all the tin paint-tube, an English invention imported into France in the early 1840s, freed him from the necessity to stay in the studio to paint. Without it, the landscapists of the Barbizon school could hardly have engaged in outdoor work to the extent they did; nor could they have done so, for that matter, without the new facilities for rapid travel that the railway offered. As industrial chemistry progressed, a whole range of new intermediate colours came on to the market, relieving the artist of much time-wasting labour mixing primary colours in a back room. Another momen-tous invention was the daguerreotype. Its repercussions on the portrait painter in particular were considerable. He was encouraged to give greater attention to colour, where the daguerreotype could not compete, less to line and shading, and to aim at a 'speaking likeness' rather than a meticulous copy. An inci-dental consequence of photography was that the portrait painter no longer needed to rely exclusively on sittings or on his memory; when Courbet was planning to visit Guernsey in order to paint Hugo's portrait, he wrote in advance asking to be sent a few photographs. The negative results of the invention were even more far-reaching. This inexpensive, rapid method of achieving exact likenesses ruined the market for many dull but dexterous painters who had formerly driven a flourishing trade in the manufacture of fussily faithful family portraits.[4] Beyond this, it is probable that photography counted for something in the process by which, very gradually, the subject of a picture came to be regarded as of lesser artistic consequence in itself; critics gave increasing attention to specifically painterly elements, and the way was open for the bolder compositional and technical experiments of the Impresionists.

Lithography, an earlier invention than any of the others mentioned, made a bigger immediate impact since its introduction coincided with the development of the popular daily newspaper. The special property of lithography that made it peculiarly suited for newspaper use was that very little deterioration occurred between the first copy taken of an original drawing and any number of subsequent impressions. Some of the major artists of the early nineteenth century—Delacroix, Géricault, and of course Goya—experimented with lithography, while the demands of commerce called into being a small army of draughtsmen specializing in the new technique. Some of them were mere copyists, turning out bad facsimiles of the more widely discussed *salon* pictures, or portraying the latest fashions in carriages or women's clothes. Others used lithography to give a fresh impetus to the ancient art of caricature. One of the first in France to do this was Carle Vernet (1758–1836), the father of the celebrated painter of battle-scenes. Henry Monnier and Gavarni—the former on account of his creation of the unforgettable Joseph Prudhomme, the latter for the sake of his portrayal of the *lorette*, that charming and light-hearted predecessor of the Second-Empire *cocotte*—won wide renown in the first half of the century. But however fascinating the record they left of the types and manners of their times, neither of them possessed an artistic genius to match that of Honoré Daumier.

In his quiet and unobtrusive way, Daumier was a man of strong though not extreme republican views. These had found expression in the savage caricatures of Louis-Philippe and his ministers which he had executed for *Le Charivari* during the first few years of its life.[5] The series had ended in 1835, when political caricature was banned by law, and Daumier turned to social satire, inaugurating his own version of the 'human comedy' which, by and large, appeared simultaneously with Balzac's publication of the series of novels constituting *La Comédie humaine*. Monnier may have come closer than Daumier to the spirit of Balzac's works, but the middle-class types that Daumier caricatured—the small *rentier*, the shopkeeper, the briefless barrister —all have their equivalents in the pages of *Les Petits Bourgeois*, *César Birotteau* and *Le Cousin Pons*; and Daumier was arguably more successful than Balzac in portraying the *petites misères de la vie conjugale*.

When, in 1848, the fetters were struck off and Daumier found himself free, once more, to use his pencil for the purposes of political comment, the good republican that he was could see very little, at first, to arouse his indignation or merit attack. One of the exploits of the working class during the February Revolution—the taking of the Tuileries Palace—was commemorated in a drawing of a Paris urchin, a forerunner of Hugo's Gavroche, sprawling on the throne with a well-caught expression of cheerful impudence on his face. 'Blimey, it ain't arf soft!' (*'Cristi, comme on s'enfonce là-dedans!'*) is the legend—possibly not actually contributed by Daumier himself. There was an apt reference to the flight of capital from France in a sketch published on March 7th, showing a banker stepping off the boat at Dover, with a heavy safe tucked under his arm. A few tars are standing on the quayside, watching him with inscrutable expressions. The caption is a variant on the famous remark attributed to Francis I after the battle of Pavia: '*Tout est perdu, fors l'honneur*'; Daumier's man of money is exclaiming: 'All is lost, save the safe'. Also worth mentioning, less for its artistic merits than for its prophetic accuracy, is the drawing of a medallion showing Louis-Philippe's head in profile, cruelly distorted and with a grossly thick neck, and the legend round the circumference: '*Louis-Philippe dernier roi des Français.*'

Daumier's best work is of a kind that dispenses with explanatory text and makes its point unaided, but if one is examining his art for the light it sheds on popular reactions to the events of the period, it is necessary to take also into account pictures drawn for the sake of the dialogue printed underneath. Some of these have their period interest, independent of the humour which may be largely confined to the small print. The revival of modes of address current under the First Republic is quietly satirized in a drawing published May 22nd, 1848, showing a horse bus retreating up a Paris street, the conductor standing on the rear steps. He faces a voluminous middle-aged woman who is clasping a fat dog to her bosom: 'Sorry, citizeness, no animals allowed.'—'Damn you for an aristocrat', she shouts back, shaking her umbrella at him. A few of Daumier's humorous series—like *Les Papas*, a gentle collection of studies of parents and children—had been inaugurated under the July Monarchy and were continued without interruption and with very little change in tone after the downfall of the régime. But new situations suggested new series, like that entitled *Les Alarmistes et les Alarmés*, designed to tease those members of the middle class who looked on political developments in the spring of 1848 with more apprehension than gratification. A frightened citizen is shown pulling at his wife's arm and urging her to walk home more quickly; his misgivings have been aroused by a group of 'armed men' (actually a procession of small boys led by one of their number beating a drum). Then there was a fresh series entitled *Les Divorceuses*: six cartoons, appearing at intervals between August and October 1848, refer to the proposals currently under discussion to legalize divorce. A series rather similar in tone was launched the following year, under the heading *Les Femmes socialistes*, showing husbands disconsolately baby-sitting while their wives attend political meetings, or emancipated wives refusing haughtily to sew on missing trouser-buttons. Daumier, one would judge, was no feminist.

He was one of the first to sound the alarm at the revival of Bonapartism in France. The cartoon *Victor Hugo et Émile de Girardin cherchent à élever le Prince*

Louis (December 11th, 1848) has already been described.[6] An earlier drawing,
which appeared on December 2nd and refers to Louis-Napoleon's return
from exile, is headed *Paquebot napoléonien*. It has a kind of children's story-
book delightfulness. A diminutive figure sitting in a huge helmet, in which
he has evidently made the sea-crossing from England, Louis-Napoleon is
being drawn up a shingly beach by a sprightly though bedraggled eagle.
There were other political figures that Daumier attacked with much greater
bitterness, notably the Comte de Montalembert, the leader of the clerical
party in the Assembly, and Adolphe Thiers, depicted in a particularly vicious
caricature entitled *Un Parricide* as a dwarf-like figure wielding a huge club
inscribed 'Press Law'. Thiers' unsuspecting victim, the allegorical figure
representing the angel of the press, sits in a kind of halo in the background,
bent over the sheet of paper on which she is writing. Few of his cartoons
display so effectively Daumier's extraordinary craftsmanship in conveying
an impression of bright light while using only the resources of line and
shading that the lithograph offered him. Another characteristic trick of style
—the propensity for arranging four figures round the rectangle, as it were at
the four points of the compass—is illustrated in two cartoons which appeared
respectively on May 8th and June 3rd, 1850. In *Légende de l'an 1850* Montalembert is shown ascending to heaven, while three cherubim, with the features
of his three political followers, flit around him. *Les Moucherons politiques*
depicts four excessively sturdy gnats, representing Montalembert, Thiers,
Berryer (the chief legitimist deputy), and Molé (leader of the Orleanists),
who are trying to blow out the candle-flame of the February Revolution.[7]

During the parliamentary vacations of the summer of 1850 Daumier
found a new subject on which to exercise his wit. The city authorities chose
that moment to begin replacing the paving stones of the principal arteries of
Paris with tarred surfaces. Macadamization, as it was called, was an invention
that commended itself to those responsible for keeping order in the capital,
since roads so treated could not be torn up to provide the material for
barricades. This aspect of the matter may not have escaped Daumier, but he
makes no allusion to it, though all the cartoons he published on the subject
stress the dire inconveniences of this method of road-making. The
Parisians, for fear of being trapped in the sticky mixture, are depicted walking
about on high stilts. A couple of property-owners are shown staring about
in despair at the huge 'To let' notices in the windows of every apartment in a
newly macadamized boulevard. The supposed advantage of the new process
was, of course, that by providing a smoother surface it would allow vehicles
to travel faster; but this was not, in Daumier's view, an unmixed blessing: a
drawing on July 19th suggests that the time would come—such are the

blessings of civilization—when horse-drawn carriages would all have to be equipped with warning-bells. There are occasions when an ironist finds himself unwittingly indulging in accurate prophecy.

In the autumn the political scene darkened once more. 'Gracious heaven!' exclaims a fond father aghast at the sight of his small son returning from a walk with a black eye; and, addressing the nursemaid: 'I'm sure, Madeleine, you must have let the child shout "Long live the Republic!" in the street.' Daumier seems to have had a sure premonition how the Republic would end and what régime would supersede it. On October 21st, 1850 a particularly daring cartoon, for which no commentary was needed, appeared under the heading: *Le Nouveau Tapissier de la Couronne.* The 'royal upholsterer', on the left of the picture, with an outsize pair of scissors in his hand, is cutting up cloth for the throne which stands behind him on a table. The point, so cleverly made, is that the vast folds of the material are all embroidered with the heraldic bee that Napoleon I adopted as one of his emblems.

The efforts of Bonapartist adherents were at this time being concerted by a fund-raising and propaganda organization known as the 'Société du 10 décembre'. Daumier launched a veritable press-campaign to denounce their activities, inventing, for the purpose, two scarecrow figures whom he named Ratapoil and Casmajou. In a cartoon which *Le Charivari* published on February 26th, 1851, the pair are shown, carrying deadly looking life-preservers, outside an apartment, the street-door of which has been half-opened by a frightened housewife. Ratapoil greets her with the customary formula used by sextons to extract offerings from the faithful: '*Pour les frais du culte, s'il vous plaît.*' Ratapoil, whom Daumier drew from a small clay model he had constructed, is an unforgettable figure, the very type of the lean, villainous ex-soldier, with his staring eyes, his whiskers that seem to sprout all over his face, his battered hat, and his long body encased in a rusty black *redingote* (a long skirted greatcoat buttoned over the chest). He was active in the country as well as in the city. A cartoon published June 20th 1851, showed him reduced to a diminutive, spindly figure in the background, while in the foreground a peasant couple in clogs stand in a field staring up at the sky with their mouths wide open. In this instance the caption is indispensable for understanding the point: 'Honest Monsieur Ratapoil promised them, if they signed his petition, that the larks would fall ready roasted into their mouths.'

His anxiety about the growing menace of Bonapartism was not so obsessive as to cause Daumier to neglect his other targets, such as the obscurantism of the clerical party. Montalembert's candidature for election to the Académie Française is the subject of a drawing in which the supplicant, wearing his usual smugly sanctimonious expression and an enormous shovel-hat, is shown knocking at the door of the Institut de France with a copy of his *Histoire de Sainte Élisabeth de Hongrie* tucked under his left arm. The caption, for once, is as neat as the drawing: 'Knock, and it shall be opened unto you.' Another protest by Daumier against the increasing interference of the Church in educational matters caused a great stir when it was published on March 28th, 1851. The lithograph was inspired by the government's action in suspending Michelet's lectures at the Sorbonne: a repulsive, red-nosed capuchin monk is depicted standing on a rostrum and declaiming to the rows of benches in the amphitheatre—his audience consisting of two bored janitors slumped in their seats, waiting for him to finish so that they can lock up and go home. It is one of the artist's most brilliant realizations: Baudelaire may have been thinking of this drawing especially when, comparing Daumier to Molière, he wrote that both shared the ability to 'aim straight at the target. The idea is given immediate shape. You have only to look and you grasp the point.' Michelet himself was delighted and wrote Daumier a touching letter of thanks, telling him that his 'admirable sketch, reproduced everywhere in Paris, has elucidated the question better than the ten thousand articles' that had been written about it. Michelet went on to refer to, analyse and praise one of Daumier's earlier cartoons, *Le Dernier Conseil des Ex-Ministres*—a delicate way of expressing his esteem for the artist, since this drawing had been published over three years previously; and he ended his letter by telling Daumier that he alone, among the many gifted draughtsmen practising the art, had guts ('*vous seul, vous avez des reins*').

However, Daumier's career as a political cartoonist was almost at an end.[8] Practically the last drawing he executed under the Republic took the form of an urgent warning to Louis-Napoleon, headed: 'What would happen in the event of a fresh attempt to cross the Rubicon.' The Rubicon was, of course, the river separating Gaul from Italy, the crossing of which with his legions involved Julius Caesar in outright violation of the laws of the Roman Republic; but in addition—though Daumier could scarcely have known this—the secret file in which Louis-Napoleon kept his plans for the forthcoming *coup d'état* is said to have been marked 'Rubicon'. The drawing shows three men fording the river in the foreground, Berryer behind Ratapoil, with only their heads showing above the water. The leading man is entirely submerged, though his plumed hat, still visible, permits him to be identified as the Prince-President. To drive the point home, Daumier has sketched in the Pont de la Concorde behind them and the Palais Bourbon on the right; a host of tiny figures are streaming across the bridge and into the building, a reminder of the two occasions in 1848 when the National

Assembly was invaded by a revolutionary mob. This time, however, Daumier had been too optimistic in his prediction.

The Artist and the 'Salon'

No other artist in France was as deeply committed to the republican cause as Honoré Daumier, if we except the sculptor David d'Angers, a member of the National Assembly in 1848, whose activities were rewarded by banishment after the *coup d'état*. In general, the artist of the time, in contrast to the poets and novelists whose case-histories we examined in our first chapter, were disinclined to regard themselves as the chosen agents of reform and revolution. Their relative indifference to political issues is explainable by the totally different ethos that governed their conditions of work. The whole system of state-training, government bursaries, official exhibitions, the distribution of medals and cash rewards and the commissioning of large-scale decorative works by the administration meant that immense pressures were at work all through a painter's career—as for that matter a sculptor's or an architect's—to compel him to toe whatever line, politically speaking, was supposed to be toed at the time. For decades, the artist in France had found it more natural to trim his opinions to the prevalent ideology, left, right, or *juste milieu*, than to strive—as a writer might—to remould the social outlook so that it should accord with his personal beliefs. The career of Louis David, the colossus whose influence was still felt in the French school of painting as late as the 1830s and whose posthumous reputation put into the shade even that of the two major artists, Ingres and Delacroix, who dominated the scene in the 1840s, illustrates the point admirably. David's first great picture, *Le Serment des Horaces*, was painted under the *ancien régime* and, revolutionary though it was in its intensity and linear austerity, enthralled the blasé courtiers of Louis XVI who were simultaneously delighting in the disturbing machiavellism of Choderlos de Laclos' *Liaisons dangereuses* and the brazen impudence of Beaumarchais' *Mariage de Figaro*.[9] When the Revolution broke out, David became its accredited artist: he was entrusted with control of the entire machinery of propaganda by art, he organized the Republic's great ceremonies and was primarily instrumental in winding up the affairs of the Académie royale de peinture and transferring its functions to the Institut.[10] The coming to power of Napoleon I served only to strengthen his position; although, as a teacher, David had raised a whole generation of talented painters (Gros, Girodet, Guérin and Gérard) who developed his style in the direction of the new romanticism, David still remained at the centre of the world of French art, and pictures like *Le Sacre* confirmed his position as the

9 Illustration from Hetzel's edition of *Les Châtiments*, published only after the fall of the Empire. The reference to Macbeth is the artist's, not Hugo's

10 'The *Salon* on a day when there was no charge for admission' (Daumier cartoon). From 1857 onwards entry money was exacted at the doors of the Palais de l'Industrie every weekday. On Sundays, in consequence, the galleries were crowded with a motley throng of shopkeepers and working-class people

11 Engraving by Millet: *The Gleaners* (The painting of the same subject was exhibited in 1857)

most highly regarded of Napoleon's court-painters. A comparison between *Le Sacre* and *Le Serment des Horaces* may serve to gauge the extent to which David was prepared to modify his manner in response to changes in the socio-political situation, such modifications being accomplished quite naturally—it would be absurd to suspect David of being a time-server; he was a finely adjusted political barometer. But once he was ousted from his position (the restoration of the Bourbons forcing him into exile) and contact with the central power was broken, then David's art lost direction and motivation; living abroad, in the last few years of his life, he was able to achieve nothing of any importance.

History itself, then, seemed to teach the young artist that—art being in any case above politics—the proper attitudes for him to adopt towards whatever authorities happened to be occupying the seats of power were deference, co-operation and caution. In periods of civil strife he should stand aside, as far as he could, and remember that in the last resort his overriding loyalty was to his art. Gustave Courbet, more than any other artist, was to reverse this attitude in the period of his maturity, but even Courbet, at the time of the February Revolution, was inclined to lie low and let the others fight it out. His shoulder-shrugging indifference persisted even through the June insurrection. 'I am not going to fight for two reasons', he wrote to his parents at this time. 'Firstly, because I have no faith in wars fought with muskets and cannon, which are against my principles. For ten years now I have been engaged in battles of the mind. I should be inconsistent if I acted otherwise. The other reason is that I have no arms, and so can't be tempted. So you need have no fears on my account.'

In 1848 commercial art, as we understand it today, hardly existed; but there were, concentrated in Paris, a small army of professionals who made a living by the exercise of their skills as engravers, lithographers, portrait-painters, carvers of religious images, and the like. They depended, like all artificers engaged in semi-luxury trades, on a certain level of general prosperity and business confidence. The slump that had set in since February meant that the well-to-do had stopped patronizing them. Unemployment was immediately translated into starvation. Their predicament was such that David d'Angers, deputy for Maine-et-Loire, laid a request before the Assembly for a vote of 200,000 francs to alleviate their distress. He was able, in his accompanying report, to show that some artists—ex-pupils of the École de Rome among them—were selling newspapers in the streets, others had been driven to enrol in the National Workshops. Conditions in these organizations were, of course, much harsher after June; the wage was pitiful and the work—navvies' labour undertaken outside Paris—strenuous and soul

G

destroying. The newspaper *Le Peuple* published on November 8th, 1848 a pitiful appeal from one of these unfortunates, writing on behalf of the others. 'There are 2,500 of us, nearly all artists, painters, sculptors, digging the Marne canal. We push the wheelbarrows, wading through water or digging in the mud'—all for a daily wage of two francs or less.[11]

By the following year even quite distinguished artists were feeling the pinch. Jean-Baptiste Clésinger, the sculptor, whose *Femme piquée par un serpent* had created such a sensation at the 1847 *salon*, had to go into hiding to escape from his creditors. Diaz held an auction sale of the entire contents of his studio, which realized a paltry 16,000 francs. The government appropriated 150,000 francs for direct relief to artists, and were further authorized by the Assembly to disburse up to 200,000 francs in commissioning and purchasing works of art. An even larger sum was raised by means of a device always dear to French hearts: a public lottery, with prizes taking the form of pictures paid for out of the proceeds.

Such expedients could provide only temporary alleviation of the artists' plight; it was more important to re-open the normal commercial channels and for this the *salon* offered the obvious means. But a fresh disappointment lay in store for would-be exhibitors: the 1849 *salon* could not open till mid-June, too late in the season to catch the wealthy patrons of art who had already left for the country. To ensure that in 1850 the exhibition should open, as it always had, in the spring, a delegation from the Association des Artistes waited on the Minister to plead their cause; but the difficulty was to find a suitable building, so many public edifices having deteriorated through neglect or been damaged in civil riot. Under Louis-Philippe the *salon* had been held in the Louvre, but this arrangement had never been popular with the Parisians, since it meant that for several weeks in the year the national art-treasures had to be relegated to the cellars to make room for the current exhibits. As a stop-gap measure the Tuileries Palace had been pressed into service in 1849; but it was badly in need of renovation. Eventually the choice fell on the Palais Royal, but it was many months before it was ready and the final solution—about the worst possible from the artists' point of view—was to hold the *salon* in the winter of 1850–51 and make it serve for both years.

The importance of this institution, the annual (or biennial) Paris art exhibition, was far greater during the period we are now concerned with than it was to become later in the century, when its functions were increasingly usurped, first by the 'independent exhibitions' which started in the 1870s, then by the private shows organized by successful art-dealers like Petit and Durand Ruel. During its heyday, the *salon* was the principal, if not the only means by which a painter, whether he already enjoyed an established reputation or whether he was still struggling for recognition, could reach prospective purchasers. In this sense, it could be described as a vast art emporium, the overheads of which were borne by the treasury. But there was nothing anachronistic in this survival from the spacious days of royal patronage, for there were sound economic reasons for the continuing lavish provision from public funds. Paris was, in the nineteenth century (and, indeed, well into the twentieth century too), the acknowledged art-centre of the world. Its schools recruited students from every civilized country, 'like the enchanted mountain that drew all swords from their scabbard', as a contemporary American art-historian expressed it lyrically.[12] Canvases by the better-known French artists of the period automatically commanded higher prices than pictures of comparable merit by painters of other nationalities. Finally, the art-market was centred in Paris: it was here that rich dilettantes from England, Russia, and the United States flocked together to attend the exhibitions and private shows, to inspect the stock of reputable dealers and to visit star artists in their studios. National pride and considerations of prestige are sufficient to account for the solicitude with which successive governments, irrespective of the régime, organized the art-life of the capital. And the focus of this activity was the *salon*.

The keen interest taken in art by the central government, normally working through the Ministry of Fine Arts, was a mixed blessing: for it involved a measure of control, and control tended to work in favour of conservatism. The *salon* was rarely, if ever, a free-for-all. In 1791 the Convention had decreed that all artists, whether or not members of the Academy, should be free to exhibit. The result was that the number of exhibits doubled, but the average quality fell off: this was one occasion when more did mean worse. It was therefore decided to reconstitute the jury, which under the *ancien régime* had acted chiefly as a guardian of public morals, and extend its functions: in future it was to decide which works were worthy of being hung and which should be refused the honour. Once re-established, the institution proved quite indispensable, if only to dam the yearly flood of submissions. There was only one other occasion, in the following century, when every work sent in was shown as of right, and this was in 1848: the same egalitarian spirit was responsible then as it had been in 1791 for giving the brilliant innovator, as well as the clumsy amateur, his chance. But the result, in sheer numbers of exhibits, was daunting. In 1791, the unjuried *salon* had shown a little under 800 works; in 1848, the paintings alone numbered 4,600. Clearly, a selection would have to be made at future *salons*, if only for practical reasons.

The drawback of the jury system was that it was a blunt instrument and tended to work to the disadvantage not just of the untalented but also of the painter whose style or subject did not accord with the prevailing conception of 'good art'. The committee that reached the decisions, acceptance or rejection, worked under extreme pressure: they were called on to pass judgement on too many canvases in too short a time. They tended also to be older men, whose powers of judgement had become ossified; this was equally true whether they were directly appointed by the ministry, or drawn from members of the Institut, or elected by direct ballot by practising artists (all these systems, and innumerable different permutations of them, were experimented with in different years). Above all, they were conscious of their heavy responsibilities as defenders of the norms that had made French art supreme. Not only the government, but the population at large, whose interest in the *salon* was comparable to that which, in our day, is aroused by certain international sporting events, looked to them to uphold the dignity of the 'grand tradition'.

The extraordinary interest taken by men and women of all classes in the visual arts was a factor of incalculable importance, both for good and ill. On the one hand it gave the painter an awareness of his wider public and discouraged the growth of coterie art; on the other hand it acted as a brake on experimentation and free development. In an age when entertainments were few and for the most part unsophisticated, the spring exhibition was a yearly event that afforded the same kind of opportunity for welcome interruption in the drab round of unrewarding toil as, formerly, did the carnival processions. With the coming of the railway and the consequent improvement in communications, the crowds of Parisians who habitually poured through the doors of the Palais de l'Industrie every spring were now swollen by train-loads of provincials up for a visit. The resultant excitement, exhaustion and congestion were something that writers of the period seldom comment on, since these things were so much taken for granted; however, one vivid account is extant, written for the benefit of a reading-public in Russia by an art-critic who had attended every *salon* from 1863 onwards. Zola was writing in 1875, but the picture he gives could, one imagines, be applied to any opening day over the previous 20 years:

What a crush on May 1st, the day the exhibition opens! From ten o'clock on, the carriages drive up one after another. The Champs-Élysées, cheerful in the bright morning sunlight, are full of a long stream of people on foot walking smartly along. At the entrance doors of the Palais de l'Industrie two turnstiles click incessantly, sounding like the sails of a windmill in a furious gale. You walk up a monumental stairway and into the galleries already full of visitors, and you blink, to start with, blinded at the sight of several hundred pictures jumbling together all the colours of the rainbow. . . . There are 25 galleries here: several kilometres of painting to be examined, in other words, if the pictures were put end to end. A labour of Hercules! For seven or eight hours you are obliged to struggle in a crowd which is growing all the time, and to elbow your way painfully to reach the pictures, stretching your neck, suffocated by the dust, the heat, and the lack of air. Even the hardiest give up the idea of inspecting everything on this round. On the first day you make do with a rapid tour of the whole exhibition. A muted hubbub arises from the rooms, produced by the shuffling of thousands of pairs of feet and recalling the roar of waves incessantly breaking on the seashore.

And yet, in spite of everything, in spite of the back-breaking fatigue, the opening day of the exhibition is a great attraction. It represents the pleasure of novelty, something people are prepared to pay dearly for in Paris. The fate of the works exhibited is decided on that day. Fashion adopts certain pictures that have produced a sensation. Groups gather round this canvas or that; the ladies utter low-toned exclamations, the gentlemen exchange comments and argue about points of aesthetics. That evening, in every drawing-room in Paris they will be talking only about the ten or twelve pictures that have drawn the biggest crowds. Downstairs, in the central garden, under a wide glass roof, room has been found among the green shrubs for the frozen world of sculpture. The men saunter down there to smoke a cigar and look at the naked goddesses. Exhausted ladies sit on the benches and watch people passing by. Great quantities of beer are drunk at the buffet. Occasionally it happens, as it did this year, that there is a downpour of rain, sometimes just at closing time. Then there is a frightful scuffle. Not a cab to be had for love or money. The women's long skirts trail in the mud. Nine or ten thousand people, collected disconsolately round the exits, watch the rain streaming down. At last the sun breaks through and the crowd, relieved, disperses and goes squelching down the Champs-Élysées in the streaming mire.[13]

Courbet under the Second Republic

This was the social and institutional background against which the realists embarked on their campaign to demolish the old and now outdated canons of academic art. Who were they? If realism means no more than the faithful rendering of nature, then we should have to include Corot, Théodore

Rousseau, and other members of the Barbizon school of landscape painters which flourished before the 1848 Revolution. But their canvases caused little commotion, their works did not affront popular preconceptions, largely because the type of picture they painted was not considered to present any kind of a threat to 'great art'. There existed a recognized hierarchy in painting, based on subjects, and landscape occupied a rather lowly position. Camille Lemonnier may have been right in calling Courbet '*un paysagiste de l'humanité*', but it was precisely because humanity, solid, ugly, ill-dressed, was in the forefront of his landscapes in place of the dainty troop of diaphanous dryads which tradition demanded, that his pictures gave such offence.[14] Besides, the Barbizon painters retained their sense of the picturesque, which conferred a familiar and thoroughly acceptable quality of romanticism on their compositions. This quality was something altogether alien to Courbet, as the most cursory inspection of, shall we say, *Les Demoiselles de village* will reveal. The difference between his approach and Corot's is dramatically illustrated in an anecdote that has come down to us of an occasion when, in the summer of 1849, both artists were staying at Louveciennes and decided one afternoon to go into the forest of Marly to paint. Corot kept shifting his position, scanning the scenery till he found a spot with a suitably picturesque vista. Courbet started sketching just where he happened to be, saying that for him any view was as good as any other: all he needed was nature in front of his easel for him to copy.

Apart from Daumier, whose realism manifested itself throughout most of his life in a different art-form and whose water-colours and oil-paintings, though they could well be classified as samples of realist art (*Une Blanchisseuse, Voiture de troisième classe*), provoked little discussion when they were exhibited, two other painters besides Courbet have some claim to be considered as members—not of the realist school, which existed briefly in literature but was never constituted among the artists—but of the realist movement. They were François Bonvin and Jean-François Millet. Both were of humble extraction—Bonvin the son of a gamekeeper, Millet of a peasant; both were in their early thirties when the Revolution broke out. Of the two, Bonvin seems to have been closer to Courbet. He frequented the Brasserie Andler where Millet seldom set foot. In 1848 Courbet and Bonvin paid Daumier a visit to urge him to enter the competition for an allegorical representation of the Republic, intended to replace the portrait of Louis-Philippe in administrative offices up and down the country. Daumier acceded to the plea of the two younger artists and entered a very fine design which did not, however, win the competition.

Bonvin came to the fore with a picture, *Femme qui taille la soupe*, which was in the 1850–51 *salon*, and he acquired a modest reputation in the early 1850s for his still lifes, his domestic scenes, and above all for his portrayals of peasant children. His realism was sentimental and nostalgic, his choice of detail uncomplicated and soothing to the eye. No awkward questions were raised by his bright, gentle depiction of the peasant class.

Millet's grasp of the realities of rural life was stronger, but even so, from the point of view of strict doctrinaire realism, his art was vitiated by an unmistakable leaning towards idealization. *Le Vanneur, Le Semeur, Les Glaneuses*[15] contrive to show the cultivator engaged on his immemorial tasks, but the fact that Millet's sower wears the kind of cap common for labourers at the time and that his winnower is in clogs makes no difference to one's general impression that it is above all the ritual *act* of sowing, winnowing or gleaning, as performed since the days of Boaz and Ruth, that Millet is showing us. The individuality, the contingency of the subject, which is the mark of Courbet's realism, is absent from Millet's painting. If this was realism, then no great rift separated realism from academicism; all Millet had done was to stir a few drops of his own brand of humanitarianism into the old mixture. Baudelaire's remarks in his *Salon de 1859*, if unkind, are not altogether unfair: 'His peasants are pedants with altogether too good an opinion of themselves. . . . Reaping, sowing, leading cows to pasture, they always seem to be saying: "Poor we may be and disinherited, we are the ones who make the earth bring forth! We accomplish a mission, we exercise a priestly function!" Instead of simply distilling the poetry inherent in his subject, M. Millet insists on adding it.'[16]

If we try to discover what contemporary opinion, which was largely hostile to it, understood by realism in art, we are bound to conclude that, at least in the 1850s, the movement was represented by one man only: Gustave Courbet. Courbet himself was content that it should be so; this isolation tickled his naïve vanity. When, on the occasion of the Paris Exhibition of 1855, the government declined to show his *Enterrement à Ornans* (though it accepted eleven other of his canvases for display), Courbet opened a private show which he proudly advertised, on a banner strung over the entrance-door: 'Le Réalisme. G. Courbet', as though it were a title to which none but he had a right. Largely self-taught, he had no desire for disciples and no wish to become a teacher, and it required nothing less than a deputation of discontented students from the École des Beaux-Arts to persuade him (in 1861–2) to set up a school of his own. A studio was leased in the Rue Notre-Dame des Champs, and some 40 students enrolled, each paying 20 francs to meet the rent. With the single exception of Fantin-Latour, none of them subsequently achieved any degree of celebrity, and the experiment was short-lived. Courbet himself found that teaching absorbed too much of his time, and the proprietor was unhappy at having oxen or horses introduced into his premises for the students to draw.

Thus, it was generally understood that realism in art began and ended with Courbet; at least, it was hoped it would end with him. The label was attached to him at an early stage, less by his defenders than by his detractors. Théophile Gautier used it—though without implying any markedly hostile judgement—in discussing his *Après-Dinée à Ornans* which created an initial sensation at the *salon* of 1849. 'M. Courbet', wrote Gautier, 'may be classified among those realists who seek counsel only of nature. His temperament is virile, robust, rather ponderous and rustic, but has all the healthy qualities of the countryman.' The critics were not too certain how they should react to this large canvas which presented a domestic scene of the kind normally found in small genre pictures. It had no elegance, no wit, but it was painted in so masterly a fashion that the judges could not do otherwise than award Courbet a gold medal in recognition; this was a distinction which—in theory at least—meant that all submissions of his to future *salons* would be automatically accepted for hanging. Grudgingly, the critic of the *Revue des Deux Mondes* admitted that 'true, M. Courbet paints well, he renders perfectly what he has in front of him. But this exactness produces nothing but a trivial truthfulness.' And a certain Jean-Louis Peisse struck a similar note of disdain, using a more brutal and lapidary formula: 'It is impossible to vulgarize art (*encanailler l'art*) with a greater sense of technique, or be more of a painter and less of an artist.' Courbet, reading this, guffawed: 'Yes, M. Peisse, art needs to be vulgarized.'

From the very start, criticism was faced with this paradox in Courbet: he broke the conventions, his art was without any discernible spiritual qualities, he seemed not to know or not to care when his picture was frankly ugly, and yet he was a first-class painter technically, perhaps the greatest craftsman operating in France at the time. Without trying to introduce any new methods or to apply any new theories—totally unlike the Impressionists in this respect—using the same conservative colour-range as the academic painters of the day, he yet appeared startlingly revolutionary simply by his choice of subjects and the manner in which he treated them. Contemporaries said he had a soulless attitude to what he painted; we should say today that he was emotionally neutral towards it. This neutrality of emotion is, of course, of the essence of realism: Flaubert, and Zola at his best, were to exhibit it in their own medium and provoke the same complaints.

It was in the succeeding *salon* (which, as we have seen, was held in the winter of 1850–51) that Courbet really set the cat among the pigeons. He exhibited nine pictures of which the three largest, *Les Paysans de Flagey revenant d'une foire*, *Enterrement à Ornans*, and *Les Casseurs de pierre*, caused more argument than anything else in the *salon*. The ordinary uneducated visitor shied away from them: they were not pretty, these hard-faced peasants with the oxen and pigs they had been buying at the cattle-fair, this long line of grimacing mourners with the parallel level line of barren cliffs in the background seeming to weigh down on them like a flat lid. People of position or breeding, confronted with Courbet's two sad stone-breakers, raised disdainful eyebrows: was the fellow trying to disseminate socialist propaganda with this silently eloquent protest against brutalizing toil? Both opinions—that Courbet's pictures were ugly and that his ideas were danger-ous—were voiced by the journalists who wrote about the exhibition. Étienne Delécluze, the champion of Ingres—a diehard classicist in other words, though a liberal in politics—Delécluze wrote disgustedly in the *Journal des Débats*: 'never, perhaps, has the worship of ugliness been more openly practised.' In the *Revue des Deux Mondes* the term 'socialistic painting' was used, while the Marquis de Chennevières confided to his readers that he had heard Courbet spoken of as 'the Messiah of democratic art'. It might be so indeed. 'If democratic painting consists in using the dirtiest and commonest tones to model the most vulgar forms selected with a view to what is most ugly, then certainly I would not deny', wrote this aristocrat among critics, 'that M. Courbet is a democratic painter.'

Courbet under the Second Empire

The next *salon* was the first to be held under the auspices of the new Empire. The code that was to govern this and future exhibitions, which was pub-lished on January 29th, 1852, embodied several important new provisions. Perhaps the most significant variation on previous practice was that each artist was now limited to three submissions. These would be judged by a committee consisting half of ministerial nominees, the rest of elected repre-sentatives; but only those artists who had had at least one work accepted at an earlier *salon*[17] were eligible to vote in the election. It was a system obvi-ously rigged to tip the scales in favour of conservatism. On the other hand, the importance the régime attached to the status of the fine arts in France was demonstrated by the announcement, made a few weeks later, that work would shortly start on the construction of a new art-gallery in the Champs-Élysées. This was the future Palais de l'Industrie, in which the annual exhibitions were regularly held for the remainder of the century.

Courbet fondly imagined that his principal submission to the 1852 *salon*,

Les Demoiselles de village, would disarm those of his critics who had been so severe two years before. 'I have thrown my judges off the scent', he declared. 'I have changed my ground and done something graceful; nothing they have been saying up till now will apply.' He was wrong. The new picture, in which Courbet had painted his two sisters giving alms to a peasant girl in a rural setting of cows in meadows, reconciled no one to realism, even though, as the catalogue indicated, the canvas had been bespoken by the Duc de Morny. Gautier was disdainfully condescending: 'These three figures are meant to be graceful, and if M. Courbet had dared, he would have made them altogether attractive. . . . But as leader of the school of ultra-realism, one has one's obligations, and it may be that a few fanatics are already upbraiding him for deserting his post. Ugliness carried its obligations.' Gustave Planche went much further: the three girls were 'frighteningly ugly. . . . *Les Demoiselles de village*, like the *Casseurs de pierre*, have nothing to do with painting taken in its loftiest sense. All they demonstrate is a craftsmanship adequate at the most for sign-painting.'

Les *Demoiselles de village* aroused, on the whole, more amusement than indignation, on account of the curious lack of proportion in the dimensions of the cattle and the human figures. Commentators less solemn than Gustave Planche made fun of these 'toy cows'. But when, the following year, Courbet exhibited his *Baigneuses*, the scandal reached homeric proportions. A real flesh-and-blood woman stepping out of a real forest pool, holding up one arm to balance herself on the slippery ascent—this was bad enough, for a public used only to nymphs and goddesses immune from the laws of gravity and to the oriental beauties in the indoor swimming pool of a Turkish harem painted by Ingres; but that Courbet should have given his model such revoltingly thick thighs, such matronly hips, this was more than could be endured. The story went round that Napoleon III, at the private viewing held before the exhibition opened, was so incensed that he struck at the painting with his riding-crop. Courbet, when this was reported to him, expressed some regret that he had not worked on a thinner canvas. 'He would have torn it and I should have sued him. That would have made a stir.' Courbet would have been capable of doing so too, with his dauntless self-confidence and contemptuous disrespect for authority. The Empress Eugénie, on the same occasion, reacted with greater restraint and good humour. The art experts who had been conducting her through the galleries had spent some time explaining to her the finer points of Rosa Bonheur's paintings of horses: they were not the graceful animals of her native Andalusia; these were *percheronnes*, big plough-horses with powerful haunches bred on the border of Normandy and the Beauce. Docile, Eugenia de

Montijo listened to the lecture, then, moving on to Courbet's bathing woman: 'Is that a *percheronne* too?' she asked.

But in spite of the uproar and the recriminations, in spite of Gautier's plaintive bleats ('Surely a girl or a young woman with a shapely, elegant silhouette and a fresh, satiny skin is just as *real* as a vast matron upholstered with adipose tissue?'), Courbet's reputation as a master went on growing. Freakish, disturbing, and vulgar he might be, but was there any other painter of his generation who seemed more likely to succeed to the inheritance of Ingres and Delacroix? The organizers of the international exhibition planned for 1855 realized well in advance that Courbet would have to be allocated a place of honour among French exhibitors in the fine arts section. Nieuwerkerke, the man responsible, thought he saw a way out of the difficulty. Courbet would be specially commissioned to execute a work for the occasion, and, to ensure that he observed the decencies, he would be required to submit a sketch first. To prepare the ground, Courbet was invited—signal honour—to partake of lunch with the Surintendant des Beaux-Arts himself, accompanied by two subservient members of the artistic establishment, Français and Chenavard.[18] All we know about this extraordinary confrontation derives from the letter to his friend and patron Alfred Bruyas that Courbet wrote immediately afterwards.[19] It appears that the painter flew into a rage as soon as he realized what was being asked of him. 'I answered immediately that I didn't understand a word of what he [Nieuwerkerke] had been saying to me, in the first place because he asserted that he was the government, and I didn't feel myself in the least included in this government, that I was a government equally, and that I doubted if his government could do anything for mine that I could accept. I went on to say that I regarded his government as a simple individual, at liberty to purchase my pictures if it wished, and that all I asked was that it should give art free access to its exhibition and stop paying out 300,000 francs to subsidize 3,000 painters who are against me.' Warming to his theme, Courbet went on to accuse the administration of defrauding him of money rightfully his: none of the considerable takings at the doors of the last *salon* had been passed on to him, though he reckoned that, since his own pictures had been the main attraction, he should have been paid something like 15,000 francs. As for the 1855 Exhibition, he said he might send along his *Enterrement*, to signify that in his view it was high time that the system of state meddling in art should be given a decent burial; but for the rest, he would hold his own, private exhibition, so that at least he would be able to put the entry money into his own pocket.

As a final gesture of independence, Courbet tried to settle his own bill for the lunch.[20]

The incident illustrates much besides the arrogance of this prickly artist, who is said to have wanted the motto *Courbet sans courbettes* ('Courbet who never bowed or scraped') to be engraved on his tombstone. It can be seen as marking an important turning-point in the history of French art, when, for the first time perhaps, the old system of state patronage, dating back to the days of Richelieu and Colbert, was decisively rejected in favour of entirely new arrangements whereby the artist was to be regarded in the light of a primary producer, dealing directly—or through the medium of middlemen—with private purchasers; in so far as the state desired his products to enrich its holdings in public art-galleries, it would have to treat with him as one customer among others, enjoying no special privileges. Courbet was able to adopt this defiant stance because his work already commanded good prices in the open market. By the mid-sixties he had even become a fashionable painter; spending the season at Trouville, doing seascapes and portraits on the spot and selling them to the wealthy clients he found there, he could earn as much money as he wished. The risk was, of course, that he would soften his manner to suit his clientèle, but at the time few signs of such concessions could be detected.

At the 1863 *salon* he quite deliberately provoked a fresh scandal by sending in a picture painted in great secrecy at Saintes (in the Loire valley), which, given the climate of religious feeling at the time, was bound to be regarded as blasphemous: it showed a group of tipsy priests, returning home after 'conferring' over too copious a lunch, and lurching about the highroad to the amusement of the countryfolk who are shown watching them. The *Retour de la Conférence* was, not surprisingly, rejected by the jury. Courbet was told the picture infringed not just the proprieties, but the law forbidding 'outrage to religious morality'; he was not even allowed to exhibit it in the Salon des Refusés which was organized that year to complement the official *salon*. Then, in 1864, he upset the jury again with a picture entitled *Vénus poursuivant Psyché de sa jalousie*. In view of Courbet's well-known aversion to representing mythological scenes, it occurred to them that the alleged subject might be simply a cover for a highly improper scene from real life: the expression on Venus's face, as she leans over the charming body of the sleeping Psyche, could as well be taken for that of a dry-mouthed lesbian as of a malevolent mother-in-law. Playing for safety, they rejected this picture too.[21]

In 1866, however, he made a triumphal return to the *salon* with two pictures. One was a woodland scene with deer, perhaps the most enchanting painting from nature he ever executed. Courbet told a visitor that they could hardly reject this canvas, 'unless they interpret it as a secret society of roebucks meeting in the forest to proclaim the Republic.' The other picture showed a recumbent nude playing with a parrot, her face—unlike that of Manet's brazen hussy Olympia, exhibited at the *salon* the previous year—modestly averted from the spectator; an arrangement which allowed Courbet to paint her magnificent head of rippling dark hair fanning out in the left-hand corner. These two offerings resulted in fulsome tributes from nearly everybody, which Courbet lapped up delightedly. 'Comte de Nieuwerkerke sent me a message to say that I had done two masterpieces and that he was enchanted. All the jury said the same thing—no complaints from anyone. I've pulled off the biggest success of the exhibition, unquestionably.'[22] There was, however, one discordant voice—that of a brash young critic writing his first *salon* review: Émile Zola. 'Courbet, this year, has rounded the sharp angles of his genius; he has put on a velvet glove, so the crowd is delighted to see him no different from anyone else and applauds, satisfied to see the master at its feet at last. . . . Think back to the time when he painted the *Baigneuses* and the *Enterrement à Ornans*, and tell me whether those two masterly canvases were not altogether stronger meat than the two delicious titbits he has given us this year. And yet, at the time of the *Baigneuses* and the *Enterrement à Ornans*, Courbet was a laughing-stock, Courbet was stoned by the outraged public. No one mocks him today, no stones are flying. Courbet has sheathed his eagle's talons, he has put a damper on his powers, and everyone sings his praises.'

Zola, who had visited Courbet's studio and seen the master's earlier works, was perfectly justified in denouncing this decline, attributable to the desire to be a popular success. Nevertheless, Courbet had not completely sold out. At heart he remained an opposition artist, as was shown in the very last months of the Empire when Maurice Richard, the new Minister of Fine Arts, announced that both Courbet and Daumier were to be made members of the Legion of Honour. Courbet, who had not been sounded in advance, declined to accept the distinction in a polite, though rather long-winded letter to the well-meaning minister. The essential passage is worth reproducing, if only because it enlarges significantly on the somewhat incoherent reasons Courbet had given Nieuwerkerke, in December 1854, for refusing to execute a commission requested by the government. 'The state', wrote Courbet in 1870, 'is incompetent in matters of art. When it takes it on itself to distribute rewards, it trespasses on the domain of public taste. Its intervention is totally demoralizing, fatal to the artist whom it misleads as to his true value, fatal to art which it makes conform to official conventions and condemns to the most sterile mediocrity. Good sense demands that the state should stand aside. The day it decides to leave us alone, it will have accomplished its duty by us.'

Daumier too refused the decoration. A group of younger artists, delighted at this double gesture of defiance, arranged a banquet in their honour; and at the culminating moment, amid wild applause, the two senior realists rose from their seats and embraced.

Courbet's defenders: Proudhon and Champfleury

The question remains how far Courbet's fanatical defence of his own independence arose from a purely temperamental dislike of regimentation, and how far it was politically motivated. Were conservative critics right in detecting subversive tendencies behind his choice of subjects and the way he handled them? Was realism, in other words, truly the proletarian counterpart to the aristocratic art of the academic painters and the bourgeois art of the genre painters?

Courbet's own utterances do not provide the most trustworthy guide to the solution of these problems. He was a great talker, but also a wild talker. Proudhon, who had listened to him as patiently as any man, said of him that 'although he speaks a lot in sequence, he reasons inconsequentially; he has isolated intuitions, more or less true, which are sometimes lucky hits, often sophistries. He appears incapable of constructive thought.' The few manifestoes he issued (the declaration of principles that was printed in the catalogue to his private exhibition of 1855, or again the letter of December 25th, 1861 which he published in reply to the art-students' request that he should open a school) were composed, almost certainly, with the assistance of Castagnary. Left to himself, Courbet was apparently quite unable to express his ideas coherently, as is sufficiently evident from the improvised lecture he gave at Antwerp, to mark the opening of an exhibition of his work in that city.[23] Essentially, this discourse consisted of a string of imprecise assertions leading up to an unsubstantiated conclusion, thus: Realism means the rejection of the ideal; to reject idealism is the first step in emancipating the individual; the emancipation of the individual implies democracy; therefore, realism is essentially democratic art.

Courbet was no worse a painter for being a poor logician. He was an acute observer of the world around him, capable of transferring what he saw, line and colour, with great precision on to his canvas; the eye and the hand worked together in perfect unison, and it mattered very little that the intellect had no part in the result. But Courbet was also vain, impressionable, and persecuted. His vanity was flattered when theoreticians spun their intellectual webs round his productions; his impressionability made him all too ready to accept as gospel what they said about his art, provided that what they said made it sound important; and, being a victim of so many violent attacks whose point and motivation he only dimly understood, he was happy to endorse any explanation that his champions offered of what he was trying to do.

He had two principal apologists, Proudhon and Champfleury, both of whom 'discovered' him at about the same time, in 1848. Neither of them saw him in quite the same light, since both wanted to use his art to illustrate their own doctrines. Eventually Courbet broke with Champfleury, but he remained on close terms of friendship with Proudhon until the latter's death in 1865. There seems to be little doubt that Proudhon was mainly responsible for shaming Courbet out of the studied indifference to political issues which, as we have noted, characterized his attitude during the early stages of the Second Republic, and converting him to socialism. For Courbet certainly thought of himself as a socialist, 'not only a socialist', as he wrote in a letter dated November 19th, 1851, 'but a democrat and a republican as well, in short a partisan of total revolution and above all, a realist, that is to say a sincere adherent of the real truth'. Whatever the 'real truth' (la vérité vraie) might be, the linking of socialism with realism at this early date is significant as indirect evidence of the influence Proudhon was already exerting over Courbet's thought.

Proudhon's views on Courbet's art were embodied in a posthumously published work entitled Du principe de l'art et de sa destination sociale. The philosopher did not claim to have any particular insight into the nature of art; but he had firm opinions about its social function, which was 'the physical and moral improvement of our species.' He analysed all the important pictures Courbet had painted to date, and declared them all to be inspired by some moralizing purpose. The Casseurs de pierre was the first socialist picture ever painted. Its value lay in its implicit denunciation of a capitalist society which can find no better use for human labour than to employ it in the deadening drudgery of breaking stones by the roadside. The Demoiselles de la Seine, with their bloated faces and animal-like poses, are intended to disgust the beholder and cure him of his hankering after such carnal pleasures as can be bought in the streets. Les Baigneuses constitute a warning against gluttony, it being incredible that the women Courbet painted could have developed such monstrous physiques short of a life time of over-eating.

It is easy to deride these naïvely didactic interpretations, but from a historical viewpoint it is important to see how Proudhon, without perhaps quite realizing what he was doing, had thrown out a life-line to the idealists struggling in the rising tide of realism. According to Proudhon, the value of realism lay in its expression of certain moral ideals cherished by all mankind in every age: such ideals as justice, continence, unselfishness, and truthfulness. Little wonder that Nieuwerkerke was impressed by the book and began once more making overtures to Courbet. As for Courbet, he took little note of the implications of Proudhon's reading of his art, being entirely satisfied with the publicity it procured him. 'It's staggering', he wrote to his parents (June 19th, 1865). 'The whole of Paris is in a state of jealousy and consternation. It's going to increase the number of my enemies and make me a man without a rival. What a shame he is dead and can't uphold the principles he has advanced!'

But, of course, this twisting of the pure realist doctrine into a new variety of humanitarian idealism infuriated the positivists. Zola wrote a damning review of Proudhon's book which he published first in the Lyons paper Le Salut public and then, in 1866, in his collection of critical essays, Mes Haines. It drove the last nail in the coffin of Champfleury's friendship with Courbet. The two had already quarrelled over Le Retour de la Conférence which Champfleury deplored as a blatant piece of propaganda painted under Proudhon's influence. When he criticized the picture, Courbet accused him of being in the pay of the government. Champfleury thereupon told him bluntly that he was talking too much (a reference to his long conversations with Proudhon) and painting too little. To this Courbet retorted haughtily: 'I cannot admit that a man should withdraw from communal action. The great figures of history who are traditionally admired have constantly been involved in what went on in their age.' There was some good sense in what Courbet said; but he did not appear to grasp that there was a world of difference between being 'of one's time', in Daumier's phrase, and engaging in a naïvely reformist art.

In any case, after Le Retour de la Conférence and Proudhon's death, Courbet painted no further works that anyone would have been tempted to take as didactic, with the doubtful exception of the somewhat sentimental genre picture L'Aumône d'un mendiant, executed in 1868.

Champfleury who, unlike Proudhon, was a professional art-critic and a good judge of painting, took justifiable pride in having been the first to announce Courbet's emerging genius. He had picked on the least noticed of the ten canvases Courbet had sent to the 1848 salon (Nuit classique de Walpurgis) to predict that the unknown man who executed it would in time be hailed as a great painter. He was equally enthusiastic about the strange portrait of Baudelaire that Courbet exhibited on the same occasion. At the next salon Courbet had already acquired a certain celebrity, and Champfleury took a pardonable pride in pointing out that he had been the first to speak of him.[24]

So far the word realism had not been mentioned. Champfleury used it for the first time in an article in *L'Ordre*, September 21st, 1850 when, referring to the *Enterrement à Ornans*, he announced: 'The critics may, as from today, prepare to do battle for or against realism in art.' In 1851, in his first full-length study of Courbet, Champfleury made the significant comparison with Balzac who was also, in his time, reproached with depicting repulsive figures, when the ugliness was in the models, not in the artist's vision as he reproduced them.[25] 'Is it the painter's fault', asked Champfleury, alluding to the mourners portrayed in Courbet's masterpiece, 'if material interests, small-town life, sordid egoism, provincial narrowness have clawed their faces, dimmed their eyes, wrinkled their foreheads, made their mouths stupid?' The article, which appeared in *Le Messager de l'Assemblée*, ended with a fierce tirade against the light-hearted conventional genre-painters, 'pastry-cooks all using the same mould,' whose art was doomed to give way to that of the realists, 'serious, earnest, ironical, brutal, sincere and full of poetry'.

In 1855 Champfleury used Courbet's private exhibition as the occasion for a fresh manifesto, perceptibly less enthusiastic than previous ones; privately, he had written to Max Buchon to describe the opening ceremony in somewhat irreverent terms. His article, first published in *L'Artiste*, September 2nd, 1855, took the form of a letter to George Sand; it was later included in Champfleury's miscellaneous collection of critical essays entitled *Le Réalisme*.[26]

By the mid-1850s the term 'realism' was already beginning to lose whatever precision it may have originally possessed. Champfleury notes that Wagner, whom he calls a 'hyper-romantic German musician', had been accused of realism in the French press.[27] We have already seen how the word was bandied about in the law-courts in 1857, in connection not just with Flaubert's *Madame Bovary* but with Baudelaire's *Fleurs du Mal* too. The following year, in an article published by *La Revue contemporaine*, J. J. Weiss applied it to the plays of Alexandre Dumas *fils*. Champfleury was surely justified in writing, as he did: 'Anyone who makes any pretence to innovate anything is dubbed a realist. No doubt about it, we shall have realism in medicine, in chemistry, in industry, in the historical sciences. M. Courbet is a realist, I am a realist: if the critics insist, why should I object?'—though he professes that at this stage the word has become virtually meaningless and that name-giving seems to him an unprofitable exercise. 'I fear schools as I fear the cholera, and my greatest satisfaction is to deal with sharply defined individualities'—like Courbet's.

Champfleury's essay is of value chiefly for its penetrating analysis of the reasons why Courbet's art had come under attack. In the first place, the

H

artist has been guilty of violating certain caste taboos. 'M. Courbet is seditious because he has painted in good faith life-size portraits of members of the middle class, peasants and village women. . . . People could not admit that a stonebreaker should be given the same importance as a prince; the aristocracy took umbrage at the allocation of so many yards of canvas to commoners; only sovereigns have the right to be painted full-size, with their medals, their gold lace, and their ceremonial expressions.' The point was an important one, though it had less to do with realism than with Courbet's instinctive reaction against the tyranny of tradition. The second reason Champfleury gives for the hostility Courbet had aroused was that he failed to take account of the widespread prejudice against contemporary costume. Historical dress, plumes, patches and points, were picturesque, 'but seriously to depict people of today with their round hats, black coats, varnished shoes, or peasant clogs', this was very strange and rather distasteful.

Finally, Champfleury mentions the charge universally brought against Courbet, that he was deficient in idealism. The apologist does not try, properly speaking, to refute it; to have done so would have been to fall into the same error as, later, Proudhon. We can see clearly enough today that it was Courbet's 'materialism', or in other words his successful revival of a genuine representational art, that placed him in the forefront of development. For a few decades at least, advanced artists stopped relying on their memory or their imagination to guide their brush, and it was Courbet who set them the example. But this was something Champfleury could not have foreseen; instead, he concentrates on Courbet's extraordinary expertise, the workmanlike qualities of his art. 'He goes to work on a huge canvas with intrepid energy, he may not charm everyone's eyes, some portions may be rough or clumsy, but every one of his pictures is *painted*.' To divert critical attention from Courbet's subjects and direct it towards his style was no doubt the soundest way to establish his reputation; but arguments along these lines could not, at this period, be generally appreciated by Champfleury's readers.

His article ends a little lamely, with some carping reservations about the picture *L'Atelier du peintre* in which, so he implied, Courbet had forsaken all the principles that had guided him until then. This was no 'realistic' representation of his studio, in the sense that his *Enterrement à Ornans* was a realistic representation of a country funeral; in any case, what did Courbet mean by sub-titling the new picture 'allégorie réelle'?—the two words, surely, were self-contradictory. Actually, as we know from his private correspondence, Champfleury was already growing disenchanted with the newest developments in Courbet's art and by the tiresome commotion caused by the arguments over realism. He declared that Courbet would have had an easier passage if he had curbed his excessive vaingloriousness. The habit that journalists had got into of continually linking his name with Courbet's began to irritate him and he complained to Max Buchon that where Courbet was concerned he felt himself rather in the same plight as a cat rushing madly down the street with a tin-kettle tied to its tail.

Champfleury and Literary Realism

The truth was that Champfleury lacked the temperament of the doughty fighter; he was not a polemicist by disposition, and his excursions into literary or artistic controversy were always a little half-hearted. It is highly characteristic of him that in the preface (dated March 25th, 1857) to *Le Réalisme* he spent much time and energy denouncing the word and all others ending in -ism, which rhyme, as he says, but lack all reason. 'I don't like schools, I don't like banners, I don't like systems, I don't like dogmas; I could not stay cooped up in the little chapel of realism, even if I were its god.' The one quality he looked for, both in art and letters, was complete sincerity. 'If suddenly a few writers appear who, tired of versified falsehoods, of the obstinate rearguard action of romanticism, confine themselves to a study of nature, extend their investigations down to the lowest social classes, free themselves from the fetters of fine language which cannot accord with the subjects they wish to treat, can they be said to constitute a school? I should never have thought so.' Champfleury goes on to name the writers he is thinking of: the list includes three Victorian novelists, Dickens, Thackeray, and Charlotte Brontë, and two Russians, Gogol and Turgenev. He mentions no French author, though one imagines Stendhal would have met most of Champfleury's requirements reasonably well.

A bias against poetry, especially romantic poetry; a concern for whatever truth emerges from the 'study of nature'; a preference for 'low-life' subjects (as he observes a little further on, in the humbler ranks of society 'sincerity of emotion, behaviour and speech is more in evidence than it is higher up the social scale'); and an unadorned style: these constitute the basis of the new literary aesthetic, together with two further principles which emerge from Champfleury's other critical writings, from his teaching and his practice. Firstly, there should never be any overt moralizing; impartiality is the watchword. The didactic novel as practised by George Sand, the propaganda novel like *Uncle Tom's Cabin* or the *Mystères de Paris*, popular songs such as Dupont's, intended to rouse the worker to a sense of his wrongs, all these are stigmatized, notwithstanding Champfleury's genuine and abiding concern for democratic values. And secondly, no novel should be undertaken without the most careful preliminary research. Here Champfleury joins hands with Flaubert, though he never took matters to the extraordinary lengths that Flaubert did over *Salammbô* and *Bouvard et Pécuchet*. For the most part, Champfleury wrote about the society of his native Laon that he had known since boyhood, and needed to undertake no special investigations into the social *milieu*; but when he selected a less familiar setting (as he did in *Monsieur de Boisd'hyver*, a novel largely concerned with the intrigues of clerics in a provincial diocesan city), he claimed to have spent several years documenting himself.

Champfleury's novels, which are so completely forgotten today that it is not even easy to locate copies, were astonishingly successful in their day. *Les Bourgeois de Molinchart* ran through four editions between 1855 and 1859: sales totalled 100,000. *Les Souffrances du professeur Delteil* had the distinction of being translated into English.[28] As early as 1857, Michel Lévy started bringing out a complete edition of Champfleury's works. If the popularity he enjoyed in his lifetime soon waned, this was less the fault of realist elements in his books than of other features that he introduced as a concession to the average unsophisticated reader of his time. He might have adopted as his own Dickens' motto: 'Make 'em laugh, make 'em cry'. Having in his youth doted on the farcical situations that enliven the novels of Paul de Kock, Champfleury was apt to repeat them, and delighted in introducing grotesque episodic figures who make no important contribution to the plot. These eccentrics are put in for laughs, while his persecuted heroes and distressed heroines are too often designed to arouse an unreflecting compassion. But the realism is there too: Champfleury reproduced what he had observed and remembered with such fidelity that the people of Laon were able to recognize themselves in *Les Bourgeois de Molinchart* or *La Succession Le Camus* with as much ease—and with as little gratification—as the people of Ornans in Courbet's *Enterrement* picture. The portraits Champfleury draws are made up of innumerable tiny details, which by their cumulative effect do provide the reader with a remarkably intimate picture of day-to-day life in provincial France at the period.

Duranty, theorist and novelist

Champfleury may not have approved of 'schools', but it was not long before he discovered that one had been founded in his name. In the autumn of 1856 a group of fervent young admirers, totally unknown in the world of letters, launched a monthly journal, *Réalisme*, expressly designed to propagate his ideas. He was not consulted in advance about its 'line' and was apparently never asked for a contribution; but his works were generously extolled in its pages and his lightest utterance was quoted with reverence. The editorial staff espoused many of his pet aversions. Any poet could be assured of rough treatment in the pages of *Réalisme*. Hugo was dismissed scornfully as a 'literary clown'. Banville's *Odes funambulesques* were described as 'a little tambourine filled with little pebbles to make a noise and please little children'. *Les Fleurs du Mal* was published just after the demise of the journal, but the opportunity was not missed for a side-swipe at Baudelaire in connection with his translation of some of Poe's *Tales of Mystery and Imagination*: Poe was compared to a Dutch cheese and Baudelaire to the rat comfortably ensconced within it. Champfleury's strictures on the intrusion of material description in the novel were strongly endorsed, and *Madame Bovary* denounced as a deplorable model in this respect. Flaubert's method was guaranteed to rob his work of all vitality, turning it into a well-oiled piece of machinery or—in the terms of the review which appeared in the fifth number of *Réalisme* (March 15th, 1857)—'a literary application of the laws of probability.' Finally, they echoed Champfleury in requiring that all novelists should write prosaically about ordinary (middle- or lower-class) people going about their ordinary business in an ordinary setting (for preference, a small country town).

The guiding spirit in this team of brash iconoclasts was Edmond Duranty, at the time a junior employee in the offices administering the Crown Estates. Present-day perspectives accord him a rather more significant place than he occupied in the estimation of his contemporaries; Duranty was a sadly neglected figure all through his life, but there are signs that he is at last being restored to his rightful place, both as a critic and as a creative novelist.[29] The journal he was largely responsible in starting failed to establish itself financially, and disappeared after only six issues. The extraordinarily aggressive tone it adopted must be interpreted as a natural reaction to the bitter hounding of everything that could be denoted as realism by high-toned periodicals like *La Revue des Deux Mondes*, the editor of which, François Buloz, was conducting in the 1850s a regular campaign against all literature that appeared not to be inspired by old-fashioned idealism. The pundits of the university world had joined in the hue and cry. In 1856, the year *Réalisme* was founded, the Académie des Sciences morales et politiques advertised a competition for the best essay on the influence of the modern novel on public morals. They awarded the prize to a magistrate who submitted a virulent diatribe in which nearly every important French novelist since Stendhal was accused of deliberately corrupting his readers.

In some ways, Duranty's position was nearer to Proudhon's than it was to

the more positivistic and morally neutral standpoint taken up by Champfleury and also, incidentally, by Hippolyte Taine a little later. Reacting
rather more violently than his elders against the tenets of the 'art for art's
sake' movement of the 1830s and Gautier's celebrated dictum: 'only what is
useless is truly beautiful; anything that can be put to any use is ugly', Duranty
saw it as an important part of the realist's mission that he should make his art
serve a social purpose. Among the works of his time that he specifically
approved—in spite of Champfleury's objections to its didacticism—was
Uncle Tom's Cabin.[30] This does not quite mean that he advocated the writing
of *romans à thèse*. The value of Harriet Beecher Stowe's novel lay in its
convincing picture of plantation society in the southern United States; that
the book might also serve the cause of emancipation was incidental. For
Duranty, every novel should be a fragment of contemporary social history,
soberly narrated, devoid of literary ornament or extraneous dramatic colour-
ing, and also purged of all moral judgements delivered by means of authorial
comment; the common reader should always be left to reach the correct
conclusions unprompted.

> Hence realism sets the artist a pragmatic and utilitarian philosophical aim,
> which is not entertainment but something nobler . . . Requiring of the
> artist that he should devote himself to the establishment of *useful truth* (*le
> vrai utile*), realism expects of him above all emotional response, powers of
> intelligent observation which allow him to *perceive* the lesson to be derived
> from, or the emotion to be aroused in, a spectacle of whatever order, base
> or noble, whatever the conventional judgement; and which allow him
> further invariably to *draw* this lesson from the spectacle, to evoke the
> emotion inherent in it, since he will have learned how to represent it fully
> and link it to the total social aggregate . . . . [31]

Duranty was actually engaged in writing his maiden novel when this
article, which embodies in somewhat abstract language his literary ideal, was
published. The novel, *Le Malheur d'Henriette Gérard*, was clearly intended to
illustrate the doctrine—unless, indeed, one takes it that the doctrine was
elaborated as theoretical justification for the novel. At all events, the 'useful
truth' embedded in the work is readily distinguishable; Duranty expressed
it, in fact, in the text itself, forgetting for a moment his own embargo on
authorial intrusions: 'Parents have the acknowledged right to treat their
children with harshness and even cruelty in the name of authority, reason
and affection; and the legitimate resentment shown by the children is condemned as rebelliousness and ingratitude. Weaker, and deprived of support,

the children see their resistance broken by the family. Or else, if they take flight, they are stigmatized.'

The case selected by Duranty in order to illustrate this 'useful truth' is an almost classic one, found over and over again in Molière, for example, whenever he wishes to show the abuses of parental authority: a girl from a middle-class family falls in love with a young man not regarded as eligible by her parents; they deny her all access to her lover and prevail on her, using every kind of moral pressure, to agree to marry an older, richer man of their choosing. Certainly Duranty succeeded in fulfilling what he had set forth as the proper aim of literary realism: the illustration of a particular social truth by means of a typical instance. The danger he incurred with the situation he had chosen was of sliding into sentimentality (one can imagine how Champfleury would have handled this theme). Duranty seems deliberately to have multiplied his difficulties by accumulating all possible elements of the most threadbare pathos. Firstly, the secret, idyllic love-affair that takes root between a young man living in poverty and a girl whose class-conscious parents will obviously never permit the match. Then, the dramatic discovery of the intrigue, the steps taken to sunder the two young lovers. After that, the long process by which Henriette's will to resist is slowly sapped, until finally she gives her consent to the marriage that has been arranged for her. And the final melodramatic double climax: Émile, the rejected lover, drowns himself in despair on the eve of the wedding,[32] while the aging Croesus whom Henriette marries is smitten with paralysis in consequence of the terrible scene she makes when she learns of this suicide.

The excruciating oppressiveness of Henriette's plight is further deepened by the utter abjectness of every member of her family. She encounters no sympathy from anyone in her circle and, of course, she can look to no one for help. Her father, completely absorbed in impractical agricultural experiments, has long since abandoned the direction of his children's upbringing to his wife; she, fussy, domineering, utterly unscrupulous, is a female bully of the worst type. In addition, Henriette has a brother who is jealous of her, taunts her, spies on her, and, when he dares, physically maltreats her. The bridegroom whom the family seeks to impose on her is a sexagenarian broken in health by a lifetime of crapulous debauchery but, of course, immensely rich.

Probably, if Duranty had chosen to idealize his heroine more than he does, his novel might have enjoyed a certain vogue; certainly Barbey d'Aurevilly, one of the few reviewers who wrote about Le Malheur d'Henriette Gérard when it was published in 1860, would have preferred it if Henriette had shown a little more spirit than to return home and submit to her family's wishes simply because she got soaked to the skin the night she tried to run away. But what Barbey called 'an aesthetic bloomer' (*une bévue esthétique*)[33] is in fact evidence of the quality that rescues Duranty's novel from banality. The relentlessness with which he denies his protagonist a conventional heroism is quite remarkable. The best part of the book is taken up with a patient analysis of Henriette's gradual moral disintegration under the barrage of specious arguments which her mother, other members of the family, and friends of the family direct against her in order to persuade her to renounce Émile and accept Mathéus. Some of the arguments are hard to refute. The advantages which would accrue from this alliance are manifest; is it not ungenerous and egoistic on her part to deny them these benefits for the sake of the warmth of a young man's embraces? Then, the young man himself, melancholy, weak-willed, recoiling so cravenly before the difficulties of the enterprise, is perhaps not, after all, the ideal lover she could wish for. She makes the fatal decision to pretend acquiescence, hoping for some miracle to deliver her before she is committed irretrievably: the costly presents her elderly suitor then presses on her, the bridal trousseau which is ordered, all these are the teeth in the trap that is closing on her. Duranty shows how her original quiet determination not to yield is replaced by self-contempt alternating with fits of violence vented on her persecutors; but the unrelenting pressure continues. She asks herself whether marriage to the senile Mathéus can be any worse than her present wavering state of mind, whether self-disgust can in any case go further than it has gone. Married, she will attain a degree of freedom she has never enjoyed; and the power she would exert, as mistress of so large an income, must be weighed in the balance. A visit she pays with her mother to the Mathéus country seat weakens still further her resolution: the beauty and elegance of the extensive grounds act powerfully on her imagination. There are few instances in the literature of the nineteenth century of so meticulous an analysis of gradual demoralization and creeping paralysis of the will.

Duranty's subject in his second novel (the only other one he wrote under the Empire) was class enmity. This was as much a social problem as the bourgeois practice of selling unwilling daughters into marriage, and therefore as deserving of treatment in accordance with the principles of realist art he had laid down. *La Cause du Beau Guillaume* is set in a village somewhere in the centre of France. Nearly all the characters, apart from the central figure Louis Leforgeur, are peasants; Louis belongs to a well-to-do family and has the introspective tendencies and nervous energy associated with the educated classes. At the beginning, when he rents a house in the village, the local rustics regard him as a 'strange animal' to be treated with respect on account of his supposed riches. They consider him to belong to a superior race, and he looks down on them as inferiors. But instead of keeping his distance, he breaks the taboo by taking one of the village girls into his house and living with her openly as his mistress; this is resented, not on account of the seduction itself (Duranty anticipates Zola in the disillusioned account he gives of the morals of country communities), but because Louis, a 'city man', has stolen from them one of 'their' girls.

To summarize the novel in this way is to describe it rather, one supposes, as Duranty wanted it to be read than as an unprepared reader would view it if he were ignorant of the author's intentions. By presenting his major theme, class struggle, under a sexual aspect, Duranty belittled it and robbed it of its immediacy; it is too easily overlooked as we watch the development of the triangular situation involving Louis, Lévise, and her disappointed and angry 'follower', the poacher Guillaume. Of the three, only Louis has any complexity of nature, with the result that the drama tends to be shown almost wholly through his eyes. This is something very different from the impartial inquiry into an abusive social institution which Duranty had conducted so convincingly in *Le Malheur d'Henriette Gérard*. Already he was falling below the standards he had set himself and, by this failure to adhere successfully to his own programme, providing a disturbing demonstration of the extreme difficulty of producing viable literary work in accordance with it.

Flaubert and Realism

It has long been recognized that the term 'realism', when applied to the novel under the Second Empire, embraces work done by men who belonged to two very disparate and even mutually antagonistic groups. We have seen how bitterly Flaubert's first novel was attacked by Duranty in the pages of *Réalisme*; but we have also seen how, judging from what was said in court, *Madame Bovary* was none the less rated a work of realism by the establishment. These apparent contradictions do, of course, arise to some extent from the proliferation of meanings the word had already assumed by 1857.[34] But they are also attributable to the simple fact that Duranty and Pinard saw different things to object to in Flaubert's novel.

It may not be unreasonable, a century later, to group together in one more or less coherent movement Champfleury, Duranty, Flaubert, and Edmond and Jules de Goncourt, on the grounds that they were all willy-nilly working together to rid prose fiction of the residual elements of romanticism which persisted, for instance, in the contemporary novels of Victor Hugo (*Les Misérables* was published in 1862, *Les Travailleurs de la mer* in 1866). Nevertheless the literary historian is still obliged to take note of, and explain if he can, the fact that these five writers saw themselves as belonging to two quite distinct factions and were remarkably unaware that there was any common denominator in their literary outlook. Arnold Hauser sees the distinction between the two groups in terms of their class orientation: one wing wrote 'for the masses', while the other, the 'mandarins' as he calls them, wrote for a cultured élite. This categorization can be corroborated by referring to the actual declarations of intent made by representatives of either camp. Champfleury, for example, confided: 'For a long time I have studied the aspirations, the desires, the joys and sorrows of those classes of society for which I feel sympathy, and I strive to render these emotions in all their sincerity. I write what they are incapable of writing; I am no more than their interpreter.'[35] Such a statement stands in the most striking contrast to Flaubert's notorious alienation from the common herd, expressed in many a misanthropic outburst in his private correspondence. 'Between us and the crowd there exists no link, unluckily for the crowd, unluckily for us above all. But since there is a reason for everything, and since the whim of an individual appears to me as legitimate as the appetites of a million men and can take up as much room in the world, it is necessary, leaving material considerations out of account and neglecting humanity which rejects us, that we should live for our vocation, climb up into our ivory tower, and there, like an Indian dancing girl surrounded by perfumes, live alone with our dreams.'[36] Flaubert's detestation of his own age is, of course, legendary; he compares it, in a violent simile, to the taste of excrement in his mouth. 'But', he goes on, 'I want to keep it there, congeal it, harden it, make it into a paste to daub over the nineteenth century, as Indian pagodas are gilded with cow-dung, and— who knows? maybe it will prove enduring.'[37] It has so proved. There is nothing in literature that has contributed more to our awareness of the maddening dreariness of provincial life in nineteenth-century France than *Madame Bovary*, or to our sense of the irretrievable collapse of idealism after 1848 than *L'Éducation sentimentale*.

It is also possible to draw a distinction between these two groups of realist writers in terms of the position they occupied in a society ruled by commercial values. Neither Flaubert nor the Goncourt brothers needed to rely on the proceeds of their published works for their livelihood; they lived in reasonable comfort on income derived from inherited wealth. Champfleury, on the other hand, made no pretence of the fact that he wrote for money; and Duranty similarly, after he relinquished his post in the civil service, became a professional writer. Hence the alternative set of terms used by Hauser to characterize the two opposing groups: *rentiers* and *bohemians*.

(One would prefer some other word than bohemian. Champfleury's connections with the bohemian group of painters and writers was severed some
time before the Second Empire, while Duranty took pride in the fact that
he had never had any dealings with them: *la vie de bohème* was essentially a
Louis-Philippard phenomenon.) It is not impossible that the Goncourts'
attitude to their age—more disdainfully, less full-bloodedly hostile than
Flaubert's—is to be explained by their social origins. The brothers accepted
realism, but as cultured gentlemen, not demagogues. Their novels are all
concerned with contemporary society, and on occasion even (as in *Germinie
Lacerteux*) with sections of that society which had always been considered too
backward, too unpolished to repay study; but what marks their work above
everything else is their refusal to allow themselves to become personally
involved in their subjects. Their self-conscious endeavours to attain an
individual style increased the impression that they were doing their best to
hold their material at arm's length. During their lifetime they were appreciated by a relatively small circle of admirers, mostly professional writers, and
since their deaths—one might even say, since Jules' death in 1870—their
works have fallen into the limbo of those more often respectfully referred to
than actually read. Anyone who opens them today is aware of a kind of
sepulchral chill wafted from the printed pages.

The really fundamental line of distinction has to be drawn not between
the two rival groups, but between Flaubert on the one hand, and all the
other novelists classified as realists on the other. And the distinction is simple:
Flaubert has survived as a major figure in European literature, the others not.
But why?

Flaubert's deepest intellectual attachments were to the scholars and
scientists of his time; he had ambitions to turn himself into a polymath, and
indeed the composition of some of his works, *La Tentation de Saint-Antoine*
and *Bouvard et Pécuchet*, almost compelled him to become one. 'Would I
were young!' he exclaimed—in his thirty-fourth year; 'how I would work!
One ought to know everything before one writes anything. We are, poor
scribblers the lot of us, monstrously ignorant. . . . The books from which
whole literatures have flowed, Homer's, Rabelais', were the encyclopedias
of their day; they knew everything, those stout fellows, and we know
nothing.' Art should mirror not just the social scene, but the whole universe;
it should be comprehensive and crystal clear. 'Art is representation, we should
think only of representing things; the artist's mind ought to be like the sea,
so wide that its limits cannot be discovered, so limpid that the stars in the
sky are reflected in its depths.'[38]

As Flaubert saw it, the domain of art was converging with that of science and the two would ultimately merge. Bouilhet's *Fossiles*, a long poem that drew its material from recent geological research, appeared to him premonitory of the poetry of the future. 'Literature will more and more take on the

A contemporary cartoon by Lemot shows Flaubert 'dissecting' Madame Bovary. It was Sainte-Beuve who first referred to the realists, and to Flaubert in particular, as 'anatomists', who wielded the pen as though it were a scalpel.

aspect of science; it will be above all else *expository*, which is not the same thing as saying it will be didactic. We must execute pictures, show nature as it is, but our pictures must be complete, we must paint the interior as well as the exterior.'[39] One has to remember that western science, at the time Flaubert was writing, had hardly moved beyond the descriptive phase. The scientist was concerned above all with collecting and classifying data, with measuring, counting, and analysing; the great syntheses that were to make so strong an impact on writers' imaginations, those of Darwin, Freud, and Einstein, had still to be constructed. Thus it was possible for Flaubert to equate scientific inquiry with the kind of coolly impartial, analytic and representational writing that he admired in others and strove to achieve in his own works.

It was only when he allowed himself to speculate on the results of the application of scientific methods to art that Flaubert succeeded in surmounting the acute depression and disgust with all things that characterized his outlook otherwise. 'Art must raise itself above personal affections and nervous susceptibility! It is time to give it the precision of the physical sciences by the application of a rigorous methodology.' And again: 'When we have, for a while, treated the human psyche with the impartiality that physical scientists display in their investigations of matter, we shall have taken an immense step forward; this is the only way for humanity to rise a little above itself. Mankind will then view itself coldly and clearly in the mirror of its works; it will be like God, judging itself from on high.'[40]

The fundamental reason why Flaubert alone, among the realists, made a lasting impression on the next generation of writers was that he understood, better than any other, that the coming age would be an age of science and that, as far ahead as could be seen, certainly for the rest of his lifetime, the aims and methods of art would seek conformity with the aims and methods of the natural sciences. Zola would launch the 'experimental novel'; the Impressionists would renovate pictorial techniques in accordance with the scientific study of the nature of light. Flaubert started his literary career at the watershed that separated a period of metaphysical speculation from one of scientific dogma. The break was as visible in political life as it was in every other area of human thought and activity: the fiasco of the 1848 Revolution produced a lasting disillusion with all systems of social betterment based on idealism, pious hopes, and fond imaginings, as opposed to impartial analyses of the harsh economic facts that governed human societies in an industrial age. If we accept, as we must, Robert Binkley's bold generalization: 'The first half of the nineteenth century was an age of philosophy; the second half of the century was an age of science',[41] then we are in a fair way to understanding why Flaubert's form of realism proved fruitful, while every other form—the sentimental realism of Champfleury, the sociological realism of Duranty, the aesthetic realism of the Goncourts—was condemned to sterility.

Notes

[1] *'Le clown! le poète! Pour qui voit superficiellement, rien qui se ressemble moins; pour qui sait voir, se dégager des apparences, c'est une seule et même personne. . . . S'élancer avec agilité et avec certitude à travers l'espace, au-dessus du vide, d'un point à un autre, telle est la suprême science du clown, et j'imagine que c'est aussi la seule science du poète'* (Banville, *Critiques*, Paris 1917, p. 422).

[2] The idea can be found in embryo in Stendhal's *Histoire de la peinture en Italie*: *'Travailler, pour un artiste. . . . ce n'est presque que se souvenir avec ordre des idées chères et cruelles qui l'attristent sans cesse.'*

[3] *Le Figaro*, November 26–December 3, 1863. Baudelaire probably composed this essay in the winter of 1859–60.

[4] In his unfinished novel *Féder ou le mari d'argent*, Stendhal gives a lively account of the career of a typical portrait artist of the pre-photographic era.

[5] *Le Charivari*, the French equivalent of *Punch*, was founded in 1832 by Charles Philipon, himself a gifted lithographer and caricaturist.

[6] See above, p. 42.

[7] Oliver Larkin (*Daumier, Man of his Time*, New York 1966, p. 99) describes the winged creatures wrongly as moths. Gnats, however, are no more given to blowing out candle-flames than moths. The point is that Daumier is risking here a pictorial pun—the word *moucheron*, besides meaning 'gnat', has obvious connections with the verb *moucher*, to snuff out.

[8] He was able to resume it, in a limited degree, under the liberal Empire and in the early years of the Third Republic, until, stricken with blindness, he was forced to relinquish the crayon.

[9] The *Liaisons* were published in 1782, the *Mariage de Figaro* had its first public performance in 1784, *Le Serment des Horaces* was exhibited in 1785.

[10] It re-emerged, as the Académie des Beaux-Arts, in 1816.

[11] Quoted by A. Tabarant, *La Vie artistique au temps de Baudelaire* (Paris, 1963), p. 131.

[12] C. H. Stranahan, *A History of French Painting from its earliest to its latest practice. . . .* (London, 1889), p. 278.

[13] Zola, *Salons*, ed. Hemmings and Niess (Geneva, 1959) pp. 148–9.

[14] As J. C. Sloane points out, people resented being shown as they were, while they could not in reason resent being shown the countryside as it was. 'The presentation of a twisted oak did not involve the *amour-propre* of the beholder as did the rough body of Millet's *Semeur* or the fleshy magnitude of Courbet's *Baigneuses*' (*French Painting between the Past and the Present*, Princeton, N.J., 1951, p. 102). It could be added that not a few of the ladies who viewed this last-named painting at the *salon of*

1853 must have been uncomfortably aware that underneath their corsets and their crinolines their bodies were rather like those of Courbet's stout bathing-women.

[15] Exhibited respectively in 1848, 1851 and 1857.

[16] *Curiosités esthétiques*, ed. H. Lemaître (Paris, Garnier, 1962), p. 372. Gerstle Mack sums up the difference between the two painters' treatment of the peasantry as follows: 'Millet's proletarian figures were pious, resigned, spiritual; Courbet's were earthly, independent, and uncouth' (*Gustave Courbet*, London, 1951, p. 93).

[17] The 1848 'free' *salon* was not allowed to count for this purpose!

[18] Louis Français was a landscapist of some distinction who had taken lessons from Corot. Paul Chenavard, a more interesting figure, was the man who conceived in 1848 the ambitious design of decorating the walls of the Panthéon with a vast mural. He won over Ledru-Rollin to the scheme, was allocated sufficient funds and assembled a group of painters to work under his direction. Unfortunately, in 1852 Montalembert managed to have the Panthéon reconsecrated as a sacred edifice. Chenavard's murals, intended to dramatize the triumph of human reason, were plainly inappropriate now that the building was restored to its original functions. (It had been built as a church in the eighteenth century, but between 1791 and 1806, and again after 1830 it had been used as a simple resting-place for the remains of great men.) A great number of Chenavard's cartoons were, however, shown at the 1855 Exhibition and proved to be a major talking point.

[19] Reproduced in *Courbet raconté par lui-même et par ses amis* (Geneva, Cailler, 1950), II, 81–2.

[20] Courbet did in fact hold this private exhibition (see above, p. 95), and the government, far from placing any obstacles in his path, made sure that a few police were on hand to control the crowds that were expected to besiege the doors. But in fact the exhibition was poorly attended. Also, Courbet relented in his determination not to send any pictures to the Exposition universelle: he submitted 13 of which two (*Enterrement à Ornans* and *L'Atelier du peintre*) were rejected.

[21] When Khalil Bey, a wealthy Levantine collector, commissioned a copy of *Vénus et Psyché*, Courbet executed an entirely new work, in which the blonde and the brunette were shown in bed together, locked in amorous embrace. So it is possible his intentions had after all been slyly pornographic.

[22] Letter to Urbain Cuénot, quoted in G. Riat, *Gustave Courbet peintre* (Paris, 1906) p. 236.

[23] It was reported in *Le Précurseur d'Anvers*, August 22nd, 1861. See Riat, *op. cit.* pp. 191–2.

[24] *La Silhouette*, July 22nd, 1849. Champfleury's earlier article had appeared in *Le Pamphlet quotidien et illustré*, September 28th, 1848.

[25] It is well known that none of the numerous portraits executed by Courbet (of Baudelaire, as has been mentioned, of Berlioz, of Proudhon, and of Champfleury himself) pleased the sitters. Courbet was aware of this, but would shrug his shoulders and make the typical comment: '*Ils n'étaient pas beaux, je ne pouvais pourtant les faire beaux.*'

[26] This volume was published in 1857 and has recently (1967) been reissued by the reprint firm of Slatkine (Geneva). Champfleury's book should not be confused with the journal entitled *Réalisme* published by Duranty and his friends in the same year (see below, pp. 108–9).

[27] By a certain Fétis, who published a lengthy study of Wagner (castigated by Baudelaire as an '*indigeste et abominable pamphlet*') in *La Revue et Gazette Musicale de Paris*, June 6th–August 8th, 1852.

[28] *Naughty Boys: or, the Sufferings of Mr. Delteil*. T. Constable & Co., Edinburgh, 1855.

[29] Cf. L.-E. Tabary, *Duranty: étude biographique et critique* (Paris, 1954) and more especially Marcel Crouzet's exhaustive study, *Un méconnu du réalisme: Duranty* (Paris, 1964).

[30] Léon Pilatte's translation, *La Case de l'oncle Tom*, with an introduction by George Sand, was published in 1853.

[31] '*Pour ceux qui ne comprennent jamais*', *Réalisme*, no. 2 (December 15th, 1856). Quoted by Crouzet, *op. cit.*, p. 439.

[32] It seems likely that Duranty took the idea of this episode from Balzac's *La Vieille Fille*, where Athanase Granson, another impecunious and irresolute young man, drowns himself when Rose Cormon, his life's passion, marries an older suitor, like Mathéus a wealthy debauchee. Duranty's great admiration for Balzac is evident from his critical writing.

[33] *Les Œuvres et les Hommes*, 1ère série, 4e partie (1865), p. 236. The review appeared originally in *Le Pays*, September 4th, 1860.

[34] For a selection of the various definitions of realism offered by critics between 1853 and 1857, see B. Weinberg, *French Realism: the critical reaction* (New York, 1937), pp. 120–5.

[35] Champfleury, *Le Réalisme*, p. 8.

[36] Letter to Louise Colet, April 24th, 1852: *Correspondance*, nouvelle édition augmentée (Paris, Conard), II, 396.

[37] Letter to Louis Bouilhet, September 30th, 1855: *ibid.*, IV, 96.

[38] *Correspondance*, IV, 52; III, 21.

[39] *Ibid.*, III, 158.

[40] *Ibid.*, IV, 164; III, 368.

[41] *Realism and Nationalism, 1852–1871* (New York, 1935) p. 1.

12   Courbet, *Baigneuses* (exhibited 1853). See p. 98

13 Degas, portrait of Duranty (1879)

Fête Impériale

Haussmann and the replanning of Paris

There was one art not merely encouraged but actively practised by the man who controlled the destinies of France during the Second Empire: this was the art which the French dignify by the name of *urbanisme* and which we call, more prosaically, town-planning. Just as the first Napoleon left an indelible mark on the legal and educational systems of France, so the third Napoleon can be said to have left his monument in a reconstructed Paris. Cities had been created out of nothing at the behest of an autocratic ruler, as Peter the Great caused his new capital to rise from a marshy waste; but never before—or at least, never since Augustus rebuilt Rome in marble[1] —had an already existing city been so thoroughly redesigned in the course of a single reign.

Moreover, the effects were not confined to the French metropolis. What was achieved by Napoleon III and his indefatigable henchman Haussmann between 1853 and 1870 served as a model for a number of the larger provincial centres, Marseilles, Lyons, Toulouse, when the time came for them to be cleansed and beautified. The distinctive Second-Empire style of town-planning was, furthermore, exported to neighbouring countries: if the capitals of Belgium, Sweden and Spain bear a certain family likeness to the capital of France, they owe this to the impact made on civic architects all over Europe (not to mention America) by the example of what had been done in Paris. A new applied art had been founded, born partly of necessity, partly of Louis-Napoleon's vision and tenacity of purpose.

Even if the future emperor had not, during his six years' captivity in the fortress of Ham, conceived the ambition to rebuild Paris and cauterize the unsightly sores that disfigured it, the plight of a city slowly strangling itself would have compelled him to take some drastic remedial measures. A small start had been made in the previous reign: a couple of new bridges were thrown over the Seine, an area was cleared for the construction of the Central Markets, and some 70-odd miles of new sewerage were laid down. Certain monuments, started earlier, were completed during the reign of Louis-Philippe: the church of the Madeleine, the Panthéon, and the arch at the Étoile: in between the Étoile and the Place de la Concorde (now dignified by the Luxor obelisk shipped from the Upper Nile) the Champs-Élysées were beginning to be flanked by picturesque new buildings.

But the centre of the city was the same crazy huddle of narrow, crooked streets, sunless courtyards and houses staggering under the weight of super-imposed storeys, that it had been for generations. Each neighbourhood, in the poorer areas, harboured a swarming colony of artisans, crowded together in conditions that would seem revolting even in present-day Harlem; every few years, some virulent epidemic or else periodic bouts of unemployment and consequent starvation would impose nature's own harsh resolution of the problem of over-population. The high, blank walls of the buildings and the dark, miry alleyways, the rattling of heavy carts and the squealing of ragged children, the malodorous air to which they were so accustomed that they hardly recognized it as impure—these composed the only en-vironment that men and women of the lower classes ever had exper-ience of. For Paris was a difficult city to move around in; indeed, it was less a city than a cluster of juxtaposed ghettos; one could easily live one's whole life pent up in the same acre or two of mouldering stone. There was public transport—a system of horse-buses—but the fare (30 centimes) was more than the working-man could easily afford. Until 1848 one could not cross the river without paying a toll; this imposition was so resented that one of the few acts of violence committed by the mob during the Revolution was to dismantle the collectors' offices at the entries to the bridges, and sub-sequent governments never dared restore the charge. In any case, the need to move out of one's immediate neighbourhood seldom arose: the work-shops were close to hand, if a man did not actually pursue his trade in the single room which was all he could call his home. Healthful recreation was something these people had no conception of, because there was no provision for it. The only open spaces within the walls of Paris were the Luxembourg Gardens, the Jardin des Plantes where a few animals were kept in cages, and the grounds of the Tuileries and the Palais Royal. On the whole the working-class people left these walks to their betters and were content with occasional forays into the spoiled countryside just outside the *barrière*.[2]

Their habitual environment, rough, rowdy, insanitary, included a certain criminal element; drunkenness and prostitution were rife; there was widespread illiteracy—a man with education, forced to take refuge in these slums, could make a living as a public scrivener, as Balzac shows Hulot doing in *La Cousine Bette* after he fell into disgrace. But by and large the inhabitants were astonishingly law-abiding, honest, and politically mature. They were, after all, the people who made the February Revolution and who, in June 1848, died heroically and unavailingly in its defence. The dignity and restraint they exhibited during the five months in which they ruled in the streets and indirectly controlled the fortunes of the country delighted those who sympathized with their cause and earned grudging tributes even from the few who persisted in regarding them as irresponsible riff-raff. Prosper Mérimée, no blind adherent of democratic republicanism, observed with astonishment how the ragged revolutionaries who invaded the Tuileries Palace, spontaneously mounted guard in rooms stacked with priceless plate and jewellery to prevent larceny.

In drawing up his private plans for a better designed and more salubrious capital city, Napoleon was in part, no doubt, motivated by a genuine desire to improve the living conditions of its humble and hard-working lower-class inhabitants. But equally, by dispersing them and driving wide avenues through the districts in which they were so dangerously concentrated, he may have hoped to forestall any repetition of the proletarian rising of 1848. In addition, and perhaps most importantly, he wanted to prepare Paris for the vastly greater influx of travellers and merchandise which the new rail-ways were already beginning to bring to its gates and which the policy of international free trade that he favoured was to stimulate still further. Some rationalization of street lay-out would have been an inescapable requirement whatever the régime. A relatively modest scheme of reconstruction had, after much debate, actually been initiated at the end of Louis-Philippe's reign but had been halted by the outbreak of revolution. As President of the Republic, Louis-Napoleon had encouraged the Prefect of Paris, Jean-Jacques Berger, to press on with the work. Expense was the great obstacle, and Berger, prudent and old-fashioned in his approach to the funding of public works, was not the man to pour out money at the rate needed if Paris was to be transformed as speedily as the Prince-President desired. It was not merely a question of building new roads to end old bottlenecks: a fresh outbreak of cholera in 1848–9, claiming nearly 20,000 victims in Paris alone, demonstrated the urgency of large-scale rehousing schemes; in addition, since the epidemic was by some medical authorities attributed to polluted drinking-water and inefficient drainage and sewerage, it seemed that some civil engineering feats on an equally grandiose scale were going to be needed as well.

When, after December 2nd, 1851, Louis-Napoleon found himself master of France, he started looking round for a trustworthy, energetic and far-sighted man to whom he could safely delegate responsibility for the execution of his plans, which were still, at the time, a closely guarded secret. He found this ideal servant in a 40-year-old career administrator of Alsatian extraction, Georges Haussmann, who had impressed him by the devotion and skill with which, as Prefect of the Gironde in 1851–2, he had swung round the predominantly royalist population of Bordeaux to acceptance of the new imperial régime. Haussmann replaced Berger as Prefect of the Seine in June 1853; at his first interview with the Emperor, Napoleon handed him a map of Paris on which he had himself traced in coloured inks the new thoroughfares he wanted driven through the city. The relative urgency of each project was indicated by the colour of the ink. First priority was to be given to the construction of one broad through road bisecting the city along its east-west axis, while another, crossing the first at right angles, was planned to start from the new railway terminal in the north (the present Gare de l'Est) and continue south, down to the river and across it, thus completing the quartering of Paris.

The construction of the east-west road was already in hand: it had been a project of Napoleon I and had been named, after one of his early battles, the Rue de Rivoli. Its last, eastern section was decreed in September 1854, and at the same time approval was given for its complement, a continuation of the Boulevard de Strasbourg designed to cross the river opposite the Ile de la Cité by a new bridge, the Pont du Change. Because of the need to pull down so many slum tenements that lay across its path, it took four years to complete this road, which was eventually named, after one of the new Emperor's military triumphs, the Boulevard de Sébastopol. Long before it was finished, the decision was taken to extend it southwards on the other side of the river, and thus the Boulevard St Michel came into being. Simultaneously, operations started in the west, around the site of the future Opera house, in order to allow an easier approach to the western railway terminal, the Gare St Lazare, and around the Étoile as well, where the 12 magnificent avenues which radiate from it and to which it owed its name, began to stretch away in all directions.

It was not long before the road builders were at work in the more densely populated east side too. Here, the longest street constructed under Haussmann's administration, the Avenue Daumesnil, led right the way to the edge of the Bois de Vincennes, while new boulevards fanned out from the Place de la République (called, at that time, the Place du Château d'Eau) to the north-west and south-east. It would be tiresome as well as pointless to list all the road-building projects that were conceived, undertaken and completed

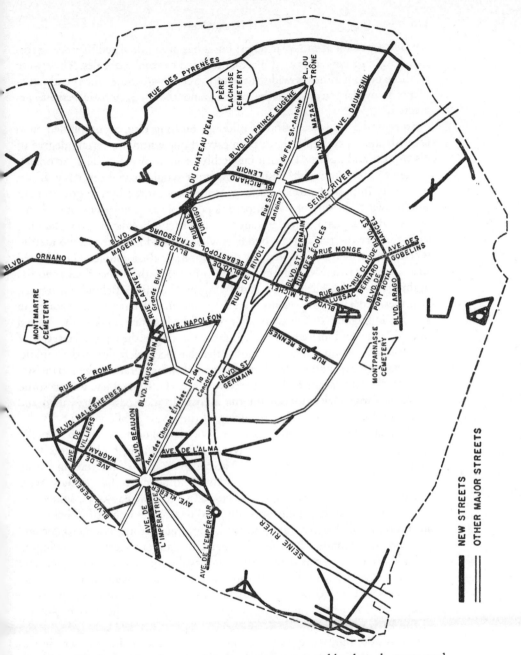

Map of Paris showing the more important new streets and boulevards constructed
under Haussmann's administration.

during Napoleon III's 18-year reign; but it has been calculated that the aggregate length of new arteries in Paris amounted to some 90 miles. They were all three or four times as wide as the old streets, with room for broad pavements in which trees could be planted and the characteristic *vespasiennes* erected.[3]

So radical a transformation of a living, bustling city, accomplished at so feverish a pace, could not have been carried out without a certain degree of discomfort and upheaval which inevitably brought protests. The cartoonists tended to take the whole business lightly; it would have been risky, if not materially impossible, to attack an operation sponsored by the government and known to be one of the Emperor's pet projects. They contented themselves with depicting, for instance, a returning holiday-maker standing aghast before the ruins of the building where he had his flat, and wondering whether his wife has perished in the demolition; or else a couple of bewildered British tourists, one exclaiming to the other that the *Times* had reported nothing about this earthquake. A drawing by Daumier, 'Behold our nuptial chamber, Adélaïde', represents a scene which might have been repeated in any city in England or Germany after one of the bombing raids of the Second World War: a middle-aged couple is shown staring at the exposed interior of a room halfway up a tenement house that has been cleft down the middle. But these gently humorous skits count as comment rather than criticism. The attacks came at the end of the reign, when Haussmann had to face some harsh parliamentary criticism for the autocratic methods he had used and especially for his unorthodox financing of these vast public works.

The manual workers were perhaps the one class of citizens who thoroughly approved of the Emperor's initiatives, even though their old haunts were subjected to such rude disturbance. The costliness of the undertaking hardly troubled them; what this furious activity implied, as far as they were concerned, was an uninterrupted succession of regular pay-days, something which, in the building trade especially, had been quite unheard of before. In an industry still largely unmechanized, the skilled stonemason, roofer and plumber, the dauntless housebreaker perched on a crossbeam and swinging his sledgehammer against the crumbling walls, the navvy with pick and shovel, spade and wheelbarrow had constant employment. If rates of pay were low and stayed low, at least the money came in steadily; and there seemed no end to the ramifying projects coming from the drawing-offices of the Paris prefecture.

It was not simply a question of new roads: new buildings were just as effective in giving the city its new look. Characteristically, where earlier régimes had left chiefly decorative monuments, statues and triumphal arches,

Napoleon III started with a strictly utilitarian building: the Halles, the covered Central Markets, the 'belly of Paris' as Zola later called it. Unfortunately the belly was placed rather too close to the heart: in other words, the Halles were sited more centrally than they should have been—though this disadvantage has become more apparent to posterity than it was to those who watched it go up.

In any case, the site had been earmarked long since, and even partially cleared during the First Empire. But the actual erection of the building had been constantly deferred and by the time Louis-Napoleon became President nothing existed except on paper. He secured a fifty-million franc loan from the National Assembly and was able to lay the foundation-stone on September 15th, 1851. The roofing of the Halles by a glass structure supported by iron girders was an architectural novelty at the time; this combination of materials had been tried out with success in the famous Crystal Palace, erected in Hyde Park for the London Exhibition of 1851, and also at one of the Paris railway terminals. Napoleon is said to have refused to authorize any design that did not incorporate it.

Another project that had been discussed for many years but never properly put in train was to link together the twin palaces, the Tuileries and the Louvre, occupying either end of the vast central site lying between the Rue de Rivoli and the Seine. These palaces were at the time separated by several old streets, one of them the Rue du Doyenné where, in the mid-thirties, the 'bohème galante' of Gérard de Nerval, Arsène Houssaye and Théophile Gautier had its headquarters. A proposal made by the gifted architect Visconti, involving considerable extensions along the north side, was adopted; unluckily Visconti died before he could complete the task, and the work of adorning the façades had to be entrusted to another man. The extravagance of the embellishments made by Visconti's successor, contrasting so sharply with the relatively severe ornamentation of the old palaces, exemplifies the contemporary love for display, though this fault was all the same less marked in the new wing of the Louvre than it was to be in Charles Garnier's Opera House. The decision to erect the latter building was taken after the attempt on the Emperor's life on January 14th, 1858 by the terrorist Orsini as he was entering the old opera house in the Rue Lepeletier. There was some initial delay, caused by argument about the suitability of the proposed site, and building did not commence until 1860. Seven years later sufficient progress had been made for the wooden screens surrounding the façade to be removed, and the extraordinary edifice loaded with fantasticated sculptures drew almost as many sightseers, enthusiastic, censorious, or merely curious, as did the building in the Champ de Mars that housed the Great Exhibition of that year.

Besides the public buildings erected by Haussmann's administration—
those mentioned, together with the unpleasing office blocks which replaced
the foul but picturesque slums of the Ile de la Cité—a vast number of
apartment-houses, hotels, departmental stores, restaurants and cafés were run
up by private building consortia along the new avenues and boulevards.
They were all very expensive looking with their gilded ironwork, lavish
wood panelling and shiny fittings. In one of his prose-poems[4] Baudelaire
describes a typical new café of the period, ironically detailing its plushy,
nouveau-riche splendours:

> The very gaslight was flaring with all the ardour of a neophyte, and shone
> with might and main on the dazzling white of the walls, on the brilliantly
> polished sheet-glass mirrors, on the gilt of the mouldings and the cornices,
> on the friezes showing chubby-faced pages holding hounds that strained
> at the leash, showing ladies laughing at the falcons perched on their
> clenched fists, nymphs and goddesses bearing baskets on their heads piled
> high with fruit, pastries, and game, while Hebes and Ganymedes held out
> at arm's length little pitchers of Bavarian cream or multicoloured sticks of
> Neapolitan ice: all of history and all of mythology pressed into the service
> of gluttony.

The cafés and restaurants have mostly been refurbished, but the apartment-
houses still stand, much the same as they were apart from the effects of time
and weather, as characteristic of Paris as its skyscrapers are of Manhattan.
Their regular façades and elevations are due to the terms of the contracts
passed by Haussmann with the architects to ensure that the houses should
present a uniform appearance, marching down either side of his wide,
straight streets like stone-and-mortar soldiers. As a rule they would have an
inner, shadowy courtyard, overlooked by the kitchens, and suites of rooms
of varying dimensions and degrees of comfort, depending on the floor level;
the garrets under the roof, reached by a service stairway, were reserved for
the maids' rooms. As for the kind of life that was led inside these sumptuous
and pretentious mansions, Zola's *Pot-Bouille* affords more than a few hints,
just as its sequel, *Au Bonheur des Dames*, conveys a vivid impression of the
backstairs life of the great new emporia, the Louvre, the Samaritaine, the
Bon Marché.

Yet another of Zola's novels, written before either of these, opens with a
colourful and impressionistic pen-picture of a scene typical of the late
Empire: the return of hundreds of fashionable carriages from the Bois de
Boulogne one autumn afternoon, with the sun beginning to sink behind
them. Appropriately, this book (*La Curée*) has as its principal theme the

speculative frenzy touched off by Haussmann's extensive building pro-
grammes; the introductory scene could not have been set in an earlier historical
period, when the Bois de Boulogne was still a royal demesne, part of the
forest of Rouvray which used to extend over a vast acreage to the north-west
of Paris. In the first half of the century, the Bois was noted chiefly as a hide-
out for wanted criminals and a conveniently secluded meeting-ground for
duellists. During his years of exile in London (1845–8), Louis-Napoleon had
been much struck by the beauty of Hyde Park, with its shady trees and lawns
leading gently down to shimmering water, a pleasance open to the meanest
citizen who wished to escape from the dusty streets. He resolved there and
then, if ever the power and opportunity were his, to endow Paris with a
public park that would rival London's. The Bois de Boulogne, partially
deforested and replanted, its long, straight rides replaced by cunningly
winding walks, and its swampy pool cleaned up and transformed into an
imitation Serpentine, became a city park on the city's edge, equipped with
restaurants and cafés, romantic grottoes and waterfalls, and even—at the
insistence of the sporting Duc de Morny—with a race-track, Longchamps,
to vie with Epsom Downs. An approach road from the Étoile was laid out,
of exceptional width, and named the Avenue de l'Impératrice.[5] It became
the fashionable parade-ground for the varnished carriages of the *beau monde*
and the *demi-monde*.

The landscaping of the Bois de Boulogne took between five and six years.
The corresponding east-side park, the Bois de Vincennes, was laid out in a
mere two years; it provided a symmetrical 'lung' available to the working-
class population who were settled at too great a distance from the Bois de
Boulogne to make the trip. In addition to these two large areas, smaller
parks were created near the centre of Paris: the Buttes Chaumont in the
north-east, where imaginative use was made of a number of abandoned
lime-quarries, and the small, restful Parc de Montsouris in the south, completed under the Third Republic.

The provision of small patches of verdure here and there within the city
and larger recreational areas on its outskirts went some way towards bestow-
ing on Parisians that rarest of urban commodities, fresh air. But the problem
was also tackled from a different direction—from underground. In 1855
tourists from abroad, visiting Paris for the first of the Great Exhibitions,
complained bitterly on their return of the insanitary odours which turned
their stomachs even in the *beaux quartiers*. 'I have seen', wrote one of them,
'persons of fashion living in Paris in juxtaposition with nuisances which
would drive the poorest mechanic in London out of the cheapest lodging
and which no earthly consideration would tempt an English cottager to

submit to.' But at the time of the next Great Exhibition, in 1867, the cleanli-
ness of the streets of Paris evoked the most favourable comment from a correspondent to the *Saturday Review*, who was prompted to suggest that the paupers
in British work-houses would be more profitably employed sweeping out
London gutters with birch-brooms than picking oakum. 'We talk about hy-
giene in London with our "Social Science Congresses" and "Health Officers"
and "Sanitary Commissioners". In France they do not talk so much but act.'[6]

It was Haussmann who realized, much more clearly than his master
Napoleon, that the art of town-planning does not stop at providing vistas
and monuments that are a joy to the eye, but includes supplying whatever
apparatus is needed to keep the town sweet to the nose. In the case of mid-
century Paris, this meant an enormously more complex and extensive sewerage system. For the first time, careful calculations were made to establish the
quantity of liquid that would be flowing through the subterranean galleries;
and novel constructional materials, notably hydraulic cement, were employed to make them water-tight. These new tunnels were large enough to
accommodate piped gas and piped water, the latter drawn increasingly from
the new reservoir at Ménilmontant which was supplied by fresh water
originating in the department of Aisne and conducted across country by an
80-mile long aqueduct—another ambitious engineering feat organized by
Haussmann and completed by 1865. The new sewers were one of the
wonders of Paris if not of Europe; few travellers arriving at the French
capital in 1867 to view the Exhibition omitted to book themselves a tour of
these vaulted underground marvels.

Town-planning is an art that has to be judged by two distinct sets of
criteria: social and aesthetic. As for the first, it is true, by and large, that the
citizens of Paris found themselves living in a less sordid, less crowded, less
obstructed environment in consequence of Haussmann's radical improvements. Considered simply from the point of view of the salubriousness of the
air and the convenience with which business could be transacted and amusement pursued, Paris had become a city which it was a pleasure to reside in
and a delight to visit, as indeed it remained up to the time when motor-
traffic reintroduced congestion and noise and started polluting the atmosphere all over again. As a piece of social engineering, 'Haussmanization' can
be criticized only because it did not, in every respect, go far enough. Certain
notorious slum areas were done away with, like the infamous 'quartier de la
petite Pologne' which disappeared when the Boulevard Malesherbes was
driven through it; this particular district had so blighted a reputation that
bailiffs refused to enter it to carry out eviction orders. But too often old
slums were rooted out simply to permit new ones to spring up in their place.

Some of the freshly erected tenement houses were little better than those that had been demolished, when assessed in terms of such elementary amenities as space, light, or ventilation. The administration did exercise careful control over the external appearance, and especially the façades, of the *maisons de rapport* that private builders were putting up; but it was no part of official doctrine that the state had a duty to lay down minimum standards of comfort for the living quarters behind the façades.

The other question to be asked is whether Paris was in all respects a more beautiful city as a result of Napoleon's planning and Haussmann's tireless labours. It was certainly a more distinctive city. The level skyline of the buildings, the streets that furrowed it in broad, straight lines, the occasional huge *place* where they converged: this conveyed the impression of something purposive, civilized, and seemed the very materialization, in wrought iron, asphalt, stone and glass, of a hard and enterprising régime. Haussmann's Paris bespeaks the Roman element always discernible in the French national character: the craving for order, durability, and magnificence. The architectural styles adopted were predominantly Roman or, at any rate, neo-classical; but here one must not overlook the tendency, already noted, to load the clean lines and surfaces with luxuriant ornamentation, a fault that strikes the eye most in the theatres that date from this period, the Châtelet, the Gaîté, the Vaudeville, not to mention once more the Opéra. It has been urged in justification that 'these new characteristics were honestly expressive of the prosperous and materialistic decades of the Second Empire.'[7] Much the same could be said of the Albert Memorial without endearing it to those who object to its ponderous tastelessness.

When so much that was new was erected, inevitably much that was old was razed, and in the process some buildings of historical or antiquarian value were lost for ever. Often these unfortunate results could have been prevented and the occasional ancient monument preserved by permitting a small deviation in the tracing of the new road; but Haussmann's fetish of the straight line allowed of no such irregularity. Sentimentalists regretted the merciless obliteration of old streets full of glamour and excitement, like the so-called Boulevard du Crime with its numerous theatres, its market booths and acrobats performing in the open air. The old Ile de la Cité, if an eyesore and a den of vice, was a fascinating relic, and the uninteresting municipal buildings put up on the site of the wicked old warren that formerly covered this 'cradle of Paris' seemed to typify Haussmann's determination to modernize with scant regard for the aura of tradition that clings to certain historic spots. The Paris that Balzac had loved and of which he had described every picturesque or sinister corner had gone, save for a few small islands of streets here and there. It was gone, not even preserved on canvas, since the fashion for painting street-scenes came in only later, with the Impressionists. It stayed only in the memory of a generation that would disappear too, and whose spokesman was, once more, Charles Baudelaire:

> *Le vieux Paris n'est plus (la forme d'une ville*
> *Change plus vite, hélas! que le cœur d'un mortel);*
>
> *Paris change! mais rien dans ma mélancolie*
> *N'a bougé! palais neufs, échafaudages, blocs,*
> *Vieux faubourgs, tout pour moi devient allégorie,*
> *Et mes chers souvenirs sont plus lourds que des rocs.*[8]

The 1867 Paris Exhibition

The Paris Exhibition of 1867 was Napoleon III's 'open day,' when he invited the world to view the transformation scene that had been wrought during his reign. The earlier Exhibition of 1855 had been an altogether more modest affair, a simple imitation of the London Exhibition of 1851. Moreover, it had been held at an inauspicious time, when the western powers were still fighting Russia in the Crimea. The new exhibition was dedicated to peace. It is true that the international outlook was again dark. The brief war between Prussia and Austria in 1866, ending in the resounding defeat of the Hapsburg Empire, had spread a feeling of disquiet throughout France which was deepened by disturbing reports of the fighting in Mexico (where a French expeditionary force was engaged in defending Archduke Maximilian's precarious claim to the throne). A war between France and Prussia did not seem likely, but the possibility could not be ruled out. The feeling of foreboding that stalked the chancelleries of Europe was compared by Mérimée to the emotions aroused in Mozart's *Don Giovanni* immediately before the apparition of the Commander. 'M. de Bismarck', he added hopefully, 'who is the Commander, will not, however, as I believe, make his appearance, and the rumours of war are without serious foundation. But there is a general uneasiness and nervousness everywhere.'[9] Spring was late that year and the Exhibition opened, on April 1st, under a lowering sky and with a chilly wind blowing. Only towards the end of the month did the gloom begin to lift, and festivities were in full swing when the summer came. But then, on the very day fixed for the grand ceremony at which the Emperor was to distribute prizes (July 1st), information reached Paris of the execution of Maximilian on Juarez's orders.

For all these reasons, there was a certain hectic feverishness about the excitement that the Exhibition aroused. Nevertheless the excitement was real, and infectious, and in general it would be true to say that 1867 was a year of high carnival which marked the apogee of the reign. It finally established Paris as the capital of gaiety, winning it a reputation which even the disasters of 1870–71 did not destroy and which stood unchallenged until the general eclipse of European civilization in 1914.

The organizational spadework had been carefully done. An imperial decree was promulgated as early as June, 1863, to make public the decision to hold an exhibition four years later. The intention was that it should be much more than a collection of trade exhibits: every branch of human activity was to be represented and, as far as possible, every nation in the world would be given the opportunity to demonstrate its own peculiar contribution to art, culture, and industry. Clearly the Palais de l'Industrie in the Champs-Élysées, which had served to house the 1855 Exhibition, was not going to be spacious enough to accommodate the much larger number of exhibits that the organizing committee expected. Only one site was available that provided sufficient space without being too far removed from the city centre; this was the Champ de Mars, a large, stony tract of land which owed its name to its use as a drill ground for the École Militaire. It seemed a singularly inappropriate setting in which to display the products of the arts of peace, but in fact it served its purpose so well that all the succeeding *expositions universelles* of the nineteenth century (those of 1878, 1889 and 1900) were held here.

What might be called the bread-and-butter of the Exhibition—the sections devoted to industry and commerce—were housed in the central building, an uninspiring structure of brick and iron, elliptical in shape. Its internal disposition, however, was a model of clarity and ingenuity: the designers had profited from the experience of the London Exhibition of 1862, where the bewildering array had left the visitor with a painful impression of chaos and confusion. All the way round it, sheltered by a broad glass roof, were arranged restaurants, bars and cafés, each devoted to the particular beverages or gastronomic specialities of the different countries. Beyond this, the infertile soil had been turned by some horticultural miracle into a spacious grassy park, with groves of trees here and there sheltering small pavilions, every one an example of the architectural style characteristic of each nation. So, one could stroll from a Dutch farmhouse to a Russian *izba*, look in at a Persian caravanserai, move on to a Hindu pagoda and round off the tour by inspecting a temple of the Nile complete with sphinxes. In those days when the tourist industry was in its infancy, most Parisians had seen these exotic structures only as engraved representations in travel-books and encyclopedias, and the delight they manifested at these mock-ups of the real thing would seem puerile only to later, more blasé generations.

Cosmopolitanism was the keynote of the Exhibition and was perhaps what made it so distinctively Second-Empire. Paris was never more a meeting-place of the nations than in the latter part of this reign, when the throne was occupied by an emperor whose father had been King of Holland, whose boyhood had been spent in South Germany and who had remained banished from France until he was 40; whose consort was a Spanish beauty, and whose court was thronged by foreigners, the native French aristocracy refusing to honour it. In the year 1867 Paris truly took on the aspect of the world's capital, as the Exhibition beckoned across the continent of Europe, over the Channel, the Mediterranean and the Atlantic, all those who had the time and money to spare for a visit. The boulevards were a babel of tongues —one might have imagined oneself in the west end of 'swinging London' during any summer tourist season a century later. It was the climax of an invasion that had been in progress already a few years: its theme-song was the chorus of foreigners in Offenbach's *La Vie parisienne*:

> *Nous venons,*
> *Arrivons*
> *De tous les pays du monde;*
> *Par la terre ou bien par l'onde.*
> *Italiens, Brésiliens,*
> *Japonais, Hollandais,*
> *Espagnols, Romagnols,*
> *Égyptiens et Prussiens . . .*
> *La vapeur nous amène:*
> *Nous allons envahir*
> *La cité souveraine,*
> *Le séjour du plaisir.*

The actual exhibits in the Champ de Mars were as cosmopolitan as the crowds that came to view them. If most of the mechanical marvels were still of British or American manufacture, there was a large and varied display of other products from all over the globe: furs from Russia, wool from Australia, silks from China, porcelain from Saxony and glassware from Bohemia. From the Ruhr came a huge cannon, cast by Krupps, which struck a sinister and discordant note among all the other delightful or ingenious exhibits; the Crown Prince of Prussia made it a point to begin his tour by inspecting this monstrous engine of war.

The organizers had had, further, the luminous idea of inviting more distant countries, particularly Asian and North African ones, to send small contingents of their nationals to demonstrate the arts peculiar to their culture. There was a Chinese theatre, a company of scorpion swallowers from Algeria, a troop of Indian dancing-girls. There were Japanese maidens moving gracefully in their soft-tinted kimonos and Sikhs wearing enormous turbans. Nor were the delights solely for the eye: Johann Strauss had brought his orchestra from Vienna and performed at promenade concerts. When all these pleasures had been sampled, the intrepid might enjoy an aerial view of Haussmann's bright new city for the price of a ticket in one of the captive balloons that made regular ascents.

In this welter of internationalism, France by common consent excelled in one art: that of painting. All schools were represented at the Exhibition, so that the extent to which French influence had permeated those of other countries was strikingly demonstrated. The rules stipulated that any picture painted since the last (1855) Exhibition qualified for inclusion. In the French section there were displayed no fewer than 13 paintings by Meissonier, the specialist in microscopic art; nine Millets, among them the *Angélus du soir*, an excellent example of this artist's good and bad qualities; four large decorative panels by Puvis de Chavannes, representing War and Peace, Work and Rest; and the highly controversial *Jeune homme et la mort* and *Orphée* by Gustave Moreau. The Barbizon school was represented by eight landscape studies by Théodore Rousseau and seven paintings by Corot. The Academy in all its splendour shone in Cabanel's display of idealized feminine flesh, in his *Naissance de Vénus*, his *Nymphe enlevée par un faune* (two canvases acquired by the Emperor at awesome prices) and above all in his *Paradis perdu*. The only cause for thankfulness here, wrote Zola bitingly, was that the King of Bavaria, who had commissioned the picture, was shortly to rid the country of it by carrying it off to Munich.

The array at the Champ de Mars was not the only picture-show in Paris that year. Ingres held a private exhibition in the Rue Bonaparte where over a hundred pictures, including the delicious masterpiece of his old age, *La Source*, could be viewed. Courbet too had his own exhibition (though he also had four pictures at the Champ de Mars), and Édourard Manet, the new *enfant terrible* of the world of painting, displayed the 50-odd works he had executed to date in a private pavilion on the Exhibition site.

Offenbach and the 'opéra-bouffe'

The chorus from *La Vie parisienne*, of which the first part has already been quoted, continues as follows:

On accourt, on s'empresse
Pour connaître, ô Paris,
Pour connaître l'ivresse
De tes jours, de tes nuits.
Tous les étrangers, ravis,
Vers toi s'élancent, Paris.
Nous allons chanter, nous allons crier,
Nous allons souper, nous allons aimer.
O mon Dieu, nous allons tous
Nous amuser comme des fous.

And so, indeed, they did. The Exhibition at the Champ de Mars was instructive, to be sure; gay and amusing; it also served the purpose of a public place of assignation. Gustave Doré drew the stock caricatural Englishman ruefully regretting that he had not come to Paris on his own: '*Moâ ennouyé d'avoir apporté mon femme.*' Others had been more far-sighted; for rich bachelors, like the Prince of Wales, and grass-widowers, Paris had a great deal to offer: the Paris, that is, of race-courses, champagne suppers, the *can-can* and the *opéra-bouffe*, the Paris depicted in such lurid colours and denounced in doom-laden accents by Daudet in *Le Nabab* and by Zola in *Nana*.

Czar Alexander II, on his way to Paris from St Petersburg, sent a telegram from Cologne to the manager of the Théâtre des Variétés, requesting that a box be reserved for him on the evening of his arrival. To their consternation, the management discovered that not a single box remained unsold; so the staff was sent scurrying around Paris to prevail on some less august ticket-holder to sell one back, at no matter what price. The Czar, alighting from the imperial train, drove first to the Greek Orthodox church in the Rue Daru and then, having completed his spiritual devotions, sped on to the theatre in the Boulevard Montmartre to pay homage to the true queen of Paris, the actress and singer Hortense Schneider, whom the irreverent nick-named 'le Passage des Princes'.

Her unofficial royalty had no serious challenger in fashionable society where, as conservatives and radicals were united in proclaiming, all the old distinctions of birth and breeding were blurred and *déclassement* ruled supreme. One afternoon she drove up in style to the entrance-gate of the Exhibition reserved for reigning monarchs. The guard walked over to her carriage-window to expostulate. 'But', explained Mlle Schneider, 'I am the Grand-Duchess of Gerolstein.' The gates were flung open and in she drove. *La Grande-Duchesse de Gérolstein* was the name of the operetta in which she was currently playing the title-part.

14 Demolition work in Paris in the late 1860s

15 General view of the 1867 Paris Exhibition

16 The Empress Eugénie surrounded by her court ladies. A detail from one of the many glamourized studies of the subject made by Winterhalter

The operetta or *opéra-bouffe* was an art-form so typically Second Empire that it rapidly withered away once the régime collapsed. In its heyday it could claim to be the truly democratic, truly international art of the age, since it appealed to all ranks of society and to Francophile foreigners as well as to the native-born Parisian and the family from the provinces paying a holiday visit to the capital. It was international too in the sense that its most memorable achievements were the product of the collaboration of a German musician (Jacques Offenbach was born in Cologne, of Jewish parents) with a succession of French librettists: Hector Crémieux at first, and later the indivisible Meilhac and Halévy. It may be noted, in passing, that at least two other 'vogue artists' of the Second Empire were foreign-born: Meyerbeer, whom we shall encounter a little later, and Winterhalter, the court portrait-painter; while the two men who had greatest responsibility for administering the arts during Napoleon III's reign were also of foreign extraction: Walewski the Pole, and Nieuwerkerke, son of a Dutch officer. The list, to be complete, should include the name of the Englishman John Worth, the greatest contemporary exponent of that most Parisian of minor arts, *haute couture*.

Offenbach was in his early teens when he first came to Paris to study music. To earn a little pocket-money, he used to play—preferably the 'cello, his favourite instrument—at private houses, and it was at one of these *soirées* that he was noticed by Arsène Houssaye. This was just after the former member of *la bohème* had been put in charge of the Comédie Française.[10] For the next five years, Offenbach was conductor-in-chief of the theatre orchestra; then, in 1855, he launched out on his own, founding the Bouffes parisiens for which he hired a tiny hall[11] in the Champs-Élysées. Managers under the Second Empire were not only obliged to obtain a licence to open a theatre, but were strictly limited as to the size of cast they could employ. Offenbach was permitted only two actors, but the sketch he put on was so enchantingly witty that it became an immediate hit. It ran to no fewer than 400 performances (it is true that the smallness of the theatre put drastic limits on the size of the audiences), and Offenbach's celebrity was consecrated when his little company was commanded to appear at the Tuileries and give a private performance before the court.

His next great success was *Croquefer ou le dernier des paladins*. He had now moved to a larger and more centrally situated theatre, the Salle Comte in the Passage de Choiseul, which was licensed for productions involving a maximum of four singers. *Croquefer*, unfortunately, had been written for five parts, but Offenbach, with his customary resourcefulness, was able to turn this difficulty to his advantage. He decided to allocate one part to a crusader whose tongue had been cut off by the Saracens when they took him prisoner.

K

When the four others joined in a chorus, Mousse-à-Mort contented himself with barking. No one could accuse Offenbach of not sticking to the letter of the regulations, while at the same time he had contrived to introduce an irresistible comic element.

Finally, in 1858, Offenbach was granted permission to produce operettas with no limitation on the number of singers. The operetta was not a creation of Offenbach's. Its invention was due to Hervé, an impresario of extraordinary verve and versatility, who not only composed the music and managed the theatre (the Folies dramatiques) in which his productions were staged, but wrote the librettos himself and even, when the need arose, joined the cast. In *Chilpéric*, notably, he sang the principal male part, opposite Blanche d'Antigny, an actress famous for her opulent bosom and flawless shoulders, as well as for the innumerable diamonds she wore on stage and the richly variegated love-life she led off it.[12] But in the duel for public favour that developed, Hervé lost to Offenbach, whose *Orphée aux enfers* (1858), after a shaky start, gradually caught on and became a major attraction. Napoleon and Eugénie came to applaud it, it had its 400 performances, and Offenbach joined the ranks of the Parisian celebrities. A thin, gangling figure, he was recognized everywhere, forever shivering under a fur coat which draped rather than fitted his bony body. Under the top-hat his long, straight hair fell on to his shoulders, and he peered at the passing crowd through a lorgnon clamped to a nose so pronounced that it seemed to have absorbed every other feature of his gaunt, triangular face.

Orphée aux enfers was blasted at the start by the critic Jules Janin, whose respect for antiquity was outraged—so he let it appear—by the irreverent treatment accorded by Crémieux to the gods and goddesses of Greek mythology. But Janin could not have been unaware that this type of comic debunking had a respectable lineage in French literature, traceable at least as far back as Scarron's burlesque mythological poem *Typhon* (1644). Janin's animadversions on *Orphée aux enfers* were more probably inspired by political considerations than strictly literary ones. Now a staunch supporter of the *status quo*, he took alarm at the impertinent allusions to the contemporary scene which the sleepy censorship had evidently not observed in the operetta and which could not, in decency, even be pointed out in the columns of the *Journal des Débats* in which he was writing. The legends of Jupiter's amours— with Danaë, with Alkmene, with Io, with Leda—were familiar to French audiences; every schoolboy knew his Ovid, and besides, the stories were frequently used as subjects for paintings. But the amorous propensities of Napoleon III were also a matter of common—if hushed—gossip. Thus *Orphée aux enfers* could well be interpreted as a satire on the sovereign and on the ease with which he maintained his ascendancy by corrupting those around him. There is a dramatic climax in the operetta when the Olympians, bored with their lives of endless pleasure, threaten Jupiter with a revolution, singing (to the tune of the Marseillaise):

> *Abattons cette tyrannie*
> *Ce régime est fastidieux.*

But Jupiter succeeds in pacifying them, they revert to a glorification of sensual delights, and all ends with a bacchanalian dance based on the *can-can*.

How seriously Offenbach intended his satire to be taken is hard to say. Though now a naturalized Frenchman, he still kept the detached viewpoint of the outsider, and it is not impossible that a somewhat sardonic assessment of the *fête impériale* underlies this gay composition. What is certain is that it conquered its public by its wit, its tenderness and its verve, rather than by whatever social implications or political warnings it may have concealed.

La Belle Hélène, produced six years later, used the same formula—the light-hearted pastiche of classical legend overlaying corrosive comment on contemporary society. For Helen one could substitute a dozen different women of fashion or *demi-mondaines*, ready for any kind of romp and reckless of consequences. Paris is the typical handsome, brutal, experienced *boulevardier* and behind the other characters, Greeks and Trojans, lurked the silhouettes of all the notorious playboys of the period. There are prophecies of impending doom—the operetta, like Giraudoux' play, ends with the declaration of war, as if Offenbach foresaw the approaching clash between France and the country of his birth, and guessed too that, just as the earlier war ended with the sack of Troy, so this new conflict would turn into a holocaust in which the voluptuous civilization of the imperial régime would be consumed in the flames. Radically minded reviewers, like Jules Vallès and Henri de Rochefort, did not miss these implications. But by the majority, *La Belle Hélène* was seen and heard at its most superficial level, as an exuberant paean to the life of the senses. Its tunes were whistled in the streets, turned into regimental marches, danced to at the *cafés dansants*. And Hortense Schneider, with her dimples and pert little face, won all hearts. She was precisely the kind of interpreter, full of bounce and high spirits, gay and winsome in turns, that Offenbach needed for his work, and he had bombarded her with telegrams and offers of fantastic fees until she consented to take the star part.

His stock never stood so high as in the year of the Great Exhibition. At the Bouffes, there was a revival of *Orphée aux enfers* which created something of a scandal, the management having acceded to the wish expressed by Cora Pearl to be given a part. She was one of the most notorious wantons of the age; but she had a magnificent figure and was said to have won first prize at a competition organized by the Duc de Morny for the woman with the most perfect bust. When she made her début on the stage, in a costume so scanty as to be hardly decent, there were murmurs of appreciation from the connoisseurs. However, these were drowned in catcalls and laughter as soon as Cora Pearl, née Eliza Emma Crouch, opened her mouth to proclaim in her atrocious English accent:

Je soui Kioupidonn . . . etc.

Scuffles developed in the hall between the music-lovers, who wanted to hiss her off the stage, and the Cora-lovers, who found her killing. In the end the actress herself swept off, after indicating her contempt of the audience with a traditional and very vulgar gesture.

However, the greatest attraction of the year—one that put the Exhibition itself into the shade—was the new production, *La Grande-Duchesse de Gérolstein.* For the first time, Offenbach risked a contemporary subject, a satire of the small German ducal and princely courts which still abounded at this period. It was rumoured that the original intention had been to caricature the court of Imperial Russia, with Catherine the Great as the heroine, but that the censors had prohibited this for fear of diplomatic repercussions. Even in the amended version, they had spotted an allusion to Prussia's lightning victory over Austria in the opening lines of one song:

Madame, en dix-huit jours
J'ai terminé la guerre

which had to be modified. And they seriously upset Hortense Schneider who, as Grand-Duchess, made one of her stage appearances in a quasi-military uniform. She had gone to considerable trouble to find a sash of the right shade which, however, she was forbidden to wear, again for fear of offending certain susceptibilities. These excessive precautions were understandable in the circumstances: the Théâtre des Variétés was crammed every night that summer with generals and ambassadors, kings, viceroys, princes and their ministers from every capital of Europe, besides the Emperor and Empress of France, who could not see it often enough. When the great ones of the earth will pay to see themselves wittily ridiculed, the art that has brought this about can be said to have achieved at least a moral victory over authority.

Grand Opera

Light opera was an art that paid: when *La Grande-Duchesse de Gérolstein,* which opened on April 12th, 1867, reached its hundredth performance on August 7th, receipts already grossed close on half a million francs. Grand opera, on the other hand, was certainly not paying its way, and had not been doing so since the reign of Louis-Philippe. When Nestor Roqueplan took charge of the Paris opera company in 1847, the accumulated deficit already amounted to 400,000 francs. Under his administration matters went from bad to worse, and by the summer of 1854 the company was in the red to the tune of little under a million. The only possible course was to wind it up and defray the cost of supporting the opera from public funds. The necessary decree was promulgated on July 1st, 1854, and thereafter the Opera became what it is now, a state-subsidized institution.

If the operatic art, judged simply by its ability to attract large enough audiences to pay its way, was in so parlous a condition, this was certainly not because the management was over-paying its employees. When Roqueplan introduced the rule that members of the orchestra should wear evening dress, as was the custom in London, Berlioz commented that, while he saw nothing wrong in the innovation, he thought it was a pity that another practice had not simultaneously been imported from England: that of paying the musicians reasonable salaries; how cruelly insulted the drummer at Covent Garden would be if he were offered a mere four shillings an evening for his services! There were various reasons why expenditure regularly exceeded receipts. The opera-house in the Rue Lepeletier was small, inconvenient, and outdated. As an evening's entertainment, grand opera had to compete not just with the straight theatre—which was in a highly flourishing condition—but with light opera at the Théâtre lyrique and with Hervé's and Offenbach's new-fangled opéra-bouffe. And finally the repertoire was conservative in the extreme. Very few notable new operas were performed under the Second Empire. Halévy, who made his name with La Juive in 1834, came forward in 1852 with a new opera, Le Juif errant, on which great hopes were pinned. A large sum, something like 150,000 francs, was expended on the production, but the work met with little favour. At the very end of the Empire two outstanding new operas were put on: Ambroise Thomas' Hamlet (1868) and Gounod's Faust (1869). An earlier work of Gounod's, La Nonne sanglante, based on an episode of Lewis's gothic novel The Monk, had aroused some interest among connoisseurs when it was produced in 1854, but had failed to establish itself; it was taken off after only eleven performances. Similarly, his Reine de Saba (1862) achieved no more than a partial success. Gounod did, however, compose several less ambitious works for the Théâtre lyrique, where his Faust had been given its first performance in 1859; they included Mireille and Roméo et Juliette, both produced in the 1860s.

To make good the deficiency of native talent, the Paris Opera invited the Italian maestro, Giuseppe Verdi, to compose a work to a libretto by Scribe for performance in 1854. Verdi came to Paris to superintend rehearsals, but his collaboration with his French *confrères* was far from frictionless, and the resultant delays meant that *Les Vêpres siciliennes* could not be shown till June 1855. Two years later, however, the composer's rescoring for French audiences of *Il Trovatore* (under the title *Le Trouvère*) obtained a considerable popular success. It was revived in 1860 and reached its hundredth performance in 1863. Then, in the winter of 1863, Verdi agreed to write a fresh opera with a French libretto, this time based on Schiller's tragedy *Don Carlos*. Once more, there were endless difficulties with the singers, the orchestra and the management, and the opening night was deferred until March 1867. The work was coldly received and Verdi left for Italy immediately after the first night.

It is hard to account for the moribund state of the operatic art in Paris after the two conspicuously brilliant decades that preceded the 1848 Revolution, without referring to the vice-like grip in which this art was held by the undeservedly popular composer Jakob Meyerbeer. Back in 1831 he had, in *Robert le Diable*, created a new type of opera, having strong affinities with the historical novels popular at the time and with the romantic verse drama of Victor Hugo. In Eugène Scribe he had found the ideal librettist, one who could add to the opera the element of the 'well-made play' so attractive to Parisians. Musically, he owed much to Rossini and Weber, but it was not the musical element that drew audiences steadily all through the July Monarchy and the Empire (*Robert le Diable* had its five-hundredth performance at the Paris opera house on March 1st, 1867—exactly a month before the Exhibition opened); Meyerbeer's operas were full of excitement and the productions were a feast for the eyes. On the placards in the Rue Lepeletier, *Robert le Diable* alternated with one or other of Meyerbeer's later works, *Les Huguenots* (1836) or *Le Prophète* (1849) all through the Second Empire, during which period the composer rested complacently on his laurels, producing nothing new barring a couple of works for the Opéra comique (a theatre for musical plays with spoken dialogue).

It is true that after 1849 his health started to deteriorate, and this partly explains why he produced so little. In addition, he may have feared that a new work, not meeting with the same favour, might compromise the renown he had won by his earlier successes. Meyerbeer's personality was full of contradictions. He was both inordinately vain and subject to bouts of intense diffidence, so that he could never rest happy with a score or a libretto, but would be continually modifying, touching up, correcting and deleting.

Rehearsals were an agony, and the critics' notices a torture in anticipation; he was even said to bribe them lavishly to ensure that these notices should be favourable. But with all that, Meyerbeer was serenely confident that no other living composer could conceivably challenge his pre-eminence—and indeed, so long as he remained in the public eye, no one else could hope to compete. Only Heine asked sardonically: 'When Meyerbeer is dead, who will there be to tend his reputation?' Rossini, the only possible rival, had long since given up the idea of making more music. He lived quietly in a comfortable apartment in Paris, where Meyerbeer would occasionally visit him, for the two musicians were on the friendliest of terms.

Throughout the Second Empire, rumours were current that Meyerbeer had a new opera on the stocks; he was careful not to deny them, since they served to keep alive public interest in his activities. On his death the score was found among his papers; his will provided that the Paris opera company (the Académie de Musique) should have first option on its production. L'Africaine duly had its *première* the year after Meyerbeer's death, April 28th, 1865. It was coolly received—perhaps expectations had been pitched too high—but gradually it made its way and at the end of the Empire was playing to audiences as enthusiastic as those that were applauding, on other evenings, Gounod's *Faust*.

However, if one is looking for the most sensational 'night at the opera' of those years, one is bound to fix on March 13th, 1861, when *Tannhäuser* was given its first performance. Wagner, who had come to Paris the year before, had given a few concerts, and music-lovers had been able to hear excerpts from *The Flying Dutchman* and *Lohengrin* as well as *Tannhäuser*. These specimens of Wagner's art had already started the controversy which was to last for two decades at least. Berlioz, reporting on the scene in the auditorium during the first concert, spoke of 'furious shouting and arguments which seemed perpetually on the verge of turning into a brawl'. Though not a convinced Wagnerian, Berlioz was disagreeably surprised—and not for the first time—at the invincible conservatism of the French in musical matters; the manner in which Wagner's innovations were received was a further proof, he wrote, 'that in our nation at least, when we are asked to appreciate music of a different nature from that to which we are accustomed, passion and prejudice alone are listened to and drown the voices of good sense and good taste.'[13]

Wagner was, however, loyally supported by the German and Austrian colonies in Paris, led by Princess Metternich, the wife of the Austrian ambassador, a lively, cultured, ugly woman, one of the Empress Eugénie's closest friends. She may have been able to exert pressure on the administration of the

Académie de Musique to ensure that, in spite of the undisguised hostility of Meyerbeer, *Tannhäuser* should be produced. Heralded by reports and rumours printed in the newspapers weeks in advance, the first performance gave every promise of being a stormy one. More spectators wished to be present than could be seated; the price of tickets soared; Wagner, optimistically, anticipated a triumph, but Mme de Metternich, rather more mistrustful, had her personal friends and supporters placed at strategic points in the auditorium. These precautions were quite insufficient to avert a disaster. Considerable consternation was caused at the very start when it was discovered that Wagner had placed the ballet in the first act. A third-act ballet was so much part of the French operatic tradition that in normal circumstances probably no new work would have been accepted which did not comply with the convention. The reason was that the men about town who were the patrons of the ballerinas and who had no interest otherwise in operatic productions, never troubled to attend the first two acts. Their disgruntlement, when they arrived to discover they had been cheated of their customary leg-show, can be imagined; it can also be assumed that they were not content simply to swallow their disappointment. They interrupted the performance with jeers and whistles; other members of the audience, already perplexed and restless, began to laugh; and Princess Metternich, glowering impotently in her box, snapped her fan in two in her fury. The next evening the audience was still more hostile; even the presence of the Emperor and Empress did not overawe them, and the last scene was played in an indescribable tumult. On the third night the curtain had to be rung down before the end. The German tenor shook his fist in rage at the audience, and Wagner left the theatre sobbing with disappointment.

In the musical journals, and even in the popular press, a scurrilous campaign against him was waged, with sarcastic caricatures in *Le Charivari* and parodies with punning titles, like *Panne-aux-Airs* which was put on at the Théâtre Déjazet only two weeks after the first performance of *Tannhäuser* at the Opéra.[14] A few brave voices were raised in his defence: Baudelaire published a splendid series of articles in the *Revue européenne* and Catulle Mendès echoed him in the *Revue fantaisiste*. The polemics were destined to continue for many years; Wagner had merely lost the first round in his battle for recognition in France.

Amateur Theatricals

It is sometimes maintained that the exceptional interest displayed during the reign of Napoleon III in all forms of dramatic art—whether straight stage plays, vaudevilles, revues, operatta or opera—by the ruling classes in France and their middle-class sympathizers reflects and betrays at the same time the essentially theatrical, false quality of life under that régime: 'the court in the Tuileries and the world of carousing bankers, dissolute aristocrats, parvenu journalists and pampered beauties had something improbable, something phantom-like and unreal, something ephemeral about it—it was a land of operetta, a stage whose wings threatened to collapse at any moment'.[15] Such an analysis owes much, of course, to the historian's hindsight: Hauser knew when he wrote it that the wings did collapse in 1870. He is right, all the same, in drawing attention to the connection that can be traced between the delight in play-acting and the hidden fragility of the Second Empire which depended so much on a sham re-enactment of the far more solid achievement of the First Empire.

Fashionable society did not merely flock to see professional actors and actresses: it strove to imitate them. The vogue for amateur theatricals was never stronger. Daumier executed a series of 16 brilliant drawings for *Le Charivari* in 1859 satirizing the more ridiculous aspects of this craze, from which one can see that it was by no means unusual for short sketches to be performed of an evening on makeshift stages in quite unpretentious drawing-rooms. The larger the house, of course, the more ambitious the productions. The millionaire Jules de Castellane erected a studio theatre with all the fittings and an auditorium to seat 400 guests in the garden of his house in the Rue St. Honoré, where vaudeville, comedies, even operettas were performed by amateur actors, sometimes with a stiffening of professionals. On occasion, new plays were given their first run here, which might well be their only run, if as often happened they defied the conventions too openly. These private productions were, in effect, a device adopted by people of wealth to circumvent the obstacles raised by a killjoy censorship. The spicier society columns were full, one week in 1856, of rumours of the scandalous *soirée des éventails* when, in front of a full house, the company of the Théâtre Français, hired for the evening by Castellane regardless of expense, performed two new plays, Dumas' *Le Verrou* and Jules Lecomte's *Le Collier*. These were so daringly packed with bold innuendoes and scabrous asides that it seems most of the ladies held their fans before their faces to hide their blushes—unless it were to conceal the fact that they were not blushing.

Another Dumas play served to inaugurate a series of entertainments offered by Delphine and Émile de Girardin. After the curtain had fallen and, in accordance with tradition, the author was summoned to acknowledge the applause, to everyone's surprise it was the author of the *Count of Monte Cristo* who stepped on to the stage. 'It's Dumas the Elder who is the younger of the two', he called out, putting into words what many people had long been thinking privately; and Alexandre Dumas *fils*, whose personal relations with his eminent but rumbustious father were never very easy, pretended not to have heard. But of course Dumas *père* had been one of the leading playwrights in France in the far-off days of swashbuckling romantic melodrama, and his works were not altogether forgotton. The Comte de Béthune organized a sensational private revival of his *Henri* III *et sa cour* in 1862, charging for admission but turning the proceeds over to charity. This started the fashion for benefit performances, and the rage for private theatricals grew even hotter now that the amusement could be colourably excused by the pretence that it was all in a good cause. For society beauties who found it difficult to memorize their lines, the *tableau vivant* was invented as an alternative to the curtain-raiser; the subject was frequently mythological,[16] which permitted them to pose in public without crinolines—and without a great deal else besides. Virginia di Castiglione, erstwhile mistress of Napoleon III, once consented to figure in a *tableau vivant*, but refused to say beforehand in the guise of which classical or historical figure she proposed to appear. This secrecy raised expectations to fever-point, for the Countess de Castiglione was a shapely woman; but the gentlemen's hopes were dashed. She was discovered, when the curtain went up, to be swathed in the disappointingly chaste habit of a nun.

Court Entertainments

The strangest stories were current about the dramatic spectacles staged for the imperial court, whether at Compiègne, the favourite country retreat of Napoleon and Eugénie, or at Fontainebleau: dryads dressed in nothing but a wisp of foliage, Venuses or Phrynes in skin-tight fleshings. In fact, the guests never seem to have been regaled by anything more startling than the sight of some pretty girl holding the pose of the dairymaid in Greuze's *Cruche cassée*. The blameless reputation of the men who regularly directed such artistic entertainments as the court required was in itself sufficient guarantee of their respectability. There was no single master of ceremonies. At various times a helping hand might be lent by a dramatist, Émile Augier, François Ponsard, or Octave Feuillet—whose plays were quite as popular as his novels —or by the ubiquitous director of the Théâtre Français, Arsène Houssaye. Viollet-le-Duc, though heavily committed to the task of carrying out the much-needed restoration of Notre Dame, would sometimes be active behind the scenes. Gounod would now and then oblige with a recital. But nothing in the least 'high-brow' was ever attempted. In a scathing article on the court at Compiègne, Zola observed, with some truth, that only 'entertainers' were ever invited there. 'M. Gustave Doré, a delightful sketcher who is past master at opening a cotillon, represents almost every year the arts. M. Edmond About, a charming story-teller whose dream is to reduce politics to naughty little anecdotes, is present in the name of French literature. Science, naturally, deputizes all those directors and professors whose salaries eat deepest into public funds. It is clear that only the averagely good are ever chosen, firstly because the above-average are unsociable, unapproachable people, and secondly because mediocrities make highly entertaining company. The genius of France can stay at home; Compiègne contents itself with amusing nonentities. Courbet, Hugo, and Littré do not exist for the court, but a great fuss is made of MM. Doré, About, and Le Verrier.'[17]

In public, no doubt, the imperial couple played the part that was expected of them in 'encouraging the arts', opening exhibitions, attending gala performances at the Opera. In accordance with the precedent set by earlier monarchs, Napoleon III made discreet gifts to establishment writers[18] and even paid out small pensions to indigent poets and poetesses who were specially recommended to him: Leconte de Lisle and Louise Colet, among others. On the other hand he ignored the appeal Sainte-Beuve addressed to him privately in 1856 for a large-scale programme of aid to struggling writers, to include the institution of literary prizes. Neither he nor Eugénie felt themselves in the slightest involved in the cultural developments of their time; they devoted no more than the polite attention to the arts that would enable them to pass as enlightened patrons among the uninitiated. The artists themselves were not deceived, and Flaubert, for instance, though he accepted the invitations to Compiègne that came his way, vastly preferred the literary and artistic *soirées* given by Princess Mathilde, the Emperor's cousin, in her house in the Rue de Courcelles or else, in the summer months, in her country retreat at Saint-Gratien; here he would read to her passages from the books he was working on—*Salammbô* or *L'Éducation sentimentale*—something that would have been out of the question at Compiègne, where eating and drinking, dancing and hunting were the principal occupations.

The letters written by Prosper Mérimée to Mme de Montijo and one or two other close friends provide as accurate and candid an account as we have of the cultural level of court life during the Second Empire. The author of *Carmen* occupied a special place in the affections of the Spanish-born Empress Eugénie, who as it happened had known him all her life. A friendship struck up with her father, while both were travelling to Madrid in 1830, had resulted in Mérimée's meeting the other members of the Montijo family.

Eugénie was then a child of four, just of an age to sit on 'Don Prospero's' knee and listen enthralled to the fairy-stories he told her.

Twenty-three years later she married the new Emperor of the French, and so, by a trick of fate, Mérimée found himself a close intimate of his country's new sovereigns, occupying the very position that Hugo had hoped for and might have secured if Princess Helen had become Queen of France.[19] He cannot be accused of having taken undue advantage of the situation. He accepted nomination to the Senate: the functions were largely honorific but the emoluments, 30,000 francs a year, were a welcome supplementation of his modest revenues. It is only fair to add that he continued his useful work as Inspector of Public Monuments, waiving the salary. Had he been a man of ambition rather than an amiable dilettante, he might have played an important part in the nation's affairs; but he resolutely declined all official positions. He was offered, but turned down, the chair of comparative literature at the Collège de France, which the special study he had made of Spanish and Russian literatures amply qualified him to occupy. He was twice proposed for Minister of Education, but on both occasions refused the portfolio. It was generally thought he would be appointed private secretary to the Emperor when the post fell vacant in 1864. *The Times* went so far as to report the appointment as an established fact; but Mérimée preferred to let the post go to another candidate. His sole function, as he himself used to say wrily, was that of court-jester.[20]

This was no sinecure. He found himself constantly on call, whenever dullness threatened to overtake the revellers. But how to keep these people entertained when the amusements considered suitable were so banal, so trivial, so tasteless? What with the eternal party games, the boating trips, the picnics in the woods, it seemed to Mérimée that the sovereigns had no more elevated a notion of recreation than the most dull-witted of Parisian shopkeepers. At the court of Napoleon I they played Corneille; under Napoleon III, the best that could be managed was the stage version of Octave Feuillet's *Roman d'un jeune homme pauvre*. In his letters to Mme de Montijo, who was a cultivated woman of cosmopolitan interests, Mérimée deprecated the low cultural standards prevalent in her daughter's entourage. The most he was ever asked to do was to compose charades, or learn a part in some slight skit written by Morny.

In September 1861 he had to take the train to Biarritz, in response to an urgent telegram. This little seaside town, where from 1838 onwards a colony of Spanish Carlist refugees of good birth had established themselves, was a favourite resort of Eugénie's.[21] She possessed a roomy villa (since demolished) where a select company of guests could enjoy a free-and-easy life untroubled by the niceties of court etiquette. Even practical jokes of doubtful taste were sometimes indulged in. One of Mérimée's letters to Anthony Panizzi, the colourful Italian patriot to whom many generations of readers in the British Museum library have had cause to be grateful, includes an account of one such trick that was played on Mme de la Bédoyère, a lady-in-waiting to the Empress, at a time when Bismarck was staying at the villa. The debonair minister from Berlin had made a strong impression on this good lady; jokingly put on her guard, she refused stoutly to credit the stories told of his profligacy. A conspiracy was thereupon hatched between Napoleon, Eugénie and Mérimée. Mérimée cut out a cardboard dummy head, roughly inked to resemble Bismarck's, and placed it on Mme de la Bédoyère's pillow. The Empress herself tied a nightcap round it and thrust a bolster down the bed. In the half-light the illusion was complete, and Mme de la Bédoyère had no sooner entered her room than she rushed out in alarm—though the joke could not be taken any further, since Eugénie, bursting into peals of laughter at the other end of the corridor, gave the game away.

In such wise did the rulers of the strongest power on the continent of Europe beguile their leisure. One wonders why Mérimée who, at 62, was hardly of the age for such pranks, consented to continue functioning as 'court jester'. Did he hope eventually to educate his hosts? He tried, one summer, to interest them in literature of a rather more elevated sort than they were used to, and, as an experiment, started reading from *Wilhelm Meister*; but Goethe's novel had to be abandoned after the fourth chapter. He then introduced them to Turgenev, whose short stories he had been translating into French; still they fidgeted. Even Musset's comedies proved too taxing, and in despair Mérimée had to fall back on Eugène Suë's *Mystères de Paris* to hold the attention of this linnet-brained, parvenu court. Still, it was a court, and perhaps this was enough—together with the enduring affection he felt for Eugénie de Montijo—to keep Mérimée in attendance, in much the same way as Marcel, in Proust's novel, went on frequenting the Guermantes family, despite their intellectual flabbiness and moral nullity.

Best-selling novelists: Feydeau and Feuillet

Nineteenth-century society, turbulent, materialistic, hard-headed and brash, driving Byron to Missolonghi and Rimbaud to Abyssinia, at no stage provided a very congenial environment for the original artist; but it was never so positively hostile to him as between 1850 and 1870. It is not sufficient to say that cultural standards fell during these two decades; the very criteria by which art is universally judged seem temporarily to have been abandoned.

This was the age of *kitsch*, of elegant rubbish, when agreeable trifles were acclaimed and ruggedly individualistic works of art treated with disdain and even disgust; an age when, outside a tiny, disregarded élite, the public ceased to concern itself with inner meaning and underlying structure and was content to allow itself to be beguiled by surface gloss and lulled by consoling messages. The old barbarians had smashed the statues and burnt the libraries; these new barbarians extolled and purchased pictures of no merit and crowded their theatres to watch the plays of dramatists whose talents were all devoted to providing neat solutions to phoney problems.

It was a society more prosperous than any previous one, in which the writer, particularly, found it harder than ever before to make a living. Though standards of literacy were steadily rising, people were reading less. Writing in the *Revue des Deux Mondes* in 1850, Armand de Pontmartin noted that even established authors like Dumas *père* and George Sand, whose novels under the July Monarchy would have been given an initial printing of 2,000 copies, were now published in first editions of 1,000 copies or less. True, in 1850 the book-trade, like other luxury or semi-luxury industries, was still suffering the after-effects of the dislocation caused by the revolution; the trouble was that it never properly recovered lost ground until well after the establishment of the Third Republic. Previously, spectacular fortunes had been made by authors—by Frédéric Soulié, by Dumas and by Eugène Suë. Victor Hugo had accumulated a very comfortable nest-egg, and so might Balzac have done if he had had a little of Hugo's canniness. Again, in the later 1870s and in the 1880s, writers like Zola and Maupassant were able to grow rich on the proceeds of their works, and numerous others managed well enough on their royalties. But the intervening period was a thin time for men of letters who, unless they had a private income (as did Flaubert and the Goncourts) needed to supplement the meagre payment they received for their literary work with more or less congenial jobs—as librarians, university teachers, or freelance journalists.

There were some best-sellers, of course, one being Hugo's *Les Misérables* (but there were special, political reasons for this), and another, Renan's *Vie de Jésus*. This sympathetic but uncanonical biography of the founder of the Christian religion had an immediate sale of 40,000 copies; the interest it aroused was stimulated in no small measure by gratuitous advertisement-by-denunciation from various fashionable pulpits. Since there were adventitious reasons for the high sales of both these books, neither can count as the typical and representative best-seller of the time.

The sociology of literature has not progressed far enough to permit analysis of the mechanism whereby an averagely mediocre novel can, appearing at the right time, touch some responsive chord in the society into which it is launched and so acquire the precarious status of a book compulsively devoured by an entire generation of readers. Émile de Montégut, the distinguished literary critic on the staff of the *Revue des Deux Mondes* at the time, explained the huge popularity of Ernest Feydeau's novel *Fanny* when it appeared in 1858, by suggesting that it should be regarded as 'the concentrated expression of the tendencies literature has been developing in recent times. In this little phial are bottled all the more or less pernicious essences of works that have won applause over the past ten years. It has everything: the affectation of a moral purpose, lascivious crudeness, sexually stimulating descriptive passages, the idolatry of matter.'[22] No reader today should go to the considerable trouble of locating or acquiring a copy of Feydeau's pseudo-masterpiece in the hope of finding in it what Montégut did. The point he was trying, obliquely, to make was that Feydeau's novel was simply Flaubert's *Madame Bovary* rehashed in a more succinct and accessible form. The words he uses to stigmatize *Fanny* had been used by Pinard to denounce Flaubert's novel the previous year; it is certain that *Fanny* was regarded by many of its purchasers as a pendant to *Madame Bovary*, even if it cannot be satisfactorily demonstrated that Feydeau deliberately tried to exploit Flaubert's *succès de scandale*.

As to the violent interest provoked by *Fanny*, Flaubert himself testified that cab-drivers at Rouen, sitting on their boxes, were to be seen reading it while waiting for a fare; he also recounts how a young man, finding the book in the hands of his fiancée, promptly broke off the engagement. *Fanny* went through 30 editions with astounding rapidity; Sainte-Beuve called it one of the bibles of the time, and the author grew so insufferably conceited that Baudelaire observed sorrowfully that even Victor Hugo seemed quite modest by comparison. 'I should hesitate less to call Hugo an ass than to say to Feydeau: You are not invariably sublime.'

The strangest thing about *Fanny* is that it should have been commonly regarded by contemporaries as a product of the realist movement: Gustave Merlet, for instance, coined the phrase 'the realism of fashionable corruption' to describe Feydeau's manner. Yet his characters, their emotions, and the situations in which Feydeau places them are so exceptional that we should today be inclined to classify the novel as the work not of a realist but of a dyed-in-the-wool romantic alert enough to profit from the greater licence won for writers by the successful publication of *Madame Bovary*: a sort of literary sheep in wolf's clothing, in other words. By none of the usual tests does *Fanny* qualify in the least as a work of realism. Feydeau did not provide it with even the most tenuous links with the social reality of his time. Roger, the hero, is a young man with, one gathers, a fair private fortune; he is following no career, he appears accountable to no one, and he has no family ties; there is never any mention of his father, though he frequently alludes to his mother whose memory he worships. Fanny's husband is a self-made man, but we never learn the nature of his business. The failure of an English banking-house at one point puts his affairs in jeopardy and necessitates an absence abroad highly convenient to the guilty pair; but the details of his financial difficulties, which Balzac would not have failed to give us, are withheld—though Feydeau, who had made a career for himself in banking and stockbroking, was quite as well equipped as Balzac to provide them. Fanny herself is a character who baffles Roger, the narrator. 'It had been ordained', he writes, 'that everything in our story would be strange, and that I should never understand anything in the conduct of the woman I loved.' But one should not be misled into thinking that Feydeau had created one more *femme fatale* to be added to the long catalogue which the literature of France in his century affords. The experienced reader sees nothing whatsoever incomprehensible in Fanny's conduct. She is a married woman with a young family, in whose interest it is vital that she should continue to enjoy the respect which society will accord her so long as she does not openly defy its conventions. At the same time, being a healthy woman in her late thirties, she is very understandably drawn to the much younger Roger with whom she can revel in the palpitating excitements of an illicit affair.

Viewed realistically, then, the situation is quite unremarkable. But, of course, as Feydeau presents it, it is very far from being viewed realistically, since the 'pseudo-confessional' form which he has elected to use and which is meant to illuminate the situation actually prevents the reader from focusing on it. Roger, who relates the events, is much too close to them to reflect them dispassionately; he is, moreover, much too intimately involved with Fanny to appreciate the dilemma in which she finds herself. For him it is unimaginable that any woman should freely consent to share herself between two men, pretending to each of them that her relations with the other are innocent. When he is finally compelled, by the evidence of his own eyes, to acknowledge the truth, the precarious equilibrium which this web of deception and self-deception had established is destroyed; he breaks down, runs away, and the affair is over.

This culminating episode is the so-called 'balcony scene'. Roger, having rented a house next door, steals into the garden of his mistress's home, climbs up to where he can look through the window into a first-floor room, and watches an intimate scene between Fanny and her husband. It was this scene of involuntary *voyeurism* that turned the book into a best-seller. Novels, like

17　Manet, *La Musique aux Tuileries*

18 Ingres, *La Source*. Completed in 1856, this work shows what could still be achieved within the framework of the academicism against which the realists were reacting

Fanny, which attain a temporary celebrity that cannot otherwise be accounted for, will often be found to embody a dramatization of some generalized neurosis of which their readers were at the time largely unconscious. Today we can recognize without difficulty in Feydeau's 'balcony scene' one of the fundamental 'primal scenes' with which modern investigations into human psychology have made us familiar: the child who spies on his father and mother as they are making love. The three actors fit their parts with an almost uncanny precision. Fanny is constantly calling Roger her child, and he tends to confuse her with his dead mother. His behaviour towards her is less that of a man in love than of a petulant, egoistic, over-possessive child; and this corresponds with her own attitude towards him, which is that of an over-indulgent mother, inclining to spoil him. Fanny's husband, finally, is depicted as a large-limbed, self-assured, virile man, older than both Roger and Fanny, capable, inscrutable, a little crude at times, at times a little cruel: a being whom Roger hates, fears, and secretly admires all at once.

There is no obvious reason why this close identification of the three characters with their traditional roles in a timeless psychodrama should conflict with the value of the book as a work of art. One must look at other features and aspects of the novel to discover why *Fanny* should have fallen into the limbo that awaits works which, after a sensational start, reveal themselves as deficient in the mysterious germ that permits survival and so turn out to be the stuff not of literature, but of literary history. For a start, Feydeau adopted a style which, even in 1858, had a distinctly 'period' flavour. Different in this from Constant's *Adolphe*, which by its form it distantly resembles, the book is full of eloquent periods and high-sounding rhetoric; the style is what Stendhal would have called *chateaubrillanté*. Heavy use is made of such outmoded devices as the pathetic fallacy and the introduction of inexplicable premonitions. A gallop through the night, for instance, is described as no one, probably, had described it for 30 years or more:

The moon illuminated obliquely the quiet road I was following, laying ribbons of silver across it and appearing to turn and watch me with its pallid, melancholy stare. The trees filed past me on either side, swift and black like spectres drawn along in a dangerous dance. The dogs sleeping in the courtyards leapt barking to the gates at the frenzied sound of my horse's hooves clattering over the pavement. And the wind that whipped at my face was whispering exciting encouragements in my ear. Everything spurred me forward, foretelling some drama in which I was to play a part.

L

Even if it were possible to accept this kind of writing as appropriate in a novel purporting to represent a contemporary domestic tragedy, it would still be hard to excuse Feydeau for using it as a substitute for the psychological notation that his subject clearly demands. Jealousy is his theme; jealousy is the primary, and indeed the only emotion he deals with; but nothing in its nature is made any clearer to us by the analysis he provides. No analysis is, in fact, provided: the passion of jealousy is treated simply as a pretext for Roger's lamentations and imprecations. But at the same time, the very shrillness with which he gives voice to his grief and fury encourages us to draw certain conclusions about Roger himself: that he is puerile in his reactions, self-pitying in his reflections, and above all a dangerous menace to the woman he loves. Our sympathy, which Feydeau unquestionably intended Roger should have the benefit of, is only too likely to be enlisted instead on Fanny's account.

Feydeau was never able to repeat the success of *Fanny*. His next novel, *Daniel* (1859), was even more blatantly byronic, and fell decidedly flat. *Catherine d'Overmeire* (1860) represented a more serious effort to comply with the realistic standards of the day; the character of Marcel, the young painter, makes it possible to regard this book as one of the first in the series of *romans d'art* which, appearing round about this period, combine to form a panoramic vista of the life of artists' cafés and studios during the important period that marked the emergence of the Impressionists.[23] Feydeau wrote and published these books in haste to justify the expectations of his admirers; he succeeded only in disappointing them. Sainte-Beuve, in particular, was most embarrassed at the way matters had turned out, and when, in 1862, Flaubert published *Salammbô*, he tried to blame his earlier erroneous judgment on Flaubert's slowness:

> A writer of talent, but of minor talent, coming after M. Flaubert and following in his footsteps, gave the impression briefly that he would draw down on his own head all that storm of argument and polemics that the former had provoked [with *Madame Bovary*]. Around the name of M. Feydeau a furious discussion developed which would have been more justifiably aroused by another work from the pen of M. Flaubert; but since it failed to appear and the author kept his public and the critical world waiting, they seized instead on the book [*Fanny*] which appeared in its stead and which in some measure usurped its place.[24]

Critics who deal with the contemporary scene are constantly risking these misadventures.

Although Feydeau, in this way, managed to get himself talked about, he was not altogether typical of the successful Second-Empire novelist, accepted and adulated in the fashionable *salons* of the capital as well as in the more conservative drawing-rooms of quiet provincial towns. Eugène Fromentin might have filled the part, except that he was too well-known as a painter and art-critic ever to be regarded as anything else; his one and only novel, *Dominique* (1863), was bound to be regarded as a little *en marge*. Instead, it fell to Octave Feuillet to maintain and strengthen the tradition of the *roman mondain*, the well-mannered novel in which passions are always tempered with politeness and everyone moves in an ideal world of rectitude and disinterestedness whose orbit hardly seems to intersect with that of the *fête impériale*. And yet Feuillet was deeply implicated in this *fête*, being as frequent a visitor to Compiègne as Mérimée, and in some ways better appreciated there than the older writer; with his blond beard and blue eyes, his dignity and tact, he cut almost as distinguished a figure as one of the heroes of his own novels. He had an additional advantage over Mérimée in that he was married, and married to a woman as delicately nurtured and with as fine a sensibility as any that he put into his books.

His first novel, *Le Roman d'un jeune homme pauvre*, was an instant success. Its sales in the first year of publication (1858) equalled those attained a little later by Renan's *Vie de Jésus*: 40,000 copies. The following year, the dramatized version of the novel proved just as successful: during its first run, there were evenings when as many as five hundred would-be spectators were turned away from the doors. The secret of Feuillet's popularity was the intriguing mixture in his work of a familiar, though by now somewhat dated elegance with a discreet didacticism which, however, happily dispensed with explicit sermonizing. The lesson readers could draw from *Le Roman d'un jeune homme pauvre* was that rigid adherence to old-fashioned standards of chivalry and honour would be rewarded in this world with the rewards that this world has to offer. This was, whatever the sceptics might say, an encouraging message.

If ever a novelist deserved to be called an idealist, it was Octave Feuillet; and yet such was the prestige of realism in the 1860s that even he felt it necessary to pay lip-service, in the opening chapter of the second part of his *Monsieur de Camors* (1867), to the doctrine of sincerity in art. It is true that the version of realism to which he here subscribed was not to be identified with Champfleury's, Duranty's, or Flaubert's. Addressing his women readers, Feuillet begged them 'not to flinch if the truth, as it may be encountered any day in society, stands revealed in these pages in stark colours, even though toned down. One must love the truth: one must veil it, but not emasculate it. The ideal is itself no more than the truth decked in the trappings of art. The novelist knows he has no right to misrepresent his age; but he has the right to depict it, or he has no rights at all. As for his duty, he believes it to consist in keeping his moral judgement inflexible and his pen chaste however delicate the scenes he may portray.' This declaration of principles represents perhaps the extreme limit to which a writer might go in the direction of realism without compromising his status as a fashionable novelist.

Monsieur de Camors, a longer work than *Le Roman d'un jeune homme pauvre*, is also a stronger one. Feuillet imagined the case of a man who, in order to make his way in the world, in order to acquire a fortune and become a person of consequence, makes a deliberate attempt to crush every moral scruple except such as are dictated by the sense of honour, that treasured apanage of the old nobility. 'Avail yourself without compunction of women for pleasure, of men for power; but do nothing base. . . . '; this death-bed advice of his father's is what the young Camors does his best to put into practice; he wants to repeat, in the nineteenth century, the career of Molière's 'grand seigneur méchant homme' in the seventeenth. He fails, of course, largely because of the difficulty he finds in being dissolute without being dishonourable, unprincipled and yet not ignoble. He seduces the wife of an old friend who trusts and admires him; tries to stifle his guilt-feeling in a low orgy and, returning home at daybreak, pays a rag-picker a hundred francs to strike him across the face. In this rather remarkable (unfortunately rather exceptional) early episode of his book Feuillet seems almost to foreshadow Dostoevsky.

Constantly, Camors is tripped up by an inbred respect for values which, privately, he has decided are meaningless prejudices. Either he is assailed by immediate remorse after committing some act of wickedness, or else he desists from his bad purpose out of compassion for his intended victim. The book has been compared to *Les Liaisons dangereuses*: in reality, Camors has nothing like Valmont's unflinching determination to triumph over the defences of innocence, nor does his feminine ally, Mme de Campvallon, possess either the intelligence or the ruthlessness of Laclos' Marquise de Merteuil.

From the ethical point of view, the novel resolves itself into a critique of the code of honour when this code is not subordinated to, and dictated by, religious principles. The lesson Feuillet is at pains to teach is that it is not enough to be a gentleman, one must be a Christian gentleman. As the Comtesse de Camors says to her husband: 'I imagine that honour divorced from morals is no great thing, and that morals divorced from religion are nothing at all. All these are linked in a chain together: honour hangs from the last ring like a flower; but, if the chain is broken, the flower falls with the rest.' So far so good, but one might be forgiven, reading Feuillet, for deducing equally that it is not enough to be a Christian unless one is a gentleman as well. Almost the only prominent character in *Monsieur de Camors* who is not well-born or well-connected—Camors' secretary, Vautrot—is also almost the only character guilty of really underhand dealing. All the others stand a little above ordinary humanity. Criminals they may be, but never cads; and when they sin, it is in the name of Lucifer rather than in the name of Mephistopheles.

That Feuillet should choose to deal exclusively with members of the upper classes is not in itself a weakness: Proust did very much the same thing. But whereas Proust brought to bear on the Guermantes circle a dispassionately critical gaze, charged with the irony of cool appraisal, Feuillet judged his gentry with unfailing indulgence. Only when they disappoint him by derogating from the principle of *noblesse oblige* do his critical faculties come into play; and even then, how circumspect, how apologetic even is his indictment! Camors' villainy is all but wiped out by his courtesy.

During their short period of popularity, both Feydeau and Feuillet won every kind of honour and financial gratification because in their separate ways both provided the middle-class reader with the kind of fare he craved for most: not strong meat, but meat served up with an agreeably piquant sauce, easily digestible if a little cloying. It was the kind of cultural nourishment that would not keep anyone awake at night or give anyone bad dreams. As it happened, in the same year that Feuillet published *Monsieur de Camors*, Zola brought out his first naturalistic masterpiece, *Thérèse Raquin*, designed, in his own words, to 'give all Paris nightmares'. Whether or not the book achieved this declared purpose, it is curious that the spiritually-minded Feuillet, setting out to describe the career of a man who deliberately tries to regulate his life on the principles of atheistic materialism, succeeded in conveying nothing like the same impression of the reality of moral evil as did Zola, the declared materialist and agnostic. Great literature and poor literature alike spring from other sources than the philosophical intentions of their creators.

Notes

1 '*Urbem ... excoluit adeo, ut iure sit gloriatus marmoream se relinquere, quam latericiam accepisset*' (he wrought such improvements in the city, that he could rightly boast that he left it marble, having found it brick). This sentence of Suetonius was frequently applied by his flatterers to Napoleon III.

[2] Thus, in the eighth chapter of Zola's *L'Assommoir*, Gervaise and Goujet, a laundress and an iron-worker, wander up to Montmartre and discover, 'between a mechanical sawmill and a button factory, a strip of meadow still green, with yellow patches of burnt grass: a goat, tied to a post, tramped round it, bleating: beyond, one dead tree was disintegrating in the shushine. "It's a fact", Gervaise murmured, "you could practically imagine you were in the country".'

[3] These were not a Second-Empire invention: they had been created in the mid 1830s by one of Haussmann's predecessors, Rambuteau. They were named after the Emperor Vespasian (A.D. 9–79), credited with having erected the first public urinals in Rome.

[4] 'Les Yeux des Pauvres', *Nouvelle Revue de Paris*, December 25, 1864.

[5] Now the Avenue Foch.

[6] 'A Few Days in Paris, by John Brown, shopkeeper', *Tait's Edinburgh Magazine*, August 1855; *Saturday Review*, September 7th, 1867. Both quoted in F. C. Green, *A Comparative View of French and British Civilization* (1965), pp. 113–14.

[7] David H. Pinkney, *Napoleon III and the rebuilding of Paris* (Princeton, N.J., 1958), p. 219.

[8] 'Le Cygne', *Les Fleurs du Mal*, LXXXIX.

[9] Merimée, *Correspondance générale*, 2e série (Toulouse, Privat, 1559) VII, 629.

[10] See above, p. 44.

[11] Appropriately called the Salle Lacage.

[12] She was Zola's principal model for the character of Nana. Two contemporary memorialists (Jacques Mardoche and Pierre Desgenais) summed up the difference between her and Hortense Schneider as follows: 'Mlle Schneider was exciting, modern, ironic, the froth of champagne. Blanche d'Antigny . . . represented the apotheosis of Matter' (quoted by Joanna Richardson, *The Courtesans* (1967), p. 20).

[13] *Le Journal des Débats*, Feb. 9th, 1860. Reprinted in Berlioz, *A travers chants, études musicales* (1862), pp. 291, 292.

[14] See André Ferran, 'Tannhäuser à l'Opéra de Paris: caricatures et parodies', pp. 189–197 in *Mélanges d'histoire littéraire offerts à Daniel Mornet* (Paris, 1951).

[15] Arnold Hauser, *The Social History of Art* (New York, 1952) p. 806.

[16] Maxime and Renée, in Zola's *La Curée*, are principal actors in a *tableau vivant* called *Les Amours du beau Narcisse et de la nymphe Echo*.

[17] *La Tribune*, Nov. 22nd, 1868. Le Verrier, the mathematician (1811–77), had made his name in 1846 with the discovery (inferred from irregularities in the orbit of Uranus) of the planet Neptune.

[18] Thus, Ponsard received a gratuity of 25,000 francs in 1858, paid out of the Emperor's privy purse.

[19] See above, p. 13

[20] When he sent the bound manuscript of his story *La Chambre bleue* to Empress Eugénie, he wrote on the fly-leaf: '*Composé et écrit par Prosper Mérimée, fou de S.M. l'Impératrice.*'

[21] It was, of course, much later (from 1889 onwards) that Queen Victoria and,

subsequently, Edward VII started the fashion of spending the season at Biarritz, drawing thither the cream of London society.

[22] *Revue des Deux Mondes*, vol. XVIII (1858), p. 200.

[23] The series includes the Goncourt's *Manette Salomon* (1867) and Zola's *L'Œuvre* (1886), besides others largely forgotten today: see Theodore R. Bowie, *The Painter in French Fiction* (Chapel Hill: University of North Carolina Press, 1950).

[24] Sainte-Beuve, *Nouveaux lundis*, vol. IV (Paris, 1865), p. 33.

The Artist as Pariah

Manet and the 'Salon des Refusés'

The untidy studios and noisy cafés in which the Paris *rapins* worked and met for relaxation were the scene of unusual excitement one spring day in 1863 as creased and beer-stained copies of the official newspaper, *Le Moniteur universel*, were passed from hand to hand. Down one column of the issue for April 24th was a bald announcement to the effect that the Emperor, having noted with pain the loud and frequent complaints made by painters whose submissions to the Salon were rejected, had decided that special provision should be made for those whose entries had fallen below the standards required by the judges, but who wished them to be exhibited nonetheless. Such pictures would be hung, separately from the others and at a slightly later date, in an annex of the Palais de l'Industrie, so as to give the public the opportunity to decide for itself whether the dissatisfaction voiced by disappointed competitors was justified.

These were the circumstances in which the celebrated Salon des Refusés was called into being. It was an imaginative attempt to defuse an explosive situation. Over the previous years, irritation at the obstructionist policies of the academic jury had been mounting. The news that in 1863 it was rejecting 2,800 out of the 5,000 works submitted precipitated a crisis. There was a general feeling that the average standard of accomplishment could not possibly be as low as the figure for rejections suggested. Louis Martinet, a dealer with a gallery conveniently situated in the fashionable Boulevard des Italiens, had offered, only ten days before Napoleon III's sensational decision was made public, to show a proportion of the canvases declared inadmissible by the jury; he could not show them all, his premises not being large enough, so he coupled this offer with the warning that he would not be prepared to extend facilities to 'mediocre' artists. The implication was that he was setting himself up as a one-man jury; even so, most of the innovating artists of the time would have preferred to trust his judgement rather than that of the herd of bald-headed pachyderms at the Institut led by the egregious Signol. Martinet had already demonstrated his liberalism by arranging an exhibition of 14 of Manet's paintings in his gallery during the months of February and March. The pictures included the notorious *Musique aux Tuileries*, an *œuvre de combat* which delighted the few eager youngsters, like Claude Monet, who saw it, and even caught the fancy of the old revolutionary Eugène Delacroix, who exclaimed loudly in the hearing of the scoffing bystanders that he was sorry his failing health did not allow him to attend the meetings of the *salon* jury and speak up in favour of Manet.

La *Musique aux Tuileries*, now in the National Gallery, had been executed in 1860. The scene it depicts, one of the open-air concerts that were popular at the time, had as it happens inspired a few poignant lines in one of Baudelaire's prose poems, 'Les Veuves'. Manet's pictorial representation must have been composed at very nearly the same time as Baudelaire's poetic record, and the connection between these two works, each an outstanding specimen of its particular medium, is rendered all the closer by the fact that the poet's features are recognizable in one of the figures in the foreground of Manet's canvas.[1] Baudelaire himself was not enthralled by the picture, though it may have been he who urged the artist to attempt the subject. But he was sufficiently impressed by another work by Manet in Martinet's exhibition, the portrait of the Spanish ballet-dancer Lola de Valence, to compose a quatrain in honour of this *bijou rose et noir*.

Zola reported that 'an exasperated art-lover went so far as to threaten to take violent action if La *Musique aux Tuileries* was allowed to stay any longer in the exhibition-hall.'[2] In the 'sixties, Manet was the biggest thorn of all in the flesh of a philistine public and, for that very reason, the hero and the reluctant standard-bearer of the *avant-garde*. This unwanted apotheosis had begun long before the first Salon des Refusés, when his *Buveur d'absinthe* was rejected by the jury of the 1859 *salon*. Manet painted this canvas partly with the intention of signifying his emancipation from the tutelage of Thomas Couture, whose student he had been for six unprofitable years until, in 1856, he left to embark on a tour of the European art-galleries. The picture still bore traces of Couture's influence, as Baudelaire was astute enough to see, but was all the same sufficiently defiant in conception to cause the gruff old master to lose his temper when he visited Manet's studio to view it. 'My dear fellow', said Couture, 'there's only one absinthe drinker here, and that's the painter who perpetrated this monstrosity.' Couture, who was a member of the jury, refused to vote for his pupil's work; on this occasion, both

Whistler and Fantin were similarly denied the official stamp of approval. The art students, enraged by these rejections, demonstrated in front of the Institut, and the police had to be called in to disperse the little band of rowdy protestors whistling under Nieuwerkerke's windows.

Manet himself stayed aloof from this and all other public manifestations of rebelliousness. His was a curious case: he had all the instincts of the career artist without the ability to distort his native talent and dilute the acid of his temperament so as to accommodate his art to the exigencies of the academic formula. He came from a prosperous middle-class family and would have liked nothing better than to justify their expectations. His considerable private fortune allowed him to dress like any other wealthy young dandy of his age, and to take his refreshment at the fashionable Café Tortoni; it would not have occurred to Manet to allow himself to be seen at such bohemian establishments as the Brasserie des Martyrs where Courbet at this time kept court. His closest friend among the painters was Degas (Edgar de Gas, as the name was then written), another young man of independent means whose work, at this period, was almost conventional, consisting for the most part in family portraits and historical scenes. Only quite recently had Degas' association with Duranty propelled him in the direction of modernism, which for a brief period resulted in a curious mixture of styles: the subject of his *Jeunes Spartiates s'exerçant à la lutte* (1860), another of the National Gallery's treasures, was obviously derived from Plutarch; but the foreground figures wear an incongruously contemporary appearance, attributable to the care that Degas took to reproduce realistically the plebeian faces and skinny frames of the Montmartre slum children whom he seems to have used as models for his Lacedaemonian gymnasts.

In 1861 the patience with which Manet had accepted his rebuff at the previous *salon* was seemingly rewarded: his *Chanteur espagnol* was accepted (along with a portrait of his father and mother), and attracted such favourable notice that it was moved from the spot near the ceiling where it had first been hung and given a place of honour in the centre of a panel. Gautier ventured to give it as his opinion that the artist had 'a great deal of talent'; when the awards were made, Manet was given an honourable mention.

It is not certain that he was altogether gratified when a deputation of young painters subsequently visited his studio to congratulate him; but the gesture was well meant, and their jubilation very understandable. The natural restlessness of youth, forever seeking what is new, was at this point in history reinforced by the unformulated conviction that art was on the threshold of unimaginable developments—in style, technique, and subject-

matter. The invincible inertia of the guardians of public taste—the members
of the Institut—continued to dam the mounting flood of innovation seeking
an outlet. The authorities could sense the growing irritation of the new
generation and tried to react in the time-honoured way by clamping down
on what they regarded as unseemly ebullience. Count Alexandre Walewski,
one of the first Napoleon's bastards and Minister of State to the third
Napoleon, gave no encouragement at all to the fractious young rebels who
were no longer disposed docilely to submit to the dispiriting dogmatism of
the École des Beaux-Arts. In the customary speech which he delivered at the
award-giving ceremony that year (July 3rd, 1861), he posed the rhetorical
question: 'Should it be encouraged or discouraged, this tumultuous throng
that pours along all the avenues of free art, spurred on by youthful exuber-
ance and fond hopes?' If it were left to the individual artist to pronounce on
his own merits, few indeed would have the modesty and honesty to admit
that they had been lured into attempting work for which they lacked the
talent. It was therefore a positive duty, 'for those entrusted with the mission
of supervising the progress of arts and letters, to struggle courageously
against false gods, even if these have the advantage of a temporary popularity
and are worshipped by a misguided public.' Walewski, in his peroration,
urged the members of the *salon* jury not to shrink from fulfilling their clear
obligations. 'Do not allow yourselves to be deterred', he told them, 'by those
incessant, trite laments which the strong never utter, since they are the means
by which the weak console themselves.'[3]

In view of the inflexibly reactionary stand of his minister, it is all the more
surprising that when the time for the next *salon* came round, two years
later, Napoleon III, shifting his chair Canute-like further up the beach, should
have left Walewski standing where he was to get his feet wetted in the rising
tide. The Emperor's decision to institute experimentally a Salon des Refusés
remains mysterious, like many another *proprio motu* issuing from the cabinet
of this quirky but well-meaning autocrat. That he was actuated by a sincere
conviction that good pictures were being excluded from the *salon* for no
sound reason is inherently improbable. There is no evidence that the patron
of Cabanel was any more reliable a judge of painting than his predecessor on
the throne.[4] But like all usurpers Napoleon III was careful about his popular
image, and he may have seen an opportunity to earn himself rather cheaply
the reputation of a liberal-minded and enlightened ruler. According to the
story that gained common credence, what happened was that when the
Emperor, accompanied by an aide, took his customary walk on the morning
of April 20th, he bent his steps in the direction of the Palais de l'Industrie,
went inside, viewed a few of the pictures that had already been hung, then

passed on to the sorte-room where the rejected canvases were stacked in readiness to be returned to their owners. His indifferent or untutored eye could detect little difference between what had been admitted by the jury and what had been eliminated. He returned to the Tuileries and issued his edict.

The historical importance of the Salon des Refusés lies in the fact that, for the first time, the public at large was invited to make explicit its own likes and dislikes in art, instead of merely exercising its discrimination among painters previously screened by the Institut. The task of appreciation became more complicated. This change was, of course, in line with emergent developments in the functioning of the art market, as the old system of state patronage was at first supplemented and then all but replaced by a new network of enlarged private patronage. But it was not merely the consumer who was put on his mettle: the primary producer too was faced with an unfamiliar problem. Each individual artist was henceforth obliged to opt between continuing as a potential client of the state-patronage system, or else throwing in his lot with the independents. The original announcement in Le Moniteur made it clear that any rejected artist who preferred not to exhibit in the Salon des Refusés was free to withdraw his work; and many did so, realizing that otherwise they ran the risk of being blackballed by future juries for their act of defiance.[5] Those who were prepared to accept this risk, and whose works were accordingly displayed when the Salon des Refusés opened, included a handful only of talented men besides Manet: Pissarro, Jongkind, Whistler, Guillaumin and Cézanne. The great majority, unfortunately, were painters of no talent at all; daubs certainly outnumbered the good pictures hidden there and made it that much harder to identify and appreciate them.

Cool appraisal was rendered all the more difficult by the outrageously derisive behaviour of the huge crowds who filed in to stare and mock.[6] One eye-witness, Émile Zola, in a work written many years after the event, put on record his recollection of the opening day, perhaps slightly contaminated by the memory of numerous subsequent occasions in the 1870s when the exhibitions of the independents were marked by similar disgraceful scenes. L'Œuvre is, admittedly, a fiction, but one more solidly based on verifiable fact than most, even in Zola's output. In the fifth chapter of the novel the hero, Claude Lantier, goes along to the Salon des Refusés to see how his picture is being received by the public. This picture, called Plein air, bears a strong resemblance in subject and composition to Manet's Déjeuner sur l'herbe (which was catalogued as Le Bain in the real Salon des Refusés). This is how the scene appears to Lantier:

As soon as the visitors came through the doorway, he saw their jaws open, their eyes pucker up, their faces swell, and heard the heavy snorts of stout men, the rusty grating of thin men, topped by the shrill, fluty squeaks of the women. In front of him young fops were leaning against the wall, squirming as if their ribs were being tickled. One lady had just collapsed on to a bench, her knees pressed together, suffocating, trying to get her breath back, her face buried in her handkerchief. Rumours about this comical picture must have been spreading, people were storming in from every corner of the exhibition hall, arriving in droves, pushing and shoving, anxious not to miss the fun. 'Where is it?'—'There, you see!'— 'God, what a joke!' And the witticisms flew thicker and faster than anywhere else, it was the subject, in particular, that provoked the merriment: they didn't understand, they thought it crazy, fit to make you laugh yourself sick. 'Tell you what it is, the lady is too hot, while the gentleman has put on his corduroy jacket in case he catches cold.'—'No, she's blue already, the fellow's just fished her out of a pond, and he's resting some way off, holding his nose.' . . . It was turning into a scandal, the crowd kept growing bigger, the faces reddening in the warmth of the room, each with the round, stupid mouth of the ignoramus pronouncing judgement on art, all of them together uttering every idiotic remark, incongruous reflection, inane and malevolent guffaw that the sight of an original work can arouse in the vacant mind of the bourgeois.

It is arguable that *Le Déjeuner sur l'herbe* was the first truly modern painting, even though it is very much a museum picture in inspiration: the critics of the time thought it had been modelled on Giorgione's *Pastoral Concert* which Manet had undoubtedly seen in the Louvre, but the arrangement and poses of the figures suggest rather a copy of part of Raphael's *Judgement of Paris*, which the artist had not seen but of which he had an engraving to hand. The novelty lay in the treatment: in the absence of half-tones, in Manet's technique of indicating shapes by opposing colours instead of separating them by lines in the prescribed manner; in his bold concentration on the pallor of the woman's body in the very centre of the canvas, forming so startling a contrast with the darkness of the trees and the men's clothing, while at the same time this bright vision was refreshingly balanced on one side by the patch of sunlit water and the flesh-tints and white shift of the second girl, and on the other by the array of bright colours in the left foreground provided by the big straw hat lying on the grass and the basket of fruit negligently scattering its contents over the discarded clothing. All this was staggeringly new, a revelation to the few who had eyes to see. But those few were for the most part inarticulate painters; one critic only, it appears, Zacharie Astruc, was prepared to give Manet his due as providing 'the *éclat*, the inspiration, the powerful flavour, the surprise' of the *salon*. Mostly the critics stopped short at the subject, which shocked them because they could not interpret it in the way they were accustomed to interpret a picture involving human figures. The habit of looking for references outside the frontiers of the self-contained work, which was basically the *littérateur*'s way of appreciating a foreign medium, was still almost universal and affected even the judgement of so skilled a critic as Castagnary who, for example, chose to write of Whistler's *Girl in White* (also exhibited in the Salon des Refusés) as though the artist had intended to depict the emotions of a young woman the morning after her bridal night. Such an approach to *Le Déjeuner sur l'herbe* was bound to lead to bafflement. Literally interpreted, the scene was immodest if not downright improper (the Empress Eugénie passed by, it was said, with eyes modestly averted). The expression on the faces of the three main figures was at once self-conscious and inscrutable. It was all too obvious that Manet was not interested in them as human beings, but only as coloured shapes forming part of a broadly decorative composition. But years needed to elapse before this unpalatable fact could be accepted and digested. In the meantime, the most charitable explanation that contemporary critics could offer was that Manet was misguidedly seeking notoriety by producing paintings deliberately designed to outrage the ordinary, middle-class *père de famille*. Nothing could, in fact, have been further from the truth: Manet wanted only to be accepted on his merits, which were outstanding but of so unusual a kind that they eluded recognition.

The Salon des Refusés as a whole was widely judged to have vindicated the Academy. Some critics forbore disdainfully even to allude to it,[7] thereby justifying the name 'Salon des Parias' given it by Louis Leroy. Others held that its only value had been to prove that complaints about the jury's severity had been altogether baseless: on the contrary, remarked Du Camp, the public owed that much maligned committee a debt of gratitude for sparing them in previous years the sight of so many lamentable abortions. Both Du Camp and Louis Énault (writing respectively in the *Revue des Deux Mondes* and the *Revue française*) protested hypocritically at the cruelty involved in exposing such artistic aberrations to the mockery of the crowd: it was a reversion to the bad old days when lunatics were exhibited in fairgrounds.

On the other hand, the Emperor's liberal gesture could not be reversed: the absolutism of the Institut, already weakened by Courbet's successful campaign of defiance over the previous 14 years, had suffered a further blow.

From then on, wavering between policies of indulgence and renewed severity, its edicts failing more and more to command assent, it became increasingly an embarrassment to the central authority until finally, in 1881, the state expressly relinquished all control of the annual *salon*, arrangements for which were henceforth left entirely in the hands of the artists' own professional society. A whole generation had to pass, however, before this final solution was reached. In the meantime the independent artists could draw comfort from the fact that their works had at least been hung and had been seen by thousands. Moreover, it appeared that the government was genuinely disposed to improve their opportunities of making contact with the public. A decree promulgated on June 24th, 1863, making the *salon* once more an annual, instead of a biennial event, gave deep satisfaction to con-servatives and revolutionaries alike: at a stroke the possibilities of exhibiting were doubled. The news that the hated Count Walewski had resigned delighted the 'pariahs' even more. A group of daring art students succeeded in smuggling into the Palais de l'Industrie a man-size cardboard cross, painted black and bearing an inscription in large white letters: 'Here lies the Jury of the Institute'. They set it up at the entry to the annex where the Salon des Refusés was housed and began a mock-solemn funeral chant, until the custodians, alerted by the hubbub, rushed out and drove them away. But the students kept their cross and when, later in the year, the Institut was stripped of its ancient right to judge submissions, this duty being assigned instead to an elected jury, they took it out of its hiding-place, set it up on the embankment opposite the Institut building, and performed a grotesque war-dance round it.

The Impressionists before Impressionism

Manet, we may be sure, neither encouraged nor participated in these un seemly street demonstrations. Proud, retiring, and sensitive, he stood quit aloof at this time from the younger intransigents who nevertheless regarded him as their champion. Though he craved recognition all his life, he wanted it to come through the recognized channels and from the recognized pundits. No matter what rebuffs he endured, he went on submitting his works to the *salon* and persistently refused to join with the independents when they organized their own exhibitions after the war. He envied the facility of second-rate painters like Carolus-Duran who were 'taken up' by fashionable society, and was never so pleased as he was when, in 1873, his jolly portrait of the engraver Bellot hiding behind a tankard of beer won general acclaim. Even though, after 1870, he altered his style to accord with that of the

Impressionists, became converted to open-air painting and for a period went so far as to set up his easel alongside Renoir's and Monet's at Argenteuil, he was never truly one of the Impressionist 'fellowship'.

This fellowship was formed of five young men, all born between 1839 and 1841: Paul Cézanne, Alfred Sisley, Claude Monet, Auguste Renoir and Frédéric Bazille; and one a few years older, Camille Pissarro. Pissarro's seniority, and even more his gentleness and moral earnestness, caused him to be generally revered, but it was Monet who, in these early years, tended to take the leadership. Closely associated with them all, in the role of publicist, was Émile Zola, who was of the same age (being born in 1840) and had been an intimate friend of Cézanne's ever since their schooldays together in Aix-en-Provence.

The whole history of art yields scarcely another example of a group of painters quite so close-knit as this was in its beginnings; one that remained, moreover, in spite of divergencies of temperament and aims, in spite of quarrels about tactics, a broadly united phalanx so long as Impressionism retained its importance as a movement. It has even been argued that the history of Impressionism is properly less that of painting than of these friendships 'with painting as its common denominator'.[8] This is perhaps an extreme view, but it is undeniable that Impressionism was nurtured in a culture of human sympathies, that it was a social as well as an artistic movement. The fact is all the more remarkable when one considers the very diverse class origins of the members. Some, like Cézanne, a banker's son, and Bazille, sprang from well-to-do families,[9] and if they were short of money in their earlier years, this was only because their parents, disapproving of their activities, kept them on short commons. The others had no fortune and no expectations. Pissarro's father ran a general store in the distant isle of St Thomas, in the Danish West Indies. Monet's father was a grocer in Le Havre. Renoir's family circumstances were even humbler. The son of a poor tailor in Limoges, he began life apprenticed to a painter on porcelain and, being gifted for this work, saved up enough money to pay his own enrolment fee at the École des Beaux-Arts.

They came from all parts of France—from Provence, from Normandy, from the Limousin—and even from overseas; only Sisley was born in Paris, of English ancestry. But it was in Paris, of course, that they all met, and mostly in one or the other of two art-centres: the Académie Suisse, and the school run by the academician Charles Gleyre. The Académie Suisse was not so much a school as a practice studio, situated near the Pont St Michel, where for a small charge it was possible to draw from the living model. Courbet and Manet had both used it in their time, and it was here that Pissarro met

19 Daumier's cartoon shows a disappointed *salon* entrant crying: 'Ungrateful country, you shall not have my work!' In reality, rejected canvases were marked with a single R on the back

20 Renoir, *La Grenouillère* (executed 1869). See pp. 175–6.

Monet, shortly after the latter arrived in Paris in 1859. Monet had already distinguished himself in his native town by drawing caricatures of the local notables which a picture-framer undertook to sell for him. Eugène Boudin, who many years before used to own the picture-framer's business, and who still dropped in at the shop to leave his seascapes with the present owner, met the 17-year-old youngster on the premises and encouraged him to study nature and to try and give himself a serious art education in the capital.

The friendly overtures of Pissarro—who could claim the distinction of having exhibited in the 1859 *salon*—must have gratified Monet, but before the acquaintance made in the Académie Suisse could ripen he was conscripted into the army and left for Algeria. Since the normal term of service was seven years, Pissarro resigned himself to seeing no more of this promising beginner. Another interesting young art-student he met in the Académie Suisse—Paul Cézanne—became quickly discouraged and returned to Aix, in spite of Zola's pleading, only a few months after he arrived in Paris (in 1861). Yielding to parental pressure, he entered the family banking business.

It was only after Monet returned to Paris that the group was properly formed. At the beginning of 1862 he fell ill in Algiers and was sent home to convalesce. Apparently his doctor warned the elder Monet that if his son returned to North Africa his health might be irreparably damaged; so the grocer scraped together the necessary money to purchase his discharge. Since the young man seemed as determined as ever to follow his vocation, his father despatched him once more to Paris, this time insisting that he enrol under a recognized art-teacher. Thus it was that Monet found himself the unwilling pupil of Gleyre, a man with a great reputation for turning the children he painted into cherubs and the young ladies into angels.

Gleyre's studio was open every weekday for four hours in the morning and two in the afternoon. The principal business was drawing from the living model—male or female, in alternate weeks. There were worse masters than Gleyre; he charged his pupils just enough to cover the rent of the studio, and made no income out of them; and he left them mostly to their own devices, though he could get irritated if he felt they were paying insufficient attention to the supreme art of drawing. This did not mean, as Monet soon discovered, that one was expected to draw the model as one saw it: the model might be ugly. Nature was only a starting-point; the mission of art, as the ancients had shown, was to proceed by selection, work towards the attainment of ideal beauty, and breathe spirit into gross matter.

It can easily be imagined how Monet, mindful of the precepts of his earlier, unofficial teacher Boudin, reacted to this advice. Equally discontented with Gleyre's teaching was Renoir, who entered the studio in 1862: the

M

emphasis on draughtsmanship, the slight importance attached by Gleyre to colour, ran counter to all his instincts even at this early stage. A light-hearted, easy-going young man, he soon made friends with Monet and with Bazille, another student who had recently come up from Montpellier. The fourth member of the quartet, Sisley, had been sent by his father to London, as soon as he was 18, to learn the business of a counting-house; but visits to the National Gallery during his leisure hours had instilled in him an enthusiasm for Turner and Constable that totally obliterated his residual interest in a commercial career. His parents, more understanding than Manet's or Cézanne's, had not opposed his desire to follow his bent, and he too had registered as a student of Gleyre's in 1862.

The young men, with few interests outside their art, supplemented their hours in the teaching studio with visits to the Louvre, where they practised copying the old masters. At the time this was an occupation more assiduously pursued than it is today: prints of the period show the galleries crowded with young men and women perched on stools, with brushes, palette and easel, studiously transferring to their own canvases likenesses of the master-pieces on the walls. Manet could be found here, together with Degas and Whistler; and it was here that Renoir made the acquaintance of Fantin-Latour, who urged him to copy for all he was worth. Through Fantin the young painters heard about Manet's work, though they were not able to make personal contact, as yet, with the young master. However, they visited Martinet's exhibition of his work in 1863 which, as we have seen, impressed Monet especially.

Cézanne, after a brief and unsatisfactory spell at his father's bank, had returned from Aix to Paris in 1862, rejoining his old friend Zola with whom he toured the *salon* in 1863. He introduced Zola, at that time an employee in Hachette's publishing firm, to the painter Antoine Guillemet, whose acquaintance Cézanne had made at the Académie Suisse; the two artists took the future critic round the studios, introducing him to Pissarro, Renoir, Bazille, and Monet. Zola listened attentively to their talk, picking up the technicalities and the slang, and learning much about their hopes and fears. He heard about the rumoured intrigues that preceded every vote cast by the selecting committee, and about the manoeuvres made by unscrupulous teachers to ensure that their pupils' work was received. Even if one's sub-missions found favour in the eyes of the all-powerful jury, there still remained the risk that they would be hung in some ill-lit corner or else too high for proper inspection. To guard against misfortunes of this sort, it was recommended to grease the palms of the custodians in the Palais de l'Industrie.

Much more was involved here than mere prestige. If an artist had no private fortune or was not backed by a well-to-do father, he needed to sell to pay his rent and (in Pissarro's case, for instance) to feed his family. Zola, with his own livelihood to make and a widowed mother to support, appreciated the point. There was a large market for works of art, to cover the walls of the new apartment houses in Paris, and mass-production of colour prints being still in the future, the banker, factory-owner or shopkeeper in a flourishing state of business bought originals. In addition, there was a thriving export trade, especially to Great Britain and the United States. Another lucrative sideline was the renting of pictures, not usually directly from an artist's studio but via some middleman, a paint-merchant or an antique dealer. The hostess wanting to impress her guests, the mother of a clutch of growing girls who needed to practise copying at home, were the obvious clients. But to tap these sources of income it was necessary first to exhibit in the annual *salon* and to earn good notices from reputable critics. Dealers and public alike had a touching faith in the decisions of the jury. It could hardly be doubted, by the experts and by the artists themselves, that many a bad picture was hung in the *salon* and that much better paintings were excluded; but for the ordinary picture-buyer, a canvas that had failed to meet the standards of the *salon* jury was not one they were prepared to pay hard cash for. It was not unknown for a painter, having made a sale, to be asked by the client to take the canvas back and refund the purchase money when the picture was rejected by the jury.

A few artists, of course, were in a position to snap their fingers at the arbitrary decisions made every April by the committee of balding professors and painters *emeriti* whose judgements were regarded with superstitious awe by an ignorant public. But for the majority it was a matter of the gravest concern: steady rejections were not just a humiliation, they could spell despair and destitution. A painter called Jules Holtzapfel blew out his brains in his studio in 1866 and in his suicide note declared: 'The members of the jury have refused my work, therefore I am without talent . . . and must die!' But it is likely that Holtzapfel really was without talent. The artists we are concerned with were sustained by the knowledge that, in the long run, fame and fortune would be theirs; moreover none of them—except Cézanne —were consistently and regularly rejected in the years between 1863 and 1870. Even so, most of them went through difficult times. In the summer of 1866 Monet, despite the fact that both his exhibition pictures had been accepted that year, found himself in serious financial difficulties, exacerbated by the fact that his mistress Camille Doncieux was expecting a child. His father, to whom he turned in his predicament, agreed to help him only on condition he broke off his irregular liaison, left Paris and boarded provisionally with an aunt at Sainte-Adresse. Monet remained here, doing seascapes, until in the winter of 1867–8 he defied the parental veto and rejoined his mistress and the baby son who had been born to her in the interval. They spent as much time as possible in bed together—for one thing, there was no money to pay for coals. In the spring his morale was raised by the news he had won a silver medal for the work he showed at an exhibition held in Le Havre; of more practical value was a remittance of 40 gold napoleons from Arsène Houssaye, who had decided to buy the superb portrait of Camille in a green dress which had attracted such favourable attention at the 1866 *salon*. Unfortunately, this small windfall was entirely swallowed up in the payment of outstanding debts, and in addition his creditors seized all his pictures after the Havre exhibition and had them put up for auction. Monet was reduced to such despair, indeed, that he tried to drown himself when with Camille and the child, he was evicted from the inn where they were staying because of his inability to settle the bill.

Those other members of the group who had no private income and enjoyed no regular allowance endured ordeals only a little less harsh than Monet's. Even though Renoir had one picture accepted by the jury in 1868 and Pissarro two, the latter was reduced to painting window-blinds while the former, unable to get further credit for canvas, was glad to accept a commission to decorate one of the ceilings in Prince Bibesco's Paris house.

In the summer of 1869 Monet was at Bougival, on the Seine, bitterly disappointed at the jury's rejection of both his submissions that year. He wrote to Houssaye, beseeching him to make a further purchase: but Houssaye was no longer interested in the products of this erratic bohemian. Unable even to buy paints, Monet wrote to Bazille, who was in Paris, begging him to send a few tubes. He was joined in these months by Renoir, who in August was buying him food, Monet having been without bread for a week. It was a case of the poor man giving alms to the beggar: Renoir himself could not afford to eat every day and did not always have the *sou* that it cost to frank his letters to Bazille. But side by side the two starving artists set up their easels by the river bank and painted those euphoric pictures, which they had no real hope of selling, of holiday-makers bathing and picnicking at La Grenouillère, fixing, by means of a revolutionary technique that they had together worked out for themselves, the carefree, sunlit, glinting scenes of gaiety, the final record of an age of carnival which was shortly to come to an end in the roar of cannon, the bursting of shells, and the smoke billowing up from gutted buildings.

Open-air painting

It was in part the desperate poverty dogging these painters that drove them to the unusual expedient of doing much of their work entirely in the open, summer and winter alike. To rent a studio in Paris was expensive; so, while Manet, Degas, and Bazille continued to produce indoor painting, the others were driven by the force of circumstances out of Paris into the country.[10] Pissarro, of course, had been painting landscapes since before the younger members of the group had started their careers; it was a landscape of his that was accepted for exhibition in the 1859 *salon*. Monet had practised the art, under the supervision first of Boudin, later of Jongkind, at Le Havre, and it was he who persuaded the friends he had made at Gleyre's studio to accompany him to Chailly, on the edge of the Forest of Fontainebleau, in the spring of 1864. Neither Renoir, Sisley, nor Bazille had had any experience of this kind of work, and it was Monet who initiated them. It is true that they had before them the example of the Barbizon school of landscape painters, who had been working in different parts of the forest for a genera-tion. But there was one significant difference between their method and that which Monet favoured and encouraged his friends to follow. The older painters relied partly at least on their memory; they would sketch a picture out of doors, or take notes, but it would be finished in the studio. Millet went so far as to paint entirely from memory after mentally photographing the scene that he wished to reproduce. Only Daubigny, who was not at that period working at Barbizon, painted his landscapes directly from nature, without troubling to give them the finishing touch in the studio. Precisely for that reason they looked 'unfinished' to the ordinary academic critic, and Gautier, for example, complained petulantly: 'It is really too bad that this landscape painter . . . should be satisfied with an *impression*, and should neglect details to the extent he does. His pictures are no more than rough drafts, left in a very unfinished state.'[11] There was no one to point out to Gautier that an *impression* cannot be rendered otherwise than by a picture that looks unfinished, since the 'finished' look destroyed the spontaneity and delicate freshness of the appearance. But even if some apologist had come up with this explanation, it is unlikely that the critic would have changed his mind: to count as art at all, a picture needed, at this time, to look as though it had been carefully worked over, with every detail made clearly recogniz-able. This was one of the difficulties that Monet and his friends had to contend with, though it made itself felt in a more acute form when they started exhibiting together after the war.

Another favourite rallying-ground for the younger painters was the

stretch of coast around Honfleur; here again they had been preceded by the
Barbizon group—not only by Daubigny, but by Corot, Diaz, and Troyon
as well. Monet settled here with Bazille in the summer of 1864, until his
friend had to return to Paris to take his medical examinations. It was at this
time that Monet began experimenting with renderings of the same scene in
different weather conditions: a country road at first under snow, then in the
summer, beneath a dull sky. These two compositions prepared the way for
other more famous series (views of poplars, haystacks, and of Rouen Cathedral seen under different lighting effects and in different atmospheric conditions), which Monet was to execute in the 1890s.

   More and more he was becoming interested in the transformations
wrought by sunlight as it played over objects. The spring of 1865 found all
four young men back in the Forest of Fontainebleau, with Monet busy on
his most ambitious project to date, the depiction of an open-air picnic scene
in the woods: a dozen young men and women in contemporary costume,
some standing, some sitting, some sprawling around a tablecloth laid on the
grass in a glade. It was an excuse for studying light effects, especially on the
bright crinolines and the white table linen, as the sun filtered its rays through
the dense foliage above. In spite of the interruption caused by a leg injury,
which forced the artist to stay in bed and submit to the ministrations of the
newly qualified doctor Bazille, this summer of 1865 probably counted as one
of the happiest seasons of Monet's youth. For the first time he had entered
two works for the *salon*—views of the Seine estuary at Honfleur—which had
not only been accepted but were highly praised on all sides. He planned to
send in his big picnic scene the following year; unfortunately Courbet
dropped in on him at Chailly before the work was completed and suggested
some minor changes, which Monet was unwise enough to incorporate.
Dissatisfied with the altered aspect of his picture, he rolled it and left it with
the landlord of the inn instead of taking it back to Paris with him. So as to
have something for the 1866 *salon* Monet executed at speed the full-length
portrait of Camille Doncieux which was later, as we have seen, acquired by
Arsène Houssaye.

   The impact of Courbet on these young painters was considerable at the
time; he interested himself in their work and gave them the benefit of his
advice which they were sometimes a little too ready to take. This was
particularly true of Renoir, whose gregarious and relaxed temperament
made him peculiarly suggestible: the attractive portrait of his mistress Lise,
presented as a *Diane chasseresse* and inexplicably rejected by the jury in 1867,
bears a strong likeness to the alluring nudes that Courbet was turning out at
the time.

Monet, however, was chary about accepting Courbet's direction after the unlucky experience in Chailly. While he was painting the large open-air picture, *Femmes cueillant des fleurs* (another work rejected in 1867 which is now in the Louvre), Courbet chanced to visit him and asked why he was sitting in front of his canvas doing nothing. Monet explained that he was waiting for the sun to come out from behind a cloud. 'But surely', asked Courbet, 'you could fill in the time doing some work on the background?' Monet had to explain to the disbelieving master that a picture done out of doors could have no unity unless every part of it was painted in the same conditions of light.

Other members of the group were making their own discoveries as they practised open-air painting: Bazille as he worked at Montpellier on the large canvas representing members of his family on the terrace of their house—a picture exhibited in the 1868 *salon*—Renoir with the new portrait of Lise, standing in strong sunshine, her face shaded by a parasol, which was seen in the same exhibition. This picture proves that Renoir had advanced beyond Monet in his analysis of the colours of shadows as they were cast by the thin fabric of the painted parasol on to the young woman's face, neck and shoulders. It was realized that the diffraction of sunlight in the air meant that shadows were never quite black: pure blacks and whites were artificial abstractions, hardly ever encountered in nature. Nor could shadows be truthfully rendered by simply darkening the colour of the object which was in shadow. They were what the painters at last, rubbing their eyes, saw them to be: possessed of different, but complementary colours, often with bluish tints if the sky was clear. The snowscapes undertaken simultaneously by Monet, Pissarro and Sisley in the winter of 1868–9 were essentially experiments to discover what happened when objects cast shadows on the white expanse in strong or weak sunlight.

All this, and much else, sprang from the revolutionary step they took when they decided to look at nature with their own eyes and forget—as Manet found it so difficult to forget—how all other artists since the Renaissance had seen, or at least shown, such simple things as grass, trees in leaf, the skin on women's arms and faces, the shimmering of wind-blown water. Not only did everything need to be looked at afresh, but the rendering of this new universe demanded a new and different use of tried techniques. The smooth brush-strokes had to be abandoned, since they had originally been developed as a consequence of the superstition, now exploded, that each object had its own particular (so-called local) colour, unaffected by the colours of surrounding objects. Instead, Monet and Renoir, working together at La Grenouillère, discovered the potentialities of the short brush-stroke, the hachure, the blob, the twirl, to represent the broken surfaces of reflections in rippling water and the hazy outlines of animated faces and bodies in motion, of details that the eye glides over and that the retina causes to swim together in a vivid kaleido-scope.

After this fashion was Impressionism born, though it had still not been baptized. In this way did the visible world suddenly become a brighter, more intense and gayer place, or at least so it seems to us who can look back at that moment when the revelation was made. Those who saw it being made were, as so often happens, unaware of what was happening. Their eyes were too tired, or they were blinded by prejudice or pomposity; or else they had lived too long to learn new ways of looking at old things. Besides, who were these self-styled innovators? striplings not yet in their thirties, truants from school. But one or two older men, who remembered that they had been young once, and revolutionaries too, when the last of the Bourbons was still reigning, were not so sure; they blinked, had doubts, and wondered. Nothing that Théophile Gautier ever wrote in his voluminous art-criticism has quite the same poignancy, nor does him quite the same credit, as the remarks about the 1868 *salon* which he published in *Le Moniteur universel* on May 11th. In 1868, thanks largely to Daubigny's efforts, the committee not only accepted Manet's submissions, but allowed Monet, Pissarro, Renoir, Sisley, together with Degas and Berthe Morisot, to figure in the exhibition. Gautier made no secret of his extreme dislike of the new fashion in painting, which he found most blatantly exemplified in Monet's *Navires sortant des jetées du Havre*. He showed himself quite aware of what Monet was aiming to achieve; in fact, he sums up with considerable insight the principal techni-cal innovations of Impressionism; what he will not allow is that these qualities are compatible with pictorial art as he understood it:

> To confine oneself to an arrangement of *patches*, as current jargon has it, which, even though one may grant them accuracy of tonality, do no more than indicate the external contours, the silhouette of objects—this really constitutes an unacceptable simplification of the artist's mission. That at first glance, canvases treated in this fashion may produce an *impression* (another modish word), is something we would not deny; but they do not stand up to close examination . . . they amount to nothing, more than a decorative piece designed to make an impact, which has to be viewed from a distance in a favourable light.

Having formulated his reservations, Gautier seems to waver. This is not painting as he understands it; judged by traditional criteria, it is rough, blunt, and primitive. But what if the traditions are played out? Supposing it were true that the great art of the past has today degenerated into mere formalism? What if it needs to be rescued from decadence by a bold bid to change all the rules?

Faced with this paradox in painting, one may give the impression—even if one does not admit the charge—of being frightened lest one be dismissed as a philistine, a bourgeois, a Joseph Prudhomme, a cretin with a fancy for miniatures and copies of paintings on porcelain, worse still, as an old fogey who sees some merit in David's *Rape of the Sabines*. One clutches at oneself, so to speak, in terror, one runs one's hand over one's stomach or one's skull, wondering if one has grown pot-bellied or bald, incapable of understanding the audacities of the young. . . . One reminds oneself of the antipathy, the horror aroused some 30 years ago by the paintings of Delacroix, Decamps, Boulanger, Scheffer, Corot, Rousseau, for so long excluded from the *salon*. . . . Those who are honest with themselves, when they consider these disturbing precedents, wonder whether it is ever possible to understand anything in art other than the works of the generation of which one is a contemporary, in other words the generation that came of age when one came of age oneself. . . . It is conceivable that the pictures of Courbet, Manet, Monet, and others of their ilk conceal beauties that elude us, with our old romantic manes already shot with silver threads.

Though it would be too much to say that the critic was recanting, this passage could fairly be read as a kind of abdication.

Writers' reactions to War and defeat

At the beginning of this study we saw with what universal fervour and delight men of letters of all ages and of every political persuasion hailed the advent of the Second Republic. It lasted rather less than four years. The Third Republic, which was proclaimed on September 4th, 1870, endured for 70 years, but was ushered in with nothing like the same confidence or optimism. Even those who had expended the best of their energies in the effort to pull down the imperial régime felt anything but triumph as they watched, under a grey sky, the crowds massed in front of the Palais Bourbon, the bourgeois in his black suit and the workers in their blue or white overalls, some carrying leafy branches and others with sprigs in their hats, waiting to hear the names of the members of the provisional government. Once again, the mob poured into the Tuileries Palace, and along its wall, on the south side of the Rue de Rivoli, a wag had chalked in huge letters: *Logement à louer*.

Despite superficial resemblances, this was not another 1848. For in 1848

France had been at peace, and the internal struggle for power could proceed without the threat of interference from abroad. In 1870 the nation was locked in a deadly struggle with Prussia, who would henceforth be regarded as the hereditary enemy; for 1870 led to 1914 as surely as 1918 led to 1940. Notwithstanding the huzzas on September 4th and the waving of hats, the general mood was more desperate than enthusiastic and if thoughtful people looked for historical precedents, they were more inclined to think of the downfall of the *ancien régime* and the proclamation of the First Republic than of anything that had happened when old Louis-Philippe fled the country in a panic in 1848. Patriots—and Paris as a whole was seething with the fiercest patriotism—hoped for the same miracle as had occurred in 1793 when Jourdan, Hoche and Kellermann swept the foreign invader out of France. They forgot that the coalition which had formed with the object of crushing the Convention commanded only mercenaries, outnumbered by the revolutionary armies. The Prussians in 1870 headed a different kind of coalition, a gathering of the Teutonic tribes who at last, after centuries of division, were coming together to form a new and formidable nation-state.

Certainly the invader's progress was not halted one instant by the magic formula: *La République est proclamée*. After a cruel siege, which neither the half-hearted efforts of the French armies *extra muros* nor the desperate sorties of the defenders within the city could break, starved, frozen, and subjected to a merciless bombardment, Paris finally capitulated and France sued for peace. In the ensuing disorder, with the seat of government first at Bordeaux and later at Versailles, the mood of the Parisian working-classes became more and more embittered. Finally the city decided to make a bid for autonomy. Civil war broke out, and, with the occupying German troops contemptuously holding the ring, after some of the bloodiest street-fighting that had ever been seen in a civilized capital, the Republic crushed the Commune. All these events, from the first declaration of war on Prussia on July 19th, 1870 till the final massacre of the remaining *communards* which took place among the tombstones of the Père Lachaise cemetery on May 28th, 1871, had extended over little more than ten months. At the end of it all, conservatives and progressives were in a state of shock, punch-drunk.

No one in the world of art and letters mourned the Second Empire when it so abruptly and unexpectedly disintegrated. Given the policies its leaders had adopted, given the trivialization of cultural life and the impoverishment of intellectual life, this was perhaps inevitable. But the *faute de mieux* republic that took its place commanded no great loyalty either. The truth was that far too little thought had been given beforehand to consideration of what was to succeed to autocracy. The naïve theory that if power were simply restored to the masses, via the ballot-box, a more humane and progressive society would automatically emerge, had been miserably exploded in 1848, when the politically backward provinces had blocked the advance towards greater economic justice. To prevent a repetition of this 'rural backlash', the best solution that radical thinkers could propose was that Paris should form herself into a separate city-state; hopefully the working population of other French cities would follow suit and in due course a federation would be formed. This was the thinking that lay behind the creation of the Paris Commune; the historical precedents were the Swiss cantons which had joined together in the Helvetian Republic and, further back, the alliances made between the Italian city-republics of the Middle Ages.

In truth, the thrust of events, the dislocation of communications, the hardships, disappointments, and uncertainties allowed little opportunity for rational discussion and for the emergence of a freely consented common policy. The impression one has is of a nation overwhelmed—less by the foreign enemy than by the relentless pressure of history. In all the various eye-witness accounts that we have—those written from day to day, those composed years after the events—there is hardly a line of cool, constructive analysis; and if the intellectual élite of the nation could react with nothing better than futile gestures and impassioned jeremiads, it is scarcely surprising that the country as a whole missed the chance of making 1871 a turning-point in its social organization.

If we follow the same procedure to explore the reactions of writers to these cataclysmic occurrences as we used in treating of the 1848 Revolution, we find no shortage of testimony, but it is perhaps better to confine the examination to four witnesses: two writers who belonged to the *rentier* class and who had passively accepted the imperial régime: Edmond de Goncourt and Gustave Flaubert; and two others who had striven to overthrow the Empire and re-establish republican institutions: Victor Hugo and Jules Vallès. Of these four, two (Goncourt and Vallès) spent the whole of the ten months within the fortifications of the capital. Hugo was in Paris for part of the time, while Flaubert remained in Normandy throughout, apart from a brief visit to Belgium.

Edmond de Goncourt's record of his experiences is enshrined in the famous diary which he bravely continued to keep after the death of his brother Jules on June 18th, 1870. As a chronicle of the contemporary scene, it is detailed and illuminating, for Goncourt was a practised observer; but it is also written in a blackly pessimistic mood, traceable in part to his recent bereavement but attributable even more to his generally misanthropic and class-conscious outlook. In the first flush of excitement aroused by the proclamation of the Republic he remained unmoved and full of foreboding. He failed to discover in this rowdy rabble (*cette plèbe braillarde*) the grandsons of the revolutionary soldiers who had first marched to the strains of the Marseillaise: 'They seem to me simply sceptical hooligans, out on a joyous spree, a political smash-and-grab; hooligans with little heart for large patriotic sacrifices.' He is astonished at the widespread light-heartedness: no one would dream that this was a beleaguered city, shortly to be put to fire and sword. Nothing has changed: 'the same gaiety, the same futile talk, the same hubbub of lightly ironical conversations in the restaurants and cafés. Men and women are the same frivolous creatures as they were before the invasion. At the most one notices a few women looking cross because their husbands won't put the paper down.'

The Indian Summer, exceptionally fine that year, helped to sustain the fallacious mood of optimism even though the first signs of the coming food shortage were already apparent, with the shops selling off tins of boiled beef and mutton, articles of consumption which the fastidious Parisians would never have sampled in normal times. On October 10th Goncourt drew his ration card. But he notes with an artist's eye the beauty of the russet trees and of the soft blue of the zenith fading towards the milk-white mists on the city's horizons, with all the buildings bathed in a faintly violet light. The uniforms of the military added an unusually brilliant note to the colour-scheme: 'The red képis and the red trousers, the greyish brown shirts, the glistening rumps of the horses, the clusters of sabres hitched on to the branches, the brass helmets with their plumes outspread; and in the midst of it all, one officer in his crimson dress-uniform, with a red flannel cape flung negligently over his shoulders, sitting in his chair in an attitude at once jaunty and indolent.'

But as the month of October wore on, the excitement faded. 'Never reading anything but the predictable bulletins of a miserable war, never finding anything in the newspapers but tedious commentaries on defeats decked up under the name of *offensive reconnoitring* . . . deprived of all that used to constitute the intellectual recreation of the educated city-dweller, of every novelty, of every chance of self-renewal; vegetating, in a word, in this brutal and monotonous wartime existence, the Parisian in Paris is seized by the same *ennui* as if he were living in a provincial town.' It was the gloom of the unlit streets which, as the days grew shorter, depressed Goncourt more than anything; this had nothing in common, of course, with the black-outs imposed in later wars—it was simply a consequence of measures taken by the authorities to conserve supplies of gas, needed as much for heating and cooking as for illumination. He remembered how formerly the city could be seen at ten leagues distance by the light it projected on to the night-sky; now, even the newly built districts are made to look dilapidated and decrepit by the deep shadow that falls over everything as soon as the sun has set.

Goncourt was standing on the steps of the Théâtre Français, on the last day of October, when he learned the news of Marshal Bazaine's disgraceful capitulation to the Prussians at Metz. He joined the crowd of citizens who were converging through the rain on to the Hôtel de Ville. In the square, armed men were shouting *Vive la Commune!* The historic building had already been invaded by the workers, some of whom were sitting in the open windows, their legs dangling. Others—presumably typographers—were taking down from dictation the names of the proposed members of the Committee of Public Safety which was to take over from the Republican government. Goncourt went home with a heavy heart, to write in his diary: *Finis Franciae.* In fact, had he stayed, he would have seen the attempted *putsch* foiled by battalions of the National Guard alerted by Ernest Picard, who had succeeded in slipping out of the Hôtel de Ville unobserved. With the assistance of a few detachments of Breton militiamen, they evicted the insurgents within hours and set the ministers free. The orders that had already been issued for an immediate election were countermanded, and the republican government, back in the saddle, set about planning the repressive policies that did much to fan the flames of class warfare in Paris over the next few months.

A small and rather ludicrous part in this abortive rising was played by Jules Vallès. While Félix Pyat was drumming up his contingents of national guardsmen in the working-class districts of Montmartre and Belleville in preparation for the march on the Hôtel de Ville, Vallès decided to conduct an independent operation and, with 30 followers, seized the Mairie de la Villette in the 19th *arrondissement*; when the rightful mayor appeared, he locked him up in a cupboard in his own office. The following day he realized he had acted too precipitately, evacuated the building with his men and went into hiding.

Vallès composed his own memoir of the events of 1870–1 as the concluding part of an autobiographical novel, *L'Insurgé*, published posthumously in 1886. In its entirety this book, written with immense verve and steeped in sardonic humour, commemorates better than any other written record the grim underside of the *fête impériale*, for Vallès counts assuredly among the most persecuted of the literary pariahs of the time, of the *réfractaires*, the malcontents, to use his own term. He is also the best example we have of the socially committed writer at a time when the police and the censorship between them had all but succeeded in imposing a complete embargo on any discussion of matters that might embarrass the government. Vallès had originally come up to Paris from Nantes, where his father taught in a school, in September 1848. Though only 16, he was already a convinced socialist. In 1850, among the students who crammed the lecture-hall at the Collège de France to listen to Michelet, he stood out as the most fearlessly devoted champion of that recalcitrant professor; and when the course was suspended by government order,[12] he drew up a protest which was signed by hundreds of his classmates and headed a procession through Paris to hand it in at the Chamber. Police interference was rendered unnecessary by the torrential rain which dispersed the demonstrators—the conservative press laughed off the march as '*la manifestation des parapluies*'.

About the same time Vallès enrolled in a secret society with an innocuous enough name, *le Comité des Jeunes*, whose aims were to defend republican institutions from whatever quarter they were threatened. But he found, when the *coup d'état* took place, that he was the only member of the society bold enough to go into the streets and harangue the workers. He also discovered that the workers had lost the will to resist, and after a half-hearted attempt to build a barricade he returned home to Nantes. Back in the capital a few months later, he was implicated in a conspiracy against the Emperor and sentenced to six months' solitary confinement in the fortress of Mazas.

On his release he lapsed into a vague bohemian existence from which he emerged, in 1857, to start his career as a freelance journalist. He could never stay long on any one paper, the bitterness of his satire invariably frightening his editors, however much they appreciated the vigour of his style. A humble job as registrar of births and marriages helped to eke out his irregular earnings as a writer; but he lost his post when he fell foul of the authorities over a public lecture on Balzac, whom Vallès presented in an unconventional fashion as one of the great revolutionaries of the century. He was rescued from destitution by Villemessant who recruited him to the staff of his booming paper, *Le Figaro*. From there Vallès moved to Ernest Feydeau's *Époque*; Feydeau paid for him to go on a short visit to England where Vallès was, by his own account, delighted to breathe the air of political liberty. On his return he joined *L'Événement*, a new paper just launched by Villemessant; it was in *L'Événement* that Zola published his notorious *Salon de 1866*.

Vallès' prose was too vivacious to be permitted to moulder in newspaper files; he collected the best of his articles and published them in two volumes, the first entitled *Les Réfractaires* and the second *La Rue*. The latter included a notable essay on Courbet in which Vallès recalled the emotions that had filled him when he first saw *Les Casseurs de pierre*: 'We had always felt a deep respect for the suffering and the vanquished and we asked of the new art that it too should assist in the triumph of truth and justice. This picture, with its grey tints, with its two horny-handed, swarthy-necked figures, was like a mirror reflecting the drab and painful lives of the poor.'

He used the same title, La Rue, for the newspaper which he founded in June 1867, having finally reached the conclusion that it was pointless looking for an editor bold enough to take his copy. La Rue did not lack for subscribers, but the police were on the alert and it was not long before street sales were prohibited. The authorities seized one issue, that of November 30th, 1867, on account of an article entitled 'Cochons vendus'; the term was a slang expression applied to the remplaçants—the men who, not being themselves liable for military service, accepted money to serve in place of some rich young man who had drawn an unlucky number. Vallès, taking the disobliging words in another sense, applied them to all those teachers, writers, and politicians who agreed to support the régime in return for a pension, a decoration or a portfolio. La Rue was finally killed off at the beginning of 1868; no official action was taken, but Vallès suddenly found it impossible to persuade any printer to set it up.

After emerging from prison in February 1869—he had incurred two separate sentences for articles published in Le Globe and Le Courrier de l'Intérieur—Vallès started a new daily paper, Le Peuple, and tried to enter parliament. He was crushingly defeated at the polls, an experience which should have taught him once and for all that he was never likely to serve the popular cause except as a journalist and polemicist. But Vallès, by now, had become almost indifferent to defeat and inured to disappointment; the combination in him of mocking self-pity and indomitable courage, together with his genuine admiration for the oppressed classes whose spokesman he had made himself, allowed him to weather every storm and endure every kind of persecution. His adult life was one long series of punishments, as his childhood had been.[13]

As a pacifist, he was opposed to the declaration of war in 1870; and as a fearless propagandist he made no secret of his views. With a few comrades, he organized a march across the city with white banners inscribed Vive la paix! in black ink. The bellicose citizens of Paris fell on them, and the police intervened in the scuffle—but not in defence of the demonstrators. A few days later Vallès was arrested in the course of another pacifist rally, but was released from custody when the disastrous news from the front came to justify his defeatism. He witnessed the proclamation of the Republic with as little joy as had Goncourt, though the reasons for his despondency were very different: when Vallès tried to shout: Vive la République . . . SOCIALE! he was told to keep his mouth shut if he did not want his nose bloodied. The names of the members of the Government of National Defence inspired him with scant confidence: they were all, he judged, bourgeois opportunists who had been quietly waiting in the wings since 1851; once the Empire had bit the dust, they seized power greedily, with both hands. Henri Rochefort, who had been his fellow prisoner at Sainte-Pélagie and had edited the paper *La Marseillaise* for which Vallès was writing immediately before the outbreak of war, was not, of course, in the same case, but Vallès suspected that his friend was being merely used as a 'front' by people like Gambetta and Jules Ferry. The real revolution was still to come, and meanwhile, there was work to be done in organizing it clandestinely. Vallès was active in the socialist clubs, founding one himself in Belleville. As the Germans encircled Paris, Flourens, Blanqui, Félix Pyat and other dedicated revolutionaries formed a 'Central Republican Committee' of the 20 *arrondissements*, and on September 20th passed a number of highly patriotic resolutions: that there should be no negotiations until the enemy had evacuated French territory, that Paris should be destroyed sooner than surrendered, and that a *levée en masse* should be decreed forthwith. It was with the object of giving these decisions effect that the revolutionaries had invaded the Hôtel de Ville and attempted to seize power on October 31st.

During the few hours in which Blanqui and his band believed themselves to have triumphed, they sent a deputation to the house where Victor Hugo was staying, inviting him to accept the presidency of the new government; as matters turned out, it was as well that the old poet declined.

Hugo had left the Channel Islands on August 15th, guessing that a military collapse was impending, but unwilling all the same to re-enter France until it was certain that his old enemy Louis-Napoleon would never set foot on the soil of the homeland again. He crossed to Brussels, called on the French embassy and requested a passport, which was delivered him without difficulty on the presentation of a visiting-card. Then, not even troubling to unpack, he settled down to await developments. His friends in Paris were asked to send him a telegram as soon as they judged it advisable that he should return. The telegram arrived on September 5th, the day after the proclamation of the Republic, and Hugo took the next train to Paris. He was welcomed on the station by a huge crowd . . . and by Judith Gautier, the handsome, 22-year-old daughter of Théophile, whom a little later Hugo, though well into his seventies now, was to add to the incredibly long list of his conquests. He was urged to address the crowd, who were reciting lines from *Les Châtiments* and shouting that he should be carried in triumph to the Hôtel de Ville. Hugo spoke to his supporters from the balcony of a small café opposite the station, telling them that he had come not to displace the government of the Republic, but to lend it his support. This was also the answer that he gave on October 31st to Blanqui's emissaries.

Edmond de Goncourt paid him a courtesy visit on November 7th and found him, and all his circle, pessimistic about the chances that Paris would be able to withstand a winter siege. Hugo was more sanguine about the long-term prospects, however, predicting a rapid recovery and a settlement of accounts with Germany after 'four or five years'. But he had little confidence in the Government of National Defence and even less in the military commander in Paris, a stalwart Catholic called Trochu whom he described witheringly and wittily in the verse collection, *L'Année terrible*, published just after the war, as

> *brave, honnête, pieux, nul,*
> *Bon canon, mais ayant un peu trop de recul.*

Goncourt, too, was growing more despondent than ever; his account of the last two months of the year is sombre. His mistrust of the proletariat, the *blousiers*, the *gens de Belleville*, deepened every day; he wondered whether there would not be a reaction, the old provinces of France rising against Paris, so that the entire country would disintegrate and cease to exist as a unified state. The spirit of 1793 seemed utterly dead, killed by the individualism, the corrosive scepticism, the corrupt materialism of the Second Empire. Goncourt in the face of national defeat reacted in the same way as did, in 1940, a great many men and women of his class, seeing in the disasters that had befallen them something like the chastisement of heaven for their blind pursuit of selfish enjoyment under the previous régime.

He could see little to admire in the current mood of stoical indifference. 'Posterity would do well not to be misled by tall stories of the heroism of the Parisians of 1870. All their heroism will have consisted in eating rancid butter with their runner beans and sirloin of horse instead of sirloin of beef—but without really noticing the difference, the Parisian being far from fussy, at the best of times, about what he eats.' All the same, references to the worsening food situation become more and more frequent in the diary; some of them are of a very curious character. Goncourt tells how he watched one worthy citizen riveted in front of a shop-window where a particular substance was on display which the poor fellow was obviously in an agony of indecision about buying for use in his frying-pan: it was cocoa-butter, normally sold only as a contraceptive preparation. This was still in October; by the end of November he would not have been so squeamish: cats, by then, were retailing at six francs a carcase, rats for one franc each and dog-

N

meat for one franc a pound. On November 28th Goncourt watched men with nets drawing the carp from the pool in the Luxembourg Gardens. The following day, his cook being unable to make edible the salt-meat on the ration, he was forced to decapitate one of his own chickens, much to his sorrow; he did it in style, however, with a Japanese ceremonial sword, one of the pieces from his collection.

Men were having to have their trousers taken in at the waist, and the corpulent Théophile Gautier lamented that he was finding it necessary, for the first time in years, to wear braces. On Christmas Day, a goldsmith was displaying expensive jewellery cases, each open to show a fresh egg nestling inside in cotton-wool. Only the stocks of wines and spirits seemed inexhaustible, and on New Year's Day the streets were as noisy with revellers as ever. It is true that, for the very rich, it was still possible to buy game and poultry at certain provisioners and Goncourt is staggered—and a little contemptuous—that the starving population does not pillage such shops instead of passing by with a mildly ironical jest. By January 21st even the bakers had nothing for sale, and Goncourt was accosted in the Rue St Nicolas by a girl offering herself 'for a crust of bread'.

On top of all this there was the shelling which had started just after Christmas and went on day after day. Even so, there were poor women standing in queues before bakers' shops who were crying: 'Let them cut the bread ration, anything, rather than give in.' But it could not go on. On January 28th Thiers signed an agreement with Bismarck: Paris had capitulated.

All this time, Goncourt's friend and fellow novelist Flaubert, stuck in the family house at Croisset, on the Seine, which he shared with his old mother, was fuming, fretting, bewailing his fate, and even more the fate of France. The Prussians did not actually reach Rouen until early December; when they did, the author of *Madame Bovary* found ten men, three officers and their horses quartered on him at Croisset. His impotent rage and indignation can be inferred from the remarks he had already made about the invaders in his letters, particularly those to his old friend George Sand. He had disapproved of the declaration of war as strongly as had Goncourt and Vallès and indeed all thinking men, whatever their political creed. He declared himself 'sickened, wounded to the soul' by the stupidity of his fellow countrymen and by the fresh example of the ineradicable savagery of civilized man. 'The fearful butchery which will ensue has not the slightest pretext to justify it—it is fighting for fighting's sake.' The constant error of the intellectual élite, he went on, was that they foolishly believed that the masses were made in their image and could therefore be trusted with the direction of affairs.

It was an unproven assumption which had given rise to a superstitious belief in the virtues of universal suffrage. 'Do you suppose that if France, instead of being governed, as it has been essentially, by the common people, had been in the control of the mandarins, we should be in this plight?' George Sand could hardly agree with such anti-democratic sentiments, and when the republic was founded she wrote to Flaubert to tell him to pluck up heart. 'You make me weep', he replied, 'you with your enthusiasm for the Republic. When we are on the point of being vanquished by the most practical positivism, how can you go on believing in such fantasies?' For if there was any conviction that Flaubert still clung to after this catastrophe, it was his old conviction in the supremacy of science and logic, since it was by the use of scientific method and logical reasoning that Prussia had made herself the dominant power in Europe. And France's only hope now was to imitate her, to give up its frivolous faith in meaningless abstractions and political panaceas; the French would have to become a nation of pragmatists. 'The whole evil arises from our inconceivable ignorance. What should be examined is taken on trust. Instead of scrutinizing, we make assertions. The French Revolution must cease to be a dogma and must be dealt with scientifically, like everything else in human affairs. If people had been more scientific, they would not have believed that a mystical formula was capable of bringing whole armies into the field and that the magic word "Republic" had the power to put to flight a million well-disciplined soldiers.'

Not that Flaubert felt any love or admiration for those well-disciplined soldiers, led by the scientifically minded von Moltke and inspired by the positivist Clausewitz. He was impaled on an excruciating dilemma: 'Of what use is science' he asked, 'since this nation, with its scientific education, is committing atrocities worthy of the Huns and worse than theirs, for the Prussians' atrocities are systematic, coldly and deliberately executed, and have not the excuse of passion or hunger?' All the same, the French would have no alternative, in the future, but to follow suit; the whole country would become a barrack-room, the arts of elegance would wither, and there would be no room for literature. 'Literature', he told George Sand, 'seems to me a vain and useless thing. Shall I ever be in a fit state to write any more? Ah! if only I could emigrate to some country where there were no uniforms to be seen, no drums to be heard, no talk of carnage, where one was not forced to be a citizen! But the earth is not habitable any more for the poor mandarins!'[14]

The Commune

A new National Assembly was elected on February 8th, largely representative of the monied and propertied interests who realized they had nothing to gain by a prolongation of hostilities. Power passed from Gambetta, with his policy of heroic resistance to the last drop of French blood, to the prudent Thiers who wanted a patched-up peace followed by as rapid a national recovery as could be organized. But Gambetta was all the same elected to the Assembly, together with a brave band of those men who had been prominent in the Provisional Government of 1848 or had distinguished themselves later by their stalwart opposition to the Empire: Arago, Ledru-Rollin, Edgar Quinet, Félix Pyat, Jules Simon and Vallès's friend Rochefort. They constituted the nucleus of the left-wing opposition and, once the session had opened at Bordeaux, they chose Victor Hugo as their parliamentary leader.

The old poet had arrived in the ancient capital of Aquitania on February 13th: he was given as vociferous a welcome as he had received in Paris the previous September. But whatever the popular feeling in his favour, the majority of his fellow delegates regarded him with deep mistrust, and his speeches in debate were rarely listened to without some signs of impatience. He refused to vote in favour of ratifying the treaty that Thiers had concluded with Bismarck and, on March 1st, made an inflammatory prophecy of the coming *guerre de revanche*. 'Starting tomorrow, France will be filled with one idea only . . . to recover her strength, to raise a new generation and nurture in holy anger those children who will grow to be men; to forge cannon and to form citizens, to create an army which will be a nation . . . ' so as ultimately not merely to wrest back from Germany the lost provinces, Alsace and Lorraine, but to occupy the whole left bank of the Rhine. It is remarkable that the prospect that filled Flaubert with foreboding—that France would become one vast Spartan camp filled with citizen-soldiers—should have moved Hugo to lyrical fervour. One is tempted to speculate on the reasons for the difference. Some have to do with questions of temperament, others with personal history. Hugo was in a large measure a prisoner of his own legend. In the course of his long exile, he had come to regard himself as the personal incarnation of a superior patriotism; it was, in fact, for that very reason that he was attacked by those men in the republican ranks who placed social justice above national self-interest.[15] Flaubert, on the other hand, had made his peace with the Empire and, as far as possible, ceased to think about political issues: hence his disgust and disgruntlement when they forced themselves on his attention.

Before long Hugo, exasperated at the recurrent interruption of his speeches in the Assembly, resigned his seat. On March 17th he had in any case to return to Paris, when the news was brought him of the sudden death of his son Charles. Goncourt saw him briefly at the funeral which was held on the very day when Thiers tried to make a show of force in the working-class suburbs of Paris and then, alarmed when his troops started to fraternize with the workers, ordered the total evacuation of Paris not only by the military but by all departments of the civil service. The elected government now had its seat in Versailles, the Germans—neutral in this domestic dispute—were camped on the other side of the city, at Vincennes, and Paris was faced with a second siege. Goncourt, plunged into an even deeper depression by this new turn of events, felt tired of being French, as he put it. Like Flaubert, with whom he had had no contact since before the war, he experienced 'a vague longing to go off in search of a country where the artist could be left in peace to meditate, without being disturbed at every turn by the stupid agitation and idiotic convulsions of the destructive mob.'

The power vacuum left by Thiers in Paris was filled by the Central Committee which promptly set up its own administration. In the elections that were held to determine its composition Vallès succeeded, this time, in securing a seat. The other representatives were all men of his stamp, if not more intransigent in their outlook: they included, inevitably, Auguste Blanqui with his motto 'Neither God nor boss'; Gustave Flourens; Félix Pyat who, like Hugo, had resigned from the National Assembly; and the anarchist Arthur Arnould, who believed that the source of social evil was not to be looked for in the principles that inspired the government of a state, but in the very existence of the state. There were also a fair number of manual workers in the Commune; noticeably absent from the Provisional Government formed after the February Revolution of 1848, their strength in this new revolutionary committee testifies ironically to the advances in popular education made under Napoleon III.

Edmond de Goncourt, reading the list, can be forgiven for deciding that the Commune was nothing more nor less than a proletarian junta. 'Perhaps, in accordance with the great law of change in human affairs, the workers represent, for modern societies, what the Barbarians stood for in ancient societies: convulsive agents of dissolution and destruction.' The myth of the barbarian proletariat, gathering to sack the cities of the bourgeoisie as the Goths had ravaged the Roman Empire in the fifth century, was, as we shall see, destined to become firmly rooted in the minds of a whole generation of writers during the next 30 years, contributing significantly to the apocalyptic frenzy that gripped France during this *fin-de-siècle*.[16]

Goncourt noted with sardonic glee the appointment of Vallès as Commissioner for Education under the new régime. In fairness, he granted Vallès more talent and sense of responsibility than any other member of the Commune (in fact, he distinguished himself by his moderation and his readiness to combat the extreme measures mooted by the wilder elements); still, remembering the intermittent campaign against classical education that Vallès had conducted in the press, Goncourt decided it would be amusing to see what changes he would initiate—if he were granted time. But it seemed unlikely that time would be granted him. On April 2nd Thiers' troops started bombarding the city. 'Thank God!' wrote Goncourt. 'Civil war has broken out.' He even feels regretful that the Commune is so soon to be crushed; if it had lasted a little longer, the country would perhaps have been sickened for good of mob-rule and of the two institutions that had made it possible: universal suffrage and a free press. In an extraordinary passage, Goncourt (who can hardly have forgotten his own persecution under the press-laws of the Empire) expressing his loathing of the very concept of the freedom of the press. 'In my view, the political newspaper is nothing but an instrument of falsification and incitement. In my view, the literary journal . . . is nothing but an instrument of moral degradation and intellectual abasement.'

Throughout April and May, Goncourt's mood was compounded of two elements: dread of the 'cohorts of Belleville', shambling down the boulevard opposite Tortoni's, almost embarrassed in their hour of triumph and keeping their eyes fixed on the dilapidated boots in which their bare feet were thrust; and a ferocious contempt for that of his own class, who accepted the imposition of working-class rule with a show of indifference that merely masked their pusillanimity. 'Oh, the Parisians of today! You could rape their womenfolk before their eyes, you could do worse, you could steal their purse from their very pocket without changing them in the least: they would remain the most abominable moral cowards I have ever seen.' On the publication of the decree making service in the National Guard compulsory for all males between the ages of 18 and 40, many of the men had gone into hiding; but one saw a fair sprinkling of foreigners, tourists who had poured back into Paris immediately after the armistice, and at the Étoile the diarist's eye was caught by the dauntless Englishwomen standing up in their victorias and watching through their binoculars the Versailles cannon firing at the barricade of the Pont de Neuilly.

Sunday, May 21st was fine and sunny. A charity bazaar was being held in the grounds of the Tuileries Palace; on the *quais*, the usual crowd of anglers were sitting with rod and line. As night fell, the theatre-goers made their

f'ami Sionel

'Communard', pen-and-ink sketch by Gustave Doré: an unsympathetic vision of
the proletarian in arms.

way unconcernedly to their favourite *salle de spectacle*. Hardly anyone knew that the intelligence services of the Versailles army had discovered an undefended gate (the Porte Saint-Cloud) and were at that very time busy establishing themselves in the western districts of the city. On Tuesday, a few barricades were hastily thrown up, but not all of them held. After some murderous street-fighting in the Rue de Rivoli and the Rue Royale, the Tuileries were surrounded; the communard leader in charge of the defence gave orders for the apartments to be soaked in paraffin, and the ancient palace, together with the adjoining library of the Louvre, went up in flames.[17] The fires spread—or more were lit—along the Quai d'Orsay; even Notre-Dame was threatened; and with a terrifying eruption, the powder magazine of the Luxembourg, on the left bank, exploded. Crazed by the heat, blinded by smoke, and driven by blood-lust, the armed men on both sides stopped waiting for orders and fired indiscriminately. No quarter was given either to prisoners or hostages.

Vallès, meanwhile, wandered helplessly around, horrified at the excesses he was forced to witness, and risking being lynched by his own side because he urged moderation. On May 26th he was forced to watch the cold-blooded execution of 50 hostages, including many priests, in the Rue Hoxo. He helped defend one of the last barricades to hold out, but was disappointed in his hopes of an heroic death; in fact, of the 79 members of the Commune only eight, it would appear, lost their lives in the fighting or in the summary executions that followed.

He was given shelter for a night in a herbalist's shop. The following morning, wearing the uniform of a major in the regular army, he set off driving an ambulance round Paris to pick up the dead and the wounded and take them to hospital. At one point he was recognized in the street by Maxime du Camp, who had the decency not to denounce him. The rumour went round that he was dead; obituaries—some of them defamatory in the extreme—were published in the papers, and this circumstance no doubt helped Vallès to pass undetected. He took refuge through the summer in the house of a friend, the sculptor François Roubaud; then, in December, with a false passport, he crossed the frontier and made his way to Brussels. But there was no safety here. Even Hugo had been expelled from Belgium for making a public appeal for clemency to be shown to the *communards*. So the poet found asylum in the Grand-Duchy of Luxemburg while Vallès crossed to England, remaining there until, in 1880, a general amnesty made it possible for him to return to France.

One other member of the Commune whose fate interests us is Gustave Courbet. Unlike the writers whose reactions to the events of 1870–1 we have just analysed, Courbet seems to have remained optimistic almost to the end. Though not unpatriotic, he was prepared to argue that the invasion of France was a cheap enough price to pay for ridding the country of the imperial régime. No sooner had the Republic been established than he found himself designated to take charge of the national art-galleries and museums, thus replacing his old enemy Nieuwerkerke; and he displayed exemplary energy in organizing the safeguard of the public monuments and art treasures housed in Paris when at the start of the siege they came under the threat of the German guns. On April 16th he was elected to the Commune and in a letter to his parents dated April 30th described himself as 'up to his neck' in politics. He confessed himself sometimes at a loss to understand the complex machinery of administration but, for all that, 'I am enchanted. *Paris is a veritable paradise*; no police, no outrages, no quarrels, no exactions of any kind. Paris is moving under its own steam, as smoothly as you could wish. We must try and always be like this.' The gulf between Courbet's optimism and Edmond de Goncourt's embittered pessimism could scarcely have been wider.

Even so, the violence of his colleagues on the Commune seems to have clouded Courbet's serenity, and he resigned his seat some time before the Versailles troops broke into the city. During the fighting he remained on guard at the Louvre and was arrested, tried and sentenced to six months' imprisonment. With some difficulty he managed to obtain permission to practise his art inside the walls of Saint-Pélagie, executing for the most part still lifes of flowers and fruit. The prison governor, doing his rounds, was startled one morning to see a girl's head resting on the pillow of Courbet's pallet; he had been entirely deceived by a masterpiece of *trompe-l'œil*, the artist having painted the picture on the wall next to his bed.

The two works he submitted to the 1872 *salon* were both refused. Meissonier, one of Napoleon III's favourite painters, bullied the other members of the jury into rejecting the pictures on the grounds that Courbet, by his participation in the Commune, had forfeited the right to exhibit. This extraordinarily petty victimization of one of France's greatest living painters boded ill for the prospects of a more liberal treatment of artists under the new régime, but there was worse to come. On May 24th, 1873, after a dramatic clash with the reactionaries in the Chamber, Thiers resigned the presidency and was succeeded by Marshal MacMahon. One of the first acts of the new ministry was to decree the re-erection of the Colonne Vendôme which had been dismantled under the Commune. As early as September 14th, 1870 Courbet, on behalf of the artists' commission of which he was president, had petitioned the Government of National Defence to have this monument to Napoleon I's victories removed, since it was 'devoid of all artistic value', anti-republican by what it symbolized and 'contrary to the genius of modern civilization and to the idea of world-wide brotherhood which, henceforth, must prevail among the nations'. No action was taken, however, until in the middle of the second siege of Paris the Commune decreed the demolition of the Column. This was on April 12th, four days before Courbet was elected to that body, so that there can be no question of his having been directly responsible for the act of which the Bonapartists in the post-war Assembly accused him.[18] Fearing a second prison sentence, Courbet left France and settled in Neuchâtel; but the French courts condemned him *in absentia* to pay the costs of the restoration of the monument, carefully calculated to reach the grand total of 323,091 francs, 63 centimes. What property he had left in France was seized; a sale of his pictures by the government took place on November 26th, 1875, when Courbet was already struck down by a fatal illness; he died on the last day of the year.

Zola, novelist and art-critic

The period of clerical reaction, which Flaubert had foreseen so clearly (the only alternative, the rule of the Internationale, being equally distasteful in his eyes) was initiated by the ministry of the Duc de Broglie and lasted until 1877, when the country, in fresh elections, overwhelmingly repudiated the alliance of monarchists and Bonapartists by which it had been ruled since just after the end of the war. Broglie's administration earned the name 'l'Ordre moral', a title derived from a sentence in the President's opening message to the National Assembly in 1873: Marshal MacMahon declared that his government would remain 'energetically and resolutely conservative', and that, with the help of God, the army, and all right-thinking men, 'we shall pursue together the work of liberating the territory and re-establishing moral order.' A national pilgrimage to Chartres Cathedral was organized immediately after the reading of the President's address; some 50 deputies marched at the head, carrying tapers. As a sequel, other pilgrimages, to Paray-le-Monial, La Salette and Lourdes were arranged, with cut rates offered to the faithful on special excursion trains. Finally, the Assembly passed a bill authorizing the expropriation of a site at Montmartre on which the Archbishop of Paris wished to erect a basilica. The site was deliberately chosen on the summit of the Butte Montmartre so that the new church, consecrated to the Sacred Heart, would be seen to exercise a symbolic supervision of the sinful city stretched beneath it.

The Republicans, of course, through their newspapers and by means of pamphlets, counter-attacked with vigour. The clerical reaction tended, indeed, to cause even those intellectuals who had little faith in ballot-box democracy, men like Renan, Taine and Flaubert, to move over to the left. *A fortiori*, a writer like Zola, who had espoused the republican cause under the Empire, was moved to inject a measure of anti-Church propaganda into those of his works that were composed during the period of the *Ordre moral*.

The case is curious since the series of novels that Zola started publishing after the war were not supposed to be set exactly in contemporary time. In 1868-9, needing to harness himself to a major work which would satisfy his craving for large-scale undertakings, he drew up his plans for writing the 'natural and social history of a family under the Second Empire'. His objectives were twofold: he wished, through this sequence of interlinked novels, to denounce the crimes and scandals that had stained the annals of the Empire; and in the second place, extending the ideas of his mentors Flaubert and Taine, he hoped to introduce something of the rigour of the natural sciences into literature. To achieve the first end, he had merely to utilize and dramatize the anti-bonapartist propaganda current in the closing years of the Empire, to which he had himself been contributing in the articles he was publishing in the opposition press between 1868 and 1870.[10] Zola spent several months, immediately before the war, working out the details of the ten novels which, at that time, he anticipated would be sufficient to contain the saga of the Rougon-Macquart family; then, having extracted from his publisher a promise of financial support, he settled down to write the initial volume, which centred on the impact of the *coup d'état* of 1851 on a small town in Provence. *La Fortune des Rougon* was written before the Franco-Prussian War broke out, but its publication had to be deferred until peace had returned; so that even before *Les Rougon-Macquart* had started to appear in print, the period in which they were all intended to be set, the Second Empire, had already receded into history.

Now it was practically an axiom of the realist novel in nineteenth-century France that it should deal with the contemporary age and with contemporary problems. *Les Rougon-Macquart*, conceived as a withering denunciation of bonapartism, could never be contemporary in this sense: Zola published his account of the Franco-Prussian War (*La Débâcle*) in 1892, by which time the events he described so graphically were only a childhood memory for those of his readers who were under 30. He turned this unexpected difficulty, which the instability of political régimes had posed him, by the simple expedient of under-emphasizing, at least in the later novels of the series, the overtly historical element. The miners' strike in *Germinal* (1885), the stock-exchange crash in *L'Argent* (1891), might just as feasibly have occurred under the Third Republic as during the Second Empire. But in the first half-dozen novels he wrote, the setting is unmistakably 'period'; modernism enters into them only, as it were, by a subterfuge.

For all that, these early novels are genuine products of the Third Republic, and specifically of the radical outlook of the *Ordre moral* period, as is clear enough once we try to account for the anti-clerical sentiment which permeates them all but is most apparent in two of them, *La Conquête de Plassans* (1874), and *La Faute de l'abbé Mouret* (1875). Both are novels about clerics, and in both the question of priestly celibacy looms large. Abbé Faujas, in *La Conquête de Plassans*, is an efficient tool of the civil power, working resolutely and discreetly to ensure that the provincial town to which he has been despatched should be swung over to the support of the new régime. Serge Mouret is a simple country priest who falls in love: *La Faute de l'abbé Mouret* relates his sinful amours and subsequent return to grace, though it is clear enough that his renunciation of the girl he has seduced is meant to arouse contempt rather than admiration in the reader. Thus in neither novel is the Church allotted a particularly distinguished part, and it is this that turns them into a sort of disguised critique of the religious revival which was in full swing in the 1870s.

Other novels show the close affinities between Zola's concept of his art and that of the painters with whose work we were concerned at the beginning of this chapter. The question of the 'impressionism' of Zola's prose style is too delicate and complex to be elucidated short of abundant illustration and commentary; but it is clear that a novel like *Le Ventre de Paris*, which Zola published in 1873, could have been written only by a man who had gained considerable insight into the preoccupations of what was called the 'Batignolles group' of painters. One of the peripheral characters in this novel is in fact a young painter, Claude Lantier; his later career will be traced in the novel, *L'Œuvre*, which Zola used as a pretext to give his own account of the history of Impressionism from the time of the Salon des Refusés onwards. In the earlier novel, it is above all Claude's interest in the picturesque aspects of modern city life that links him with certain artists whose work Zola had followed with the keenest interest in the 1870s: Monet, Pissarro, and Renoir in particular.

Zola's personal acquaintance with Monet and his friends dates back, as we have seen, to the early 1860s, but it was in 1866 that he came into prominence as the doughtiest and most devoted of their champions. The series of articles about the *salon* that he published in *L'Événement* that spring created a considerable scandal, both on account of his unheard-of impertinence in

listing the members of the jury and publicly examining their credentials—
with no respect for persons—and for the seemingly extravagant way in which
he vaunted the hotly contested talent of Édouard Manet, whose works had
been refused that year by the jury and whose situation, as Zola wrote, was
that of 'a pariah, an unpopular and grotesque painter . . . an artist whom
people pretend not to understand and who is banished from the little world
of painters like a leper.' Zola added that if he had the cash, he would buy
every canvas Manet would sell him. 'In ten years' time, they will fetch 15 or
20 times the price.' Here he was over-estimating the rapidity with which
Manet was to establish himself and when he reprinted this essay in 1879, Zola
changed this sentence to read: 'In 50 years' time . . . '.

The only other full-length *salon* that he wrote before the war was devoted
to the 1868 exhibition; this review[20] was noticeably less truculent than the
earlier one. The obvious reason for the quieter tone was that the jury, that
year, had followed a more enlightened policy: Manet's submissions were
accepted (one of them was his portrait of Zola) and it was possible to believe
that this much maligned artist was beginning to disarm his critics. 'You will
find that there will be jokes about the painter of *Olympia* in the popular
press for some time to come', Zola predicted. 'But already intelligent men
take him seriously, and the rest of the crowd will follow in their train.' Not
only Manet, but nearly all the other members of the Batignolles group were
represented that year by one or two paintings, and Zola found the right
words to express their originality, their freshness and their modernity. He
devoted an entire article to Pissarro, and most of another to Monet. Although
the latter had sent in two seascapes, Zola presents him as being above all a
Parisian artist, the painter of modern urban life:

> He delights in our city skylines, in the white and grey patches that
> houses make against a clear sky; he delights in overcoated men hurrying
> about their business in the streets; he delights in race-meetings, in the
> clattering of the gentry's carriages along fashionable avenues; he delights
> in the women of our times, with their sunshades, their gloves, their pretty
> dresses, even their hair-pieces and rice-powder, everything that makes
> them daughters of our civilization.
>
> In the country, Claude Monet will prefer a carefully tended park to a
> forest glade. He likes to discover everywhere the human touch, he wants
> to live among us all the time. A true Parisian, he imports Paris into the
> countryside, and feels unable to paint a landscape without placing in it
> ladies and gentlemen all dressed up.

It could be objected that in this passage Zola over-emphasizes certain aspects of Monet's art in his first period, but it is clear that what he prized in Monet, as also in Bazille and Renoir of whom he wrote further on in the same article, was whatever made them assimilable to the literary movement which he was preparing to head. In *Le Ventre de Paris*, it may be that Claude Lantier is only distantly modelled on Claude Monet: but what characterizes Zola's fictional painter—the love of bright colour, of the bustle of city streets, of the juxta-position of the old and the new in architecture—is enough to make him a kind of composite of all the eager young men whom Zola used to meet of an evening at the Café Guerbois in pre-war days.

The Impressionist Exhibitions

The war interrupted the careers of all of them and ended that of one of them—Frédéric Bazille, who enlisted in a regiment of Zouaves and was killed in battle. Renoir was drafted into a cavalry regiment and posted to Vic-en-Bigorre in the Pyrenees. Cézanne went into hiding at L'Estaque. Pissarro had to move out of Louveciennes, leaving his canvases to the mercy of the advancing Germans; he went first to Britanny, then to London, where Monet and Daubigny had preceded him. Another refugee in England was the dealer Paul Durand-Ruel, who had succeeded in shipping over most of his stock of the nineteenth-century French masters and had opened a gallery in New Bond Street. It was in London that Durand-Ruel first made personal contact with Monet and Pissarro and started buying their canvases to add to his holdings. When he returned to Paris he continued the same policy, buying from Sisley and Degas as well, and investing heavily in Manets. Durand-Ruel rightly believed that, given time, these canvases would appreciate in value, but in addition he hoped to earn the gratitude of the members of the group and persuade them to look on him as their principal patron. Steadily rising prices in the immediate post-war period seemed to justify his confidence. At a sale in Paris held early in 1873, a collection of Pissarro's canvases realized a surprisingly high figure. Later that year, Manet sold five paintings to the operatic tenor Jean-Baptiste Faure, including *Le Déjeuner sur l'herbe*, for which the asking price was 4,000 francs, and *Le Bon Bock*, for which he received 6,000 francs. The latter portrait had been exhib-ited that spring; Manet never achieved a greater popular success with any of his *salon* pictures.

Prosperity seemed, for these struggling artists, to be just round the corner; in fact, it was further away than they imagined. In the post-war inflationary boom the general level of prices paid for works of art showed a natural tendency to rise. But then the over-stretched economy suddenly contracted, business slackened off, the price of securities fell, and Durand-Ruel had no choice but to draw in his horns and cease buying. The painters found themselves in the same financial difficulties as before.

The harsh logic of their situation required them to exhibit, since wares that are not displayed can never attract purchasers. But under the Third Republic the *salon* was just as unsatisfactory an institution for this purpose as it had been under the Second Empire. The eight or ten canvases they might, in a good year, hope to have exhibited were all too easily lost in the ruck; moreover, the fact that *Le Bon Bock*, a work altogether uncharacteristic of the new tendencies, was the only painting of Manet's to achieve a real success in the *salon* suggested that no headway could be made unless the young artists were prepared to soften the asperities of their art.

In the circumstances the idea of a separate group exhibition commended itself to a few of them—though not to Manet. The notion was first publicly mooted by Paul Alexis in an article in *L'Avenir national*, May 5th, 1873. Alexis was a young writer who had close ties with Zola, and the paper on which he worked was currently employing Zola as its theatre critic; so it is possible that the scheme was a brain-child of the author of *Les Rougon-Macquart* who was in any case a great believer in group action and was even then laying plans for the formation of his own nucleus of naturalist novelists, to include Alexis. Monet was immediately attracted to the idea, and wrote to *L'Avenir national* in support of it; Pissarro too felt that salvation might lie in an annual group exhibition.

A limited liability company was accordingly formed, with a list of statutes and a name (*Société anonyme des artistes peintres*) deliberately chosen for its colourlessness, since it was no part of the exhibitors' intentions to pose as revolutionaries. In fact Degas insisted, as a condition of his participation, on the abandonment of the original stipulation that only artists prepared to boycott the official *salon* should be eligible to exhibit with the *Société anonyme*; Degas had no wish to give the press the opportunity to stigmatize the society as a group of incompetents who chose this method of exhibiting because their art fell below the standards required for admittance to the *salon*. Fear of incurring the ridicule of insensitive critics even led to an attempt on the part of some members of the society to blackball Cézanne; only earnest pleading by Pissarro persuaded the others to allow this gruff, shy, tormented genius to join their ranks.

The exhibition was located in a set of studios off the Boulevard des Capucines belonging to the photographer Nadar, who let them rent-free to the society. It opened on April 15th, 1874 and provoked immediate comment in the press, mostly unfriendly when it was not downright offensive. The most effective review was the gently ironical skit that appeared in *Le Charivari* under the heading: '*L'École des Impressionnistes*'. The author, Louis Leroy, later plumed himself on having invented the word; though his claim may be allowed without difficulty, the term *impression* was, as we have noted, commonly bandied about before the war in connection not only with Monet's style but, even earlier, with reference also to Daubigny's; and three days before Leroy's famous article appeared Armand Silvestre, defining the vision common to three landscapists in the group (Monet, Sisley and Pissarro), declared that it differed from that of earlier masters in respect of the 'effect of *impression*' which these painters were exclusively concerned with, 'leaving the quest for *expression* to the zealots of the line.'[21]

Leroy's article took the form of an imaginary dialogue between the journalist and a landscape painter of the old school, loaded with years and honours, whom he is conducting round the exhibition. On first confronting Monet's *Boulevard des Capucines* the venerable visitor exclaims: ' "That's an impression, or I'm much mistaken! But could you please explain to me what all those little black threads in the bottom of the picture are meant to be?"—I answered that they were people walking along.—"You mean that's what I look like when I am walking along the Boulevard des Capucines? Confound it, sir! are you making game of me?" ' There were more intelligent comments than this on Monet's masterpiece, including one from the pen of a critic, Ernest Chesneau, who counted as a recent convert, his earlier observations on the work of the Impressionists having been decidedly unsympathetic. 'Never', wrote Chesneau, 'have the impalpable, the fugitive, the instantaneous qualities of movement been caught and fixed in their prodigious fluidity as they have been in this extraordinary, this marvellous rough study (*ébauche*) that M. Monet has catalogued under the title *Boulevard des Capucines*.'[22] But even for Chesneau, the work was only a 'rough study'; he could not grasp that the effect it has on the observer, this 'prodigious fluidity' as he called it, had been obtained only by giving it what, by earlier canons, would be judged an 'unfinished' appearance. His review continues: 'Obviously this is not the last word in art, nor even in this particular art. It will have to contrive to transform the sketch into a finished work (*transformer l'esquisse en œuvre faite*).'

The middle-class critics with whom Impressionism had to contend were constantly putting forward, usually in less measured and more scathing language than Chesneau used, the same objection: that these artists were either lazy or impatient, but at all events slapdash; they would not take the trouble to learn how to draw, or to work on their canvases until they had the smooth, glassy texture that constituted a 'finished' appearance. There

The demolition of the Colonne Vendôme, depicted here, was decreed by the mmune on 12 April 1871 (see p. 194). The monument had been erected in 1810 commemorate the battle of Austerlitz

22 Paris in flames during the *semaine sanglante*, 21–27 May 1871. The Tuileries Palace, totally destroyed and never rebuilt, is seen here from the left bank of the Seine

could be no good art without hard work: this was axiomatic for the bourgeois who, after all, expected and exacted careful workmanship from the joiner, the plumber, the furniture-maker whom he employed. The purchasing public, made up of members of the same class, entirely agreed; who wanted to hand over a sheaf of crisp blue one-hundred franc notes for a canvas on which the brush-strokes were still visible? The deadly meticulousness of Meissonier, on the other hand, corresponded precisely with the bourgeois idea of value for money.

The accusation of carelessness, or of inability to learn the elements of his craft could be levelled with as much justification against Manet, and indeed had been for many years. The cry was raised again at the 1874 *salon* over the single picture of his that the jury accepted, *Le Chemin de fer*. The most effective refutation of the charge was made, on this occasion, by Stéphane Mallarmé,[23] whose essay dealt not merely with the canvas that the jury had grudgingly accepted, but also with the two that it had refused: *Le Bal de l'Opéra* and *Les Hirondelles*. The execution of *Les Hirondelles*, Mallarmé admits, might have been judged a little rudimentary, a little unvarnished: 'to use a colloquial expression, "the picture has not been pushed far enough", has been left unfinished.' He answers the objection by posing the question: 'What is a work that is "not pushed far enough", when there exists a harmony among its elements which gives it unity, when it has a charm that the addition of a single extra touch would quickly dispel?' Mallarmé concluded his article by making yet a further appeal for a more liberal policy in the organization of the official exhibition. Talent, he argued—perhaps a little too glibly—is readily recognized, and should be the sole passport here; the jury should reject only the untalented artist.

The Impressionists continued to show themselves unwilling to trust the *salon* jury to confine their activities to excluding the untalented (which in any case was no doubt what the jury had always imagined it was doing). Their experimental private exhibition had not been an unqualified success; but neither had it been an outright failure: at least they had established their existence as a group in the eyes of the public. Their stock was still low: this was cruelly demonstrated by the derisory prices reached at an auction sale in 1875, in which Monet, Renoir and Sisley participated, along with Berthe Morisot, now Manet's sister-in-law. Some of the pictures went for sums that barely covered the cost of the frames, and the behaviour of those members of the public who attended the sale to boo rather than to bid was so unruly that the auctioneer had to call in the police for fear of open brawling.

On the other hand, new private patrons were beginning to come forward. There was the cultivated Dr Gachet, with a private practice in Paris and a large house at Auvers; he had taken an intelligent interest in the work of the group since the days when they used to meet of an evening in the Café Guerbois, where he would join them and listen to their discussions. He gave particular encouragement to Cézanne, who in 1873 moved from Pontoise to Auvers in order to be near him. Then there was Georges Caillebotte, an engineer with a private fortune who was also an amateur painter; he not only purchased pictures from Monet and Renoir but sent his own careful, insipid compositions for display in their group exhibitions. But perhaps the most enlightened collector of all was Victor Chocquet who, though his means were limited (he depended for his livelihood on his job in the civil service), spent all he could spare on their canvases, especially on those of Cézanne. Moreover, Chocquet engaged in active propaganda on behalf of the Impressionists, attending their exhibitions and engaging any unconvinced or clearly hostile visitor in violent and persuasive argument.

A second independent exhibition was decided on in 1876 with 20 exhibitors joining in, showing a total of some 250 works. The critics were as scathing as ever; a note of frenzied exasperation underlay the usual contemptuous irony. The right-wing press dubbed the Impressionists 'the revolutionary school' and insinuated that they had entered into an unholy alliance with the rump of the *communards*. Albert Wolff informed his readers in *Le Figaro* that the exhibition was the work of 'five or six lunatics, including one woman', a statement which so enraged Eugène Manet, the husband of the woman alluded to (Berthe Morisot), that it was with difficulty that his friends could restrain him from issuing a challenge. But for all that, there were signs that Impressionism was being taken seriously in some quarters, and was even beginning to achieve an international reputation. Zola despatched a report on the exhibition to *The European Herald* of St Petersburg in which he contrasted the qualities of youthful challenge and burning conviction that he found in the Rue Lepeletier with the 'chilly, formal, dark halls of the official exhibition' at the Palais de l'Industrie. He singled out for particular praise Monet's *Japonnerie* and *La Prairie* and characterized Renoir as 'a Rubens bathed in the brilliant sun of Velazquez'. In the *New York Tribune* Henry James admitted that he found the Impressionist exhibition 'decidedly interesting' even though 'none of its members show signs of possessing first-rate talent.' James drew an interesting analogy, far-fetched though it may have been, between their attitude to the subject-matter of art and that of the Pre-Raphaelites. Both groups had rejected the traditional view of the beautiful, and for the same reason: that it was 'a metaphysical notion, which can only get one into a muddle and is to be severely left alone.' Instead, the artist's function was to 'give a vivid impression of how a thing happens to look at a particular moment'. But there was a difference between the realism of Holman Hunt and Millais and that of Degas, Monet and the others. The English school endeavoured to compensate for their infidelity to the 'more or less moral proprieties and conventionalities' of neo-classical art by exquisite craftsmanship and laborious attention to detail. 'But the Impressionists, who, I think, are more consistent, abjure virtue altogether, and declare that a subject which has been crudely chosen shall be loosely treated. They send detail to the dogs and concentrate themselves on general expression.'[24] Although it is certain that James was mistaken in thinking that there was any *arrière-pensée* of this sort in the Impressionists' adoption of the blurred outline and the dissolving contour, at least he does not attribute these features to mere carelessness or defective technique, as most contemporary critics were still inclined to do.

Naturalism and Impressionism

By the time the third exhibition was held, in 1877—the first to be boldly announced as an *Exposition des Impressionnistes*—it was evident that a change of attitude in the public was under way. There was no lack of scoffers among the visitors, but there were also women in fashionable clothes and critics disposed to take this new art seriously and to acknowledge that some of the exhibitors, Renoir and Degas at least, had talent, even if Monet, Pissarro and Cézanne remained beyond the pale. Renoir, in fact, was beginning to achieve the prestige of a fashionable portrait-painter. He had found a new patron in Georges Charpentier, the publisher, who commissioned him to execute a portrait of his wife and children which, when it was exhibited in the 1879 *salon*, very nearly became the 'picture of the year'. Now Charpentier was Zola's publisher; the other authors on his list included most, if not all, of the *médanistes*, the group of young writers gravitating around Zola who took their name from the little hamlet where he had his country retreat. Impressionists and naturalists hobnobbed in the Charpentiers' drawing-room and the links between the two movements were now visible to all. Manet completed his portrait of the actress-courtesan Henriette Hauser in the winter of 1876-7, at the same time as *L'Assommoir*, appearing in instalments in the newspaper *Le Voltaire*, had reached the chapter where Zola describes Gervaise's scapegrace adolescent daughter at the start of her life of vice; and Manet, profiting by his old friend's new-won celebrity, decided to call his picture *Nana*.

It was with the publication of *L'Assommoir*, the seventh volume of the *Rougon-Macquart* cycle, that naturalism became a universal talking-point.

The earlier volumes had been politely received or politely ignored by the critics; none of them had achieved the kind of shocked attention which Zola's pre-war sex-and-murder thriller, *Thérèse Raquin*, had earned. Zola had his share of the neurotic ambition common among men who suffer from a deep-seated insecurity feeling, and this cold neglect exasperated him far more than even the most violent hostility or misunderstanding. Edmond de Goncourt, recording an occasion when Zola, at dinner with him and his friends Alphonse Daudet and Ivan Turgenev, was reminiscing about the privations of his youth, tells us in his diary how, when the novelist spoke at length and bitterly about 'the suspicion with which he is regarded, the kind of quarantine in which his works are kept', the others tried to cheer him up, telling him he had nothing to complain of and that he had not done so badly, for a man still in his early thirties. Zola answered: 'You will think me a child, but I can't help it. . . . I shall never be decorated, I shall never be elected to the Academy, I shall never obtain a single one of those honours which set a seal on talent. In the eyes of the public, I shall always be a pariah, yes, a pariah.' And, added Goncourt, 'he repeated the word four or five times: a pariah.'

The dinner-party at which this outburst occurred took place in January, 1875. Two years later Zola had become one of the most notorious of French writers, bitterly attacked but read by everyone, and certainly a pariah no longer. *L'Assommoir* was so startling a novelty that it could not fail to break through the barrier of indifference. For the first time, men and women of the working class—the very types who had control of Paris during the 73 days of the Commune—were given the leading parts in a specimen of that hitherto exclusively middle-class literary form, the novel. Even the narrative passages were written in their racy, ugly dialect. Zola's very audacity in bringing out such a book, so eloquent an indictment—however indirectly formulated—of the exploitation of the worker through the operation of *laissez-faire* capitalism, was breath-taking enough. Fortunately for his personal security, perhaps, the year in which *L'Assommoir* was published was also the year in which new elections swept the conservatives from office, ended the *Ordre moral*, and banished the spectre of a reversion to a monarchical system of government. Presidential democracy was now firmly established in France, with a coalition of left and left-centre parties in power, and the Republic was assured of continued existence at least for a few more years; it took the threat of a military coup by General Boulanger, in 1889, to end this euphoric interlude.

Zola consolidated the position he had won with determination and energy. A press-campaign to popularize the virtues of naturalism, not just in

Gill's cartoon, 'The Birth of Nana-Venus' (1880), an obvious distortion of Botticelli's famous picture, represents a typical contemporary comment on what was felt to be the outrageous frankness of Zola's naturalism.

the novel but in the drama too, was undertaken in *Le Voltaire* and *Le Figaro*. A small body of disciples and adherents, some of them writers of great talent, others little more than cultured journalists, gathered round him; the naturalist school was born and in 1880 produced, in the collection of short stories entitled *Les Soirées de Médan*, the literary equivalent of the group exhibitions of the Impressionists. Naturalism was exported abroad, to Italy, to Germany, eventually even to the British Isles and the United States once the Anglo-Saxon reading public had been conditioned to accept the repellent immodesty of a physiological interpretation of character. Strindberg claimed to have launched naturalism on the stage, a feat which Zola himself had attempted with less success. The reaction came eventually, of course, but that story can be left to our concluding chapter.

Impressionism achieved no such spectacular break-through. It was more a case of the gradual attrition, through custom, of critical opposition. The independent exhibitions continued; there were eight in all, the last being held in 1886. But though they served their purpose of keeping the new developments in painting before the public eye, they were also a cause of inner dissension within the group itself. After the fourth exhibition (in 1879) Monet deserted the others in order to follow Renoir's example and exhibit in the official *salon*. Neither Renoir, Monet, Sisley, nor Cézanne had any part in the sixth (1881) exhibition; only Pissarro and Degas remained out of the original band, together with Berthe Morisot; and there was one notable new recruit, Gauguin. All along, difficulties had been caused by Degas' Csistence on the inclusion of his personal friends, who except for Mary inassatt were depressingly unoriginal artists. Only in 1882 when, thanks to the exertions of Caillebotte and Durand-Ruel, Pissarro was finally persuaded that Degas' publicity value to them was less than his nuisance value, could a more or less representative collection of Impressionist paintings, mostly drawn from Durand-Ruel's extensive holdings, be shown.

The following year Manet died. Right at the end of his life the elusive recognition he had been pursuing for so long seemed at last to have been attained. His old friend Antonin Proust, having been appointed Minister of Fine Arts in Gambetta's new cabinet, secured for him the coveted red ribbon of the Legion of Honour (1881). The two pictures he sent to the *salon* of 1882 (*Un bar aux Folies-Bergères* and *Jeanne*) were universally praised; even Albert Wolff, who in times past had shown himself among the most violent critics of the new painting, made amends on this occasion. 'The exhibition hall is full of young men to whom Manet has taught the modern art of open-air painting', he wrote. (In point of fact, it was Claude Monet who, at Argenteuil, had shown Manet the elements of this art.) *Jeanne*, said Wolff, was 'ravishing in the impression it leaves. One cannot deny that M. Manet's art is truly his; he has not borrowed it from the museum, he has wrested it from nature.'

It fell to Zola, his first defender, to write Manet's principal obituary; a retrospective exhibition having been arranged, he was asked to provide the preface to the catalogue. It is possible that a more enthusiastic panegyrist could have been found; but it was undeniably appropriate that the leader of the naturalists should have been chosen to render a supreme homage to the artist who, in spite of his constant refusals to be associated with them, must count as the first and probably the most influential inspirer of the Impressionists.

Notes

[1] Other contemporaries portrayed by Manet in *La Musique aux Tuileries* include Théophile Gautier, Offenbach, Champfleury, the art critic Zacharie Astruc, and his own brother Eugène.

[2] *Salons*, ed. Hemmings and Niess, p. 95.

[3] Quoted by A. Tabarant, *Manet et ses œuvres* (Paris, 1947), p. 42.

[4] It is said that when Louis-Philippe was inspecting the new decorations that Delacroix had undertaken for the Palais du Luxembourg, he asked whether they were painted directly on to the walls. When told they were canvases he was heard to murmur: 'Thank God for that, we can have them removed.'

[5] Of the 2,800 works that the jury were supposed to have rejected, over half (1,600) were withdrawn by the artists and therefore not displayed at the Salon des Refusés.

[6] An estimated 7,000 on the first day (May 15th).

[7] Gautier wrote 12 articles in *Le Moniteur* on the official *salon*, none on the Salon des Refusés.

[8] F. Mathey, *The World of the Impressionists* (1961), p. 38.

[9] As did Berthe Morisot, who exhibited with the Impressionists after the war; she was the daughter of a rich magistrate.

[10] Monet did, however, share briefly, in 1864–5, Bazille's studio in the quiet little Rue de Furstenberg, behind the church of St Germain-des-Prés, which is now a Delacroix museum, Delacroix having used the premises for some years before his death in 1863.

[11] Quoted by E. Moreau-Nélaton, *Daubigny raconté par lui-même* (1925), p. 81.

[12] See above, p. 87

[13] See his novel *L'Enfant*, the first part of the autobiographical trilogy entitled *Jacques Vingtras* of which *L'Insurgé* is the last part; and also the exhaustive biography written by Gaston Gille: *Jules Vallès, ses révoltes, sa maîtrise, son prestige* (Paris, Flammarion, 1941).

[14] Flaubert, *Correspondance. Nouvell eédition augmentée*, vol. VI (Paris, Conard, 1930), pp. 134–5, 138, 148, 184–5, 215–16.

[15] Thus, Vallès delivered a stinging attack on Hugo in his paper *La Rue* on the occasion of the revival of *Hernani* in 1867 (see above, pp. 74–5), calling him 'une statue creuse, . . . sur laquelle on frappera, comme les paysans sur les casseroles, pour rappeler ou maudire les abeilles,'—a reference, of course, to the bees as emblem of the Napoleonic Empire.

[16] The first factor in the equation (proletarian = barbarian) had been established long ago. Paul Lidsky (*Les Ecrivains contre la Commune*, Paris, 1970, p. 24) quotes Saint-Marc Girardin who back in 1832 wrote in *Le Journal des Débats*: '*Les Barbares qui menacent la société ne sont point au Caucase ni dans les steppes de la Tartarie, ils sont dans les faubourgs de nos villes manufacturières.*' Public opinion had been shocked by the events in Lyons, November 1831, when the silk-workers reacted violently to an enforced cut in their wages, took over the city, and had to be dispersed by the military.

[17] The partial destruction of this library (or, perhaps, of the library of the Hôtel de Ville a day or two later) occasioned one of the more celebrated poems in Hugo's *L'Année terrible*, '*A qui la faute?*' The poet violently upbraids one of the incendiarists for such a crime against humanity; the man answers him crushingly: '*Je ne sais pas lire.*'

[18] In fact it was Félix Pyat who, according to a claim he made in a letter to *The Times* (June 24th, 1864) bore chief responsibility for the destruction of the Colonne Vendôme.

[19] Especially in *La Tribune*, *Le Rappel*, and *La Cloche*. See Henri Mitterand, *Zola journaliste* (Paris, 1962), pp. 81–121.

[20] Published in *L'Événement illustré*, May 2nd–June 16th, 1868 (7 articles).

[21] *L'Opinion nationale*, April 22nd, 1874. Philippe Burty, writing in *La République française*, April 25th, similarly emphasized, in a eulogistic review of the exhibition, what he called the '*qualité des impressions*'. See Jacques Lethève, *Impressionnis es et symbolistes devant la presse* (Paris, 1959), pp. 63–4.

[22] *Paris-Journal*, May 7th, 1874. Chesneau actually wrote here—as he did thro ughout his article—Manet where he meant Monet. This confusion was constantly being made, more to Manet's annoyance than Monet's, and on one occasion led to a near-crisis in Zola's relations with Manet. (For details, see my article 'Zola, Mane t, and the Impressionists', *PMLA*, vol. LXXIII (1958), pp. 407–417.

[23] 'Le Jury de peinture de 1874 et M. Manet,' originally in *La Renaissance rtistique et littéraire*, April 12th, 1874; reproduced in the Pléiade edition of Mallarmé's works (ed. Henri Mondor and G. Jean-Aubry, 1945), pp. 691–700.

[24] James, *The Painter's Eye*, ed. John L. Sweeney (London, Hart-Davis, 1956), pp. 114–115.

six

Widening Horizons

The Myth of the Decadence

There is no clearer indication of the mistrust with which thoughtful men in France confronted the broad spectrum of social and cultural developments during this half-century, than their persistent belief that they lived in an age of decadence. The country was obviously growing steadily richer; the benefits of education were spreading; communications were improving all the time, and technical changes were following one another faster than they could be properly absorbed. And yet, among writers who took time to reflect and consider, the prevailing mood was one of foreboding. If one compares this period with the Age of the Enlightenment in the previous century, which covered roughly the same span of time (from 1734, when Voltaire published the *Lettres philosophiques*, till 1789) the contrast could hardly be more marked. The earlier era was one of steady national decline combined with growing self-confidence and optimism on the part of the bourgeois intelligentsia; the later period shows the exact reverse—broadly speaking a prosperous and contented population and a self-confident administration, whose cultural spokesmen were none the less filled with gloom and despondency and apt to indulge in the direst predictions. What they foretold, however, was not quite the catastrophe which in the event overwhelmed France and Europe in 1914. The prophecies had nothing apocalyptic about them: the end was to come not with the roar of a cosmic explosion but with the wheeze of a slow puncture.

Versed as they were in ancient history, they saw a close and menacing parallel between contemporary trends and the events that preceded the fall of the Roman Empire. Round the shores of the Mediterranean some 2,000 years before, there had spread a vigorous civilization which (it was supposed) had after a few centuries grown enervated through over-luxuriant development, so that, when the hordes of barbarians stormed the frontiers, the Romans of the decadence could oppose no effective resistance, and allowed themselves to be slaughtered, their daughters to be ravished and their city to be laid waste with scarcely a protest. The same thing was to happen again; the only point in doubt was the form to be taken by the new barbarian invasion. Before 1870, those who thought destruction would come from across the frontiers were inclined to cast their eyes in the direction of the Russian Empire. The annihilation of the Grande Armée in 1812 and the occupation of French soil by Cossack troops in 1815 was still a scar in the collective memory; while the more recent clash in the Crimea had strengthened the idea that Russia was the hereditary enemy. But more imaginative minds saw as the greatest threat an internal, moral or psychological collapse. The frenetic pursuit of material wealth, the fading of all generous idealism and the replacement of religious faith by universal scepticism would be sufficient to doom the race.

> Ce n'est pas que, le fer et la torche à la main,
> Le Gépide ou le Hun les foule et les dévore,
> Qu'un empire agonise, et qu'on entende encore
> Les chevaux d'Alarik hennir dans l'air romain.

> Non! le poids est plus lourd qui les courbe et les lie;
> Et, corrodant leur cœur d'avarice enflammé,
> L'idole au ventre d'or, le Moloch affamé
> S'assied, la pourpre au dos, sur la terre avilie.

Leconte de Lisle wrote these two stanzas in the very early years of the Second Empire.[1] At its heyday, the Goncourt brothers expressed the same kind of apprehensions in their novel *Les Hommes de lettres*.[2] The hero is shown in conversation with a garrulous medical practitioner whose diagnosis of the current *mal de siècle* can be assumed to approximate closely to the theories dear to the two authors: essentially, the doctor holds that the pace of modern life is responsible for the high incidence of anaemia, especially among artists, intellectuals, and men of affairs, all of whom belong to the class of those who 'live their lives almost solely through impressions, pleasures, satisfactions, disappointments, setbacks of a moral order'. The significant passage runs as follows:

Anaemia is on the increase, that's a positive fact. The human race is degenerating. It's the same thing, projected from families to the species, as occurs to royal dynasties at the end of the line. You must have seen those kings of Spain in the Louvre—how they show every symptom of thinning of the blood. Possibly that was the sickness of the Roman Empire; you can see even in the bronze effigies some of the emperors with features that seem to have run together. But in those days there was the remedy to hand. When a society was dying off, exhausted physiologically, an invasion of barbarians descended on it to transfuse the young blood of Hercules into its old veins. Who will save the world from the anaemia of the nineteenth century? Will rescue come from an invasion of society by the workers in a few hundred years' time?

The analogy between the destructive raids of the Goths and Huns in the fifth century and the short-lived triumph of the manual workers in the streets of Paris in 1871 was almost bound to occur to Edmond de Goncourt when he witnessed it.[3]

The quality of the pessimism that darkened the French literary scene in the 1850s is best apprehended when one compares the books and poetry written at that time, under the aegis of Parnassianism or realism, with the typical products of the Romantic era, even though that earlier period had a well-deserved reputation for morbidity. Thus, the characteristic curve of family fortunes in Balzac's *Comédie humaine* is ascendant. The Claës clan in *La Recherche de l'Absolu*, the Hulots in *La Cousine Bette* endure misfortunes and come near to disaster, but at the end of each of these novels they have overcome the threat and are shown recovering strength and cohesion. Just as characteristically, in Flaubert, the curve is descendant. Emma Bovary's robust father, the farmer Rouault, has as his one surviving daughter a nerve-ridden, suicidally inclined woman, whose only child Berthe already shows signs of some pulmonary affection before the book is ended; on the last page, after her father's death, we are told she has been sent to work in a textile factory where we may be sure the conditions of labour obtaining at the period will bring her short life to a premature end. *Madame Bovary* is, among other things, a chronicle of family degeneration.[4]

The myth of decadence, whether at the level of the family, the nation, or the entire race, had gripped the imagination not only of poets and novelists, but of philosophers and social thinkers too, well before the military disasters of 1870 came to confirm and vindicate their pessimism. The ruin of liberal hopes in 1848 no doubt helped to foster the idea, but it was not only liberal thinkers who contemplated the future with the gravest misgivings. Claude-Marie Raudot, whose treatise *La Décadence de la France* was published as early as 1850, was a Catholic conservative who had no reason to repine at the way progressive policies had been reversed after June, 1848;

even so, he could take little comfort from the spectacle of a France whose agriculture was on the wane, whose birth-rate was falling, and whose male population, as the recruiting statistics showed, was suffering from a steady decline in physique. For Arthur de Gobineau the decadence of the race was self-evident; he was more concerned with elaborating a theory to explain it, and so he evolved his hypothesis of a fatal contamination over the centuries of the pure Aryan stock (the Franks) by the inferior Mediterranean breed. Gobineau found confirmation of his ideas in the fact that the dominant nation at the time was clearly England, a country inhabited—so he sturdily maintained—by fair-haired Aryans, industrious, inventive, prolific and aggressive. Gobineau's fanciful analysis, presented in his *Essai sur l'inégalité des races humaines* (1853–5) did not, it is true, win many adherents when it was published, though in the following century, adapted and perverted by such forerunners and apologists of National Socialism as Houston Stewart Chamberlain and Alfred Rosenberg, it did achieve a certain sinister notoriety.

Under the 'liberal' Empire the myth of national decadence was exploited by anti-establishment writers, who argued from analogy between the relaxed and permissive moral tone of the régime and the orgiastic excesses of ancient Rome: nemesis would overcome the court of Napoleon III, as it had dogged Nero and Caligula. The fact that pagan licentiousness had, in Rome, coincided with the greatest extension of imperial power, while the fall of the Western Empire had occurred three and a half centuries later, at a time when the Mediterranean world was completely Christianized and therefore (presumably) clean living, was an awkward historical fact invariably glossed over. Thomas Couture's grandiose portrayal of a Roman revel[5] was an anachronism, at least if one attaches any importance to the title, *Les Romains de la décadence*; any reader of Gibbon could have told Couture that the same stretch of time separated the reign of Heliogabalus, considered to mark the high tide of depravity in the ancient world, from the sack of Rome by Alaric the Goth, as separated the reign of Henry of Navarre from the French Revolution. But these chronological niceties were ignored by all and besides, the distinction between the politico-historical connotations of the term and its moral overtones was never very firmly drawn. When Henri Rochefort brought together between the covers of a book the spicy newspaper articles he had been inditing on current society scandals, it was not felt to be anything but highly appropriate that he should have entitled the volume *Les Français de la décadence*.

The customary line taken by publicists of Rochefort's political persuasion was that only the Empire was decadent: France itself was healthy and would recover its vigour once the Napoleonic régime had been swept away.

'Let us found the Republic and you will see how we shall purify the moral life of France', wrote Eugène Pelletan, the author of a heavy diatribe against the corruption of the age entitled *La Nouvelle Babylone*. But in the meantime no denunciation of the wickedness of the times was too harsh for the puritans of the left. In the private letters he was writing in the early 'sixties, Proudhon sounds like a veritable Old Testament prophet, predicting every kind of disaster on hand to smite an idolatrous people. 'Our nation has been in a period of decadence for *thirty years*', he asserted. 'They tell me sometimes that people's minds are beginning to wake up and their consciences to murmur a little, but after the ten years that have just passed, during which our countrymen have been covered in shame, I see nothing for them but continuing decadence.' France, he declared in another letter, presented the spectacle of 'a society falling into dissolution, a civilization on the point of extinction, a crumbling world. Eighteen centuries ago, mankind was in travail, as today: but then, the form this decomposition took was a wild debauchery; today its characteristic is *cowardice*. Everywhere there is cowardice, vileness, ignobility and baseness from the sovereign to the beggarman. If it was not of the Roman decadence that Proudhon was reminded, it was of the decline of Spain in the seventeenth century. 'I am three quarters convinced', he wrote to Félix Delhasse, 'that France today is at the same stage as Spain after Philip II; it is rotting; its destiny is to limp behind the other nations'; and again, to another correspondent: 'France is today where Spain was after Philip II: it has been declining since 1830; today, its decadence is proceeding at an ever faster rate: conscience, intelligence, character, all its qualities are perishing; already the other nations are deriding ours.'[6] Yet Proudhon remained optimistic as to the long-term prospects; he hoped for great things once science had finally dethroned religion; like most other nineteenth-century progressives, he had an unreasoning, unshakable belief in the upward march of humanity.

It was primarily among men of letters, who cherished no ambitions to alter or reform the government of their country, that the myth of national decadence attained its most lavish efflorescence. Moreover, they were less inclined to view the phenomenon with alarm; on the contrary, many of them derived a perverse satisfaction from imagining themselves the singers of a dying race. Whereas Leconte de Lisle professed despair at the spectacle of degeneration and anathematized his crass and degraded contemporaries, a younger poet, Stéphane Mallarmé, appeared to revel in the twilight atmosphere of irreversible decline. The mood in which he wrote his *Plainte d'automne* (composed in 1864) is not one of revolt, nor even of resignation, but rather one of morbid delectation:

Since Maria has left me to dwell in another star—which? Orion, Altair, or thee, green Venus?—I have ever cherished solitude. What days I have spent alone . . . with one of the last authors of the Latin decadence; for since that white girl is no more, singular to relate I have loved whatever is embraced by the words: decline and fall. Thus, of all the seasons of the year I favour most the last, languid summer days that immediately precede autumn; and of all times of the day, the hour when I take my walk is when the sun rests before sinking, its yellow bars reflected on the grey walls and its coppery rays on the window-panes. Likewise the literature to which my spirit turns when it carves delight will be the dying poetry of the last moments of Rome, though only so long as it in no wise breathes the rejuvenating approach of the Barbarians and has not started to babble the infantile Latin of the first pieces of Christian prose.

This passage—as is to be expected, coming from a young poet—is not exempt from literary reminiscences. The allusion to the dead companion, Maria, at the beginning, echoes Edgar Allan Poe, some of whose poems Mallarmé was later to translate. The title, 'Plainte d'automne', harks back to Baudelaire's 'Chant d'automne' and to his 'Sonnet d'automne':

> Comme moi n'es-tu pas un soleil automnal,
> O ma si blanche, ô ma si froide Marguerite?

It is significant that it was Baudelaire who, in the preface he wrote for a collection of Poe's stories which he had translated, championed the cause of 'decadent literature' which, he said, compared to the literature of classicism, was an unforgettable, elegantly attired beauty compared to a 'rustic matron, repellent in her good health and virtue'. And, in a further and even more suggestive analogy, he wrote:

This sun which, but a few hours ago, was crushing all things under its direct white light, will shortly flood the western horizon with variegated colours. In the effects of the dying sun, certain poetic spirits will encounter new delights; they will discover in them dazzling colonnades, cascades of molten metal, fiery paradises, a melancholy splendour, the pleasures of regret, all the wonders of dream, all the memories of opium. And the sunset will indeed seem to them the marvellous allegory of a soul laden with life's experience, and sinking below the horizon with a rich provision of thoughts and dreams.[7]

Even though Baudelaire was prepared to celebrate the beauties of 'decadent literature', if thereby he could further the interests of his favourite foreign poet, it by no means follows that he thought of his own poetry as being decadent; at the most he might have been prepared to concede that, as a modernist born into a decadent age, he could not avoid exploring the subject. Nevertheless, to Mallarmé's generation and to the symbolists in the 1880s, Baudelaire certainly appeared the father-founder of French decadent literature. He owed this reputation principally to the preface that Théophile Gautier wrote for the first posthumous edition of *Les Fleurs du Mal*: a preface reprinted in all subsequent popular editions for the rest of the century, and regarded as an inspired text by the younger poets who, with one accord, looked on Baudelaire as their spiritual ancestor. Gautier's essay contained very little beyond the idea that decadence was the supreme quality of Baudelaire's poetry. Civilizations, he argued, age like individuals; corruption sets in, and mephitic vapours are exhaled from the decaying humus of the graveyards of nations. These are Baudelaire's themes: the depravity and perversions of an age of overripeness. In a suggestive and frequently quoted passage, Gautier analysed Baudelaire's poetic style from the same point of view, calling it

> ingenious, complex, and learned, involving deep research into shades of meaning, for ever pushing back the boundaries of the language, borrowing from every technical vocabulary, taking colours from every palette and notes from every keyboard. . . . This style of the decadence is the final stage reached when language is required to express everything and is stretched to the ultimate point of tension. One may recall, in connection with it, the Latin of the Lower Empire, gamy and already blotched with the greenish hues of decomposition, and the intricate refinements of the Byzantine school, the ultimate form taken by Greek art after it had fallen into deliquescence; but such is truly the inevitable and necessary idiom of those nations and civilizations in which artificial life has superseded natural life.

This account of Baudelaire's style is, of course, highly fanciful: the vocabulary of *Les Fleurs du Mal* is by no means remarkable for its virtuosity or its excessive use of technicalities and neologisms.[8] Nevertheless, Gautier's presentation of Baudelaire as the master of modern decadent style was universally accepted. The study of Baudelaire which Paul Bourget published in his *Essais de psychologie contemporaine* (1883) included a section expressly entitled '*Théorie de la décadence*'. As Bourget interpreted it, decadence was the inevitable consequence of too cerebral a way of life; the nervous system took control, the sinews atrophied; physical degeneration led to sterility and hence to the extinction of the race. But Bourget did not agree with those pre-war prophets of doom who saw nothing but evil in the ravages of the decadent spirit. 'If the citizens of the decadence are inferior as promoters of the greatness of a nation, are they not far superior as artists of the inner realm of the soul?' This line of apology had been pressed by Bourget for years, in critical articles published in various literary periodicals.[9]

Literary decadence had thus been provided with a precursor (Baudelaire) and an apologist (Bourget); but, apart from rare, inconclusive, and in any case almost inaccessible samples provided by Mallarmé, a recognizable modern specimen had still to make its appearance. The first—and perhaps the only—decadent masterpiece was finally published in 1884: it was Huysmans' revolutionary *A Rebours*.

The style of this novel, to begin with, was 'decadent' in Gautier's meaning of the word, though Huysmans in his later works made even further progress along the path of the strange preciosity invented by the Goncourt brothers and named by them '*le style artiste*'. Then the hero, Des Esseintes, who became the very prototype and image of the nineteenth-century decadent: like Barbey d'Aurevilly, like Baudelaire himself, a dandy, withdrawn, impassive, contemptuous of public opinion; a man whose cynicism bordered on depravity—witness the notorious apologia for abortion, or the story of his attempt to pervert the slum-boy Auguste Langlois by paying his expenses at a high-class brothel. Des Esseintes was decadent in his unreflecting egoism, in his impotence, in his indolence,—but above all in his aesthetic tastes, which ran entirely on the rare, the morbid, and the artificial: among modern painters, Gustave Moreau and Odilon Redon alone found grace in his eyes, and among modern writers, after Baudelaire, chiefly such fluid and hallucinatory poets as Verlaine, Tristan Corbière and Mallarmé. Des Esseintes invariably prefers the bizarre and the outlandish or, as he puts it, 'the Byzantine efflorescences of the brain and the complex deliquescences of language'. Balzac is too robust for him, Hugo too banal. Finally, he shares with Mallarmé a love of the Latin authors of the decadence, that is, of the fifth century A.D., whose obscure names and insignificant works Huysmans reels off with pedantic gusto. 'Des Esseintes' interest in the Latin language did not slacken even when, in the last stage of putrescence, it hung, losing its members, running with pus, conserving in the general corruption of its body only a few solid hunks which the Christians hacked off, to marinade them in the brine of their new language.' This passage in the third chapter of *A Rebours* is echoed in the fourteenth, where Huysmans salutes Mallarmé as incarnating, 'in the most consummate and exquisite fashion', the decadence of French literature. There was, however, one striking difference between the decline of Latin and the decay of French,

23 Emile Zola, age 30

24 Joris-Karl Huysmans, as he appeared about the time he wrote *A rebours* (1884)

25 The picture, *Les Romains de la Décadence* (1847), by Manet's teacher Thomas Couture, sums up the popular nineteenth-century image of decadent hedonism

the former spread over four centuries, while the latter had taken place as a sudden decomposition, a precipitate purulence, so that 'the spotted and superb style of the De Goncourts coexisted in Paris with the gamy language of Verlaine and Mallarmé'.

Barbey d'Aurevilly, who had been accorded his meed of praise in *A Rebours*, observed in reviewing it that the book was 'one of the most decadent we can find among the decadent books of this decadent century. For an author as decadent as this to make his appearance, . . . we must really have become what we are—a nation on its death-bed.'

'Les Rougon-Macquart'

Huysmans, who had predicted that *A Rebours* would be 'the biggest fiasco of the year', was as astonished as he was gratified at the sensation it caused. This 'breviary of the Decadence', as Arthur Symons called it, became the bedside book of a whole generation, not only in France but in England too; for the decadents, unlike the naturalists, found ready disciples on the other side of the Channel. George Moore referred to *A Rebours* in his *Confessions of a Young Man* as 'that prodigious book, that beautiful mosaic', while Oscar Wilde paid Huysmans the dubious compliment of citing his novel as one of the principal agents in the corruption of Dorian Gray.[10] Most of his literary friends—Bourget and Maupassant, Verlaine and Mallarmé—wrote Huysmans enthusiastic letters: only Zola had reservations, which he frankly communicated to his disciple, in a long, detailed analysis of his impressions on first reading the book. Huysmans' reaction to these mild reproaches was curious but rather characteristic—for the author of *A Rebours* had his share of deviousness: he declared he had given Des Esseintes views that were 'diametrically opposed to those I hold, so that no one would dream of attributing them to me . . . and this complete reversal of my preferences allowed me to put forward some quite unwholesome ideas and to celebrate the merits of Mallarmé—which seemed to me rather a good joke.'[11] It is doubtful whether Zola was satisfied by this pretence that *A Rebours* was only a hoax; when Huysmans visited him at Médan that summer Zola taxed him, in a friendly fashion, with disloyalty to the creed they had both subscribed to hitherto. Huysmans, forced to come into the open, had to admit that he could see no future for naturalism, a movement of which he had been one of the founder members.

Of course, *A Rebours*, with its loose construction, the poverty of its narrative development, its total concentration on one very exceptional central character, and above all its repudiation of the modern world in

P

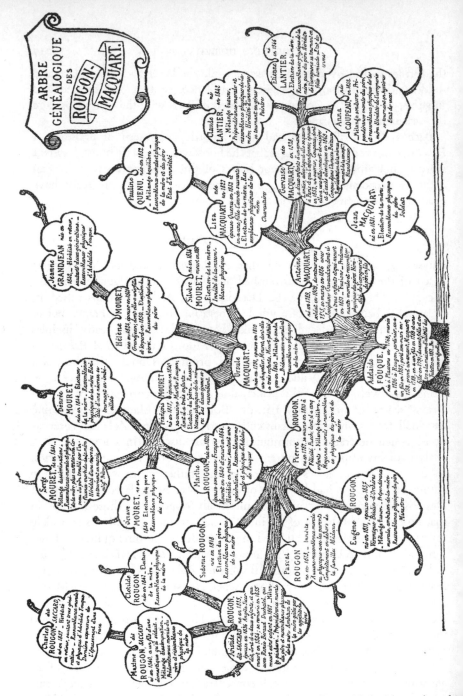

The Rougon-Macquart family tree (see p. 218-22) was first published by Zola in his novel *Une Page d'Amour* (1878).

favour of an aesthetic ideal of fastidious self-cultivation—*A Rebours* had little enough in common with the run-of-the-mill naturalist novel, or indeed with Huysmans' own earlier contributions to the genre: *Marthe, histoire d'une fille*, an unvarnished account of the life of a brothel-inmate; *Les Sœurs Vatard*, the story of the unhappy love-lives of two working-class girls employed in a book-binding establishment; *En ménage*, a desolating account of a young writer's conjugal and extra-conjugal misfortunes; and the equally pessimistic *A Vau-l'Eau*. And yet, although it had been clearly Huysmans' intention, with *A Rebours*, to break out of the straitjacket of naturalism, the work is not altogether devoid of vestigial traces of the earlier aesthetic. Des Esseintes is not a mere bookish eccentric, a Sylvestre Bonnard lacking the geniality of Anatole France's amiable recluse. Portions of the novel are taken up with retrospective accounts of the hero's childhood, the earlier stages of his illness, the curious perversions into which his failing virility traps him. His oddities are explained, in accordance with normal naturalistic procedure, by reference to his diseased heredity. In the strictly medical sense he is, as the term was used at the time, a degenerate.

Now the whole of Zola's major work, the *Rougon-Macquart* cycle of novels, was based on a theory of degeneracy. Choosing a particular family, he imagined how the seeds of congenital idiocy and alcoholism might have been sown in its earliest ancestors: though the first Rougon was of stable temperament, his wife Adélaïde was a hysteric and Macquart, the father of her two illegitimate children, a habitual drunkard. Tracing their posterity generation by generation, Zola was able to illustrate, in his 20 novels, all the different aberrations which the initial flaws produced. The forms that degeneracy may take are many and varied, so that in a single branch of the family (in the children of Gervaise Macquart) we find a painter of genius condemned to artistic sterility (Claude in *L'Œuvre*); a working-class agitator subject to uncontrollable fits of rage and violence (Étienne in *Germinal*); a homicidal maniac (Jacques in *La Bête humaine*); and a courtesan (Nana) whose irresistible sexual magnetism is similarly attributed to her warped ancestry. Or again, tracing another line down from father to son, we observe Adélaïde's legitimate son, Pierre Rougon, a stolid tradesman dominated by an ambitious wife, whose second son, Aristide (Saccard), grows up as an unscrupulous financier, elaborating frenzied schemes for self-enrichment, some of which succeed. In the third generation, Saccard's son Maxime makes his appearance: a languid, effeminate youth, utterly corrupted by the licentious atmosphere of Paris under the Second Empire. 'He represented', wrote Zola in *La Curée*, 'a refinement in the race of the Rougons, mutating into something delicate and vicious. . . . This family was living too fast; it was dying already in this frail creature, of uncertain sex, who was not motivated, like Saccard, by the lust for riches and enjoyment, but typified the slackness of those who feed on fortunes made by others; a strange hermaphrodite emerging at the appropriate moment in a cankered society.' As for Maxime's son Charles, he is the last of the line. Fifteen years old when he is introduced into the only novel in which he has a part, Le Docteur Pascal, he has a mental age of five and is described as possessing 'a slender, delicate grace, like one of those anaemic, stunted kings at the close of a dynasty, with a crown of long, silky fair hair. His big eyes were empty, his disturbing beauty was overcast with the shadow of death. And he had neither mind nor heart, he was nothing but a vicious puppy rubbing himself up against people to get them to fondle him.' This beautiful idiot, representing the last stage in the degeneracy of the Rougons, is in addition a haemophiliac; and he dies one afternoon when left unattended, having cut himself with the scissors he was playing with. Ultimately, the decadence of a race shows itself in its inability to reproduce itself: in the third generation the Rougon-Macquarts number 11, in the fourth 13, but in the fifth and last only three are named. They are Jacques-Louis Lantier, the hydrocephalic son of Claude Lantier, the painter, who dies at the age of nine; Louiset Coupeau, the sickly child of Nana, who dies in babyhood of smallpox; and Charles Rougon who, as we have seen, bleeds to death before attaining maturity.

It would, of course, be wrong to list Les Rougon-Macquart among the products of the decadent aesthetic; but it is arguable that decadence was its main theme, both on the level of pathology, in the almost morbid interest Zola took in the waning vigour of his central family, and on the social level, since he obviously subscribed to the theory current among left-wing republicans like himself, that the state of France during the reign of Napoleon III could be fairly equated with that of Rome under the later Caesars: the notion that moral turpitude among the effete ruling classes would prove to be their undoing is implicit in several of his novels, notably La Curée, Nana, Pot-Bouille and La Débâcle. The difference, however, between Zola and the decadents was that Zola sternly denounced these enervated voluptuaries, whereas they were more inclined to associate themselves complacently with the tired patricians of the fifth century composing their elegant verses as they watched the tall, fair-skinned barbarians file past.[12]

In 1884, the year Huysmans published A Rebours, Zola brought out the twelfth novel in his series, which he entitled La Joie de Vivre. Appropriately, it is in this novel that he explored all the current themes of decadence, aesthetic as well as pathological. The young hero, Lazare Chanteau, is not a member of the Rougon-Macquart family,[13] but is as subject as they to a vitiated heredity. His father is a permanent invalid, he himself is neurotic and lives in terror of death, and when finally he marries, he has a sickly son of whom he predicts: 'he'll suffer from gout like papa and his nerves will be in a worse state than mine. Look how puny he is: it's the law of degeneration.' Lazare is a dilettante, dabbling first in medicine, then in industrial chemistry and land reclamation, but too quickly discouraged to carry any of his projects to a successful conclusion. He is interested in music, but never composes anything but a funeral march. He is attracted to Schopenhauer's pessimism, and believes strongly that the promises of science will never be kept. He is the very type of dispirited, impotent, introspective intellectual that Zola saw as typical of the decadent movement: the kind of man with whom he had little patience and for whom he felt even less sympathy.

Zola confided to the pages of *La Joie de Vivre* all his misgivings about the philosophical and cultural trends of his time. But however he resisted, the current was firmly set by now against the scientific positivism on which naturalism had been founded. For the next few years, all the important manifestations of literary and artistic life would be marked by the irrational and mystical elements which he had been combating throughout his whole career. To a large extent, this new tendency would be determined by forces acting on the French cultural scene from abroad: for the first time since the Romantic era, foreign influences were starting to make themselves powerfully felt, and the winds of change were blowing from across the frontiers.

Wagnerism

In 1883 Richard Wagner died in Venice and Ivan Turgenev in Paris. Neither of these foreign celebrities had any ties with the other, but, as not infrequently happens, their disappearance opened the way for a reappraisal of their own art and (in the case of Turgenev) of the art also of his great compatriots. The Wagnerian cult, and the vogue of the Russian novel, were two outstanding examples of the kind of effervescent cosmopolitanism that the *fin-de-siècle* generation was perhaps a little too apt to indulge in. A third instance is the interest aroused by the Scandinavian dramatists, and by Ibsen in particular, at the very end of the century. In each case it is noteworthy that the French 'discovery' of these European masters was made some time after their reputation had been securely established in the other cultural centres of the Continent. It is as though the final stamp of approval conferred on their work by the Paris *élite* had to be withheld until they had gained preliminary recognition elsewhere; but a more plausible explanation of the phenomenon would be that the French, with their ingrained cultural isolationism, were reluctant to acknowledge outstanding distinction in any contemporary foreign artist. In the 1880s and 1890s, however, this traditional chauvinism was largely breached.

Various reasons can be adduced for the greater readiness of the French to pay attention to what was happening in the cultural scene abroad. Some were, in a loose sense, political: reverses on the battlefield in 1870 and the humiliating peace settlement that followed had ended French hegemony, and the younger generation found it easier than had their fathers to view their country as forming but one component in the European cultural complex, enjoying no special privileges and no monopoly of literary, artistic or musical excellence. Then again, there was an ill-defined feeling everywhere that horizons were widening as the twentieth century approached. As against the few who feared the onset of a new barbarism, there were many who grew excited at the prospects opened up by a developing technology;[14] and there was, in consequence, a greater disposition to take seriously any novelty, however outlandish in appearance and provenance. Finally, it was in this period, which later earned the name of '*la Belle Époque*', that the custom grew up among the wealthier sections of the community to spend the summer months in various fashionable centres of artistic life abroad instead of remaining quietly at home on their country estates. The process was, of course, assisted by the steadily improving railway system, and even more by the erection of luxury hotels, smart casinos, and similar establishments all over Europe.

One such centre was Bayreuth, the small town in northern Bavaria where, in 1876, Wagner opened the *Festspielhaus* which had been designed to present his operas under ideal staging conditions. In the first year the festival was visited by a mere handful of French musicians and music-lovers; but among them were Vincent d'Indy and Saint-Saëns, and also Catulle and Judith Mendès. We have seen how Catulle Mendès, with Baudelaire, had been one of the few who took up cudgels in defence of Wagner after the fiasco of the *Tannhäuser* production at the Paris Opera in 1861. With his wife Judith, *née* Gautier, and Villiers de l'Isle-Adam, he had paid Wagner a visit just before the war, when the old maestro was living in semi-retirement at Triebschen, on the banks of the Lake of Lucerne. Wagner beamed on them, compared them to the Knights of the Grail, and was evidently touched by the interest they displayed in his work. After witnessing performances of some of the operas in Munich, the trio returned to Paris and sent accounts of their experiences to the press, Mendès in a series of '*Notes de voyage*' which appeared in *Le National*, Judith Gautier and Villiers in articles published in *Le Rappel*. A first performance of *Lohengrin* the following year in

Brussels was the occasion for a fresh pilgrimage, and for renewed dithyrambs in the French papers.

The wave of Germanophobia that followed the war placed serious obstacles in the way of the dissemination of Wagner's musical ideas. The composer himself, when it became known that he was the author of a satirical farce which made fun of French military pretentions so drastically deflated in 1870, forfeited the goodwill of many patriots, including Catulle Mendès.[15] Such attempts as were made to perform extracts from the operas at popular concerts during the 1870s almost invariably led to trouble: either the orchestra refused to play, or the performances were interrupted by catcalls and whistles from the auditorium.

In the following decade, and particularly after Wagner's death, public hostility died down and the mood became more receptive. It is true that when Carvalho tried to have *Lohengrin* performed at the Opéra-Comique the opposition was so violent that he gave up the idea; but another director, Charles Lamoureux, was bolder and staged the work at the Eden Theatre (May 3rd, 1887). There was such an uproar in the hall that no more than one performance was attempted. However, it was observed that the objectors did not appear to be drawn from the same social circles as usually made up an operatic first-night audience. In fact, Wagner was already becoming almost a vogue cult in upper-class society. Rumours were spreading about the group of devotees, under the leadership of Judith Gautier, who were meeting privately in Nadar's studio to discuss Wagner's ideas and listen to fragments of his music. The annual 'pilgrimage to Bayreuth' was by now attracting not merely musicians (Fauré in 1883, Debussy in 1888 and 1889) but avant-garde writers like Bourget and Robert de Montesquiou and, increasingly, society hostesses, who made the trip in the company of the titled and wealthy snobs of their acquaintance. 'People go to Bayreuth to be seen, to make their way in society, or in search of amusement', wrote Barrès in 1886, adding that this was hardly what Wagner himself had intended or anticipated when he inaugurated the festival. In the 'nineties it was as fashionable to visit Bayreuth during the season as to go to Monte Carlo, Baden-Baden, or any of the other 'Roulettevilles' of Europe, and the company was much the same: aristocratic, cosmopolitan, paying no more than lip-service to the art of which they pretended to be devotees. 'What are you doing here at Bayreuth, my dear duke? I didn't know you liked music.'—'It's true', replies the member of the Jockey Club, 'it's true, I can't stand music, but I adore Wagner.'

The influence of Wagnerian opera on the development of French music was neither very profound nor very long-lasting. Édouard Lalo, a man now in his sixties who—like César Franck, for that matter—had had a somewhat undistinguished earlier career, made an attempt to incorporate Wagnerian orchestration in his opera *Le Roi d'Ys*, the story of which was derived, again in accordance with Wagnerian prescriptions, from folk-legend. *Le Roi d'Ys* was greeted, when performed in 1888, with no more than polite applause: the imitation was too flagrant. Two other unsuccessful attempts to adapt Wagner's formula to the French tradition were made by Emmanuel Chabrier, in *Gwendoline* and *Le Roi malgré lui*. Chabrier's decision to embark on a career as a composer was reached as a direct result of hearing a performance of *Tristan* in Munich: he was so overwhelmed that he resigned his post at the Ministry of the Interior in order to devote himself entirely to his new vocation. Even though nothing he composed while he remained under the spell of Wagner is musically of much importance,[16] Chabrier counts as an outstanding illustration of the trend towards a general overlapping of interest in the arts that was so characteristic of the century's end and can be loosely connected with Wagner's advocacy of the *Gesamtkunstwerk*. Besides being a talented musician, Chabrier was a close friend of Manet's and collected his pictures (he was the first owner of the famous *Bar aux Folies-Bergères* which Manet painted in 1881–2), and he also knew and frequented a number of the Parnassian poets, Leconte de Lisle and Banville, Verlaine and Anatole France.

Wagnerism was, indeed, a literary cult no less than a musical one. More than one zealous Wagnerian, like Villiers de l'Isle Adam, was a prominent figure in the symbolist movement—as was also Élémir Bourges, the author of the weird, decadent novel with the Wagnerian title *Le Crépuscule des dieux*. Certain elements of Wagner's work reappear in literary symbolism: the fascination with the medieval concept of sin and evil found in *Tristan* is duplicated in *Là-Bas* and Huysmans' later novels; and certain symbolists were not averse to treating of the perverse passions which have their place in some of the operas and to which Verlaine drew attention in his sonnet 'Parsifal':

> *Parsifal a vaincu les Filles, leur gentil*
> *Babil et la luxure amusante—et sa pente*
> *Vers la chair de garçon vierge que cela tente*
> *D'aimer les seins légers et ce gentil babil.*

This poem had been commissioned by Édouard Dujardin for one of the issues of *La Revue wagnérienne*, where it appeared together with Mallarmé's sybilline 'Hommage' and six other sonnets by less reputed poets, all supposedly inspired by Wagner's work. Dujardin launched his review in

February, 1885; a young dandy, with monocle and well-trimmed beard, he liked to affect brilliant waistcoats embroidered with Wagnerian motifs: the swan from *Lohengrin*, and certain bars of music. He owed his initiation in large part to the Anglo-German Wagnerian Houston Stewart Chamberlain; in Munich, meeting in beer-houses between performances of *Parsifal* and the Tetralogy, they talked endlessly about the corpus; it may have been Chamberlain who suggested to Dujardin the idea of founding a musico-literary periodical to propagate the faith when he returned to Paris. Dujardin himself had had some musical training—he had attended the Conservatoire at the same time as Debussy—and in Téodor de Wyzewa he had at any rate one collaborator with some competence as a musicologist. But for the most part those who wrote for the *Revue wagnérienne* were men of letters, though they included two of Wagner's earliest champions in France: Catulle Mendès and Champfleury. Mallarmé who, besides the sonnet just mentioned also sent the *Revue* a prose rhapsody, 'Richard Wagner, rêverie d'un poete français', almost certainly admired the German composer on no firmer grounds than that Baudelaire had written a panegyric on him. It was above all Wagner's suggestive manipulation of mythology and allegory that appealed to the symbolist generation; for many of them, one fears, the music was no more than a stirring noise.

As for the musicians, one reason why, on the whole, they were able to resist Wagner's influence was that, for the first time in generations, a strong and self-reliant native group of musicians was coming together in Paris; this group drew on a variety of inspirational sources, but above all followed the old tradition of treating the medium as a self-contained matrix of melodious forms rather than as an instrument for emotional expression. Some of these men were interested enough in Wagner to make the necessary trips abroad to see productions of the operas; but few were so powerfully affected as to imitate Lekeu, who swooned away after first hearing the prelude to *Tristan* and had to be carried out of the theatre. Vincent d'Indy's visit to Bayreuth in 1876 certainly left him with a strong impression and the work that he composed on his return, *La Forêt enchantée*, testifies to the fact. More typically, Gabriel Fauré combined a keen admiration for Wagner with a robust imperviousness to his influence. He visited Cologne in 1878 to hear *Das Rheingold* and *Die Walküre*, and in Munich the following year he was in the audience listening to the entire tetralogy. But the compositional work he was mainly engaged on in the 1880s bore no relation at all to what he had heard in Germany: it consisted of the piano settings he made of poems by the Parnassians Leconte de Lisle and Sully Prudhomme and, later, of the saccharine love-ditties taken from Verlaine's *Bonne Chanson*; together with the *Requiem* for his parents and some chamber music. Similarly Debussy, though profoundly impressed by what he heard on the first pilgrimage he made to Bayreuth in 1888, returned in a somewhat disillusioned frame of mind after his second trip, which took place the following year. He was on the whole more drawn to the music of Tchaikovsky and Borodin which he heard during a visit to Russia and again at concerts conducted by Rimsky-Korsakov at the 1889 Paris Exhibition. But, like Fauré, he turned to French poets for his immediate inspiration; not to the same poets—Debussy belonged to a younger generation and had friends in the symbolist circle—but to such modernists as Mallarmé, Pierre Louÿs and Maurice Maeterlinck.[17] The graceful sensuality of the *Prélude à l'Après-midi d'un faune*, a work which obtained an immediate and striking success when it was first performed in 1894, was as un-Teutonic as could be imagined and, in so far as it can be described as tone-painting, has obvious affinities with what the Impressionists had been attempting in pictorial art; once more it can be seen how, as the century drew to its close, all the arts appeared to be converging or, at least, borrowing from one another.

Debussy, born in 1862, was a brilliant newcomer. Over the period we are concerned with, the dominant figure in French music until his death in 1890 was a man 40 years older, César Franck, who however wrote all his most important works in the last decade of his life: the Symphonic variations for piano and orchestra (1885), the Symphony in D minor (1888) and the three so-called symphonic poems, *Le Chasseur maudit*, *Les Djinns*, and *Psyché*. Franck's influence on the younger men he gathered round him was as much spiritual as musical: the atmosphere among his pupils was almost too highly charged with emotional strenuousness. A native of Liège, of Walloon parentage, he had his full share of the moral earnestness associated with northern races. He admired but feared Wagner's music—admired it for its brilliance and inventiveness but feared it for the dark passions that underlay it. When he died his place was taken easily by Vincent d'Indy, who already had to his credit some important orchestral works, including the popular *Symphonie sur un chant montagnard français* which, by its use of native French folk-music, contrived a complete break with foreign (and particularly German) influence. D'Indy was the very embodiment of moral sanity. A firm Catholic—not of the morbidly mystical type that Huysmans personified—he had a drily intellectual side to his nature and was a born teacher. It was natural that he should have taken charge of the school that he founded with two others[18] in 1894, the Schola Cantorum which, originally intended as a society for fostering interest in the sacred music of the past, evolved before the end of the century into a seminary for composers, duplicating the functions of the Conservatoire but discharging them with rather more devotion.

The Russian Novel

The impact of the Russian novel on the French reading public was quite as violent as the impact of Wagner on the French musical public; it took place at about the same time (in the mid-1880s) and left as little trace on the native literature as Wagner on the indigenous French musical tradition.

Turgenev, whose death in the same year as Wagner we have noted, had been an established feature of the Parisian literary scene since 1856, when he took up semi-permanent residence in the French capital. He was on friendly terms with most of the leading prose-writers of the period: with Mérimée, George Sand, Flaubert, the Goncourt brothers, Alphonse Daudet and Émile Zola. Everyone appreciated his genial good nature and many admired the lyrical qualities and well-knit structure of the novels of Russian life that he went on writing through these years and which were regularly turned into French as they appeared. He was virtually the sole interpreter to the west of the *mores* of his countrymen, and hence was commonly regarded as the only living Russian writer of importance. Turgenev, who knew he owed this reputation simply to the ignorance of his hosts, was loyal enough, and a good enough patriot, to do his utmost to secure a French readership at least for the works of Tolstoy. But, of course, Turgenev's good opinion could only be taken on trust so long as Tolstoy's works remained untranslated; and it was not until 1885 that French versions of *War and Peace* and *Anna Karenina* (published in Russia in 1863-9 and 1875-7) were made accessible in Paris. As for Dostoevsky, he died some years before the translators got to work on the products of his pen.

As soon as the novels of these two Russian masters appeared on the boulevard bookstalls, they were pounced on and devoured with an eagerness that astonished and delighted their promoters. In September 1885 *Le Figaro* reported that 'for the past 18 months the French have become passionately interested in Russian literature.' The following February Maurice Barrès, in an article significantly entitled '*La Mode russe*' which appeared in *La Revue illustrée*, commented sardonically: 'Everyone knows that over the past two months any man of taste and education is obliged to exclaim, no sooner than the first compliments have been exchanged: "Ah, my dear sir, are you reading these Russians?" You take a step backwards and say: "Oh, Tolstoy!" whereupon the other, advancing towards you, breathes: "Dostoevsky!" And this is how you show you have a cultivated mind in this

year of grace 1886.' In December Wyzewa predicted that 'the zeal of
Parisian publishers in translating the Russians will doubtless be the principal
literary phenomenon of the year 1887, as it was the principal phenomenon
of the year that has just gone by'. Within a very short space of time, all
Tolstoy's fictional work was available in French; some titles were even
issued twice over within a few months by competing publishers. As for
Dostoevsky, the four great novels were translated between 1884 and 1888,
and in September 1888 a stage version of *Crime and Punishment* caused a
mild sensation when it was put on at the Odéon.

Nor were the secondary novelists forgotten in the rush to satisfy this
apparently insatiable demand for things Russian: an earlier translation of
Goncharov's *Oblomov* was reissued in 1886, together with versions of his
two other, relatively feeble novels, *The Precipice* and *A Common Story*;
Garshin's *Nadezhda Nikolaevna*, published in Russia in 1885, was translated
into French in 1888, while in the 1890s the French were introduced to Leskov
and Korolenko. The more conservative critics protested at this shameless
exploitation of a foolish craze. 'Who will rid us', sighed Armand de Pontmartin, 'of the Russian novel, of this eternal Tolstoy, of that sempiternal
Dostoevsky? You begin to think it's all finished—but no. After the positively
last appearance, there are more to follow; and I am inclined to imagine there
must be in the background some workshop or factory where publishers,
lured by false hopes of profit, pay hacks to turn out pseudo-Tolstoys and
spurious Dostoevskys.'[19] Pontmartin's suspicions were not altogether
unfounded: there were, at any rate, translators unscrupulous enough to
detach a chunk of *The Brothers Karamazov*, change the names of the characters,
give it an invented title and issue it as a separate work by Dostoevsky.[20]

Underlying this astonishing wave of interest in Russian prose fiction was
a certain general curiosity about a country with which the political leaders
of the Republic were currently seeking a diplomatic *rapprochement*. The
disastrous outcome of the Franco-Prussian War had demonstrated the dangers
to France of remaining isolated among the European powers. In the immediate post-war period, however, there was nothing that the Quai d'Orsay
could do to remedy the situation: Germany was watchful for any move that
could be construed as a renewal of hostile postures and, besides, in an age
when every other state in Europe had its crowned head (Switzerland and
San Marino excepted), the French Republic found itself in a kind of diplomatic quarantine. Nowhere was this distrust stronger than at the Court of
St Petersburg. Both the new tsar, Alexander III, who had acceded to the
throne in 1881, and his foreign minister Giers were totally averse to an
alliance with an unstable and probably revolutionary clique of Frenchmen

whose ambassadors—contrary to universal custom—were not always titled aristocrats.

Nevertheless, the French government quietly pursued its objective. Certain cards could be discreetly played. The Russian Empire had an under-capitalized economy, and in 1888 a loan of 125 million roubles, the first of a series, was successfully floated on the Paris Exchange. In the same year the old German Emperor died; his successor, Wilhelm II, clashed violently with his grandfather's minister Bismarck and brought about his resignation. The 'dropping of the pilot' caused a tremor to run through the chancelleries of Europe; in the upshot, the secret treaty binding Russia and Germany fell into abeyance, and France was finally able to obtain the defensive alliance with Russia for which she had been patiently working. The negotia-tions took a long time, of course, and were not eventually concluded until 1894. But throughout the intervening years, French russophilia had been gathering strength, feeding on hopes that were finally realized, and these purely political developments probably played some part in stimulating the sudden and unprecedented interest the public took in Russian literature and, to a more limited extent, in Russian music.

Some corroboration of this hypothesis comes from the fact that the critic and literary historian whose writings helped most to acclimatize Tolstoy and Dostoevsky in France was himself a career diplomat who had been appointed, in 1876, secretary to the French Embassy at St Petersburg. Eugène-Melchior de Vogüé's book, *Le Roman russe*, was published in 1886; but its individual chapters, on Turgenev, Tolstoy, Dostoevsky and Gogol, had appeared, in that order, in the *Revue des Deux Mondes* between 1883 and 1885. This was a fortnightly periodical of unimpeachable respectability, to be found on every dowager's coffee-table; by writing in it, Vogüé ensured at the outset that his essays should be read by the right people, that is, by Catholic conservatives of good birth, and his presentation of these largely unknown Russian authors was deliberately biased to ensure them a sym-pathetic reception among members of the French upper classes. That their art was realistic, was something he could not deny; but this realism was so close to idealism that the difference was perceptible only to the most highly trained critical intelligence. It was realism refined by spiritual content, purged of Flaubert's inhuman pessimism and totally devoid of Zola's sordid brutality; it was the realism of a simple, God-fearing nation. Vogüé used a multitude of illustrations to bring out the contrast between the Russian and the French realist schools. In the chapter on Gogol he analyses the short story *The Greatcoat*, which he finds steeped in a compassion for humanity totally foreign to the French realists. Akaky Akakievitch, Gogol' pitiful hero, has much in common with Flaubert's two celebrated comics, Bouvard and Pécuchet; like them, he is a copy-clerk and, like them, an ingenuous simpleton. But whereas Flaubert ridicules his queer pair, caricaturing Pécuchet and making a butt of Bouvard, Gogol jokes about Akaky gently and with perceptible compassion. 'For the former, the weak-minded man is nothing but a detestable monstrosity; for the latter, he is an unhappy brother.' Turgenev, in spite of his close association with Flaubert and the French realists, maintains the sympathetic approach to his characters so typical of the Slav. Vogüé instances one of the stories in *A Sportsman's Sketches* ('Living Relics'—the sportsman comes across a peasant woman living alone in her wretched hovel and wasted with sickness, who tells him the story of her life in a tone of quiet resignation). 'In this broken body', commented Vogüé, 'there dwells a soul, purified by suffering, angelically meek, preserving a peasant's artlessness and yet uplifted on to the heights of absolute renunciation.' The critic contrasts Turgenev's treatment of the situation with what his younger friends in Paris, Zola, Maupassant, atheistic adherents of a purely physiological concept of human nature, might have made of it: in their hands the story would have become 'a lecture in pathology; they would have delighted in the dissection of those stiffened limbs, those hidden sores. They would have pointed out all the flaws in the nervous system and would have diagnosed idiocy.'

The two chapters of *Le Roman russe* that constituted its central revelation were those devoted to Tolstoy and Dostoevsky. Tolstoy's realism, Vogüé argued, is justified by the quality of his god-like irony, so far removed from the degrading cynicism that informs the works of writers like Stendhal or Flaubert. Besides which, Tolstoy never forgets that he is a Russian gentleman; the offensive crudeness of French naturalism is utterly foreign to his art. Mindful, no doubt, of the inflated sales of *Nana*, of the unsavoury successes of Huysmans' *Marthe*, Goncourt's *La Fille Élisa*, and the licentious opening story in Maupassant's *La Maison Tellier*, Vogüé makes the point that '*War and Peace* is in the hands of every young Russian girl; *Anna Karenina* unfolds its perilous subject like a manual of morality, without a single suggestive passage.' All this is fair comment. It is really only when he came to deal with Dostoevsky that Vogüé failed to do justice to his subject: the mildly progressive Catholic democrat that he was could hardly have been expected to plumb the depths of this tormented, reactionary slavophil. The picture that he drew was inevitably distorted and incomplete, but at the same time it was original and attractive and was not properly superseded until Gide delivered his illuminating series of lectures on Dostoevsky at the Vieux-Colombier in 1923.

It was in connection with Dostoevsky chiefly that Vogüé launched the concept of the 'religion of human suffering', presented as a form of Greek Orthodox Christianity stripped of all dogma but preserving the essential message of the founder of the religion. The Siberian convicts portrayed in *Letters from the House of the Dead* are 'steeped in the spirit of a New Testament which has passed through Byzantium; they are fashioned by it to asceticism and martyrdom. . . . These people come straight out of the Acts of the Apostles.' The masochism so characteristic of Dostoevsky was interpreted by Vogüé as a peculiar oriental form of propitiation through suffering. The 'religion of human suffering' finds its fullest expression in *Crime and Punishment* which accordingly ranks for Vogüé as Dostoevsky's masterpiece; it is one of the inevitable weaknesses of this chapter—and, indeed, of *Le Roman russe* as a whole—that Vogüé was compelled, in the interests of the thesis he was arguing, to dismiss the later works, *The Idiot*, *The Demons*, and even *The Brothers Karamazov*, as abortions unworthy of serious study. It was above all in Raskolnikov's final confession of his crime, and in Sonya's acceptance of exile with him, that Vogüé discovered the core of Dostoevsky's teaching: 'that suffering is a good in itself, especially suffering submitted to in fellowship, that it is a sovereign remedy for all evil.' One cannot speak of the bond that unites the student and the prostitute as love: 'we have to restore the etymological meaning of our word *compassion*, as Bossuet understood it: suffering with or by another.'

Presented in this light, Tolstoy and Dostoevsky could not fail to appeal to a large body of readers, critics, and serious-minded young writers fatigued and appalled at the cheerlessness and occasional grossness of naturalist literature. Using as his mouthpiece Durtal, the hero of *Là-Bas*, Huysmans wrote that the novel needed at all costs to be rescued from materialism; that the theory that men and women were entirely at the mercy of their animal appetites and sexual instincts provided all too narrow a platform on which to erect a flourishing literature; and that while no one wished to return to the shallow idealism of the 'genteel' novel, to the 'woolly works of Cherbuliez or Feuillet or alternatively to the tear-jerking little tales of Theuriet or George Sand', at the same time it was imperative to reinstate the incorporeal, the intangible, and to aim at what he called a 'spiritual naturalism'. Dostoevsky, Huysmans added, was about the only writer who had tried to do this.

These opening pages of *Là-Bas* spell out what a great many men of Huysmans' generation, anxious, questing, disappointed with the bitter fruits of positivism, must have been privately thinking. Looking back in 1894 on the state of mind of the French literary public when the first translations of the Russians rolled off the presses, the critic Gaston Deschamps, with a trace of exaggeration, recalled that 'in 1886 we were shut up, without hope of escape or a glimmer of light, in the dungeons of naturalism. Enormous blocks, called *L'Assommoir* and *Nana*, had been rolled up against the doors by M. Émile Zola. Other workmen had stopped up the windows with dirty linen, old papers, mortar and clay.' The breath of pure air, blowing off the steppes of Russia, 'gave us the strength to roll the stone away from the sepulchre'. It was not a reaction against realism as such, but against the heartless attitude adopted by the French masters of realism towards humanity. 'Dostoevsky, Tolstoy, are realists too; but they do not believe that "the wide world is wholly contained in a petticoat or a pantaloon." '21

The precise degree to which the Russians affected the course of development of the French novel is difficult to determine, but it hardly appears that they exerted more than a temporary pull in the direction of a more moralistic, anti-positivist art. (The influence of Tolstoy's later didactic writing on social, educational, and religious thought was of course quite another matter.22) Zola himself departed from custom to the extent of introducing into the sixteenth volume of *Les Rougon-Macquart* a highly suspect whiff of girlish innocence and church incense; but Vogüé would not have recognized in *Le Rêve* (1888) a valid specimen of 'mystical realism' within the meaning of the term as he applied it to Dostoevsky's art. On the other hand, incontrovertible evidence does exist that Zola wrote the seventeenth novel of the series, *La Bête humaine*, partly at least in order to refute the underlying premiss of *Crime and Punishment*, viz. that a man can, by intellectual reasoning, persuade himself that he has a moral right to commit a murder. The novels that Maupassant wrote after 1886 (*Mont-Oriol*, *Pierre et Jean*) are less austerely dispassionate than the two he published before that date (*Une Vie* and *Bel-Ami*); but the message that can be extracted with a little ingenuity from these later novels—that moral suffering can be spiritually ennobling—might just as well have been a concession to the taste of the fashionable public that Maupassant was courting in the later 1880s, as a sign of his conversion to the 'religion of human suffering'. Genuine converts to this creed can be found, but only among relatively minor practitioners of the art of the novel. Paul Bourget's second novel, *Crime d'amour*, deals with the salutary effect of moral suffering on a debauchee and one of his victims; his third, *André Cornélis*, repeats the situation exploited by Dostoevsky in *Crime and Punishment*: Bourget too has his murderer, undetected, who endures a prolonged interrogation and, when at last he confesses his crime, feels relief at being able to atone. Both *Crime d'amour* and *André*

26 The most widely reported of the anarchist outrages in France was the bomb explosion in the Chamber of Deputies on 9 December 1893 (see p. 241). There were no fatalities

27 Manet's portrait of Mallarmé (1877)

28 One of the numerous studies made by Rodin for the head of Balzac, 1893–7.

Cornélis were written within a year or two of the publication of Vogüé's articles on the Russians in the *Revue des Deux Mondes*.

The Swiss-born author Édouard Rod, who came to Paris in 1878, also attempted for a brief space of time to put into practice the lessons taught by Dostoevsky and interpreted by Vogüé. Rod had begun his literary career as a fervent admirer and dutiful disciple of Zola, writing the prostitute's life-history which was almost *de rigueur* for a self-respecting naturalist at the time (*Palmyre Veulard*, 1881). The novels and short stories that followed earned their author a modest reputation under Zola's wing but did not bring Rod into prominence. Then, in 1889, appeared *Le Sens de la vie*. Tolstoy himself scented a disciple when he read the book—Rod having sent him a complimentary copy—and wrote from Yasnaya Polyana an unusually effusive letter in which he thanked the young author for having procured him 'one of the happiest sensations I know: that of meeting an unlooked-for companion in the path I am following'.[23]

Le Sens de la vie is a novel of ideas with very little plot; the hero, a young married man, chances to read the works of Tolstoy and Dostoevsky, and experiences an immediate—but unfortunately only intellectual—thrill of response to their lofty moral tone, to their message of universal love, and above all to their rejection of a narrow scientism in favour of a mystical sense of the wonder of the universe. Experience teaches him, however, that he lacks the instinctive democracy of the great Russians which enables them to cross the barriers of class and to feel the same fellowship for all men, even for the most brutish and least intelligent. In the last resort, the 'religion of human suffering' is something he can admire but cannot whole-heartedly embrace; he can become a philanthropist, a good husband and a kind father, but he cannot experience the rapture of utter self-sacrifice. The pity he feels for the unfortunate is mechanical and therefore sterile: 'it is the pity of the curious dilettante, who wants to know what pity is like for the sake of the knowledge or because he thinks it a fine emotion, and who plays with it as with any other toy—art, love, vice or virtue. . . .'

In the preface to his next novel, *Les Trois Cœurs* (1890), Rod attempted to sum up what the Russians had meant to men of his generation, who had turned their backs on naturalism because of its spiritual poverty, because it was 'in its essence self-satisfied, very limited, materialistic, more curious of the social framework than of characters, of the substance than of the soul; while we were—and were increasingly to become—dissatisfied, full of yearning for the infinite, idealistic, uninterested in the social framework and searching always, among his surroundings, for the essential man'. Rod proceeds to enumerate the reasons for this trend, and lists a whole string

Q

of aesthetic and philosophical influences, all of them—interestingly—originating from abroad; the Russian novel may have been the most important, but Rod also mentions Schopenhauer's pessimism, Wagner's music, and the paintings of the pre-Raphaelites.

The last 10 or 15 years of the century were marked by these successive waves of excitement among those with interests in art and music as well as literature and thought, which were set in motion by the sudden discovery or this or that great master, the exoticism of whose work was almost a guarantee of its importance. The last to 'arrive', in this sense, were the Norwegian dramatists Ibsen and Bjoernson; but, since their works were popularized, though not actually introduced, under the banner of symbolism, we must start by casting a necessarily cursory glance at the development of the native symbolist movement between 1884 and 1891.

Symbolism in poetry

At the time *A Rebours* was published Mallarmé's name, so loudly trumpeted by Huysmans, was still quite unknown to the public at large, while Verlaine had a greater notoriety as jailbird and profligate than as poet. It is true that the first volume of *Le Parnasse contemporain* had included 11 poems by Mallarmé as well as eight by Verlaine: but the fact was remembered by few—the collection had appeared as long ago as 1866. The second issue, which came out just after the war, had included the text of *Hérodiade*, but the editors of the third (and last) volume, Banville, François Coppée and Anatole France, declined to print anything by Verlaine and turned down Mallarmé's *L'Aprés-midi d'un faune*.[24] A kind of conspiracy of silence operated where Verlaine was concerned: his collection *Sagesse*, containing the devotional poems he wrote after his conversion, was given a mere four reviews, and little was said either about the brochure he published in 1884 on the three '*poètes maudits*', Mallarmé, Rimbaud, and Tristan Corbière. This slim volume nevertheless constitutes an important document in the history of symbolism, for between its covers Verlaine quoted not only several poems by Mallarmé which had never appeared in print before, but some totally unknown specimens of the work of the already almost legendary boy-poet Rimbaud: the '*Sonnet des voyelles*' and '*Le Bateau ivre*', among others.

Ironically, the publication which was chiefly responsible for bringing the symbolist movement to the notice of the wider reading public was neither Verlaine's *Poètes maudits* nor even Huysmans' *A Rebours*, but a parody of the new kind of poetic writing, a volume published in 1885 under the title *Les Déliquescences d'Adoré Floupette*.[25] It was widely read (a second edition followed the first within six weeks) and not all its readers realized that it was a mere skit; at any rate, its appearance seems to have triggered off a whole succession of scandalized newspaper articles about the 'decadent poets' which lasted for the rest of the year. In 1886 the poets—or their apologists—counter-attacked and, after the fashion of the time (which still happily persists in France) founded little magazines in which to expound their ideas: *Le Décadent* on April 10th, *La Vogue* on April 11th. It was in the pages of *La Vogue* that Teodor de Wyzewa published his important article on Mallarmé, the gist of which was that the new poetry demanded— and had every right to demand—a creative effort on the part of the reader approximately equivalent to the creative effort expended by the poet. After all, wrote Wyzewa, 'music is certainly not appreciated by those who have received no musical education; why should poetry be set down, ready cooked, to be devoured nonchalantly by any Tom, Dick or Harry?' *La Vogue* also continued the piecemeal publication of Rimbaud's *œuvre*, with '*Les Premières Communions*' (in its first number), and later *Les Illuminations* and *Une saison en enfer*. It is indicative of the mystery surrounding the fate of Rimbaud, who had abandoned literature for a life of adventure in, probably, 1875, that *Les Illuminations* were announced in *La Vogue* as being the work of 'the late Monsieur Rimbaud': it was not realized even by those who were in possession of his manuscripts, that the god was alive in Abyssinia.

Given the small circulation of *La Vogue*, it is unlikely that Wyzewa's article attracted much notice at the time; but on September 18th, 1886, Jean Moréas published a manifesto in the most widely read of all the Paris newspapers, *Le Figaro*. Entitled simply '*Le Symbolisme*', Moréas's article[26] was at one and the same time an apology for the new movement and a summary of its aims, which he defined along broadly Mallarméan lines. 'Symbolist poetry seeks to clothe the Idea in a tangible form which, however, is not meant to be an end in itself, but remains ancillary to the Idea which it serves to express.' What could be called, for convenience, the Verlainian approach to symbolism was elucidated in another manifesto published by René Ghil in the first issue of *La Décadence*, October 1st, 1886.[27] 'To symbolize is to evoke, rather than to narrate or depict: the object holds sway only when, forgotten in itself, it is reborn ideally thanks solely to its dreamlike and suggestive qualities.' The unavoidable lack of precision of these formulae allowed the detractors to dismiss the new poets as just a band of conceited and grandiloquent humbugs. Anatole France, with rare obtuseness, advised them to take a lesson in simplicity from Lamartine; Gaston Deschamps made the inevitable pun about 'symbols' and 'cymbals' and declared that the obscurity of this poetry was simply a cloak intended to dissimulate the intellectual poverty of those who composed it. Unfortunately there was, in addition, a great deal of cross-fire between the 'symbolist' and the 'decadent' camps; so that the impression one has is of a profusion of manifestoes and indictments, with far too little poetry actually getting written. But there was at least one point on which everyone was agreed: the 'masters' of the school were, indisputably, Mallarmé, Verlaine, and the absent Rimbaud.

What did they have in common, these three poets born within 12 years of one another? A violent admiration for Baudelaire, certainly; but otherwise very little, either on the personal or the artistic plane. The three founders of the romantic school in France, Lamartine, Vigny, and Hugo, who were also, curiously enough, born over the same span of 12 years,[28] produced a much more homogeneous body of poetry. The youngest members of each trio, Hugo and Rimbaud, had in common an extraordinary precocity; but otherwise, no one would dream of associating the author of the *Odes et Ballades*, the docile supporter of throne and altar, the handsome young husband of Adèle Foucher, with Arthur Rimbaud the truant schoolboy, the shameless sponger and catamite, in perpetual revolt against everything and everyone that seemed to lay him under any constraint: his mother, social conventions, literary traditions, and the tyranny of moral and religious prohibitions.

Between 1885 and his death in 1896, Verlaine composed little poetry of the first order, though he published quantities. He was, however, a well-known figure and over these years took on the aspect of a living symbol of revolt against the bourgeois ideals of thrift, sobriety, respectability and hard work. His poverty was interpreted by his admirers as a standing reproach to the materialism of the age; his profligacy, even, a protest against the hypocrisy of current moral standards. Verlaine was a sort of walking incarnation of Dostoevsky's crapulous but saintly drunkards, a visible exemplar of the religion of human suffering.

In fact, although by this time Verlaine had run through his patrimony and had no settled source of income, his poverty hardly amounted to real distress. Unlike Baudelaire, he preferred begging to starving; he never found it difficult to wheedle money out of his friends, and his publisher, Léon Vanier, would always pay him cash on the nail for any poem he cared to send along. He was invited to lecture in Holland (1892) and in Belgium and Great Britain (1893); these tours were lucrative even though the sponsors were sometimes obliged to comb the local bars and brothels when he was needed on the platform. In September 1894 Maurice Barrès persuaded 15 patrons, several of them titled, to covenant to pay him a monthly pension of 150 francs. One of these, Robert de Montesquiou, became Verlaine's principal protector in later years.

Since June 1885 Verlaine had been lodging at the Hôtel du Midi, an establishment described by his most recent biographer as 'a brothel, catering for a motley clientèle of pimps and prostitutes, unemployed workers, drug-pushers, ex-convicts'.[29] At the beginning his mother was with him; but she caught pneumonia and died in the winter of 1886 and thereafter the poet lived with a succession of broken-down, blowzy whores who shared his fondness for the bottle. He was in and out of hospital, receiving treatment for an extraordinary variety of ailments and diseases: rheumatism, diabetes, cirrhosis of the liver, syphilis and cardiac hypertrophy. He was a cheerful invalid, much indulged: the doctors, well aware of his literary fame, were proud to be in attendance, and hospital rules did not apply to him, any more than did police regulations when he was well (the police were under instructions never to arrest him, no matter what public outrages he committed when in his cups). Admiring visitors, including all the outstanding symbolists and decadents, would visit him in the public ward or sit with him under the plane-trees, conversing as his disciples did of old with Socrates. Verlaine's appearance—his bald head, bulging brow and white beard—enhanced the physical resemblance with the Greek sage.

Over approximately the same period, Mallarmé too was holding court at the famous *mardis*, the Tuesday evening gatherings in his flat in the Rue de Rome. The visitors were received in the schoolmaster-poet's dining-room, on the walls of which hung a few chosen works by modern masters (Manet's portrait of Mallarmé, a pastel by Odilon Redon, an engraving by Whistler, a water-colour by Berthe Morisot). The furnishings were very English (Mallarmé earned his living as a teacher of English): a dresser covered with rustic pots, cane chairs, a rocking-chair, a Victorian chaise-longue. There were budgerigars in a cage and a white cat. Mallarmé stood in front of a porcelain stove, smoking his pipe and discoursing while the visitors sat around or sprawled on the floor. They included all the most promising writers of the younger generation: Gide, Valéry, Claudel, Jules Laforgue until his tragic death at the age of 27, and Gustave Kahn; and the occasional distinguished foreigner on a visit to Paris, Arthur Symons, Oscar Wilde, Stefan George. Reports of these occasions have come down to us, but no actual record of Mallarmé's fascinating conversation. It was, according to Camille Mauclair, 'limpidity itself, the most dazzling and at the same time the most pregnant imaginable. A Plato would have been required to note the words of this Socrates.'[30] With two different Socrates discoursing variously in different quarters of Paris, the city was decidedly earning the title of 'the New Athens' that was sometimes bestowed on it during the so-called *belle époque*.

Symbolism on the Stage

By 1891, the date of Rimbaud's death, symbolism had moved from the stage of being an esoteric and, in the opinion of many, a somewhat risible cult and was now universally recognized as the only valid modern poetic school. A long and serious essay entitled *'Le Symbolisme contemporain'* by Ferdinand Brunetière, one of the select group of professional critics of the time,[31] was published in the *Revue des Deux Mondes* in April and marked the final consecration of the symbolists' ideas. Brunetière stressed, approvingly, the advance they had made from the entrenched positions of the Parnassians: poetry now sought to suggest, instead of limiting itself to rational statement or plastic description; it was aspiring to the condition of music. The hitherto unified self of the poet was dissolving into a rainbow of diverse states of sensibility; the indecisive, the dreamlike, the blurred impression and the melting mood were now the staple material of all the arts.

It was in 1891 too that the first attempts were made to accommodate symbolism to the stage. In February the 19-year-old manager of the Théâtre d'Art, Paul Fort, announced that his theatre was in future to be 'completely symbolist'. Such a declaration necessarily implied taking up an anti-naturalistic stance and, specifically, setting up in opposition to Antoine's Théâtre Libre which had given Ibsen's *Ghosts* its first performance the previous year and was currently rehearsing *The Wild Duck*. The first evening's entertainment offered by Paul Fort showed a certain lack of finesse. A symbolist poetic drama by Pierre Quillard, *La Fille aux mains coupées*, in which the cast declaimed in slow monotonous voices behind a muslin curtain, was followed by a *'scène naturaliste'* showing a working-class mother driven on to the streets in order to save her children from starvation: a piece of banal melodrama intended to poke fun at the tender social consciences of the naturalists. The joke was in bad taste and fell flat. Conflicting cries of *Vive Zola!*, *Vive Mallarmé!* rose from different parts of the auditorium, in which the two men, who in private life were the best of friends, were sitting in acute embarrassment.

In May the Théâtre d'Art put on a benefit performance in aid of two impecunious artists, Verlaine and Gauguin. Gauguin, who had already escaped from France once to the tropics when, in 1887, he took ship to Panama and helped dig the canal, made up his mind this time to settle for good in the South Seas and accordingly put all his pictures up for public auction. Surprisingly—for few critics had deigned to notice his work hitherto—the sale realized nearly 10,000 francs, a sum quite large enough for the traveller's immediate needs. The proceeds of the gala night at the Théâtre d'Art—comparatively meagre, it must be said—were accordingly paid over entirely to Verlaine. As usual, Paul Fort had arranged a varied programme, including poetry recitals as well as a first performance of a one-act play, *L'Intruse*, by an unknown author from Belgium, Maurice Maeterlinck. The entertainment was more decorous this time, and the audience judged it rather tame. As the reviewer in *Le Figaro* said, the symbolists would have done better to go on saying: 'Ah! if only our works could be staged!' Now that they had been staged, people could see for themselves that the heavens were not opening.

The acting company on this occasion had been joined by a young man, stage-struck since his schooldays, by name Aurélien Lugné-Poe; he was also given a part in one of the short plays, Remy de Gourmont's *Théodat*, put on at the Théâtre d'Art in December 1891. Other works performed the same evening were Maeterlinck's *Les Aveugles*, a play that impressed everyone except the incurably prosaic Francisque Sarcey; and an adaptation of the *Song of Songs* in which an attempt was made to appeal to the senses of sight, hearing and smell simultaneously by providing a musical accompaniment to the mimed spectacle and wafting different perfumes in the direction of the audience through the nozzle of a rudimentary scent spray. Muffled laughter and an epidemic of sham sneezes were the predictable results of this ill-advised experiment in 'synesthesia'.

After one more production—of Marlowe's *Dr Faustus* in an inadequate translation—the Théâtre d'Art closed its doors. Paul Fort had given proof of enthusiasm and ingenuity but lacked experience and authority; also, he was having to run the enterprise on a shoestring, since none of his productions were expected to settle down to a profitable long run. Fortunately, his withdrawal did not spell the end of symbolist drama, since Lugné-Poe, who had watched the experiments with interest, was able to pursue them, first at the Cercle des Escholiers where he produced and acted in five plays, and then with the company that he founded in association with Paul Fort, the Théâtre de l'Œuvre. His policy, from the start, was to allow a large place in the repertory to plays by foreign dramatists: in the course of time, there were productions of works by Maeterlinck, Gerhart Hauptmann, Oscar Wilde, and by the 'Scandinavians', Bjoernson, Strindberg and, above all, Ibsen. Although, as we have seen, it was Antoine who first introduced Ibsen to the Parisians, Lugné-Poe's productions were the means by which

French audiences grew to know and appreciate the work of the great Norwegian playwright.

The first play Lugné-Poe took was *The Lady from the Sea* which, with its undercurrents of secrecy and strangeness, lent itself admirably to the kind of 'poetic' treatment that the actor-producer, remembering the Théâtre d'Art stagings of Maeterlinck, decided to give it. He insisted on the cast using a dreamy, monotonous delivery and moving about the stage slowly, 'somnambulistically'; it was something like the sleep-walking scene in *Macbeth* played without the doctor and the gentlewoman. The critics were baffled, but quite impressed. This was something altogether different from Antoine's presentation of *Ghosts* or from the production of *A Doll's House* which had won so resounding a success at the Théâtre du Vaudeville. But there was an audience in the 1890s for this sort of dream drama, an audience growing tired of anguished social problem plays about inherited syphilis and the 'woman question'. No one knew for sure whether Lugné-Poe was presenting Ibsen 'correctly' or not, but at any rate his versions were pleas-antly disturbing and undeniably moving. The spectators had the impression —an impression that the symbolists had always wanted to give in their plays, without quite seeing how it was to be done—that the actual words spoken by the characters were mere cover for what Henri de Régnier called 'spiritual eddies which suddenly open up as whirlpools and disclose in the depths of their tortuous spirals the most personal of dreams. What-ever lies latent in these people, whatever they cannot openly avow, is discovered and made manifest, and beyond the everyday, superficial being another is stripped bare and stands revealed, stranger and more authentic. The characters are, as it were, their own spectres.'[32]

Ibsen had been played all over Europe but never like this; but why should he protest, if this was how the French wanted to have him played? In an interview published in *Le Figaro*, January 4th 1893, he declared himself delighted with Paris, gratified by the care taken over the production of his plays, impressed by the intelligence of the critics and deeply sympathetic to the young symbolists because, he said, the future belonged to them. This was more than enough to establish Ibsen willy-nilly as a symbolist. The Théâtre de l'Œuvre went on to produce *Rosmersholm* and *An Enemy of the People* in 1893, *The Master Builder* in 1894 (the original, *Bygmester Solness*, had been written only two years before), *Little Eyolf* and *Brand* in 1895, *Pillars of Society* and *Peer Gynt* in 1896. A fixed style was adopted: the actors behaved as if drugged, their movements sluggish, their voices hollow and querulous in turn. The whole production was made as unnatural-istic as possible and Lugné-Poe himself, whether he was playing Rosmer,

Solness or Brand, always wore the same long black overcoat and waist-coat buttoning up to the chin, a costume which the young symbolists paid him the compliment of adopting as the unofficial uniform of their movement.

Curiously, Ibsen was at one and the same time caught up, in this fashion, by the wave of neo-mysticism that arose at the century's end, and also elevated to the status of prophet and interpreter of the intellectual and political anarchism current at the period. Most of the critics and writers who actively supported the Théâtre de l'Œuvre, men like Camille Mauclair, Pierre Quil-lard, Henri de Régnier and Félix Fénéon, were self-confessed anarchists, even though they accorded no more than theoretical support to the move-ment. Anarchism burst on the scene, taking the phrase in a quite literal sense, in the spring of 1892, when a series of bomb explosions in Paris spread alarm and consternation. The socialists were quick to dissociate themselves from the phenomenon, which the police treated simply as an outbreak of lawlessness. Anarchism, said the editor of the *Revue socialiste* (Benoît Malon), was a doctrine that ran clean contrary to socialist teaching, being in fact mere anti-state individualism and therefore retrograde, not progressive. 'We are', he proclaimed, 'the most bitter adversaries of the anarchists.' Conservatives tended to agree with Leconte de Lisle, who regarded anarchism as simply another manifestation, after decadentism, symbolism, and mysticism, of the pernicious anti-rationalism of the *fin de siècle*; the same view seems to have been taken by Zola, who told a journalist interviewing him on behalf of *Le Figaro* that 'the anarchists are poets. This is the eternal black poetry, as old as humanity, as old as evil and suffering.'

The culprits—fanatics, criminals, or martyrs, depending on one's point of view—were duly rounded up and dealt with according to the law. There was a lull for 18 months and then, on December 9th, 1893, a bomb thrown from one of the public galleries in the Palais Bourbon exploded among the deputies, causing a number of injuries but no deaths. The police arrested a certain Vaillant who, at his trial, deposed that his aim was to bring to fruition the 'ideas of justice and freedom' sown, by among other writers, Ibsen. Vaillant was led to the guillotine shouting: 'Death to bourgeois society! Long live anarchy!' Seven days after his execution, another bomb was thrown into the restaurant of an hotel near the Gare St Lazare. The police gave chase and the anarchist, after discharging his revolver at them, was overpowered and taken into custody. He was a certain Émile Henry, the son of a member of the Commune who had escaped to Spain in 1871. In the next few months, there were a series of similar outrages followed by multiple arrests. Émile Henry was guillotined on May 21st, 1894 and on June 24th the President of the Republic, Sadi Carnot, was stabbed to death in a street in Lyons by a young Italian terrorist. The horror aroused by this latest atrocity encouraged the authorities to stage a mass trial of some 30 anarchists, including many intellectuals accused of militating in favour of the doctrine; they were, however, nearly all acquitted by the jury, much to the disgust of the right-wing press.

The anarchist movement bore two aspects. It was a form of social protest: Émile Henry spoke of 'legitimate reprisals' and reminded the court of all the 'innocent victims' of the social order, 'those children who are slowly dying of anaemia in the slums because they cannot be properly fed at home, those women who grow pale and weak in your factories to earn 40 *sous* a day, thankful if poverty does not force them into prostitution'. But anarchism was, besides, an arrogant, aristocratic manifestation of revolt, a movement to emancipate the individual from enslavement to a soulless materialism. In this other guise it was close to the spirit of the Théâtre de l'Œuvre and found its truest embodiment in the hero of Alfred Jarry's *Ubu-Roi*, produced there in 1896. Ubu can be interpreted both as a satire of everything the intellectual anarchists detested (his avarice, his cowardice, are essential qualities of the stock *bourgeois*), and simultaneously a personification of the anarchist himself, in his insolent disregard of every moral or religious constraint, his pure outrageousness. In the same way certain of Ibsen's heroes, like the fiercely individualistic Solness, could be regarded as breathing the anarchic spirit; a play like *Pillars of Society* shows class-conflict at its most bitter; while *An Enemy of the People* bore as its epigraph the dictum: 'The majority is always wrong. The strongest man is he who is most solitary.' The gala performance of *An Enemy of the People* at the Théatre de la Renaissance, March 29th, 1898, was ostensibly given in honour of Ibsen's seventieth birthday; but in the electrical atmosphere of the time, it was turned into an occasion for dreyfusard manifestations. Stockman was identified with Émile Zola: Zola was 'the strongest man', the lone individual, and the majority, 'always wrong', were at that very time howling for his blood. Ironically, Zola had very little sympathy for Ibsen's message; as a social thinker he was a firm believer in democratic methods and communal action, and as a novelist his strength had always lain not in the presentation of outstanding individuals but in the portrayal of crowd scenes and mass emotion, in such works as *Germinal*, *La Débâcle* and *Lourdes*.

The 1889 Paris Exhibition

The permeability of French cultural life during the last two decades of the century to every kind of influence blowing from abroad—not simply those just discussed, but others of which we can make only passing mention, such as English aestheticism[33]—might suggest an impoverishment of national life, even a weakening of the sense of national identity. In fact, there was little sign of anything of the sort. Politically, economically, and morally the country had made a rapid recovery from the setbacks of 1870-1. The war indemnity to Germany had been paid off much faster than anyone had thought possible, and the occupying forces had in consequence withdrawn behind the frontier. French diplomacy was securing the Republic a respected place in the councils of Europe, while in the wider world French power was extending over central Africa and the Far East. Industry was expanding, and fresh technical inventions—colour photography, the cinematograph, the fountain-pen and the typewriter—were providing artists and writers with new tools and laying the foundations of new modes of artistic expression not to be fully developed until the next century. The ratification of the Berne copyright convention on September 5th, 1887 allowed a much greater measure of financial protection for men of letters and put an end to the iniquitous practice of pirating original work which had previously robbed authors of some of the fruits of their labours.

In architecture, the passage from the Second Empire to the Third Republic occasioned no immediate changes in taste or design. Charles Garnier's opera house in Paris was completed, and the building inaugurated on January 5th, 1875. Garnier went on to create the twin-towered Casino at Monte Carlo, in a sumptuous style which was widely copied in other spas and seaside resorts for public buildings intended for similar purposes. The ornate, eclectic style favoured by architects during the Second Empire continued to be used for large structures like the 'Printemps' departmental store in Paris (by Paul Sédille, 1881). As before, the occasional *exposition universelle* furnished opportunities for displaying architectural innovations. That of 1878 was responsible for one permanent edifice, the Palais du Trocadéro with its twin minarets. That of 1889 produced two sensational structures, the Galerie des Machines and the Eiffel Tower: both were made possible by the use of steel, a material cheapened in cost by the recently invented Bessemer converter process. The Galerie des Machines, with a roof-span— enormous at the time—of 380 feet, impressed everyone as the cathedral hall of the technological age. The metal tower due to Gustave Eiffel was not to everyone's taste, and a group of writers and artists signed a letter of protest which they addressed to the organizers of the Exhibition. Huysmans denounced it violently, calling it a 'solitary suppository riddled with holes'; he disliked the colour, and thought it failed even to give the impression of being really tall; in any case it looked unfinished.[34] But the man in the street was full of admiration, and maddened his wife by repeating the awesome statistics: 300 metres high, made of 12,000 separate pieces held together by two and a half million rivets. God knows what it weighed, but the total cost was said to be 15 millions; say 50,000 francs a metre. But the view from the top made it very worth while. The first up—inevitably— was that most loyal of Francophiles, the Prince of Wales, who never missed an *exposition universelle*.

The future Edward VII was one of the very few representatives of reigning houses to visit Paris in 1889;[35] in view of the fact that the Exhibition had been timed for the centenary of the French Revolution, the reluctance of kings and emperors to honour it with their presence is hardly surprising. In this respect the occasion was very different from the famous 1867 Exhibition, but in others it was not so very dissimilar. The operettas of Offenbach and Hervé were revived, though Offenbach himself was in his grave: he died three months before the last and best of his works, *Les Contes d'Hoffmann*, was given its first performance. The famous wantons of yore were replaced by a new generation—now nicknamed *horizontales*—but the tradition of gallantry seemed under no threat from republican virtue, any more than did the reputation that Paris had won under the Second Empire as the capital of gaiety. In October 1889 the legendary Moulin Rouge, built on the site of a Montmartre working-class dance hall, opened its doors for the first time. The fake red sails of the windmill beckoned a predominantly upper- and middle-class clientèle, whatever the social origins of the acrobatic dancers, the *chahuteuses* as they were called. This mixed society, given over to noisy enjoyment, has been preserved for us in the pictures and posters of Henri de Toulouse-Lautrec who, unprepossessing enough with his swarthy beard and eyeglasses, was to be seen at the Moulin Rouge most evenings, stamping over the floor on his cherry-wood walking-stick, joking with the artistes, raising his top-hat to the occasional prince or count who caught his eye, recognizable from afar, despite his diminutive stature, by the stentorian tones of his voice.

Exoticism, as we have seen, had been a marked feature of the 1867 Exhibition; exoticism was as much in evidence in 1889, especially in the colonial annex on the Esplanade des Invalides, which had sections devoted to Algeria, Tunisia, Senegal and Cochin-China: here one could examine specimens of local arts and crafts, watch them being made in the workshops, taste the culinary specialities of the various regions, haggle at open-air stalls, wander into mosques and Buddhist temples. The military and naval expeditions that secured France a foothold in these distant parts of the world had been condemned in many quarters as useless extravagance; but the stay-at-home Frenchman was beginning to feel slightly flattered to think that even though, long ago, with the fall of Quebec, he had lost dominion over pine, he might yet assume dominion over palm in whatever sub-equatorial regions the British and the Dutch had not already grabbed.[36]

The highly popular writings of a French naval officer, Julien Viaud, contributed in no small measure to the upsurge of interest in those distant ports where the tricolour flew. His first book, *Aziyadé*, published anonymously in 1879, was set in the Levant, the author having spent some time in Salonika and Constantinople three years previously. An earlier voyage to Tahiti was recalled in a second novel, *Le Mariage de Loti*; thereafter, Lieutenant Viaud used the pseudonym Pierre Loti for all his books, which included *Le Roman d'un Spahi*, set in Senegal, and *Madame Chrysanthème* in which the author used his memories of a liaison he had once contracted with a Japanese girl in Nagasaki.

Madame Chrysanthème was published in 1887; it was followed, two years later, by a travel-book, *Japonaiseries d'automne*. Loti's account of the strange, remote and fabulous Empire of the Rising Sun served to stimulate as much as satisfy a curiosity about Japan which had existed for many years among connoisseurs. Merchants with an eye to a collectors' market had been shipping back paintings, carvings, porcelain and lacquer work since very shortly after Commodore Perry had compelled the Japanese to resume relations with the outside world. An oriental shop, 'La Porte chinoise', had been opened in the Rue de Rivoli as early as 1862; the couple who ran it had lived in Japan and were able to secure a steady supply of curios. The shop was much frequented by writers and artists with a leaning to the bizarre: Baudelaire, the Goncourt brothers, Edouard Manet and Fantin-Latour. Soon, eastern motifs began to appear even in *salon* pictures. In 1865, under the title *Princesse du pays de porcelaine*, Whistler exhibited a portrait of his mistress Jo dressed in oriental silks. Manet placed two Japanese prints on the wall in the background of his portrait of Zola. Degas, more profoundly influenced by Japanese art than any other contemporary painter, refrained from betraying the fact in so obvious a way. Instead, he studied the technique of the Japanese masters, their handling of spatial relationships particularly, their occasional odd foreshortenings and the strange bias of their compositions which could lead them to allow a foreground figure to be bisected by the edge of the panel.[37]

After the war collectors increased in keenness if not in discernment. The climax came with the 1878 Exhibition: Edmond de Goncourt, in particular, was quite ravished by what he saw in the Japanese section of the Trocadéro.

Among the new generation of artists, Vincent van Gogh was the most ardent in his appreciation; he would spend hours in the shops that specialized in Japanese prints and drawings, poring over them delightedly and purchasing as many as he could afford. He even paid the artists of Japan the supreme compliment of producing copies of those of their woodcuts that particularly appealed to him. Félix Fénéon planned a history of Japanese art which in the event never got written; Edmond de Goncourt did bring out monographs on Utamaro and Hokusai. What made this enthusiasm all the more remarkable was that the French collectors' knowledge was limited to the art-production of the eighteenth and nineteenth centuries; the older and more valuable pieces, heirlooms of the noble families, were never allowed by their owners to fall into the hands of the rapacious merchants who engaged in this trade.

Rodin

The fine arts section of the 1889 Exhibition included works of the outstanding impressionists, Pissarro and Monet, and even one canvas by Cézanne, *La Maison du pendu*, though this had been smuggled in only by the exercise of judicious blackmail on the part of Chocquet: having been requested to lend some furniture, he made it a condition that the Cézanne picture, which he owned, should be displayed. But in retrospect, one is inclined to think that the most exciting exhibits must have been the bronzes of Auguste Rodin: his *Age d'airain*, his *Saint-Jean Baptiste* and his bust of Victor Hugo. The 49-year-old sculptor had at last achieved a certain degree of celebrity, though only after a hard and at times desperate struggle. For 20 years after he left the École impériale de dessin, Rodin had been battling with poverty, neglect and snubs, moving from one employer to another, working essentially as a craftsman, a sculptor's assistant or a caster, rather than as an independent artist; but this long apprenticeship undoubtedly served him well in the end.

For much of the century, sculpture had been a neglected and despised art. Baudelaire, who headed one of the sections of his *Salon de 1846*: '*Pourquoi la sculpture est ennuyeuse*', argued that it was inferior to graphic art precisely because it was three-dimensional: the sculptor was not therefore able to control the point of view of the spectator nor compel him to view the work from the angle at which it was intended to be viewed. 'Painting has only one point of view; it is exclusive and despotic; which is why the painter's expression is far stronger.' Baudelaire added that sculpture, whether -n the cathedrals of the Middle Ages or in the park of the Palais de Versailles, had always been most successful when complementing architecture; only in its primitive beginnings, when the savage carved his fetishes and totem-poles, had it existed as an independent art.

Among the sculptors of the Second Empire only one was outstanding: Jean-Baptiste Carpeaux, whose works are at least graceful and vivacious; but he died in 1875 at the age of 48. The revolution which, in painting, was carried out by a whole fellowship of painters working in close communion with one another, in sculpture had to be accomplished single-handed by Rodin, himself a laconic, retiring genius, for all his lusty appetites.

The first work by Rodin to be accepted for exhibition was a marble bust called *L'Homme au nez cassé*. This was in 1875. All the time he could spare, over the next 18 months, was given to modelling a nude standing statue of a young Belgian conscript. Originally called *Le Vaincu*, its name was changed to *L'Age d'airain* and it was hotly discussed when shown in the 1877 *salon*. The commission to execute a monument for the municipality of Calais, commemorating the six heroic burghers who delivered themselves up to Edward III to save their fellow citizens from massacre, was given to Rodin in 1884 (though the monument was not finally unveiled until 1895, partly because it proved unexpectedly difficult to raise the money to pay the sculptor the agreed fee). And in 1886 he was commissioned to produce a monument to Victor Hugo, to be placed in the Panthéon.

Neither of these commissions caused Rodin as much trouble, nor did the work that resulted provoke as much controversy, as did the project to produce a monument in honour of Balzac. The patrons in this instance were the Société des Gens de Lettres, appropriately enough, since Balzac had been one of their earliest and most energetic presidents. They launched a subscription for the monument in November 1885 and entrusted its execution to the sculptor Chapu. He died, however, in 1891 without having taken the work very far, and a new artist had to be chosen to start afresh. Zola, who had been elected President of the Société des Gens de Lettres that year, asked his close friend, the architect Frantz Jourdain, to sound Rodin about his willingness to submit his candidature. Rodin boldly promised a delivery date less than two years ahead, and the committee duly appointed him—though only by a small minority of votes, and only as the result of an impassioned plea by Zola.

A glutton for work, Rodin seems to have had little idea, when he agreed to undertake the assignment, just how difficult a proposition it was to prove. There was an extraordinary shortage of reliable contemporary portraits of Balzac—nothing, in fact, beyond an insipid likeness done by Louis Boulanger and an unexpressive bust by David d'Angers. By a stroke of luck a hitherto unknown daguerreotype in Nadar's collection came to light and proved to be of greater use than anything else: taken towards the end of Balzac's life, it showed him ill and careworn, his right hand placed outstretched over his breast.

After reading all the literature on the novelist available at the time and consulting the great specialist Spoelberch de Lovenjoul, author of a nearly definitive *Histoire des œuvres de Balzac*, Rodin reached the decision that Balzac would have to be shown draped in his famous monk's robe, with his arms folded across his chest. This garb, besides being universally associated with Balzac, had the advantage of disguising the pot-belly and the short, fat legs; for the writer's squat body and enormous head made him an intrinsically difficult subject for a sculptor. In accordance with his almost invariable practice when modelling draped figures, Rodin started by making a series of nude studies, using a suitably stocky male model who posed for him in different attitudes. Over each of the various plaster casts he tried draping cloth and, with a picture of the statue in his mind's eye, visited the square of the Palais Royal, where the monument was to be erected, to check how it would appear in its ultimate setting.

He was still at this stage when he received the visit of a number of members of the committee of subscribers, who were already concerned about reports of the slow progress Rodin was making. Introduced into the studio, these gentlemen stood aghast at the sight of the collection of roughly modelled nude figures, who looked more like heavy-weight wrestlers than studies for a romantic genius. Since the sculptor disdainfully forbore to offer any explanations they trooped out of the studio unenlightened and even more disturbed than when they arrived. A further call a few months later, at the end of May 1893 which was the deadline Rodin had given, left a still more unfortunate impression. The artist was in a depressed state of mind, partly as the result of a severe bout of influenza from which he had not properly recovered, and partly on account of private worries: his mistress Camille Claudel, the poet's sister, was giving him no peace, insanely jealous as she was at his infidelities, real or supposed. He had done hardly any more work on the Balzac statue since they last saw it, and seemed so ill and listless that the subscribers' representatives wondered whether the monument would even be ready in time for the centenary of the novelist's birth, in six years' time.

Zola's term of office as president of the Société des Gens de Lettres came to an end in March 1894. Luckily his successor, the poet Jean Aicard, was well disposed towards Rodin and exerted himself as had Zola to prevail on the members not to cancel the commission. But he could not allay their

29 Toulouse-Lautrec, *La Danse au Moulin Rouge* (1890)

30 Carpeaux' sculpture, *La Danse*; part of the decoration of the new Paris opera house, it was considered highly daring in its day

anxiety. Rodin, hearing of the agitation, sent the Society a dignified letter, returned the 10,000-franc advance he had received, but still refused to acknowledge defeat. His Balzac had him now by the throat, and the work had to be terminated no matter how long the struggle lasted: to abandon it would have been tantamount to abnegating his mission. But the Society could hardly have been expected to enter into these personal considerations; an agitation started to have the work put in the hands of a more trustworthy sculptor, and Aicard, in disgust, announced his resignation. The scandal was such that it could no longer be kept quiet: the newspapers got hold of the story and soon a public debate was raging. Rodin had plenty of rivals and secret enemies who had an interest in having him disgraced and shown up as incapable of completing a major work. The invasion of his studio by visitors and reporters made it even harder for him to concentrate on the task in hand. All through 1895 and 1896 conspiracies were rife to have the commission awarded to some other sculptor and Félicien Champsaur, making mischief as usual, brought the quarrel to a head by publishing an offensive article in *Le Gil Blas* in which he proclaimed that Rodin's reputation as a great sculptor was as overblown as Mallarmé's fame as a great poet.

Finally, in March 1898, Henri Houssaye, the new President of the Société des Gens de Lettres, was able to transmit to members Rodin's personal assurance to him that the statue would be ready within six months, and in fact the artist sent it along shortly afterwards for exhibition in the spring *salon*. But it was with a heavy heart; Judith Cladel has recalled how she watched him examining the enormous statue as it left his studio, seeing it for the first time in the open, and complaining that he was being forced to part with it before he was completely satisfied. It was set up in the Galerie des Machines, the vast hall erected for the 1889 Exhibition and still not, at this date, dismantled. Rodin had decided to show alongside it the entirely pleasing marble group called *Le Baiser*; the President of the Republic, Félix Faure, complimented him warmly on this work when he saw it at the pre-view, but turned his back on the *Balzac* without a word. On the first day of the exhibition, it was all too clear that the great majority of the public shared Félix Faure's unspoken opinion about the relative value of the two works. They milled round the towering statue, the 'monolith with a human face', turning curiously to examine the impassive creator who stood by *Le Baiser* with his hat pulled over his eyes and his great beard rendering the expression on his face quite inscrutable. Some laughed at him, others stared at him speechless with indignation. There was a chorus of vilification in the press, and the insults Rodin was forced to endure verged on the out-

R

rageous. Groups were formed on purpose to visit the gallery and make rude remarks in front of the statue, in front of this 'snowman', this 'sack-race' as it was variously called. In the streets little plaster figures roughly resembling penguins or seals raised on their tails were hawked as miniatures of 'Rodin's Balzac'. To cap it all, the committee of subscribers issued a fatuous statement refusing to recognize the statue as being that of Balzac at all.

At this Rodin's admirers rallied and opened a fresh subscription to purchase the work and have it erected on a suitable site. Funds flooded in. The controversy, for a while, vied in acrimony with the arguments about the innocence of Dreyfus and the propriety of having his case re-tried, which were at their climax during this summer of 1898, and it was significant that the majority of those who subscribed for the purchase of the Balzac were also convinced that Dreyfus had been wrongfully sentenced for high treason.

The quarrel was ended by Rodin himself who wrote to the new committee of subscribers informing them that he had decided to remain in possession of the statue and to accept no offers for it from any quarter. He also withdrew it from the Galerie des Machines. The gesture was both dignified and disinterested and, besides, Rodin probably did not have the heart to part with his Balzac. He described the work later to a journalist as 'the crowning-piece of my entire life, the very pivot of my aesthetic. On the day I conceived it I became a different man. My evolution was radical: I had forged a link between the great traditions that had perished and the art of my own time, a link which has grown stronger every day.' It is possible now to see clearly what Rodin meant. The Balzac stands at the conjunction of naturalistic and symbolistic art; it is overwhelmingly real, and yet it incorporates an idea, thus acquiring a spiritual dimension of great emotional depth. Viewed at ground level, it is crushing: a giant looking over the heads of pygmies. Seen from a raised plane, the face swallows everything, a face, as Rilke wrote, 'gazing and drunk with gazing, a face seething with creation: the face of an element.'[38] So much linked Rodin to Balzac, these two daemonic geniuses standing at the beginning and the end of the nineteenth century, each totally committed to flesh-and-blood humanity and yet each of them a brooding visionary, both utterly devoted to their art and struggling to accomplish in a single lifetime the impossible task of expressing all they felt called on to express; so much linked them that it is hardly to be wondered at that a work so unlike anything else, so fitting a culmination of an age of tumultuous and multifarious artistic endeavour, should have been born of the meeting and mating of these two spirits.

Notes

[1] They are part of the poem *'L'Anathème'* included in the collection *Poèmes et poésies* which was published in 1855.

[2] First published 1866; reissued, as *Charles Demailly*, by which title it is now usually known, in 1868. The passage quoted below will be found on pp. 265–6 of the *'édition définitive publiée sous la direction de l'Académie Goncourt'* (Paris, Flammarion and Fasquelle, n.d.).

[3] See above, p. 89

[4] It is true that the fortunes of the Homais family follow a correspondingly ascendant curve, and that Flaubert describes the Homais household, in the last chapter of the book, as *'florissante et hilare'*. But this only reinforces the point. Homais and his large brood represent clearly enough the barbarians who are about to supplant the decadent Bovarys.

[5] Exhibited at the *salon* of 1847.

[6] *Correspondance de P.-J. Proudhon*, vol. XI (Paris, Lacroix, 1875), pp. 164, 220–1, 264, 334.

[7] *Curiosités esthétiques, l'Art romantique et autres œuvres critiques*, ed. H. Lemaître (Paris, Garnier, 1962), p. 620.

[8] It is however true that in a footnote to one of the poems in his collection, Baudelaire did testify to the qualities of *'la langue de la dernière décadence romaine'* which, he said, was *'singulièrement propre à exprimer la passion telle que l'a comprise et sentie le monde poétique moderne ... Dans cette merveilleuse langue, le solécisme et le barbarisme me paraissent rendre les négligences forcées d'une passion qui s'oublie et se moque des règles.'* But Baudelaire was thinking of the kind of rhymed verse, full of conceits and puns, that appeared among Christian Latinists in the early Middle Ages, of which the poem he is referring to, *Franciscae meae laudes*, is a clever and curious pastiche. Poetry of this kind, full of religious imagery, a mixture of the mystical and the profane, is certainly not what Mallarmé understood by the literature of the decadence which he was careful to specify as pre-Christian or at least neo-pagan.

[9] Jacques Lethève (*'Le thème de la décadence dans les lettres françaises à la fin du XIXᵉ siècle'*, *Revue d'Histoire Littéraire de la France*, vol. lxiii (1963), p. 51) quotes instances dating back to 1876 when Bourget wrote in *Le Siècle littéraire*: *'Nous acceptons sans humilité comme sans orgueil ce terrible mot de décadence. Que signifie-t-il de si infâmant et de si méprisant que nous devions jeter à l'eau tout travail de l'esprit déshonoré de sa marque? Les grands siècles ne sauraient durer toujours, et ils se prolongeraient que leur effrayante monotonie fatiguerait l'admiration jusqu'au dégoût.'*

[10] See R. Baldick, *The Life of J.-K. Huysmans* (Oxford, 1955), p. 88.

[11] Zola's letter, and Huysmans' reply, have been published in Huysmans, *Lettres inédites à Émile Zola*, ed. Pierre Lambert (Geneva, 1953) pp. 102–7.

[12] Cf. Verlaine's sonnet 'Langueur' (*Jadis et Naguère*), first published in *Le Chat noir*, May 26th, 1883.

[13] The family is represented in the book by Pauline Quenu, an offshoot of the

Macquart branch, who has been left an orphan and is being brought up in the Chanteau household.

[14] Jules Verne, the founder of modern anticipatory (so-called science-) fiction, wrote his best remembered works in the late 'sixties and early 'seventies. His underlying theme is travel: air-travel (*Cinq semaines en ballon*, 1863), underground travel (*Voyage au centre de la terre*, 1864), polar travel (*Les aventures du capitaine Hatteras*, 1866), underwater travel (*Vingt mille lieues sous la mer*, 1870), extra-terrestrial travel (*De la terre à la lune* and *Autour de la lune*, 1865–70), or simply fast globe-trotting (*Le Tour du monde en quatre-vingt jours*, 1873). In many cases these journeys are undertaken in vehicles with a range and versatility theoretically feasible but not by any means achieved at the time Verne was writing; and the expeditions are usually headed by non-French leaders, even though a Frenchman often joins the party. Jules Verne succeeded in combining a sincere patriotism with a genuine cosmopolitanism of outlook.

[15] The existence of this political comedy was revealed by Victor Tissot. *Voyage au pays des milliards* (Paris, 1875). Tissot also informed the French public that Wagner had composed a triumphal march for the victorious German troops on their return.

[16] It was not until he visited Spain in 1882, where the uninhibited folk-music and popular dances came to him as a revelation, that he succeeded in composing a piece of music (*España*) that won general acclaim.

[17] Debussy first read Maeterlinck's *Pelléas et Mélisande* in 1892. The opera he wrote based on the play was not given its first public performance until 1902.

[18] Charles Bordes, a student of French ecclesiastical music of the Renaissance, and Alexandre Guilmant, an organist.

[19] *Souvenirs d'un vieux critique*, *9ᵉ série* (1888), p. 199.

[20] See my 'Dostoevsky in disguise: the 1888 French version of *The Brothers Karamazov*'. *French Studies*, vol. IV (1950), pp. 227–38.

[21] Deschamps, *La Vie et les livres*, *1ère série*, pp. 212–14. The phrase between quotation marks appears to be a reference to something Flaubert said about Charles Bovary, in the first months of his marriage to Emma: '*L'univers, pour lui, n'excédait pas le tour soyeux de son jupon*' (*Madame Bovary*, pt. I, ch. V).

[22] See the chapter 'Tolstoyism' in Hemmings, *The Russian Novel in France*, *1884–1914* (Oxford, 1950), and also Thaïs S. Lindstrom, *Tolstoï en France* (Paris, 1952), pp. 61–94.

[23] Letter dated February 23rd, 1889: quoted in Charles Beuchat, *Édouard Rod et le cosmopolitisme* (1930), pp. 275–6.

[24] The work was, however, brought out in the same year (1876) by Lemerre in an edition limited to 195 copies, with illustrations by Manet.

[25] The authors were Henri Beauclair, a journalist, and Gabriel Vicaire, a minor poet. The joint pseudonym they adopted was '*Marius Tapora, pharmacien de deuxième classe*'.

[26] It has been reproduced in Bonner Mitchell, *Les Manifestes littéraires de la Belle Époque* (Paris, 1966), pp. 27–32.

[27] Not to be confused with *Le Décadent*, the literary magazine launched six months earlier by Anatole Baju.

[28] Lamartine in 1790, Vigny in 1797, Hugo in 1802. Mallarmé was born in 1842, Verlaine in 1844, Rimbaud in 1854.

[29] A. E. Carter, *Verlaine: a study in parallels* (Toronto, 1969), p. 198.

[30] Mauclair, *Mallarmé chez lui* (Paris, 1935), p. 66.

[31] Brunetière occupied the chair of French Literature at the École Normale Supérieure. Émile Faguet, Francisque Sarcey, Jules Lemaître, Gustave Larroumet, were other noted critics of the period who similarly held university teaching posts.

[32] *Entretiens politiques et littéraires*, January 10th, 1893. Quotd by J. Robichez, *Le Symbolisme au théâtre: Lugné-Poe et les débuts de l'Œuvre* (Paris, 1957), p. 156.

[33] Represented principally by Oscar Wilde's *Picture of Dorian Grey*, the drawings of Aubrey Beardsley, and the poetry of Arthur Symons and Ernest Dowson.

[34] Huysmans, 'Le Fer', in *Certains* (Paris, 1889).

[35] The only others were the King of the Belgians and the Shah of Persia.

[36] These extensions of French overseas power were jealously watched by the jingoistic British; tension between the two powers reached crisis point in 1893 (over the question of the independence of Siam) and again in 1895, at the time of the Fashoda incident.

[37] A good early example of Degas' use of this trick of design is his *Femme aux chrysanthèmes* (1865).

[38] 'Schauend, im Rausche des Schauens, schäumend von Schaffen: das Gesicht eines Elementes': Rilke, *Sämtliche Werke*, vol. v (Frankfurt am Main: Insel Verlag, 1965), p. 197.

The Explosion of Truth

In the summer of 1897 Émile Zola wrote the final chapters of the concluding volume of the trilogy, *Les Trois Villse*, on which he had been engaged since he finished *Les Rougon-Macquart* four years earlier. He found himself in one of those periods of dead calm into which even the most assiduous and methodical worker may drift. The next task he planned was the novel about the evils of a declining birth-rate which he had long wanted to get down to; but, now that the moment had come, he felt curiously disinclined to look back over his notes. He wondered at times about his increasing tendency to deal, in his novels, with topics of immediate, everyday concern to his huge public rather than with the old, tried, intimate subjects, love and death, jealousy, despair and resignation. *Paris*, the novel he had just finished, was really no more than an unwieldy hotch-potch of editorials on such themes as urban poverty, the anarchist movement, the conflict between religion and science, and the dangers of cheap journalism. Zola had long since forgotten the precepts of his dead master, Flaubert, and was now using fiction, as Dickens and Hugo had used it, to focus attention on social abuses and suggest remedies to social problems.

But through that warm September at Médan he felt more inclined to idle the days away, with his camera, his bicycle, and his dogs, than pursue his inquiries into the reasons why French parents had stopped producing large families. His wife was abroad, visiting friends in Italy, and they would not be returning to their town house and the usual social round until she was back. So it was that when a respectable city lawyer, by name Louis Leblois, requested an hour or so's conversation with him on a matter of public interest, the novelist responded gladly enough. His visitor began by asking Zola what he knew about the circumstances of the trial and sentencing of an army officer on the General Staff, a certain Alfred Dreyfus, three years previously. Zola had one very clear memory: of a literary dinner at which

Alphonse Daudet's son, the journalist Léon, had given an excited account of how Dreyfus, after his secret trial by court martial, had undergone the humiliation of being stripped of his rank in public, his badges torn off his uniform, his sword snapped in two before his eyes. The man seemed neither crushed nor stoically indifferent: he had repeatedly shouted his innocence, regardless of the jeers and howls of the assembled journalists. Zola remembered feeling uneasy and even a little sick as he listened to Léon Daudet's reconstruction of the scene. Surely the man's punishment—life imprisonment on Devil's Island, off French Guiana, the rigours of which were not unfamiliar to Zola since he had described them 20 years earlier in a graphic chapter of his novel *Le Ventre de Paris*—was sufficiently harsh without adding to it this ferocious hounding by the crowd: the crowd, Zola's perpetual nightmare, that hideous hydra which had yet fascinated him as it had no other artist.

The question whether Dreyfus had been given a fair trial and awarded a just sentence was not one that Zola had thought it necessary to pose himself at the time, and nothing had occurred to cause him to ponder it since. The one piece of evidence that had led to the arrest had been a handwritten list of military secrets that the writer was offering to sell to the Germans. The handwriting was said to be indisputably Dreyfus's. This document, always thereafter referred to as the *bordereau*, had been published in facsimile by *Le Matin* on November 10th, 1896, but Zola had not happened to see it. In any case, an earlier article in *L'Éclair* had hinted that Dreyfus was not found guilty on the evidence of the *bordereau* alone, and that there had been other, more damning proofs, of a kind that could not be divulged without provoking a serious international incident.

What Leblois had to tell Zola was this: in June of that year (1897) he had been visited by the new head of the counter-espionage office, Lieutenant-Colonel Picquart who, on the point of leaving on a mission to Tunisia, desired to confide in him certain doubts he was privately entertaining about the legality of Dreyfus's trial. Picquart, when he took over his new functions in 1895, had been instructed to investigate the case with a view to discovering Dreyfus's real motives for betraying his country. The absence of any plausible motive was one of the most troubling aspects of the case: for Alfred Dreyfus had no known pro-German sympathies and, moreover, being possessed of a substantial private fortune, stood in no need of the small sums he might have obtained in exchange for the relatively unimportant information he was alleged to have offered to pass on. It is true that he was a Jew: but only the most rabid anti-Semite would have considered that this fact explained everything. Moreover, Dreyfus's detention had not brought the leakage of military secrets to a stop: presumably another spy was still at large. For some time, Picquart's investigations led nowhere; but then, one day, incontrovertible evidence came into his hands that a certain Commandant Esterhazy was in treasonous correspondence with the German military attaché.[1] Esterhazy was known to be living a dissolute life and to be in serious financial difficulties. Was he just another traitor? Certainly the proof of his guilt did not, in itself, suffice to throw any doubt on Dreyfus's. But in August 1897 Picquart saw two letters written by Esterhazy and realized immediately that the handwriting was the same as that of the *bordereau* which had served to incriminate Dreyfus. Here was the proof that there had only ever been one traitor, who was Esterhazy, not Dreyfus.

His chiefs, as can be imagined, were not much elated when Picquart communicated to them his discovery. To admit that a military court had made a mistake and sent the wrong man to a penal colony would prove, they feared, so damaging to the prestige of the army that it was imperative to suppress this new evidence. Picquart was horrified that the generals should be coolly contemplating leaving an innocent man in prison in order to save their own reputations. Moreover, he knew that Dreyfus's relatives were feverishly investigating the case themselves, and that sooner or later they were bound to arrive at the truth. But his protests and remonstrances to General Gonse, his immediate superior at the War Office, were unavailing; or rather, the only effect they had was to suggest to the military authorities that this officer with the inconveniently tender conscience should be taken off the case. Picquart was duly relieved of his post and sent away from the capital. A man of lesser moral calibre might have rested content with the thought that he had done all he could and that he must now bow to the wisdom of his superiors who would handle the case as they thought best. But Picquart's conscience would not let him rest. To make any public announcement of what he knew was unthinkable; he was a serving soldier, a career officer, and he knew his duty. But the situation might change, and Picquart felt it was not right that the strong presumption of Dreyfus's innocence should remain locked in his own breast. Accordingly he visited Leblois, who was a personal friend, and under the seal of secrecy disclosed to him some, though not all, of the facts that had come to light since Dreyfus's trial.

This was the gist of what Leblois had to tell Zola. The information had already been imparted to several other men in the public eye, among them the greatly respected elder statesman Scheurer-Kestner, who was vice-president of the Senate. Zola subsequently met Scheurer-Kestner at dinner, and the whole story was retraced once more. The novelist was enthralled by the real-life melodrama without being fully convinced, as yet, that there really had been a miscarriage of justice in 1894, and that, currently, high personages in the War Office were frantically taking precautions to cover up. He agreed that the whole murky affair needed investigating, and that Scheurer-Kestner, with his contacts in high places, was best placed to do this; he was, in any case, still complacent enough to believe that, with a little prodding, the army could be trusted to put its house in order. He deplored the distasteful tactics of the anti-Semitic right-wing press, engaged on a gratuitous campaign of vilification against Dreyfus, his family, and the growing band of his supporters. He could not agree either with the super-patriots who argued that, the army being the shield of France, to expose the errors and partiality of high-ranking officers was a more irresponsible course than to leave a possibly innocent man to languish in prison under a tropical sun. But at this stage, and indeed right down until January 12th, 1898, it did not occur to Zola to regard the business as anything more than an interesting and no doubt significant episode, a 'slice of life' which, duly trimmed, might furnish him with the ground-plan of a future novel. As he himself admitted, in the incomplete notes he made for that history of the Dreyfus Case which, regrettably, he never found time to write,[2] for many weeks he had looked on the whole imbroglio with the detached if not dispassionate eye of a collector of 'human documents'. Life seemed to be imitating art, spontaneously providing the shape and equilibrium that the artist is usually obliged to impose. There was this 'trio of types: the man under sentence, guiltless, far away, with all the tempestuous thoughts whirling in his brain; the guilty man, here among us, walking free, with what was going on in his mind while another was expiating his crime; and the bringer of truth, Scheurer-Kestner, silently active.' Zola published one article in Le Figaro on Scheurer-Kestner and was hoping to follow it up with two others, one on Esterhazy and one on Dreyfus—sound, useful journalist's work, such as he had written successively over the years on a variety of figures temporarily in the limelight and needing such support or denunciation as his pen could provide. But Zola did not for one moment imagine that he should abandon his prescribed role as the eloquent but essentially inactive commentator; this was the role that he and all other writers had adhered to strictly since the events of 1848–51 had proved the ineffectuality of any more direct participation in the machinery of public policy. Moulders of opinion they might be, but they were not charged with the actual responsibilities of power and had no desire to shoulder them.[3]

After January 12th, 1898 Zola stepped over this cautious demarcation line, and can be said thereby to have ended, at one stroke, the division between the writer and society which had remained in force for well on 50 years.

minable, pour égarer l'opinion et ^{37} couvrir leur faute.

J'accuse enfin le premier conseil de guerre d'avoir violé le droit, en condamnant un accusé sur une pièce restée secrète, et j'accuse le second conseil de guerre d'avoir couvert cette illégalité, par ordre, en commettant à son tour le crime juridique d'acquitter ~~un coupa~~ sciemment un coupable.

En portant ces accusations, je n'ignore pas que je me mets sous les coups des articles 30 et 31 de la loi sur la presse du 29 juillet 1881, qui punit les délits de diffamation. Et c'est volontairement que je m'expose. —

Quant aux gens que j'accuse,

The concluding folios of the manuscript of *J'Accuse*. The words in which Zola described his action in publicly denouncing Dreyfus's judges ('*un moyen révolutionaire pourhâter l'explosion de la vérité et de la justice*') can be read on the right.

je ne les connais pas, je ne les ai jamais vus, je n'ai contre eux ni rancune ni haine. Ils ne sont pour moi que des entités, des esprits de malfaisance sociale. Et l'acte que j'accomplis ici n'est qu'un moyen révolutionnaire pour en hâter l'explosion de la vérité et de la justice.

Je n'ai qu'une passion, celle de la lumière, au nom de l'humanité qui a tant souffert et qui a droit au bonheur. Ma protestation enflammée n'est que le cri de mon âme. Qu'on ose donc me traduire en cour d'assises et que l'enquête ait lieu au grand jour!

J'attends.

For on this day Esterhazy, denounced by Mathieu Dreyfus on November 14th, was unanimously acquitted by the court martial that had been convened to try him. The verdict was utterly absurd and totally unexpected. If doubts had remained in anyone's mind about Esterhazy's guilt, they should have been removed by the publication in *Le Figaro* on November 29th of a batch of Esterhazy's private letters which showed him consumed by an almost pathological hatred of the nation in whose army he served. 'If this evening', he wrote in one of them, 'I were told that I should be killed to-morrow as a captain of Uhlans, sabring the French, I should assuredly die happy.' The same issue of *Le Figaro* reproduced in facsimile the *bordereau* that sent Dreyfus to Devil's Island alongside one of Esterhazy's letters also in facsimile, so that the damning similarity could be seen by all. After this, both Zola and Scheurer-Kestner were serenely confident that the second court martial would put everything right: Esterhazy would be found guilty of the crime for which Dreyfus had been made to suffer; the real traitor would be given his due deserts, and the unfortunate victim of a tragic error of justice would be rehabilitated. What they failed to make allowances for was the short-sighted *esprit de corps* of the army men, disastrously encouraged by the anti-Jewish propaganda of a certain section of the nationalist press.

The acquittal of Esterhazy sounded like the clanging of a second set of prison doors on the unfortunate Dreyfus. Only a charge of dynamite could blow them open now. And this is exactly what Zola provided with the 'Open Letter to the President of the Republic' which, under the banner headline *J'Accuse!*, was published on January 13th in the newspaper *L'Aurore*. Zola himself called this long indictment 'a revolutionary means of hastening the explosion of truth and justice'. It was certainly revolutionary, for no piece of prose like it had been penned—not even by Victor Hugo in the relative safety of the Channel Islands—at any time during the nineteenth century. It was forced out of him by a deep but controlled emotion, which emerges in the style, hard, bare, devoid of rhetorical flourish, but so vibrant that even today, when nearly all the unfortunate men that Zola pillories have fallen into a grateful oblivion, still the serried paragraphs retain the power to provoke a shudder of excitement in the reader. Language, at last, was being used not as a mirror or an ornament or an intoxicant, but as a weapon. Zola himself said that it was a case of the pen against the sword. He was too modest. The pen itself had been tempered and sharpened and transformed into a keener blade.

Tactically, the publication of *J'Accuse* was a coolly calculated act of provocation. Zola knew he was infringing the law of libel, for which the penalty might run to a year's imprisonment. He was counting on being taken to court; indeed, unless the army leaders were to accept, meekly, his charges of deliberate fraud or culpable negligence, they would have to prosecute him. But this case could not be heard *in camera*. The trial would be public, the defence would be free to subpoena what witnesses they wished, the whole monstrous web of lies that had enveloped the luckless Dreyfus could be exposed and slashed to pieces. This, at least, was what Zola and his friends were hoping. When the trial was held, a few weeks later, it required all the astuteness of the presiding magistrate to prevent the full truth emerging. Though Zola lost his case, the revisionist cause received an impetus which eventually carried it through to victory: to adapt another of Zola's ringing phrases, 'truth was on the march and nothing could halt it.'

If *J'Accuse* had never been written it is possible that Dreyfus would never have been cleared; but for the historian of French cultural life, Zola's 'open letter' has a deeper significance. It helped every writer to recover a sense of social purpose which had got lost in the disheartening early months of the Second Republic and had never, over the five intervening decades, been really recaptured. The day after it was published there appeared in *L'Aurore* the first instalment of the so-called 'petition of the intellectuals'—a manifesto calling for the retrial of Dreyfus, signed eventually by over 3,000 writers, scholars, and artists. Zola's name was at the head, and immediately after his that of Anatole France. Why should this mild-mannered man with the caustic pen, one of the pillars of the establishment and one of Zola's bitterest critics, have suddenly thrown in his lot with the *dreyfusards*? And why, again, should it have been the rich, indolent young dilettante Marcel Proust who, with his friend Fernand Gregh, visited Anatole France to obtain his signature? Why should the signatories have included Edmond Rostand, whose stirring drama *Cyrano de Bergerac*, so archaic in its truculent romanticism, was currently enjoying an immensely successful first run? and André Gide, whose early symbolistic works published in the 1890s, the *Poésies d'André Walter* and the *Voyage d'Urien*, suggest no very urgent commitment to contemporary concerns? One thing fused together all these very dissimilar writers, the young and the middle-aged, the poets and the novelists, the naturalists and the symbolists: a realization that their common currency, the word, had suddenly been revalued. Overnight, the writer had become a power in the land.

There were probably as many men of letters who disapproved of Zola's stand and attacked the 'revisionist' line: they included men from the same literary camps, ex-decadents like Bourget and Jean Lorrain, influential critics like Brunetière and Lemaître, a Parnassian poet and close friend of Zola's, François Coppée, and among the younger generation of symbolists,

Pierre Louÿs and Paul Valéry. The painters were just as divided: Claude Monet, who had been bitterly hurt at what he considered to be Zola's harsh travesty of the aims of impressionism in *L'Œuvre* (1886), was now totally reconciled and became one of his most fanatic supporters; while Degas lapped up the anti-Semitic propaganda of *La Libre Parole* and when one of his models started talking enthusiastically about the heroism of the *dreyfusards*, hardly gave the girl time to dress before throwing her out of his studio. Maurice Barrès launched a scathing attack on the 'petition of the intellectuals' in *Le Journal*, February 1st. Gustave Kahn, on the other hand, writing in *La Revue Blanche* on February 15th, spoke of 'the noisy irruption of the writer in political life, signing manifestos, intruding on the flow of events', and asked: 'Ought action to be the sister of the dream? Ought the writer to engage in militancy? Instead of summing up his age, or singing on the sidelines, ought he to dictate the course it should take?' Clearly Kahn felt that he ought, for his essay thereafter develops into a strong attack on Barrès for his unsympathetic attitude to Zola.

Phrasing his rhetorical question as he does ('ought action to be the sister of the dream?') Kahn was deliberately, and significantly, echoing a line in one of Baudelaire's '*Révolte*' poems, *Le Reniement de Saint-Pierre*:

> Certes, je sortirai, quant à moi, satisfait
> D'un monde où l'action n'est pas la sœur du rêve;
> Puissé-je user du glaive et périr par le glaive!
> Saint-Pierre a renié Jésus . . . il a bien fait.

We saw, in our first chapter, what state of exasperation Baudelaire had reached at the close of the Second Republic when, in all probability, he composed this blasphemous poem.[4] Political developments since the 1848 Revolution had made it all too clear that the democratic 'dream' was very far from being linked in sisterly concord with political 'action'. But now, 50 years later, the dreamers and the men of action, Zola and Clemenceau, Anatole France and Jean Jaurès, had come together.[5] Charles Péguy drew inspiration for the remainder of his short life of literary and political activity from Zola's intervention in the Dreyfus Case. Proust, in his cork-lined study, meditated on those heroic days of his youth, as he wrote *A la recherche du temps perdu* in which the social repercussions of the 'Affaire' are closely analysed. Gide might never have interested himself in the Soviet experiment in Russia or waxed indignant over the colonial exploitation of Africa if it had not been for the example given him at an impressionable age of the power a writer can develop when truly caught up in an important cause. There were certain others still in the cradle or not even born at the time

J'Accuse was published: Aragon, Malraux, Sartre, Camus, to mention only the best known. Zola's 'revolutionary act' may be said to have given them the charter they needed if they were to go beyond merely commenting on the political issues of their time, and were to participate as men of action in the shaping of events. French culture, after half a century of enforced separation from political life, had struck roots at last in the solid ground of national and popular concerns.

Notes

[1] The evidence took the form of a torn-up special delivery letter. colloquially known as a *petit bleu*, addressed to Esterhazy. Why the letter was not sent, and how its fragments reached the French military authorities, are mysteries still unresolved: see Guy Chapman, *The Dreyfus Case* (London, 1955) pp. 119 and 367.

[2] Headed *Impressions d'audience*, these notes were first published by Jacques Kayser in *La Nef*, no. 39 (February 1949) pp. 55–66.

[3] Jules Vallès, of course, was the one shining exception to this rule. He had died in 1885.

[4] This dating is favoured by Antoine Adam: see pp. 420–1 of his edition of *Les Fleurs du Mal* (Paris, Garnier, 1959).

[5] Anatole France met Jaurès in the Salle des Pas perdus of the Palais de Justice during Zola's trial, while both were waiting to be called as witnesses for the defence. Jaurès subsequently took France along to meetings of the Socialist party and to workers' meetings; eventually, after 1900, France found the courage to address such gatherings and even to participate in election campaigns on behalf of the socialists.

Bibliography

Standard political and social histories, biographies, memoirs, diaries and collections of letters relating to the period have not been included in this bibliography, which is intended simply as a guide to the more important general works dealing with the development of literature and the arts in France during the second half of the nineteenth century.

BECKER, George J. (ed.). *Documents of Modern Literary Realism*. Princeton, N.J.: Princeton University Press. 1963.

BELLESSORT, André. *Les Intellectuels et l'avènement de la Troisième République*. Paris: Grasset. 1931.

BELLET, Roger, *Presse et journalisme sous le Second Empire*. Paris: Armand Colin. 1967.

BEUCHAT, Charles. *Histoire du naturalisme française*. 2 vols. Paris: Corrêa. 1949.

BILLY, André. *L'Époque 1900*. Paris: Tallandier. 1951.

BINKLEY, Robert C. *Realism and Nationalism, 1852–1871*. New York: Harper. 1935.

BOUVIER, Émile. *La Bataille réaliste, 1844–1857*. Paris: Fontemoing. 1913.

CAHUET, Albert. *La Liberté du théâtre*. Paris: Chevalier-Marescq. 1902.

CARASSUS, Émilien. *Le snobisme et les lettres françaises de Paul Bourget à Marcel Proust*. Paris: Armand Colin. 1966.

CARTER, A. E. *The Idea of Decadence in French Literature, 1830–1900*. Toronto: University of Toronto Press. 1958.

CHAPMAN, J. M. & Brian. *The Life and Times of Baron Haussmann: Paris in the Second Empire*. London: Weidenfeld & Nicolson. 1957.

CHARLTON, D. G. *Secular Religions in France, 1815–1870*. London: Oxford University Press. 1963.

CHARVET, P. E. *A Literary History of France*. Vol IV. *The Nineteenth Century, 1789–1870*. Vol. V. *The Nineteenth and Twentieth Centuries, 1870–1940*. London: Benn. 1967.

CHASSÉ, Charles. *Le Mouvement symboliste dans l'art du XIXe siècle*. Paris: Floury. 1947.

CŒUROY, André. *Wagner et l'esprit romantique. Wagner et la France. Le wagnérisme littéraire*. Paris: Gallimard. 1965.

COLLINS, Irene. *The Government and the Newspaper Press in France, 1814–1881*. London: Oxford University Press. 1959.

COOPER, Martin. *French Music from the death of Berlioz to the death of Fauré*. London: Oxford University Press. 1951.

CORNELL, Kenneth. *The Symbolist Period*. New Haven: Yale University Press. 1951.

CRUICKSHANK, John (ed.). *French Literature and its background*. Vol V. *The Late Nineteenth Century*. London: Oxford University Press. 1969.

DEFFOUX, Léon, & ZAVIE, Émile. *Le Groupe de Médan*. Paris: Payot. 1920.

DELHORBE, Cécile. *L'Affaire Dreyfus et les écrivains français*. Neuchâtel & Paris: Victor Attinger. 1932.

DESCOTES, Maurice. *Le Public de théâtre et son histoire*. Paris: Presses Universitaires de France. 1964.

DIGEON, Claude. *La Crise allemande de la pensée française*. Paris: Presses Universitaires de France. 1959.

DUMESNIL, René. *L'Époque réaliste et naturaliste*. Paris: Tallandier. 1945.

EASTON, Malcolm. *Artists and Writers in Paris: the Bohemian Idea, 1803–1867*. London: Arnold. 1964.

FRASER, Elizabeth. *Le Renouveau religieux d'après le roman français de 1886 à 1914*. Paris: Les Belles Lettres. 1934.

GRAÑA, César. *Bohemian versus Bourgeois. French Society and the French Man of Letters in the Nineteenth Century*. New York: Basic Books. 1964.

GRANT, Elliott M. *Victor Hugo during the Second Republic*. Northampton, Mass.: Harvard University Press. 1935.

GREEN, F. C. *A Comparative View of French and British Civilization, 1850–1870*. London: Dent. 1965.

GRIFFITHS, Richard. *The Reactionary Revolution. The Catholic Revival in French Literature, 1870–1914*. London: Constable. 1966.

GUICHARD, Léon. *La Musique et les lettres au temps du wagnérisme*. Paris: Presses Universitaires de France. 1963.

GUILLEMIN, Henri. *Lamartine en 1848*. Paris: Presses Universitaires de France. 1948.

S

HALLAYS-DABOT, Victor. *La Censure dramatique et le théâtre, histoire des vingt dernières années.* Paris, Dentu. 1871.

HAMILTON, George Heard. *Manet and his Critics.* New Haven: Yale University Press. 1954.

HAUTECŒUR, Louis. *Littérature et peinture en France du XVIIe au XXe siècle.* 2e édition. Paris: Armand Colin. 1963.

HEITMANN, Klaus. *Der Immoralismus-Prozess gegen die französische Literatur im 19. Jahrhundert.* Bad Homburg v.d.H.: Gehlen. 1970.

HEMMINGS, F. W. J. *The Russian Novel in France, 1884-1914.* London: Oxford University Press. 1950.

HÉRAIN, François de. *Les grands écrivains critiques d'art.* Paris: Mercure de France. 1943.

HERBERT, Eugenia W. *The Artist and Social Reform. France and Belgium, 1885-1898.* New Haven: Yale University Press. 1961.

KRACAUER, S. *Offenbach and the Paris of his Time.* London: Constable. 1937.

LABRACHERIE, Pierre. *La vie quotidienne de la bohème littéraire au XIXe siècle.* Paris: Hachette. 1967.

LACRETELLE, Pierre de. *Vie politique de Victor Hugo.* Paris: Hachette. 1928.

LARNAC, Jean. *George Sand révolutionnaire.* Paris: Éditions hier et aujourd'hui. 1947.

LAVER, James. *French Painting and the Nineteenth Century.* London: Batsford. 1937.

LEHMANN, A. G. *The Symbolist Aesthetic in France, 1885-1895.* Oxford: Blackwell, 1950.

LÉON, Paul. *Mérimée et son temps.* Paris: Presses Universitaires de France. 1962.

LETHÈVE, Jacques. *Impressionnistes et symbolistes devant la presse.* Paris: Armand Colin. 1959.

—— *La Vie quotidienne des artistes français au XIXe siècle.* Paris: Hachette. 1968.

LIDSKY, Paul. *Les Écrivains contre la Commune.* Paris: Maspero. 1970.

MARTINO, Pierre. *Parnasse et symbolisme.* Paris: Armand Colin. 1947.

—— *Le Roman réaliste sous le Second Empire.* Paris: Hachette. 1913.

MAYNIAL, Edouard. *L'Époque réaliste.* Paris: Les Œuvres représentatives. 1931.

MITCHELL, Bonner. *Les Manifestes littéraires de la Belle Époque.* Paris: Seghers. 1966.

MOSER, Ruth. *L'Impressionnisme français. Peinture, littérature, musique.* Geneva: Droz—Lille: Giard. 1952.

MOUQUET, Jules & BANDY, W. T. *Baudelaire en 1848.* Paris: Émile-Paul. 1946.

PAILLERON, Marie-Louise. *George Sand et les hommes de 48.* Paris: Grasset. 1953.

PAYNE, Howard C. *The Police State of Louis Napoleon Bonaparte, 1851–1860.* Seattle: University of Washington Press. 1966.

PINKNEY, David H. *Napoleon III and the Rebuilding of Paris.* Princeton, N.J.: Princeton University Press. 1958.

POMMIER, Jean. *Les Écrivains devant la Révolution de 1848.* Paris: Presses Universitaires de France. 1948.

POUILLIART, Raymond. *Le Romantisme, III. 1869–1896.* Paris: Arthaud. 1968.

RAYNAUD, Ernest. *La Mêlée symboliste.* 3 vols. Paris: La Renaissance du Livre. 1920.

REQUE, A. Dikka. *Trois auteurs dramatiques scandinaves devant la critique française, 1889–1901.* Paris: Champion. 1930.

REWALD, John. *The History of Impressionism,* revised edition. New York: Museum of Modern Art. 1961.

—— *Post-Impressionism from Van Gogh to Gauguin.* New York: Museum of Modern Art. 1956.

RICHARD, Noël. *A l'aube du symbolisme.* Paris: Nizet. 1961.

—— *Le Mouvement décadent.* Paris: Nizet. 1968.

ROBICHEZ, Jacques. *Le Symbolisme au théâtre. Lugné-Poe et les débuts de l'Œuvre.* Paris: L'Arche. 1957.

ROBIDA, Michel. *Le Salon Charpentier et les impressionnistes.* Paris: La Bibliothèque des Arts. 1958.

SLOANE, Joseph C. *French Painting between the Past and the Present: Artists, Critics and Traditions from 1848 to 1870.* Princeton, N.J.: Princeton University Press. 1951.

SOURIAU, Maurice. *Histoire du Parnasse.* Paris: Spec. 1929.

SWART, Koenraad W. *The Sense of Decadence in Nineteenth-Century France.* The Hague: Nijhoff. 1964.

TABARANT, A. *La vie artistique au temps de Baudelaire.* Paris: Mercure de France. 1963.

TERNOIS, René. *Zola et son temps.* Paris: Les Belles Lettres. 1961.

THIBAUDET, Albert. *Histoire de la littérature française de 1789 à nos jours.* Paris: Stock. 1936.

TISON-BRAUN, Micheline. *La Crise de l'humanisme: le conflit de l'individu et de la société dans la littérature française moderne. Tome I. 1890–1914.* Paris: Nizet. 1958.

WEINBERG, Bernard. *French Realism: the critical reaction, 1830–1870.* New York: Modern Language Association of America. 1937.

WEST, T. W. *A History of Architecture in France*. London: University of London Press. 1969.

WHITE, Harrison C. & Cynthia A. *Canvases and Careers: Institutional Change in the French Painting World*. New York: Wiley. 1965.

WILENSKI, R. H. *Modern French Painters*. London: Faber. 1940

ZÉVAÈS, Alexandre. *Les Procès littéraires au XIXe siècle*. Paris: Perrin. 1924.

Index

Where no sub-headings are given references to pages of particular importance are set in **bold** type.

Baudry, Paul, painter (1828–86) 74
Bazaine, François-Achille, Marshal (1811–88) 181
Bazille, Frédéric, painter (1841–71) 168, 170, 172, 173–5, 198, 207
Beardsley, Aubrey 253
Beauclair, Henri 252
Beaumarchais, Pierre-Augustin Caron de 43, 88
Bel-Ami [Maupassant] 4, 232
Belle Hélène, La [Offenbach] 139
Bellot, Émile 167
Béranger, Jean-Pierre, poet (1780–1857) 78
Berger, Jean-Jacques 123–4
Berlioz, Hector, composer (1803–69) 119, 141, 143
Bernard, Thalès, poet and hellenist (1821–72) 32–3
Berryer, Pierre-Antoine, politician (1790–1868) 85, 87
Bête humaine, La [Zola] 219, 232
Béthune, Comte de 146
Billault, Adolphe, minister (1805–63) 60
Binkley, Robert 117
Bismarck, Otto von 132, 149, 186, 188, 229
Bjoernson, Bjoernstjerne 234, 239
Blanc, Louis, politician and historian (1811–82) 7, 17, 33
Blanchisseuse, Une [Daumier] 94
Blanqui, Auguste, revolutionary (1805–81) 17, 23–4, 35, 65, 184–5, 189
Bon Bock, Le [Manet] 198–9
Bonheur, Rosa, painter (1822–99) 98
Bonne Chanson, La [Verlaine] 225
Bonvin, François, painter (1817–87) 78, 94–5
Bordes, Charles 252
Borodin, Alexander 226
Bossuet, Jacques-Bénigne 231
Botticelli, Sandro 205
Boucicault, Dion 50
Boudin, Eugène, painter (1825–98) 169, 173
Bouilhet, Louis, poet (1822–69) 14, 116, 120
Boulanger, Gen. Georges-Ernest (1837–91) 204
Boulanger, Louis, painter (1806–67) 177, 247
Boulevard des Capucines, Le [Monet] 200
Bourgeois de Molinchart, Les [Champfleury] 108

Bourges, Elémir, novelist (1852–1925) 224
Bourget, Paul, novelist and critic (1852–1935) 215–16, 217, 223, 232, 251, 261
Bouvard et Pécuchet [Flaubert] 108, 115
Broglie, Jacques-Albert, duc de, statesman (1821–1901) 194
Brontë, Charlotte 107
Brothers Karamazov, The [Dostoevsky] 228, 231
Brunetière, Ferdinand, critic (1849–1906) 238, 253, 261
Bruyas, Alfred 99
Buchez, Philippe, statesman (1796–1865) 27
Buchon, Max 105, 107
Buloz, François, literary editor (1803–76) 109
Burty, Philippe, art-critic (1830–90) 208
Buveur d'absinthe, Le [Manet] 161
Byron, Lord 9, 149

Cabanel, Alexandre, painter (1823–89) 81, 135, 163
Cabet, Étienne, social theoretician (1788–1856) 23
Caillebotte, Gustave, painter (1848–94) 202, 206
Camus, Albert 263
Caprices de Marianne, Les [Musset] 46
Carey, Sir Stafford 73
Carnot, Sadi, President of the Republic (1837–94) 241
Carolus-Duran (pseud. Charles Durand), painter (1837–1917) 167
Carpeaux, Jean-Baptiste, sculptor (1827–75) 74, 247
Carvalho (pseud. Léon Carvaille), theatre director (1825–98) 223
Cassatt, Mary, painter (1845–1926) 206
Casseurs de pierre, Les [Courbet] 97–8, 103, 182
Castagnary, Jules-Antoine, art-critic (1830–88) 78, 102, 166
Castellane, Jules de 145
Castiglione, Virginia di 146
Catherine d'Overmeire [Feydeau] 154
Catherine the Great of Russia 140
Cause du beau Guillaume, La [Duranty] 112-13
Cause du peuple, La (newspaper) 20
Cavaignac, Eugène, soldier and statesman (1802–57) 25, 26, 29
Cézanne, Paul, painter (1839–1906) 3, 164, 168–70, 171, 198–9, 202, 203, 206, 246

Gounod, Charles, composer (1818–93) **141,** 143, 146

Gourmont, Remy de, literary critic (1858–1915) 239

Goya, Francisco 82

Gozlan, Léon, dramatist (1803–66) 48

Grande-Duchesse de Gérolstein, La [Offenbach] 136, **140**

Greatcoat, The [Gogol] 229

Gregh, Fernand 261

Greuze, Jean-Baptiste 81, 146

Gros, Baron Antoine-Jean 88

Guérin, Baron Pierre 88

Guillaumin, Armand, painter (1841–1927) 164

Guillemet, Antoine, painter (1843–1918) 170

Guilmant, Alexandre 252

Guizot, François, statesman (1787–1874) 19, 36, 53

Guys, Constantin, illustrator (1805–92) 81

Gwendoline [Chabrier] 224

Hachette, Louis 170

Halévy, Fromental, composer (1799–1862) 141

Halévy, Ludovic, librettist (1834–1908) 137

Hamlet [Thomas] 141

Hauptmann, Gerhart 239

Hauser, Arnold 114, 145

Hauser, Henriette 203

Haussmann, Baron Georges, prefect of the Seine (1809–91) 121, 124, 126, **128–31,** 135, 158

Heine, Heinrich 143

Helen of Mecklenberg-Schwerin, Princess **11,** 13, 148

Henri III et sa cour [Dumas *père*] 146

Henry, Émile 241–2

Hernani [Hugo] **74–5**

Hérodiade [Mallarmé] 234

Hervé (*pseud.* Florimond Rongé), composer and librettist (1825–95) **138,** 141, 244

Hetzel, Jules 68

Hirondelles, Les [Manet] 201

Histoire de la Révolution de 1848 [Lamartine] 29

Histoire d'un crime [Hugo] **68–9**

Hoche, Louis-Lazare 178

Hokusai, Katsuhika 246

Holtzapfel, Jules 171

Homer 35, 115

Homme, L' (newspaper) 73

Homme au nez cassé, L' [Rodin] 247

Hommes de lettres, Les [Goncourts] 210

Hostein, Hippolyte, theatre director (1814–79) 21

Houssaye, Arsène, writer and theatre director (1815–96) **44–6,** 47, 64, 74, 127, 137, 146, 172, 174

Houssaye, Henri 249

Huber, Aloysius 23

Hugo, Adèle 69

Hugo, Charles 27, 69, 189

Hugo, François-Victor 27, 69

Hugo, Mme Victor (*née* Adèle Foucher) 69, 73, 75, 236

Hugo, Victor, poet (1802–85) 8, 10, **11, 13–14,** 20, 22–3, **25–9,** 32, 42, 44, 47, 51, **67–74,** 76, 78, 79, 82, 83, 109, 113, 142, 147, 148, 150, 151, 179, **184–5, 188–9,** 192, 207, 208, 216, 236, 253, 254, 260

Huguenots, Les [Meyerbeer] 142

Hunt, Holman 203

Huysmans, Joris-Karl, novelist (1848–1907) **216–19,** 220, 226, 230, 231, 234, 243

Ibsen, Henrik 221, 234, **238–42**

Idiot, The [Dostoevsky] 231

Illuminations, Les [Rimbaud] 235

Illustrated London News 81

Indy, Vincent d', composer (1851–1931) 222, 225, **226**

Ingres, Jean-Auguste-Dominique, painter (1780–1867) 88, 97, 98, 99, 135

Insurgé, L' [Vallès] 181

Intruse, L' [Maeterlinck] 239

J'Accuse [Zola] 8, **260–1,** 263

James, Henry 202–3

Janin, Jules, critic (1804–74) 44, 48, 68, 75, 138

Japonaiseries d'automne [Loti] 245

Japonnerie [Monet] 202

Jarry, Alfred, dramatist (1873–1907) 242

Jaurès, Jean, politician, (1859–1914) 262–3

Jeanne [Manet] 206

Jeune homme et la Mort, Le [Moreau] 135

Jeunes Spartiates s'exerçant à la lutte [Degas] 162

Joie de vivre, La [Zola] **220–1**

Jongkind, Johann Barthold, painter (1819–91) 164, 173

Jourdain, Frantz 247

278

INDEX

Rambuteau, Claude, comte de, Prefect of the Seine (1781–1869) 158
Raphael 165
Rappel, Le (newspaper) 222
Raudot, Claude-Marie, historian (1801–79) 211
Réalisme (periodical) 78, **108–9,** 113
Réalisme, Le [Champfleury] 105, **107**
Recherche de l'Absolu, La [Balzac] 211
Redon, Odilon, painter (1840–1916) 216, 237
Réfractaires, Les [Vallès] 182
Régnier, Henri de, poet and novelist (1864–1936) 34, 240–1
Reine de Saba, La [Gounod] 141
Renan, Ernest, historian (1823–92) **56,** 150, 155, 195
Renoir, Auguste, painter (1841–1919) **168–70, 172–6,** 196, 198, **201–3,** 206
Restif de la Bretonne, Nicholas-Edmé 81
Retour de la Conférence, Le [Courbet] **100,** 104
Rêve, Le [Zola] 232
Revue blanche, La 262
Revue contemporaine, La 105
Revue de Paris, La **58–9**
Revue des Deux Mondes, La 45, 76, 96, 97, 109, 150, 151, 166, 229, 238
Revue européenne, La 144
Revue fantaisiste, La **64,** 144
Revue française, La 61, 166
Revue illustrée, La 227
Revue socialiste, La 241
Revue wagnérienne, La **224–5**
Rheingold, Das [Wagner] 225
Richard, Maurice, minister (1832–88) 101
Richelieu, Cardinal 100
Richepin, Jean, poet (1849–1926) **66**
Rilke, Rainer Maria 250
Rimbaud, Arthur, poet (1854–91) 64, 149 **234–6,** 238, 253
Rimsky-Korsakov, N.A. 226
Robert le Diable [Meyerbeer] 142
Rochefort, Henri, journalist (1830–1913) 139, 184, 188, 212
Rod, Édouard, novelist (1857–1910) **233–4**
Rodin, Auguste, sculptor (1840–1917) 3, **246–50**
Roi d'Ys, Le [Lalo] 224
Roi malgré lui, Le [Chabrier] 224
Romains de la décadence, Les [Couture] 212
Roman d'un jeune homme pauvre, Le [Feuillet] 148, **155,** 156
Roman d'un spahi, Le [Loti] 245

Roman russe, Le [Vogüé] **229–31**
Romieu, Auguste, pamphleteer and administrator (1800–55) **46–7**
Roqueplan, Nestor, theatre manager (1804–70) 141
Rosenberg, Alfred 212
Rossini, Gioacchino 142, 143
Rostand, Edmond, dramatist (1868–1918) 261
Roubaud, François, sculptor (1825–76) 192
Rouland, Gustave, minister (1806–78) 56, 63
Rousseau, Théodore, painter (1812–67) 93–4, 135, 177
Royer, Paul-Henri-Ernest de 63
Rubens, Peter Paul 202
Rue, La (newspaper) **183,** 207
Rue, La [Vallès] 182

Sacre de Napoléon, Le [David] 88–9
Sagesse [Verlaine] 234
Saint-Arnaud, Jacques Leroy de 71
Saint-Jean Baptiste [Rodin] 246
Saint-Marc Girardin (*pseud.* Marc Girardin) 208
Saint-Saëns, Camille, composer (1835–1921) 222
Saint-Simon, Henri de 9
Sainte-Beuve, Charles-Augustin, critic (1804–69) 24, 56, 60, 63, 74, 116, 147, 151, **154**
Saison en enfer, Une [Rimbaud] 235
Salammbô [Flaubert] 108, 147, 154
Salon de 1846 [Baudelaire] 80, 246
Salon de 1859 [Baudelaire] 95
Salut public, Le (newspaper) 104
Sand, George (*pseud.* Mme Aurore Dudevant), novelist (1804–76) 8, 10, **18–20,** 22, 26, **30–1,** 78, 81, 105, 107, 120, 150, 186–7, 227, 231
Sand, Maurice 19
Sarcey, Francisque, theatre critic (1827–99) 239, 253
Sardou, Victorien, dramatist (1831–1908) 47, 49, 51
Sartre, Jean-Paul 263
Scarron, Paul 138
Scheffer, Ary, painter (1795–1858) 177
Scheurer-Kestner, Auguste, senator (1833–99) **256–7,** 260
Schiller, Friedrich 142
Schneider, Hortense **136,** 139, 140, 158
Scholl, Aurélien, journalist (1833–1902) 62
Schopenhauer, Artur 221, 234